G000151944

REAL PUNKS DON'T WEAR BLACK

REAL PUNKS

THE UNIVERSITY OF GEORGIA PRESS   ATHENS AND LONDON

DON'T WEAR BLACK

MUSIC WRITING BY **FRANK KOGAN**

Permissions for the use of copyrighted material
appear on page 346, which constitutes an extension
of the copyright page.

Published by The University of Georgia Press
Athens, Georgia 30602
© 2006 by Frank Kogan
All rights reserved
Designed by Mindy Basinger Hill and Anne Boston
Set in 10.5/14 Adobe Garamond
Printed and bound by Maple-Vail
The paper in this book meets the guidelines for
permanence and durability of the Committee on
Production Guidelines for Book Longevity of the
Council on Library Resources.

Printed in the United States of America

10   09   08   07   06   C   5   4   3   2   1

10   09   08   07   06   P   5   4   3   2   1

Library of Congress Cataloging-in-Publication Data

Kogan, Frank, 1954–
Real punks don't wear black / music writing
    by Frank Kogan.
p. cm.
ISBN-13: 978-0-8203-2753-2 (hardcover : alk. paper)
ISBN-10: 0-8203-2753-0 (hardcover : alk. paper)
ISBN-13: 978-0-8203-2754-9 (pbk. : alk. paper)
ISBN-10: 0-8203-2754-9 (pbk. : alk. paper)
1. Music—History and criticism. I. Title.
ML60 .K619 2006
781.64'09—dc22   2005022124

British Library Cataloging-in-Publication Data
available

DEDICATED TO CHUCK EDDY

CONTENTS

Preface: Contamination ix
Preface to the New Edition xvii

PART ONE **BOUNCE ROCK DEATH ROLL**

1 The Autobiography of Bob Dylan 3
2 The Electric Kool-Aid Contortions Test 5
3 Death Rock 2000 12

PART TWO **HERO OF FEAR**

4 The Kingston Trio 25
5 Junior High 31
6 Bob Dylan Song Meanings 43
7 Roger Williams in America / The What Thing 45
8 The Wind from My Head 93
9 Boys in Makeup / Hurled in Their Fun 108
10 Twelve Varieties of Worms (lyrics, poems, 1977–1985) 124
11 Radio Shack 130

PART THREE **OUR BAND COULD BE YOUR LIFE—
BUT THEN YOUR LIFE WOULD *SUCK!***

12 PBS & the Lonely Hearts Club 135
13 The Disco Tex Essay 155
14 Kung-Fu Fighting 179
15 Danger on the Dance Floor 180

PART FOUR **THE GREAT WRONG PLACE**

16 The Presentation of Self in Everyday Life 189
17 How Music Creates Ideas 198
18 Wasted 201
19 The Trouble with the Sociology of Pop 204
20 Photo Disregards Its Negative 207

21 The Psychotic Carnival 209

22 A Trip to the Mountains 211

23 Here We Go (Pazz & Jop 1999) 214

24 And *Your* Bird Can Sing 219

25 Superwords Revisited 223

26 Sometimes Good Guys Don't Wear White 240

PART FIVE **STUPID STORIES**

27 The Conversation 249

28 Maybe That's What They Meant 250

29 The Great Rainstorm 252

PART SIX **FUCK MACHINES AND RAZOR BLADES:**
REVIEWS AND CRITICISM 1985–1990 253

Spoonie Gee; Sex Don't Love Nobody; the Godfather; Fucked (Pazz & Jop 1987); My Dream Date with Teena Marie; New Perspectives on Ornette Coleman; To Scare a Trendy; Nietzsche with Tits; Public Enemy (Pazz & Jop 1988); Going to Die; Squeezed from the Tube; Raze; Donna Summer; Let MTV Ring; Real Punks Don't Wear Black; Fuck Machines and Razor Blades

PART SEVEN **ERNEST BORGNINE, SONGWRITER:**
REVIEWS AND CRITICISM 1991–1998 285

Mariah; Martika; Whitney; Corina; Bonnie Raitt; What Becomes of the Broken-Hearted; Sophie B. Hawkins; Quarterflash; Swept Away; Cheekbones; Super-model; Soundgarden; Fabulosos Cadillacs; Divine; Out-of-Date Items in Fridge; Joke; Dancing Horses; Cynthia; Debbie Deb; Barber Poles; Paris Grey; Pussy; Throat Cancer; Ernest Borgnine; Plastics; Rave-Ups; Rubber Trees (Pazz & Jop 1998); Failed Revulsion

PART EIGHT **LEGEND OF THE GLOCKEATER:**
REVIEWS AND CRITICISM 1999–2004 303

Dan Duryea; Medusa and Childe; Legend of the Glockeater; So This Guy Walks into a Bar; Gore Gore Girls; Britney; On-Ramp to Style; Quiet Desert Storm; Count Five, Have a Psychotic Reaction; Fodder Bites Cannon; Alone Again, Naturally; Death Takes a Holiday; Scarred Old Slaver (Country Music Critics Poll 2003); Nashville Stalwart Dons Rose-Colored Glasses for Miss Emily; Top 11, 2004

Acknowledgements, Thank Yous, Explanations 337

CONTAMINATION

I told a big lie, back in *Why Music Sucks* #7, saying, "I don't care if my words are 'personal' or 'impersonal,' so long as they do what I want them to." Actually, I care about little *else* than whether my words are *my* words or *their* words. Somehow the words never come out feeling like mine. I die every time I write. And I know how potentially great my writing could be. I estimate my abilities as high as anyone estimates them. My potential greatness is a giant tower and I stand in its shadow.

Or so I wrote Chuck Eddy in December 1991. And, two sentences later, having already contradicted myself once—I mean, which is it, do I want to speak *my* words or do I want to speak *great* words, words that are *better* than my words, at least better than anything I'm presently calling "my words"?—I said, "I think the real problem is that I try to *will* my writing into existence. And this maybe gives me a special sensitivity to the role of 'discourses' (to use the buzz word of the day, or of yesterday). I need a conversation to come in and speak me, you know? But I'm the puritan little American boy, and I'm not really willing to hook myself into other conversations, to flow, to let the thing take me. No, I've got to do it myself, brain my way ahead, butt myself forward."

To wring some truth out of all this: Obviously, I *do* care that my words be personal, be mine, speak my style rather than the editor's or the reader's; but I care about other things more, and I was right the first time: I care that my words do what I want them to, which is to make you think, and I'll use any persona that does the job. And I also want a strong, living conversation to seize me and speak through me, to create prose and ideas in me that I can't create on my own. But such a conversation doesn't exist right now, and isn't going to unless I and people like me bull our way through and set the fire. If we want to call forth the roar of language on our behalf, we're going to have to first prime the language with our own roar.

But I'll put that quest in brackets for the moment, to ponder this: The sentence "I die every time I write" came from my pen, but I'm a product of my environment, and so is that sentence. So, what do I *gain* by being such a person, by writing such sentences? And what does a *society* gain, by producing people like me—by producing such sentences?

I'd asked the same basic question a few months earlier, in my review of Sara Cohen's *Rock Culture in Liverpool*:

> *The musicians here seem haunted by the sense that any note they play, any word they write, is potentially contaminated. An obvious question is how does one come to feel this way. But these people aren't just feeling this way, they are defining themselves: We are human beings with the potential to be compromised. So a better question would be: What do they gain by defining themselves in this way? What does this do for their art, their lives?*
>
> *It was the songwriters and de facto band leaders who had a morbid fear of sounding like normal rock or pop bands; the other band members didn't care, but maybe it's no coincidence that these others didn't generate the musical ideas.*

And again, we need to push the question further: What does a *society* gain by getting people to define themselves as potentially contaminated? For instance, if child-rearing practices produce such self-definitions, then maybe those definitions prepare one for a particular type of adulthood.

Not all the writing in this book asks that question directly, but much is haunted by it. I'm giving you not just "essays" and "record reviews" but the whole mess of Frank: emails, diary excerpts, hate letters, chatroom postings, high-school jottings. Arguments, stammers, soliloquies, puns. Off-the-cuff rants. Up-the-butt intellectualizing, w/ schmeer. Relentless analysis and reckless screaming. You get me whole. No dodging or expurgating. The mess is a big hunk of the message; it tells us we can walk and chew gum at the same time, and we'd better, or our brains will freeze and our torsos will shrivel.

But isn't the claim "You get me whole" suspect? And not merely because you're getting, along with *my* words, the words of those aliens who seize my body and put their extra-alive or extra-dead hand in place of my own, but also because there's always some asshole up the chain of command (as I've indicated, that asshole is sometimes me, apparently) who thinks that some of what I do contaminates and contradicts the rest, and makes it all illegit?

And this book is not an overview or a representative sample. To give it some coherence, I emphasize the punk Frank and pillage high school for my ongoing metaphors. So I give short shrift to the amazing musical changes of the last thirty-five years (dub, dancehall, disco, hip-hop, freestyle, house, rave, Europop, metal, etc.), changes that my g-g-generation is by and large too stupid to notice. I've said lots on such music, but I'll have to save it for my next collection, *Real Men Don't Worry About Who Another Nigga Fucked*. In the meantime, I obsess on the following themes:

The Great Wrong Place: Choose any piece of mine at random. Whether it's about PBSification or Superwords or hallway-classroom splits, or junior high school and style wars, or the struggle for style in my own writing (humor being a stand-in for personality), there's usually this backdrop: Something's fucked, something's suppressed, something's being evaded, and it's my job to counter the evasion, to smash the whatever-it-is into your face or lure and entice you over my trap door, so that you'll fall in it. But once again, accompanying this theme is the insight that, in moving floorboards and smashing faces, I'm a social product: I grew up in a college town—Storrs, Connecticut—that was off in the boonies but still something of a quasi-suburbia, so academia and suburbia are my proto Great Wrong Places. But bohemia and journalism are just as wrong—in fact, they're the Great Wrong Place in parts three and four of this book—and almost anyone can define his place as the Great Wrong Place and live a neurotic or glorious dynamic similar to mine. The only thing atypical about me is the doggedness with which I push. You see, suburbia/academia is no more fucked and evasive than anywhere else, but it tends to *define* itself as fucked and evasive and to teach punk-boho types like me to act out its romanticism for it. (And again, what does a society *gain* by producing people like me who call ourselves, and it, fake?) So we assign our music a double role: It's supposed to feed our world but it's supposed to emanate from another world and take us out of our own.

A piece of music can be many things, often at once: decoration, diversion, distraction, conversation piece, mood enhancer, mood alterer, narrative signal (in the movies), theme song, guide to physical movement (on dance floor), guide to social interaction (ditto), message to the gods, tool of the gods, mnemonic device, conveyor of lyrics, social bond (sing-alongs), social marker, scene disrupter (blasted out of car windows), self-expression, etc. Not all these roles sit at ease with one another. When the music promises to change our life or take us into a new world, then, with the music also acting as a social marker ("I'm the sort of person who listens to this sort of music"), it decorates us not only with who we are but with who we aren't but could be. If you want to know how problematic this can get, listen to the second Eminem LP. Its first single, "The Real Slim Shady," comes with instructions for how to use it: "In every single person there's a Slim Shady lurkin'; he could be workin' at Burger King, spittin' on your onion rings, or outside in the parkin' lot circlin', screamin' 'I don't give a fuck!' with his windows down and his system up." And a couple of lines later he urges us (whom? the spitter or the eater?) to be proud to be out of our minds and out of control. And *then*, in his next single, he's out-of-control Stan, killing wife and baby and launching himself off the bridge into dead, wet nowhere. And then he's drunk and jealous Marshall Mathers himself, slicing his own wife's throat, crazy, defeated, proud of nothing.

"What could be" promises to be daring and raving but risks being pathological and stupid.

Terror and Social Division: The obvious questions emerge: "Contaminated by what?" "What is being suppressed and evaded?" I almost want to say, "What have you," and simply direct you to the rest of this book. There's no single answer, since you choose your contaminants from whatever's available; and once you're in motion, the process takes you pinging all over the place with ongoing reversals of who gets to be the contaminant and who the contaminated. But here's one example, one way to start it moving:

Everclear's Art Alexakis sings, "I will never be safe, I will never be sane /I will always be weird inside, I will always be lame," swearing not to put his own young daughter through the poverty and pain he claims his own dad inflicted on him. This conveys one of the promises of the 'burbs, and of America in general: not just a wealthier life, but a safer one for our kids, a less destructive one. But Alexakis is vowing something that's not in his control. First, he has no way of knowing that he himself wouldn't have felt just as lame and broken even if his dad hadn't abandoned him to fatherlessness and poverty; and second, it's simply not in his power to guarantee his daughter's happiness. In fact, Alexakis has also recorded a song where he imagines his daughter grown up into a self-hating addict like he once was, just as Eminem (who's in the 'burbs now where he's reported to be a responsible, attends-community-board-and-parent-teacher-association Dad) does one where he foresees himself on his porch knocking back 40s and drunkenly supervising his grandkids while his daughter is out getting smashed. So it's not only pale conformists who worry that the dangers of city and country will follow them into the suburbs.

To some extent the suburbs keep their promise: Not too many suburbanites are nostalgic for rickets and lead poisoning, I don't think. But of course suburbia has life's normal terrors, and social stratification and social conflict, and people who hurt each other. So that's one type of contaminant, the Terror and Social Division (not to mention drugs) that are already mucking up the nicey-nicey suburb. We believe that Terror and Social Division ought to be somehow curable—like, through therapy. This delusion is a great trampoline for the Iggys and the Eminems to bounce off of. Nyaaah nyaaah, you can't cure me. (Sticks out tongue.) And if a parent's self-esteem depends on his daughter's happiness, this is a burden on the child and almost guarantees that she will feel the parental concern as an invasion, a contaminant. And self-destruction will feel a bit like self-assertion, as it defies the concern.

So we've created a flip-flop: Portraying itself as "safe," suburbia declares unhappiness an interloper and defines itself as fearful, as averse to risk and adventure. And in reaction to its own supposed fearfulness, suburbia makes "suburban" a pejorative. I've never heard "suburban" or "safe" used to praise a pop song. Suburbia itself is the contaminant, its supposed blandness and uniformity infecting whatever it touches. So suburbia is contaminated by danger and contaminated by safety.

But its sense of being doubly contaminated speaks less to its shame than to its ideals: that we and our children not be terrorized or ruled by social stratification, *and* that our life be a field for romance, bravery, and excitement.

A flight from "contamination" can also be a search for riches. It's not so much a fleeing from what's there as an attempt to incorporate what's missing. Notice how in my opening paragraph I shift inexplicably from insisting that my words are contaminated to envisioning the potential—but absent—greatness of my writing. It's almost the logic of a dream, that my words be simultaneously subject to invasion and capable of glory.

Failure to Spark Social Debate: The major defect in my work isn't my inability to create a Tower of Greatness but my failure to inspire a conversation about social categories. Lester Bangs once challenged us, in regard to Iggy's death trips, to examine why and what we were loving. In my fanzine, I tried to press the question further, to ask about the social characteristics of "we" who loved listening to Iggy destroy himself and about the economic and institutional environment in which such loving occurred. And I subsequently raised the issue of "high school" to see if we could use the high-school vocabulary of social groups (freaks, greasers, burnouts, skaters, preps, jocks, et al.) as a springboard to discuss social conflict in music and in rock criticism. I got a lot of great submissions about school, but not many takers on the subject of social categories. When you read any rock criticism, whether in the newspapers or the alt-rags or the fanzines, blogs, and chatrooms, it becomes obvious usually within a paragraph that there's a connection between musical taste and social allegiance. But try to get people to analyze their *own* attitudes and their "visceral" responses to music, and the conversation disintegrates, as most people feel that their opinion is sufficient unto itself and get really offended and inarticulate when you question them on where the opinion comes from.

Superwords: One way to use words is to argue over word usage. This arguing plays a crucial role in social life and social differentiation. Meta-use is use. "Jay-Z is pop not hip-hop 'cause he raps about situations that aren't real and never happened. The only reason that people like Jay so much is because he rhymes about money and girls, which is what sells right now. He raps to eleven-year-old white girls mainly." The concern here is not just with Jay-Z, but with what hip-hop is. For some, it's a genre at risk, one of the many that's too fragile to withstand the ear of that dangerous creature, the eleven-year-old white girl.

Such hot-button words (e.g., names of musical genres) often morph into what

I call Superwords. A Superword is a word that can run forward, ahead of any possible embodiment. Every genre title will get used as a Superword for as long as anybody cares about the genre, since all that's required for it to be super is the belief that any performer—and *all* performers—can fall short (in someone's eyes) in the attempt to be punk or techno or metal or hip-hop or _____. I'm a big perpetrator of this, having once argued that the only two punks left in the world were Axl Rose and Michael Jackson. The social dance that sets this ball bouncing can go something like this: "The punk rock I like is more real than the music *you* like" and "The punk rock I like is more real than *I* am," leading to "Real punk rock no longer exists/hasn't yet come into existence, since all the pretender musics are too much like you and me." So think of the fan or musician or critic reaching down to grasp a concept such as "punk" or "hip-hop" but simultaneously pushing his foot forward so as to kick the concept just out of reach. And what do you gain, chasing this who-knows-what while simultaneously kicking it ahead to protect it from being contaminated by your embrace? Well, among other things, you progressively modify your musical forms. And think of "social category" as analogous to "genre." You progressively modify your social forms.

The Double Contamination of Frank: There's a double contamination of Frank, analogous to the double contamination of suburbia. On the one hand, my prose is contaminated when other voices, seemingly of their own accord, creep into my writing, so that it takes on the tone of the *Village Voice* or of *Spin* (i.e., my words either freeze into stiffness or take on these horrible kind of gonzo antifreeze mannerisms that ultimately seem just as stiff, like they're frozen into some hideous simulacrum of "liveliness"), or it's full of rock-critic hardy har and dead I-have-to-explain-it-all-to-the-reader exposition and authoritative pronouncements that give no sense of how my mind actually moves. And, on the other hand, my prose is contaminated because it contains *too much* of my voice, say because that voice is too close to the tone of the *Village Voice* or *Spin* anyway, and too full of hardy har and exposition and pronouncements, which actually very much reflect my character; or because it contains too much of my fear and hermeticism and private intellectual obsessions and beloved personal tropes, the very things that the hardy har and exposition and pronouncements are endeavoring to break me out of. And so what's dead in my prose is that it's *me* in the prose and not the Real Slim Franky or mad, stupid Stan or whoever it is I'm afraid to be or don't know how to be.

As for what I *gain* by this sense of contamination: On the days that it doesn't paralyze me, it makes me fluid and flexible, goads me to expand my repertoire.

OK, But What Do We Really Gain? Not that I ever truly answer the question "What do we gain?" There isn't a single answer. I'd say this book itself is an answer, as is the music. "It rocks" is an answer. And here's an answer I gave in 1991:

Sir Walter Raleigh was an explorer and adventurer who heard about a city of gold called El Dorado and went searching for it. He spent a lot of time and money doing that, adventuring around in search of riches and whatnot, and finally got his head cut off. You could summarize Sir Walter Raleigh by saying, "He went looking for El Dorado and it wasn't there." Yeah, but what a trip he had! What sights! What adventures!

Life is fun, wish you were here.

Frank Kogan, 2004

PREFACE TO THE NEW EDITION

(which edition has been specially prepared, with a new preface and new introduction by the author, who obviously had the urge come upon him to express himself to large numbers of people but, rather than act on that urge by writing something new, chose instead to revise a piece he wrote almost a decade ago; he'd already whiffed on Pazz & Jop for the second consecutive year; then, when asked by Jill Blardinelli to contribute a ten-best list to her fanzine *Stupid and Contagious*, he suddenly found his voice)

NEW PREFACE, BY THE AUTHOR

I would like to point out that the previous paragraph is obviously the new preface itself.

THE PREVIOUS PREFACE

I feel it necessary to add yet another preface to clear up any confusion created inadvertently by the previous preface (the new preface), wherein it is stated that the previous paragraph is the new preface. This is not precisely the case, given that the previous preface supersedes the previous paragraph, making the previous paragraph merely the previous preface, and the previous preface itself the new preface.

AMENDMENT TO THE PREVIOUS PREFACE

Unfortunately, it is necessary to amend this preface (the preface entitled "the previous preface") in light of the fact that the new preface—the one, that is, that precedes the previous preface and is preceded in turn by the previous preface—is superseded by this preface (the previous preface), which itself supersedes both the new preface and the previous new preface, which had been redesignated the previous preface in the previous preface. Therefore, the new preface is now the previous preface, and the new preface, which is the previous preface, is now the new preface.

I prefer the Beatles' second album to the Beatles' second album, though I'll admit that both the second album and the second album are quite good and also that the second album has some persuasive adherents, those who would take its high spirits and audacity over the second album's dark rage.

Excerpts from Frank Kogan's Music Ballot for the Year 1995 for Jill's Magazine

SINGLES:
 1. Hole "Violet"
 2. Fun Fun "I'm Needin' You"
 3. Lordz of Brooklyn "Saturday Nite Fever"
 4. Mo-Do "Eins, Zwei, Polizei"
 5. Rednex "Wild and Free"
 6. Mariah Carey "Long Ago"
 7. Rancid "Salvation"
 8. Real Joy "La Danse d'Helene"
 9. Gillette "Mr. Personality"
 10. Gillette "You're A Dog"

I pulled in a ringer or two from the previous year—always happens, especially with European stuff—and I cheated and threw on a couple of LP cuts: "Wild and Free," because it's uniquely weird and it's better than "Cotton-Eye Joe"; "Long Ago," because any list with Hole needs to have Mariah on it too so that I can compare Mariah and Courtney and because Mariah's genuine singles from the last couple of years have been too much from the air-freshener section of her repertoire.

Courtney Love has a great, commanding voice; she's absolutely one of the handful of truly exciting hard-rock singers ever: Jagger, Burdon, Grace Slick, Iggy, Johnny Rotten, several more. She's really *edgy*, too; I mean her singing, not just her life. (I probably know less of her bio than does almost anyone reading this—and since her life and that of her dead husband's contributes to how her music is perceived, what it *does*, I'm not proud of knowing so little, but I just can't get myself to read the rock press; it's no longer a positive experience for me. There's a fear that Courtney's going to hurt herself or hurt others or die, isn't there?) But I wish she trusted her voice more. I wish that she were more like Mariah and that Mariah were more like her. Not that they should try to sing like each other, which would be absurd. But Courtney is too responsible—to the song, the mood, the stance, whatever she's trying to convey. This limits the music, cuts too much out—sometimes cuts the music out of her music (as Chuck Eddy would say). When she sings "Someday you will ache like I ache," yes, you really get it, there's the ache, underscored and in italics. But, you know, everything else turns off, the juice and the splash of music disappear while she's delivering the ache. I wish she'd just *sing* and let the ache take its natural place in the sound. It's in her voice anyway, she needn't will it into existence. (A great song, nonetheless.)

Mariah's at the other end. Mariah's totally irresponsible, she's splashing all over the pool and off the planet, leaping buildings and outracing bullets. The emotions get passed by, the words are just a coincidence. I didn't even notice these lyrics—almost identical to Courtney's but written a couple of years earlier—until Chuck reprised them in Pazz & Jop 1992. "On the most depressed day of my year, one of the most depressed days of my life, the day the hacks at Harmony Books decided they didn't want to publish my second book, which I'd spent a year on, the first record I played to help me cope was Mariah Carey's *MTV Unplugged EP*. She balanced my lithium somewhat, but mostly she reflected my rage à la '60s punk rock: 'Someday, someday, the one you gave away will be the only one you're wishin' for. Someday, yeah, boy you're gonna pay 'cause baby I'm the one who's keepin' score.'"

Once Chuck apprised me of them the words became part of the emotion of the song for me, just as "You're all I know/I can't let go" became part of their song when my ex-wife Leslie reviewed it in *Radio On*. ("A good song to get a divorce to. Just ask Frank.") Nonetheless, I wish that Mariah would . . . well, not tone down her exuberance, then she'd stop being Mariah, but allow the feelings to accompany her voice whenever she launches it over the sky.

Still, Mariah matters to me more than Courtney does, at this moment. I guess I just don't need my alienated sensibility affirmed for the six zillionth time. I'd rather have my exuberance affirmed and hope that someday, someday, the rage and the cruelty and the ache and my ripped face will show up in it.

[I justify calling this "the preface to the new edition" because, though this is the book's first edition, it is indeed a new one, as well. You can't, after all, claim that this is older *than some other edition, can you?]*

PART ONE

BOUNCE ROCK DEATH ROLL

CHAPTER 1

THE AUTOBIOGRAPHY OF BOB DYLAN

When I first listened to Bob Dylan's mid-'60s stuff I thought it was especially *honest*. It was honest to me because the vocals weren't pretty and didn't sound like singers were supposed to sound, and mistakes were left in. The lyrics to "Visions of Johanna," "Memphis Blues Again," etc. were honest because they were self-destructive. The earlier protest stuff, attacking power, prestige, and everyday commonplaces, fit into a genre of "folk" music; the electric stuff seemed more individual and true. Dylan got to be "honest" not by attacking power, prestige, and everyday commonplaces, but by attacking Dylan.

This "honesty" had nothing to do with the honesty of everyday life. If someone asks you what you're feeling you can say "I love you" or "I hate you" and the answer will be honest or dishonest depending on how you feel. But the honesty of personal life has nothing to do with the honesty of music. And in 1965 "I love you" was contaminated, was dead, had dropped away from honesty-in-song-lyrics. Dylan and Jagger and others like them had discovered the aesthetic power of hate and self-destruction; these feelings were new to pop music and were a big surprise, a shock. Jagger developed a routine in his song lyrics: The first lines of a song would set up what the song seemed to be about, then the rest of the song would smash what had been set up. Destruction/self-destruction was a reliable emotional rush, a guaranteed show-stopper, like the James Brown cape routine. In Dylan's words: The only beauty was in ugly.

The power—the honesty and power of self-destruction—wasn't Dylan's or Jagger's power, honesty, or self-destruction. It was something outside, from their lives, from the lives of the audience. They discovered something in the *language*, that love was dead and destruction lived, and they exploited this discovery. But it wasn't in their control. It was power they got from making music in a *context.*

The true autobiography of Bob Dylan isn't an account of his life, or how *he* got to be that way, but of how *it* got to be that way, how *we* got to be that way—it would be the autobiography of language/music, not of a person; it would be the account of the everyday life of the rock *audience,* and of how self-destruction came to be the truest noise on the radio and came to be marketed as such.

Dylan dropped out of his autobiography in 1966, but by then he wasn't needed;

hundreds of garage musicians could become the autobiography's focus. The Stooges' shows in the late '60s were an extension of this; Iggy's hurting himself, hurling himself at the audience, trying to get the audience to do (see/hear/feel) the unexpected, was the physical embodiment of Stones/Dylan music and words. When James Brown "collapsed" onstage it was a show-biz move; Iggy made it a real-life move. Real life. Real self-destruction.

The Stooges' music was a lot narrower than Dylan's. (This isn't a value judgment; I listen to the Stooges a lot more than to Dylan.) The Stooges had to ignore certain possibilities of words and possibilities of music that had been open in Dylan's music four years before. No fooling around with metaphors and rhymes, no blatant borrowing from honky-tonk and blues. "Poetry," "meaningfulness," and "complexity" had been contaminated by years of superficial Dylan imitators. Trying to sound like Dylan was like trying to please the teacher. So the Stooges had to pretend to be simple in order to be perceived as real.

The same thing happened more recently. To be expressive within a constricted social space, the Dolls had to disguise their poetry as bad grammar, bizarre conversation. To draw on the rock and blues tradition without being contaminated by it, the Contortions had to disguise their music as "no wave." Greg Ginn had to disguise his music as hardcore.

So now so many musicians conform to the idea of truth that says that truth is raw, ugly, and primitive that this primitiveness is a cliché, it's a new brand of deodorant, punk-hardcore deodorant; ultimately, it's nothing. Punk isn't punk anymore, it's a bunch of musical/clothing signs that symbolize punk. It's closer to literature or advertising than to music. The Stooges played complex, sophisticated music; they made it *seem* simple because they wanted their music to be felt directly, they didn't want ideas like "poetry" or "artistry" to clog up the audience's perception. But now people play their idea—their mistaken idea—of the Stooges, instead of playing the music. If any punk band really played "1969" in its rhythms, they wouldn't be called a punk band, they'd be called a *funk* band or an *art* band.

Hiding from Sixteen Friends of the Cometbus #20, 1985

CHAPTER 2

THE ELECTRIC KOOL-AID CONTORTIONS TEST

I've taken LSD twice in my life, had a blast both times. I'm not likely to do it again, though, since it aestheticizes everything and I'd hate to become an aesthete. You see, when I have an insight on acid, the insight parades before my eyes like a handsome glorious thing, and I'm reduced to waving at it in admiration. Also, the aesthetic judgment can supersede other equally pertinent ones. (John Wójtowicz: "A 'rule' that I think LSD might erase by accident is 'if you leap out of a window or from the top of a high object, you will get killed or maim yourself for life.' And I can easily imagine myself, while tripping, reasoning, 'Yes, but after all that's just one little criterion, and just one single jump!'") In any event, this was the first time. I was twenty-four, in New York City.

It's 1978, and we're going to see Wire and the Contortions at CBGB. Teresa says, "I've got some acid. Want some?" I say sure, which amazes Rich, who a week earlier had chided me for not taking speed with him, for being too careful to do anything new ("Peer pressure! Peer pressure!" Teresa had chanted).

We walk over to CBGB, a bar on the Bowery, not much more than a dive, right by a flophouse for derelicts and drunks and a gated parking lot with a sign consisting of the names of three Jamaican toastmasters: "U USE, U LOCK, OR U R OUT."

It turns out Wire are held up by immigration, get pushed back to the following week. So the Contortions now top the bill, and a band called the Stumblebunnies signs on to open and close for them. Inside the club, we meet Rob, a sweet-looking fresh-faced nineteen-year-old who works with me at Strand Book Store, and his sweet fresh-faced girlfriend in a cute quasi-punked-out torn sweatshirt. Rob and girlfriend are trying on punk to see how it fits. (I don't mean this derogatorily at all, since punk has always worked better as an impulse than an identity, and tentative punks are more truly punk than the real punks. E.g., my non-"punk" friend Lisa, who answered my question "Do you identify with Sid and Nancy?" by saying, "Yes, and I hate myself for it.") So there's a light in Rob's eyes. We've seen the Contortions before. We know what's coming, and we know that most of the audience doesn't. The Contortions have gotten practically no press, except for a *Voice* Choice or two. So most people are here because of the Choice, or because they intended to see Wire and decided to stick around, or because CBGB is now world famous—it's just a dark bar, the toilets often don't work and you wouldn't want to use them anyway, since there are no bathroom or stall doors (this is to deny junkies the privacy to shoot up, I presume), but it's where the Ramones, Television, Talking Heads, Blondie worked out their riffs a couple of years back and where edgy, creative types lurk (exemplary bathroom graffito: "I Like Girls Bomb Washington"). So you have tourists ready to check a hip "dangerous" scene—again, I don't mean "tourist" to be derogatory—and music guys willing to try a band that's nothing but a name on a poster; and of course the few who know of the band.

The Stumblebunnies get onstage and play subdued bluesy country rock (that's what I remember, anyway), not bad, but too recessive; I'm thinking they aren't *doing* anything with it. Wait, I have to say this right. I'm twenty-four, on acid. And. The. Stumblebunnies. Aren't. Doing. Anything.

Stumblebunnies off. We look around. Rob says, "These guys don't know what's going to hit them." The acid makes everything stand out. The mode of dress isn't slashed shirts and punk jackets but more like "We're the supercilious netherworld weirdos." But there are also people dressed in their normal casual "We're out at a club" or "We're from Jersey" attire. Or maybe it's the ones from Jersey who are dressed like Lower Manhattan netherworld weirdos.

After the usual long wait, the Contortions come on. Jody Harris scrapes his guitar pick along a metal guitar string—makes a grating, insinuating, disturbing sound—and the band jumps in, an onslaught of noise. But it really moves, has an r&b/rock 'n' roll undertow that's propulsive and compelling. (I've seen them a number of times already and am starting to learn how they do it—to hear expert counterrhythms, riffs, tonal relationships in the noise. Jody is my supervisor at the Strand, and I pepper him with questions about what he listens to, what gauge guitar strings he uses, and so forth.) James Chance looks contemptuously at the audience, dances as he sings, and he's an incredible dancer, fast, and he's shimmying across stage on one leg, then smashing his body down on the floor but bouncing back up in a sharp motion, elbows and legs out in all directions but always moving. He and his band are in slick dress suits, which I interpret as "We don't have to dress in the punk or weirdo Disturbance Uniform, since we *are* disturbed," though Rich points out later that they're done up like a mid-'60s r&b outfit. The band is sounding like mayhem, but in double time (I mean, compared to usual regular-speed mayhem). James is putting wiggles into his moves, he squirms and twirls and contorts, on and off the floor with an insect's ability to move on any surface. And then—we know this is coming, this is part of our delightful fear-energy—he slithers off the front of the stage into the audience, taunting people, cuffing them, slapping them around, while the band continues its rhythmic havoc. First gig I'd seen them, James had let loose a load of snot into his hand and then rubbed it on some tough in a leather jacket, and the tough got enraged and came after James to beat the crap out of him, but the band got between the guy and James, brandishing their instruments as weapons, until the guy finally stalked off.

During this summer of '78, I have wildly ambivalent feelings about James's act. On the one hand, not only have Iggy & the Stooges done it already, they've done it more meaningfully. Sure, James enters into the audience's territory, challenges us to participate and not just sit around like a bunch of frozen-stiff white people. (Story is that the first time James assaulted an audience the band was playing an art space, and the audience was just sitting lamely there like, "Come and present your piece for us," so James waded in and started hitting. I understand his motivation, and if as you're reading this you suddenly feel a hard whack against your ear, it's probably me.) But James's aggression, unlike Iggy's, seems there as a given, is provoked by nothing *we'd* done and doesn't play off our responses, as far as I can tell. He's taunting us, but the taunts are grade-school, boring. E.g., someone yells "Tell us a joke" and he says "You're a bigger joke than any I could tell." He's hitting us with a barrage of contempt and disgust, but I don't see how it pertains to who I am any more than would a rock that rolls down a hill and knocks me over. (Teresa perceives more here; she interprets him as feeling the world is detestable and we're sitting around being part of it, so he's going to hit us in the face with it.) But I like the act far more than I'm repelled by it. For one thing, there's an incredible *wit* to his movements, his relation to the surrounding social space. The way James looks, he could be the impish sidekick in a Saturday-morning cartoon. My friend Luc Sante, who like Rob and Jody is working with me at the Strand, tells me, "James is a little runt with red hair, who plays on his utterly unimposing physicality, as well as his whiteness, and whose aggression is both self-parody and the desperate bravado of the perpetually overmatched. James is using himself as, among other things, a sight gag." James's taunts are a tease, a threat to the psyche, not the body. So the real danger isn't in what he's going to do, but what *we* might do in response.

The Contortions make almost all other bands seem phony in comparison, not only because other bands play worse, but because those bands hang back on the stage and wait for our judgment and applause. The audience embraces passivity and concedes all the action to the bands, while the bands concede all the judgment to the audience. Why should rock 'n' roll put up with that? Jody'd once told me that James *had* to do something wild, or else the Contortions would be viewed as just another art band.

Michael Hersh, another friend from the Strand: "James seems to have an asshole radar that allows him to focus in on those who need to be attacked for their complacency. Of course, this also reinforces my neurotic need to believe that I'm cool for not being attacked myself—though I'm coming to realize that in a random audience attack, the odds of hitting an asshole are overwhelming."

My friend Rich is by no means wrong when he types me as someone afraid to step into the unknown. I nonetheless crave shows and bands where what's to happen to me is as uncertain as what will happen onstage. I think of James's forays into the audience as his way of acknowledging his dependence on us and of demanding that we make interesting demands on him; it's his search for a good dance partner (and I assume I'm not up to it, and hang back on the sidelines).

So there's a not-altogether-serene energy in the room. Between the stage and tables is a clear space—small, just a yard or two. James dances down there a lot, and potential fans and enemies work their way towards him. CBGB has a big, broad bouncer in a hard hat who places himself right in that space, as if using his massive front to announce, "Nothing will get out of hand here"—which actually makes the atmosphere more tense, as if fights are *expected*. So James is slithering around that floor space, and he slithers right up the bouncer, right up the bouncer's chest, like an insect. This is a *brilliant* move. The bouncer breaks into laughter and abandons his guard post, decides he can just let things happen.

Off to the side, not far from the stage, is a frat boy, bouncing along to the music. He's built like a rugby player, no pretense to hip style, and he thinks the whole thing is *great!* He's just dancing away there with a grin on his face, no edge to him at all, and you wonder, watching him get a kick out of this show, if there's any *real* edge to it, since he—normal frat guy—can take it so casually. Sitting behind us is a downtown freak, who's got multihued hair and plucked eyebrows and absurdly long, thin arms and legs. He must be thinking, "How dare this happy frat boy enjoy our music," so he winds his way to the front and launches himself at the frat boy, wraps spider arms and legs around him and tries to wrestle him down. Frat Boy squares his shoulders a little, causing Spider Guy to fall off, and the bouncer is there immediately to step between them. Spider Guy wends his way back to his seat, so Happy Fratty, who's fairly soused and still full of good will, goes to the lip of the stage and reaches his hand out to shake with James, no hard feelings. James kicks the hand, and Fratty shrugs and goes back to bouncing along with the beat, as happy as ever.

Everyone but Fratty remains on edge. James, a sax player as well as a singer, plays in scraggly, flapping squawks. Someone throws a shot glass; James grabs it, flings it down, smashing it on the stage floor. There's some ruckus back at the bar. I don't recall much else. Keyboardist Adele Bertei tells me when I meet her a couple of months later that this had been one of the most depressing evenings of her life, and Jody tells me the day after the show that musically the thing was ragged. I myself had not noticed any musical letdown.

Anyway, the band's set is over, they're backstage, but suddenly James is onstage again, blood running in lines down his face, and he shouts into the mic, "I don't care if you guys are cowards, I'll take 'em on by myself." Then he throws down the mic and stomps off. (The next day, I describe this to my friend Jay, and she says "Oh, that happens all the time on acid; I'm always seeing blood crisscrossing people's faces." "No, no. You don't understand. It was *real blood*.") Seeing James's bloodstreams, electric fear runs through me. I'm extra alert, my vision is double sharp, I think to myself, "It finally happened! Someone went back there and smashed a bottle into James's face." And a realization is stretching itself in front of my eyes. "This is a human being! People whom I know associate with him! And care about him! And every time he performs, he goes out there, to get hurt!" Rich and Teresa are ready to leave, but I insist we stay. "We've just seen something incredible." But why stay on? "No. We've seen something incredible. People have to *take it into account*." They look at me doubtfully. I tell them, "The Stumblebunnies final set, they can't just do it normally." The Stumblebunnies? Anyway, we stay, we wait (me, Rich, and Teresa). I insist there will be an effect. Finally, the Stumblebunnies shuffle themselves back out, the singer says something sardonic, "Broke up three fights in the last half hour," and now they're playing like before, but even more subdued, their reaction to the preceding strife being nothing more than to dull themselves out and detach. This bores me. They're not doing anything. Teresa looks at me like, "What'd you expect?" After two numbers I say, "Let's go," apologize for making them stay.

(The next day at work, Jody tells us that no one had attacked James with any bottle; James had accidentally cut himself on pieces of that smashed shot glass, while throwing himself around the stage. And afterwards, blood had seeped out. "So James was just grandstanding?" asks Rob. Jody nods.)

We clear out of CBGB, head back to Rich and Teresa's, feeling let loose. Rich is talking animatedly and walks right into a sign post, conking himself on the head but not hurting himself badly. Back at his place, he sits me in front of a record player and puts on James Brown and says, "Listen. *This* is what the Contortions are doing." I'd barely heard James Brown up until then, Brown having had no impact on white Connecticut where I grew up. Rich wants to form a band with me, and he wants me to deepen my sense of music. He explains, "When white guys fuck they just go straight in wham wham wham, while black guys put a wiggle in it." (And then the Contortions put a contortion into the wiggle.)

James Brown's "Papa's Got A Brand New Bag" had reconfigured r&b and soul and reggae and was working its way into jazz via Miles Davis and into African music via high life, but despite rock-leaning funkers like Funkadelic and Sly (and even David Bowie, of all people), rock really didn't know funk. But rock was a vanguard in one way: To overdraw the distinction, r&b is a dance among musical elements (and among the people who participate in it), while rock can also be a *battle* among musical elements (and among the people who participate in it). The Contortions took in jazz as well as funk, and jazz already had battle experience, musicians cutting each other onstage and turning their backs on the listeners. But James Chance was playing off of r&b and rock rhythms, not jazz, and Jody Harris drew heavily on Miles's guitarists David Creamer (*On The Corner*) and Pete Cosey (*Pangaea*), who were doing the same. Guitarist Pat Place and keyboardist Adele Bertei were officially "nonmusicians," but Adele had sung in soul bands and rock bands, and she and Pat obviously knew rhythm and funk. James was improvising into noise from a bedrock of r&b honking, squawking, and riffing rather than from a tradition of jazz melodic soloing, even if he drew on jazz-soloing-into-noise as inspiration. He steered clear of legato, played the sax like a drum. It's no surprise that in the wake of the Contortions, jazz guys like James "Blood" Ulmer were inspired by the "no wave" scene of which the Contortions were a part, since it seemed an alternative to jazz's relentless descent into being just a fine-art music for critics or make-out music for what was left of its public. No wave promised to take the jazz battle back to the people, back to the dance floor. (Then, of course, hip-hop superseded everything.)

The four Contortions cuts on 1978's *No New York* compilation (not included in the new *Irresistible Impulse* box) got the Contortions' sound, but Eno mixed the thing onto tissue paper, and it's too damn thin. It's still jarring and extraordinary, and by far the best record of what the band actually sounded like. James had lots of good ideas for 1979's *Off White* and *Buy The Contortions* but he botched the production by making everything too clear. Those albums are crawling with inspiration nonetheless. Among other things, James throws in disco moves and camp silliness, adding the sha-la-la-la spirit of pop music rather than just playing tough. Those two albums are the first half of *Irresistible Impulse*. The rest is James with sidemen, mostly recorded in the early '80s after the Contortions broke up, and it's far too legit—expert jazz and funk musicians, complex horn arrangements. James is singing and playing better (his voice had been scrawny in the early days), but what's lost is the Contortions' ferocious welding of sound and spewing it out. On record you can discern the lyrics, however, which are smart where his stage patter was dumb. It's as if he'd heard the Stones' "Under my thumb is the girl who once had me down" and understood that "had me down" was the greater part of it.

The Contortions' sound was unique: The rhythm had a push like no jazz band and a speed like no rock band, so it kicked the music into contortedness years before rave and jungle. And it brought the noise a decade before Public Enemy, and anticipated lots that's going on in hip-hop right now. Neptunes fans: Go listen to "Jump" on Mystikal's *Let's Get Ready*, but imagine the riffs doubling up on themselves with nightmares thrown on top. That's what the Contortions sounded like. Except no one else really sounds like the Contortions. Their two guitarists had this beautifully fucked playing, Jody splattering us with hard notes while Pat unsettled us with eerie slides. The band provided momentum that James undercut when he resorted to overdubs, and which none of the "real" jazzbos and funkbos (Bern Nix, Joe Bowie) could give him post-Contortions. But James gave the Contortions its center, its reach into our hearts and guts and minds, and a lot of its form. Definitely a whole-beats-sum-of-parts deal, and I'm sad that the band members weren't all shanghaied into band counseling and forced to stick with one another. (I should talk; I never stayed in a band more than a year.) There's much beauty in the solo sets—in clearing out the band sound, James made room for horn charts and jazzy interplay. But he didn't *have* to clear out the band sound to do this.

Someone once asked Jody what he thought Miles would think of the Contortions. "He'd call it a third-rate version of what he'd done several years earlier." I jumped to the Contortions' defense: "No. Miles is too diffuse. You guys are rock 'n' roll."

The Village Voice, April 8, 2003

CHAPTER 3

DEATH ROCK 2000
SAY IT LOUD—GET OFF OF MY CLOUD: DANCING WITH MR. BROWNSTONES

In the opening scene of Scarface, *we are shown a successful man; we know he is successful because he has just given a party of opulent proportions and because he is called Big Louie. Through some monstrous lack of caution, he permits himself to be alone for a few moments. We understand from this immediately that he is about to be killed. No convention of the gangster film is more strongly established than this: it is dangerous to be alone.*
—Robert Warshow, "The Gangster as Tragic Hero"

I once wrote a controversial review for *Spin*—that no one ever commented on—about James Brown where I claimed, in effect, that rather than being a "root" or a "source" of the present in black music, he was instead—and more interestingly—an indigestible problem for modern r&b and hip-hop. His funk had become the putative format for a lot of black music, but it was a format that no one could quite use. Funk at its invention was *really* extreme; *everything* became rhythm, foreground became background and vice versa, nothing simply supported a "lead" instrument or singer. The vocals were drumbeats, the drums punctuated and completed the vocals. The horns and guitars were staccato percussion. The beats were not evenly spaced: Instead, even more than in the rest of rhythm and blues, everything was in complementary note clusters, no instrumental part replicating another, each tumbling over the others in a perpetual-motion machine. Basically anything by James Brown from "Papa's Got a Brand New Bag" onward (r&b no. 1, pop no. 8, 1965) that wasn't a ballad fits this pattern. And most everything in "funky" black music since then has been something of a compromise or an amalgam—people wanting the funk but also wanting the song on top or the rap on top.

So even the hard funk of Funkadelic and Kool and the Gang had a somewhat straighter groove, and in hip-hop and r&b you always—until recently—had a loud drum nailing down the backbeat, or even a one-two-three-four (the more discofied r&b), with the song or rap back on top and most of the funk relegated to the bass guitar or bass keyboard. With the backbeat/one-two-three-four anchoring whatever was on top, some of JB's propulsive tumble was lost. So I think the tension in much of the world's music in the next century will be: "We don't want to give up song form or the Euromelody tradition, or we don't want to give up an out-front rap, or an out-front guitar solo, or an out-front wall of noise, or an out-front dance collage, or _____ (from whatever music tradition), yet we also want to have the tumbling funk and never-ending groove, so what do we do?" I hope it stays a problem. I can't imagine it being "solved."

I've gotten into email discussions about this with my friend Mark Sinker, a music historian in Britain, who electronically nods his assent ("some conflicts oughtn't to be resolved"). Mark says, "Black music generally (with a very few exceptions, though JB is a key one) is and always has been more casually magpie-ish than a succession of projective fantasies from its white commentators (pro or con) like to imagine." Mark goes on to cite Robert Johnson performing Bing Crosby for his black audiences but getting only his blues songs recorded by the white record company. Probably more to the point are forms like doo-wop and soul and . . . well, almost all African-American forms, which seem to be able with no effort to incorporate Euro-American harmonies and chord progressions into what are essentially black syncopation and call-and-response.

I've wondered why James Brown's funk was so accessible, why it charted so high—why it didn't itself sound difficult to a lot of people. I think basically this was because he wasn't putting a "song" on top (except in his ballads, which reverted to a more standard, less funky rhythm) but rather exhortations, chants, and so forth, so that the note clusters bubbling forth from everywhere didn't seem to *disrupt* a melody or rap that the listener was trying to latch onto.

Anyway, in general, after 1965 Brown's music became much less magpie-ish, much less eclectic from any source, Euro-American or Afro-American, and I doubt this was due to any disinclination to be either magpie-ish or Europeanized, but rather due to his total commitment to funk. In the vocals, guitars, horns, everywhere, everything was rhythm, and really there was nowhere to put much in the way of standard songs, melodies, rock guitar solos, polyphony, and so on. He did actually explore complex European chords; horn blasts and guitar chords tended to be ninths and elevenths, which would not have been possible if he hadn't taken in—probably by way of jazz—the high-art European scale.

And hip-hop and r&b continue to take in anything they can, and I see a never-ending tension in contemporary black music, which wants to keep the funk but *also* the song and the stream-of-talk on top. But if you've been listening to "urban" radio recently you'll notice that there is much less reliance on the backbeat and that vocalists and melodies are diving into the rhythm much more, crossing measure bars and ending at off-beats and so forth. And this music is breaking out of r&b and onto the pop charts. "What Ya Want" (Ruff Ryders featuring Eve and Nokio) got into the Top 30, and "Bills, Bills, Bills" (Destiny's Child) preceded Christina Aguilera's "Genie in a Bottle" as number one, which means that to many mainstream listeners this stuff is no longer difficult or challenging or radical. And even "Genie" is moving in this direction: yes, a really obviously loud backbeat to hammer everything in place, but also a tumble of fast drumbeats at the end of every other measure to dislodge the rhythm and make the song fall forward into the next measure. You'd never have gotten such prominent off-beats in a number one back in '89.

To my ears, there's a deliberate disruptiveness in Destiny's Child's music—that's their solution to the "problem": *Let* the top and the bottom disrupt each other a bit, pull the beats away from the groove and have them follow the singers, or have the singing go chase the bottom beats. Or (e.g., in their followup hit "Bug a Boo") place "orchestral" stabs in the background and have the voices run in front as if trying to out-race these stabs. What seems "challenging" is that the bottom and top aren't quite integrated, so you can marvel at the dexterity with which the singing dives after the rhythm or outruns the beats or fends off the accompaniment. Which makes this something of an up-market music (in my mind; I don't know how it plays out with its prime audience), like jazz: young black sophisticates putting forth pseudowisdom about male-female relationships, tied to sophisticated rhythms. I don't intend any of this as criticism, except that I hear fun but no warmth in Destiny's Child. In a way, these women play with the "problem" rather than trying to solve it, in that they don't put full funk and full song together but instead have each disarrange the other somewhat.

Unlike Destiny's Child, the performers who record for Ruff Ryders Records (such as DMX and Eve) seem more interested in presenting themselves as people who can fuck you or kill you than in showing off their musical dexterity. Fact is, though, that the music is some of the richest around, a lot of the richness due to frequent producer Swizz Beatz. The background music he creates—long developing riffs, usually taking up several measures—really is a foreground; the riffs *are* the drama in the music. (Or maybe they're just more comforting for me to attend to; they help me avert my ears from the ugly sounds and thoughts coming out of the rappers' mouths. "I hope you ain't tongue-kissing your spouse, because I be fuckin' her in the mouth." I don't dismiss or necessarily dislike such lyrics, by the way. I'm just ambivalent about them.) Since he's working with rappers rather than singers, Swizz Beatz has extra leeway, because sometimes rapping can be the steadying element, can be the one-two-three-four or hit hard on the backbeat, freeing up the drums to play around with off-beats. But when Swizz Beatz goes to a melody song like "What Ya Want," using a rapper, Eve, who emphasizes off-beats, the music still sounds effortless and at ease, even while it refuses to honor the measure bars and the main beats. The background melody seems to be going off on its own dance, but then when the chorus comes around, the singers jump right on top of the melody and it becomes their dance too. And, as I said, this song has been all over the radio.

In my *Spin* review I mentioned the paradox of James Brown's being the out-front star of the show *and* his being radically dependent on his surrounding musicians. If they fluff their notes, the whole structure unravels. Of course, the way I've written this assumes a live performance, or at least a group situation—whereas, in fact, most music is heard prerecorded (over the radio, through a home stereo system, in a car, at a dance club, in a supermarket, etc.), and many beats these days are programmed, not played by a group. But I don't think that this is a problem for my argument. It just makes my argument frankly metaphoric, the live model being a metaphor for how (some) people take in the music psychologically, feel it at home, use it at a dance club, sing along with siblings in the car, wherever; for the way society takes in the music. Whatever.

About fifty years ago, Robert Warshow wrote an essay that I've found unendingly useful, "The Gangster as Tragic Hero," about crime movies. "The initial contact between the film and its audience is an agreed conception of human life: that man is a being with the possibilities of success or failure. This principle, too, belongs to the city; one must emerge from the crowd or else one is nothing." I'll suggest by analogy—*real tentatively*—that the musical paradox in modern black music may be a social one as well. The music is one of group interaction, with no role inherently more central than another; yet it *needs* a star, an out-front center of attention to focus the music. But the emergence of a star, a dominant lead singer, potentially violates the form (and there are those pesky note clusters in the rhythm instruments to unmoor the star and pull him down, if he takes up too much space). James Brown bowled over these contradictions through the force of his personality, but his musical legacy is that a lot of people live in a world where the star has to adjust to his supporting players, the song has to adjust to the accompaniment.

In his essay, Warshow wrote, "Modern equalitarian societies . . . whether democratic or authoritarian in their political forms, always base themselves on the claim that they are making life happier." And so public displays of unhappiness and failure are seen as disloyal. (I'd say, that is, that public displays of unhappiness and failure that are not reducible to supposedly solvable social problems, to some category like "poverty" or "mental illness," are considered disloyal—or at least incomprehensible.) The appeal of the gangster movie is that it allows the audience to experience failure vicariously, because in such movies success leads *inevitably* to failure. To succeed is to be alone—but to be alone is to get shot, "for success is always the establishment of an *individual* pre-eminence that must be imposed on others, in whom it automatically arouses hatred." I'll ask (and I doubt that there is a simple answer) whether any of this is relevant to hip-hop—you know, where rappers emerged as the stars in a form invented by DJs; where rappers and producers share or compete for credit (which is it? share? compete? both?). I'm thinking of the Eve album, where she's proclaimed the Ruff Ryders' First Lady, but the rest of the posse comes along and supports her/drowns her out half the time. There is probably a lot to say here about the death and violence that permeate Ruff Ryders lyrics, but someone who feels the music more deeply than I should be the one to say it. I'll suggest the following: The lyrics don't just convey "I'm strong, I'm going to fuck you, I'm going to kill you," but also "We (the Ruff Ryders) need to stick together or we'll die." And rapper DMX adds, without negating the first part, that he's weak, he's sliding, he's going to die anyway. He's on the Ruff Ryders *Ryde or Die* compilation; for him the title could be *Ryde AND Die*. I don't know if these personas correspond to the rappers' actual lives. In "The Convo," DMX says that he has the God-given ability to rhyme, he has the choice to rhyme or to shoot, and with God's help he'll rhyme not shoot. But his death is part of his persona in a way that death wasn't part of the pre-posthumous persona of, say, Johnny Ace or Sam Cooke or Frankie Lymon or Marvin Gaye. In decades past, death personas—at least in popular music (jazz is another story)—have been more a rock thing, a white thing.

Okay, now for the white thing. My idea is that the Rolling Stones are relevant to the year 2000 not so much because they have been absorbed but because, in some ways—like James Brown—they haven't. Of course, musically they're regarded as either classic or moot, which makes them a dead issue, fully absorbed or not worth absorbing (though if the word *hard* is anywhere in your musical self-description—hard rock, hard beats, hardcore—then you're influenced by the Stones no matter what your genre). But there's a tendency in what they did—I'll call it the punk-rock tendency—which is still potent and problematic, still interestingly impossible.

The Stones took call-and-response form and turned it on its head. A brief description of call-and-response: A preacher says or sings (calls) something, the choir and often the rest of the congregation sing out a standard response, the preacher says/sings something else, the choir/congregation sings out the standard response again, etc. The audience is part of the form of the music, the structure; no audience, and the call gets no response. On record, the backup singers substitute for the audience; James Brown calls, "Say it loud!" and the singers respond, "I'm black and I'm proud!" In general, this form permeates black music, even when there's no congregation or backup singers. Chuck Berry says, "Go Johnny go, go," and his guitar plays a riff in response. Or Robert Johnson sings a phrase and his guitar finishes it for him. To speak loosely: Even when the music isn't precisely a call and a response, it is musical elements in conversation, voices and instruments playing off of each other, leaving space for each other.

Call-and-response is premised on a shared psychological space between singer and responders, between performers and audience. The Stones shattered that unity, set the relation between performers and audience as one of potential unresolvable conflict. *And that's what attracted them their audience.* "Don't hang around 'cause two's a crowd" attracted a crowd. The Stones were two mints in one, a come-here mint and a fuck-off mint, and the combination was involving, irresistible. (I think it was irresistible because it mirrored a split in the listener's—e.g., my own—psyche.) (And, well, probably a thousand different things attracted them their audience; different fans liked different things. But this was one.)

I'm talking metaphorically here, since I'm not claiming that the song—"Get Off of My Cloud," 1965, the same year as "Papa's Got a Brand New Bag"—created any predetermined response in the listener. Probably most listeners, when they got to the call-and-response part, "Hey (hey) you (you) get off of my cloud," simply identified with the singer and believed they were addressing the same "you" as the Stones. As it happens, the metaphor captures what *I* felt when I first heard the song, performed by a rock band at a junior-high-school dance, my nemesis and ex-friend Jeff playing drums and screaming out the words. And what I felt was that the band were a bunch of scary cool creeps who were yelling at people like me, and that maybe I—teacher's pet, emotional weakling—deserved to be yelled at. So part of me was up there with the band yelling, and part of me was the "you" that was being yelled at. But the thing is, people like me weren't the outsiders; we became the Stones' primary audience, or a big hunk of it. And the kids up there in that junior-high rock band were probably as conflicted as I was, as unsure as I where they were in relation to the "heys" and the "yous." The lead guitarist hanged himself several years later—I know nothing about it. And Jeff—probably the most charismatic guy I've met in my life—turned himself off, at least in public, took himself down to zero for the rest of high school.

In 1969 I got my first Stones album, *Big Hits (High Tide and Green Grass).* Shortly afterwards I heard that Brian Jones had died. I didn't know any of the Stones' names except for Jagger. I didn't know which one Brian was. I looked at the pictures on *Big Hits.* One of the band members, the one with blond hair, had a flat, cool, blank kind of face. It reminded me of my friend the drummer. I hoped that this one, the blond one, would be Brian, the dead one, because he scared me the most.

Here's the schema: (1) "Hey (hey) you (you)" is a call-and-response; this means that the audience is participating in its own rejection, if it wants, when told "don't hang around 'cause two's a crowd." (2) So the sing-along isn't merely an "Us vs. Them" chant; it can be an "Us vs. Us. vs. Them," an audience dividing against itself, trying to overcome and deny itself, being empowered and unified in self-division and self-destruction. And I think that this catches the Stonesiness of the era, the punk tendency within '60s rock, the audience (some of it) needing to feel rejected (in part) or attacked (in part) as a sign of the superstar's integrity (and feeling a common bond with and distance from the other listeners who felt the same way, and with the band that was doing this to them, maybe).

Mick Jagger liked to participate in his own rejection. "Heart of Stone" is apparently obvious irony, the singer claiming he's going to make the girl cry when you know that it's the girl who's making *him* cry. Except, the way Jagger sings it, the guy really is as tough and scary as the words say he's pretending to be. "Back Street Girl" does it the other way around: The words say it's about ownership, the rich married man laying down the rules to his mistress like she's property, telling her he wants to fuck her but doesn't want her to enter into and dirty up his tidy upper-class life; but in the music it's the most beautiful love song the Stones ever recorded. Another example: the live "Midnight Rambler" in which the swaggering Rambler-sociopath-narrator-killer is boasting, "Honey, it's no rock 'n' roll show," thereby denigrating the actual rock 'n' roller who wrote and is singing the song and the mere rock 'n' roll show at which he's singing it.

In Stanley Booth's great book on the Stones (called alternately *Dance with the Devil* and *The True Adventures of the Rolling Stones*) Alexis Korner and Ian Stewart recalled the Stones' early days.

> KORNER: "[Brian] used to jump forward with the tambourine and smash it in your face and sneer at you at the same time. . . . Brian achieved what he wanted to achieve by his extreme aggression, and it was extreme, it was incitement, when Brian was onstage playing he was inciting every male in the room to hit him. . . . It was Brian who made the blokes want to thump him. He would deliberately play at someone's chick, and when the bloke got stroppy, he'd slap a tambourine in his face."

> STEWART: "Brian could have been killed a few times."

Of course the Stooges and Sex Pistols and scores of other punks elaborated on this call-and-response, bands and audiences flouting each other's authority, spitting, cutting, hitting, making noise, and presumably at times getting a kick out of the whole process. At Stooges shows, instead of the fans mobbing the band—like in the Beatles' teenybopper days—you had Iggy going after the audience. He would dive into the crowd, smash his body down onto the floor, flop around like a spastic, jab the mic into people's faces and demand they sing into it, lie down on broken glass, pour hot candle wax over himself, provoke people into hitting him. So this is the call-and-response turnaround: Instead of black audiences prepared to be part of the music, you have white audiences forced into being part of the show whether they want to or not. "*I* am the audience," Iggy claimed in one of his interviews. The guy behind me at the Stooges and Blue Öyster Cult New Year's Eve show, December 31, 1973, kept yelling over and over, "Come back here Iggy and I'll kill you, come back here Iggy and I'll kill you." Lester Bangs, musing back on a particularly violent Stooges show: "Jungle war with bike gangs is one thing, but it gets a little more complicated when those of us who love being around that war (at least vicariously) have to stop to consider why and what we're loving. Because one of the things we're loving is self-hate, and another may well be a human being committing suicide." But anyway, I want to consider the social environment of this death thing, in which the *we* splits up, the psyche divides.

Brian, Keith, Dylan, another Keith, Lou, Iggy, Johnny Thunders, Peter Laughner, Sid Vicious, Axl, Kurt, Courtney, plus scores of lesser-knowns and probably a bunch of goth chicks and industrial guys I've never listened to—though some of these people realized that failure was no success at all and so decided to live, or perhaps secretly led a life of blissful mental health, self-destruction was nonetheless part of their image and part of their appeal.

Leaning again on that Warshow essay, I'd say that though this music may emerge in urban bohemia, it has its emotional roots in the suburbs from which the bohemians come. Warshow was writing from the point of view of second-generation immigrant Jews whose world of success or failure was the garment district, drugstores, the move into academia and the professions. I'm third generation, and the world of success or failure is high school, college, the business job or professional/academic career that's expected (rather than a sought-after achievement). And the agreed conception of human life—at least among would-be bohemians, freaks, goths, and probably a lot of the normals, too—is that human beings have the potential to be compromised, contaminated, that you don't succeed unless you kiss the teacher's ass or the boss's ass; but if you do so you haven't really emerged from the crowd, you've just become a teacher's pet. Becoming a "rock star" is maybe a way out of this, since it's not the teacher or boss who's judging you anymore (supposedly). But you have to please the audience—and so, to emerge from that crowd, you have to attack your audience. And as I'm suggesting, certain audiences will want you to attack them, to assert your independence from them (and in so doing you act out for them their long-lost integrity). But then you've just pleased them anyway, and if you're a real punk like the Stooges and the Sex Pistols you want fans to resist, to hit back. But either the fans kill you or (this is what audiences really do) they walk out on you. Then you're nothing, you're an obscurity. Or they don't resist you, they continue to appreciate you. So the only way to really resist their appreciation, to emerge from that crowd, is to die. And I (the fan) want you to, because otherwise you're still kissing my ass. (I'm not saying this is true, mind you; I'm just explaining the logic of its appeal.)

Anyway, I don't know if this Stones dynamic (and by the Stones I mean the Stooges-Pistols-GN'R as well) will remain a central tension for music in the twenty-first century, since punk nihilism-insanity-despair needs a social context of *optimism* to react against, an irrational sense that we're heading towards utopia and can break through all limits. I hope the world retains this optimism, as its legacy from America and Western Europe, but the real legacy might be economic collapse and ecological disaster, and Iggy & the Stooges just might not make any more sense. That would be sad.

I've been listening a lot to Turbonegro's *Apocalypse Dudes*, which is in competition with Kid Rock's for my rock album of 1999. And on the surface and in the sound it's part of the Stones-Stooges tradition. "Selfdestructobust"—yeah, they're going to kill themselves or die trying. But really, they're just unreconstructed layabouts, sitting at home with their Dolls and Stooges records, imagining that the world has stopped. So they're on their own cloud all right, but there's no call out to the world, no reason to respond, certainly no challenge to the would-be layabouts and pseudo-seven-day weekenders in their primary audience, or to anyone. And actually I'm baffled that this album is so *good*, given its insularity.

I don't know how overwhelmingly relevant this "two's-a-crowd" dynamic is at the moment, with Cobain laid to rest as a total denial and Courtney maybe having found her equilibrium. Eminem seems to be the guy now. "This guy at White Castle asked for my autograph so I signed it 'Dear Dave, thanks for the support *asshole*.'" I think Eminem's voice—a slow talk, unlike "real" rap not heavily into rhythm and rhyme—is perfect for what he's trying to do, for laying out his social pathology flat before us. (He's criticized for not being a good rapper, which is just stupid. I remember 2Pac getting criticized for analogous reasons, as if he didn't have the *right* to be emotionally effective since he wasn't dancing his tongue with the technique of a Rakim.) His lyrics are hyperbolic: "Since age twelve I felt like I'm someone else 'cause I hung my original self from the top bunk with a belt. Got pissed off and ripped Pamela Lee's tits off and smacked her so hard I knocked her clothes backwards like Kris Kross." On the one hand Eminem *detaches* himself from his narrator Slim Shady, which means that my emotional feelings towards Slim Shady's conspicuous dysfunction are tempered by my knowledge that there's a probably nondysfunctional guy (or at least one not completely owning to Shady's dysfunctions) pulling the strings of this puppet. But nonetheless I recognize that Eminem gets some poetic-intellectual-funny effects that he couldn't have gotten out of a more believable narrator. As for Slim Shady, there's a generational cool here—I'm young, I'm sharp, I'm slim, I'm a mess, isn't that cool?—with the last question very nonrhetorical, since Slim Shady *is* cool but simultaneously way too massively fucked-up to *be* cool, any possible self-control and grace under pressure long since thrown out the window. I'm your mirror. He straps himself into bed, with a bulletproof vest on, and shoots himself in the head. One's a crowd on his cloud.

Making note of the fact that Eminem's a white guy in the border country between hip-hop and rock, I'm thinking that in the future a Stones-like "Get Off of My Cloud" dynamic might become more relevant to blacks, to hip-hop, to r&b, since maybe in these genres the dynamic won't yet have been played through to its impossibility. I just bought the Kelis "I Hate You" song (which is really "Caught Out There" but I don't know anyone who calls it that). As the lyrics per se go, it's a standard r&b war-between-woman-and-man thing that doesn't enter the Stones' two's-a-crowd dynamic. Too much of a shout-along, an us vs. whomever we happen to hate. That's the lyrics per se. But the *listening experience* is a whole other thing: The I-HATE-YOU-SO-MUCH-RIGHT-NOW jumps right out and away from r&b, from black culture, from music. It's not about empowerment, getting even, taking control—it's not cool, not grace under pressure, not wit and wisdom of wronged sisterhood. It's just plain a scream of hate. She's *losing it.* Just completely losing it. Out of control. And that's where the song seems more white than black—not that whites lose control more than blacks, but that whites *in music* lose control more than blacks, because, for some whites, losing control is freedom, breaking out of oneself and one's world, from the inner contamination that binds one to the world. At the extreme this losing control isn't just going wild to the beat, it's Iggy Pop half bragging and half hating himself for being the most fucked-up guy on the block, the one who's going to die. It's about taking oneself *out.* Whereas for blacks, in general, freedom is about gaining control, not losing it. (BTW, I think that Kelis sounds *great* when she's breaking down, breaking out—far beyond most riot grrrrls (most of whom just sound mannered or ugly and self-righteous).)

I'd say that DMX more than Kelis is self-consciously fucked and making an issue of it: "You know he hurt before he died/And you wonder if he lost his shirt before he died/Only two knew the answer, and one of us is dead/So anyone who seeks the truth can get it straight to the head/Then you and him can discuss what I did/Yeah, it was wrong dog but I slid/I will pay one day, just not right now." He certainly doesn't take it into Stones-Stooges territory, where the audience participates in its own rejection. But with DMX, like Kelis, it's not so much that in the words he's portraying himself as out of control, it's the *sound*, his voice; and *sounding* out of control is what, maybe, is relatively new to black music.

In older gangsta rap, no matter what was going on in the lyrics, the rappers tended to hang back, sound cool. For instance, Dre and Dogg sounded cool and controlled in "Nuthin' But a G Thang." But DMX, when he wants to emphasize a lyric, moves his voice from smooth to clumsy. He doesn't, of course, get to white land, where losing control is a kind of letting loose, a break into freedom. For DMX it's more like he's breaking down—he can be a danger, he can be in danger. And this is why, no matter what the shit he's saying, there's a vulnerability to him. Which I guess lets me onto his cloud (unless he shoots me or something).

The Village Voice, January 18, 2000

PART TWO

HERO OF FEAR

CHAPTER 4

THE KINGSTON TRIO

The first record I bought for myself was most likely something by the Kingston Trio. This is hard to say for sure, since I may have bought the Kingston Trio records for my brother Richard, for Christmas or his birthday. We'd buy each other what we really wanted for ourselves: I'd buy him Kingston Trio, he'd buy me Chad Mitchell Trio. It made no difference, since there was only one record player, and the records were all stored on the same rack. In any event, the Kingston Trio's were my favorites.

This was age nine and ten. What was going on in my life at the time? A lot of things, so I'll just choose a couple anecdotes from fourth grade, 1963-1964.

The first anecdote is triumph. In reading class Mrs. Trevithick gave us a list of vocabulary words and instructed us, for homework, to write a story that incorporated those words. I went home and dutifully wrote a little story, as did all the other kids. She had us read our stories aloud to the class; I remember this as a quiet, uncomfortable experience. A few days later she gave us another list of words and the same assignment. At home that night I had an inspiration: I'd write a little playlet featuring an exasperated sergeant and a stupid private. *Gomer Pyle* wasn't on the air yet, so I don't know where I got the idea, maybe from the Beetle Bailey cartoon strip. I wrote funny dialogue, and when my turn came next day, I got up and acted out both parts, the sergeant getting upset and the private speaking in a ridiculous high-pitched squeak. And as I launched into this, acting with hand gestures and squeaks, the class went into hysterics. Mrs. Trevithick bent over double, she was laughing so hard. I asked a friend of mine, later, about a particular part of my dialogue, and he told me that he hadn't actually been able to hear what I'd been saying, the laughter was so loud and my voices so bizarre. It was the fact of what I was doing, up there making faces and squeaking and bawling, that was so funny.

I'd broken the dam. After that, all the boys came to class with funny, imaginative stories. Oddly, the girls continued on with quiet, dutiful ones.

This was probably the peak of my writing career. I'm sad that I couldn't have had the same effect on rock criticism.

To set up the second anecdote, I need to say that I'd been a very successful boy in elementary school, up till then. By "successful" I'm not referring to things like my story triumph, which had simply been an eruption of personality and creativity. Rather, I mean that I did well in sports: At recess when we picked teams I was either the first or second pick, and my friend Jeff would be the other one, either first or second, because you couldn't put us on the same team or we'd slaughter the other side. And I got good grades and did my homework well and usually knew the answers when I was called on in class. And I rarely got in trouble, almost never got reprimanded except sometimes for talking too much when I couldn't contain my exuberance.

But that word *successful* should sound odd. A successful boy? A successful fourth grader? I use it because it reveals how I felt then. I worked, emotionally. I worried. I argued over minor rule violations when my team lost in baseball. I was hurt by reprimands and by the occasional low test score, and I was afraid of them. I double-checked my answers before handing in tests. Also, on the other hand, I looked forward to getting tests back, my grades usually being better than most everybody's. My mom praised me for my work habits: She told me that mine were better than my brother's, since he only worked on the subjects that interested him, whereas I worked on them all.

I remember that once in class, as I was sitting down, I glanced at the boy behind me and felt a wave of pity for him. I wondered what it was like: I imagined that he must have felt desolate at not being one of us. "Us" meant people like me and Jeff, the ones who got praised and always won and were friends with each other.

So here's my second anecdote, from the other side.

There was a national day, probably known only to school teachers, called Arbor Day. The teachers had taught us a song, about trees, I guess, and had us participate in a little ceremony at which a tree would be planted and all of us fourth graders would sing the song. Normally, I'd have just stood in line and sung the song and been bored. But the boy next to me, Scott Bailey, was laughing instead of singing, and was giving me looks like, "Isn't this stupid!" So I laughed along with him, at the stupid song. But my laughter didn't come from within me, if you know what I mean. Scott wasn't someone I thought about much—he was one of those boys in the desert area away from me and Jeff and our sports club. But something must have been compelling about his laughter. Maybe I just felt that he'd think I was a sissy if I sang the stupid tree song and didn't laugh. When he started laughing I recognized the absurdity of the song—I wouldn't have recognized this if he hadn't laughed—and so I recognized that there was a whole other view. But, as I said, I wasn't laughing from within myself, even if I understood that the thing was laughable. I was laughing in response to Scott's laughing, just as I'd have sung the song in response to my teachers. Scott was next to me and laughing, he was my context, while the teachers wouldn't notice me, as far as I knew.

Later in the day, though, I was in the hallway standing on line with my home-room class, when Mrs. Trevithick came up to me out of the blue and said, "Frank, I hear you've been very bad today." And Mr. Nielson, my home-room teacher, said, "Yes, he's been bad all day." This stunned me—it was without explanation. Mr. Nielson often got irritated by me, but Mrs. Trevithick, though she was sometimes demanding, was always fair and never mean. But here she was, she'd come up to me specially, she'd told me I was bad, and she didn't even tell me why. And, as I've said, I took reprimands as failures, and I hated to fail, which is why I remember the incident. A while later Jeff came down the hall and said, "Ronnie West told on you, he told Mrs. Trevithick that you were laughing at the song." This solved the mystery, but created another. Why in the world would Ronnie West tell on me? We'd never had any arguments; I'd always been nice to him. Of course, now I can think of plenty of reasons, me being who I was and Ronnie being one of the kids who always got picked last. (I remember that one recess, when we'd had too many people for a basketball game, he and another boy didn't get chosen at all, and they were near tears; so we promised to make them the captains for the next day's game.)

So those are my two incidents, the first being one where my creativity reshapes the world, the second being an early inkling (this was 1964) that all hell was going to break loose, that I would forever lose my sense of place.

Pop music had meant nothing to me—I don't think I'd known it existed—until my brother, Richard, started listening to it on the radio. He was thirteen and I was nine, and I tended to follow him in what he did. I've never thought to wonder why he started listening then—maybe he got his own radio.

I was listening in early 1963. My favorite song, the first song I loved, was Skeeter Davis's "The End of the World." It was a sad but sweet song. We had a puppet set from Italy, and I once made the puppets do a little dance for joy when "The End of the World" came on. "Surfin' USA" by the Beach Boys was a hit then, too; I thought it was "Servin' USA," like in the Peace Corps, until Richard told me otherwise. The line "two girls for every boy" from Jan and Dean's "Surf City" struck me as being drastically intense, though I don't think I had any idea what it was about. Even more emotional was "Mecca," with the line "she lives on the east side, he lives on the west side," if I remember correctly, and the feeling that it was mysterious and tragic. I thought the singer was a woman, though I see in Whitburn it's by Gene Pitney. I wouldn't have bought any of these records, since my parents' record player didn't work anymore, it had been broken for several years. I liked Lesley Gore's "It's My Party" because of its energy, even though I felt there was something childish about its catchiness and about the crying stuff. "Judy's Turn to Cry," the follow-up, was just stupid, I thought; and over the summer I got bored with the radio, pop songs didn't interest me anymore. Or maybe my brother got bored, and I followed him in his boredom. So pop music was pretty much over for me. Six months later, when the Beatles appeared on *Ed Sullivan*, I was the only one in my fourth-grade home room who didn't watch it; I just didn't care. When Jimmy and Edith Kort down the street got "I Want To Hold Your Hand," I recognized that the song was catchy, but still the whole genre was silly to me by then. "She Loves You" with all those "yeah yeah yeahs" seemed really stupid, and when *The Saturday Evening Post* or one of those magazines printed excerpts from Lennon's *In His Own Write* (with introductory lines about how he was born while the nasties were bombing London but they didn't get him), I didn't understand the parody or the puns and I thought that the guy was a moron. But by then I was listening to a whole other genre. We'd discovered the Kingston Trio, and folk music; that was back in the summer of 1963, through some friends of my parents who'd let our family stay with them for a week at their summer place and who'd played us their records. And several weeks later my parents bought a new record player, and bought us a Kingston Trio record for it. (The timing of the purchase was no coincidence; my parents didn't think much of pop music—they listened to classical music on the radio—and, my mother told me several years later, had waited for us to outgrow pop music before getting the stereo. I didn't buy a pop record until I was thirteen, in 1967: *Sgt. Pepper's*, by the Beatles. I actually asked my father for permission to buy it—this moment was very scary for me, I'd had trouble getting the courage to ask him, and I was almost certain that he wouldn't let it into the house. But he merely told me that if I wanted to waste my money on that garbage I could.)

You could divide the folk music movement roughly into two camps: the alienated beatnik types (Ramblin' Jack Elliot, Dave Van Ronk), often leftist, played coffeehouses and bars and tried to root their music in authentic rural blues and country (i.e., in old records); and the slick commercial types (the Chad Mitchell Trio, the Limeliters), liberal, provided "sophisticated" (and slightly risqué) entertainment for patrons of "nightclubs" and were interested in punch lines more than authenticity. Naturally enough—or artificially enough, I should say—I think the slicksters were better than the beatniks (excepting my favorite beatniks, the Holy Modal Rounders and Bob Dylan). Not that I had any such opinion at the time, since I hardly knew of the beatniks' existence. Anyway, the Kingston Trio were the best of the nightclub groups, though as sophisticates go they were pretty square—really, they looked like cleancut young students ready to join the Peace Corps. I can imagine them providing an on-campus alternative to trashier surf-and-party music.

But I liked them because they were rousing, they were exciting. Listening now I realize that a reason I preferred them to the Top 40 music of summer 1963 was that *they rocked harder.* They didn't need bass or drums—they used bongos on some of their Latin and African stuff, but the acoustic guitar is actually a fairly percussive instrument. And anyway a lot of their energy came from the banjo, which on their fast stuff always seemed to charge forward pell mell.

They played two basic types of music: fast stuff, which I liked, and slow stuff, which I didn't. The fast stuff usually had one guy doing low harmony and comic commentary (if the song was meant to be funny), one guy holding the melody, and a guy on high harmony putting in background wails at crucial spots. I never liked their slow, sensitive songs. Yeccchy love songs. I liked their fast love songs, however. My favorite song of theirs was "Little Maggie," which I now think might be about a prostitute (I still can't figure out if the guy's got ten dollars to "make her mine" or to "pay her fine," if it makes a difference—and at age nine it didn't, since I had yet to be made aware of the concept "prostitute"), but at the time I just assumed it was a sailor's tribute to a long-lost or abandoned darling. "She's drinkin' away her troubles, oh lord, and foolin' another man." It's got the usual crazed banjo stampede, comic noises, and a wonderful bit of New England chauvinism: "Pretty girls were made for Boston love/Surely Maggie was made for mine." (Unfortunately, I've figured out now that they're saying "boys to love" not "Boston love," reducing it to mere *male* chauvinism; but back then "Boston love" is what I heard and "Boston love" is what made sense.)

As for their connection to what was going on in my life: none. And that is the point; the music was about my imagination, not about my life. I suppose there was some similarity between their music and my little playlet in reading class; they liked to put on voices and tell jokes just like I did; but, actually, the Limeliters and the Chad Mitchell Trio—not to mention out-and-out humorists like Tom Lehrer and Allen Sherman—were funnier. But I liked the Kingston Trio more because they were more emotional.

And as I said, it was about my imagination. Adventure songs. Songs about sailing ships. (I'd read a lot of sea stories as a child, where people used words like *bosun* and *lubber* and slept in hammocks and buried their treasure and stuck their arms into whale gut.) "Heave her up and away we'll go," and I thought of rolling sails and billowing waves (or is it the other way around?). "Remember the Alamo"—this song reminded me of a crucial early moviegoing experience, Texas volunteers in desperate hand-to-hand combat as Mexican soldiers swarmed over the walls and obliterated them.

They sang about murder: Mean John Hardy took his razor and slashed a man in Mobile Town; a long black rifle was used by a suitor to kill a groom; mysterious Tom Dooley killed a woman for no reason that was ever explained, and got caught and waited to die. They had a real eerie vengeance song, too, in which the ghost of poor beheaded Anne Boleyn was harassing old King Henry, was walking the bloody tower *with her head tucked underneath her arm.*

I mentioned above that they liked to put on voices. They did calypso, hillbilly, Hispanic, African, and this was often their best stuff. But, on their live records, they'd always introduce these songs with an edgy, condescending commentary, yukking it up, pretending for laughs that this material was primitive. Maybe they were ashamed of these songs or frightened by them. Yet when they did this music it really unleashed their energy. Their version of "The Lion Sleeps Tonight" came out a year before the Tokens' and kicks the Tokens' butt.

Not that I puzzled over or even noticed these contradictions. I just put it all into a story of energy and adventure. The whole country was on a Hero Story (that's the way it seemed on TV), shooting men into space and standing against the Russians and fighting for civil rights against hoses and dogs and whips in the evil South. And this Hero Story seemed to fit into the adventure books I liked to read, Daniel Boone and Davy Crockett and detective stories and sports stories—I don't mean to make all this seem simpleminded, since some of the stories were complex. I remember a sports novel that had as its climax a track star's decision *not* to run a race, since he didn't like all the crap and commerce that accompanied it. And there was a book about a young Jew, a musician, who goes underground as a spy in Nazi Germany, and he keeps repeating a line to himself, perhaps from a song or poem, "Go straight to the heart of danger, for there you will find safety." He ends up playing piano at the request of a Nazi captain: He plays Gershwin, and the Nazi criticizes it for being written by a Jew. Later, the captain overhears a piece that the musician is practicing, a piece the musician had actually written himself. The captain praises the piece and wonders that he'd never heard it. The musician tells him, "It was written by a Jew."

There was search for adventure. Life was on the line and people did things, and I assumed that this would be my destiny, when I got older. So my Hero Story, the one in my mind, really didn't have much to do with my being a puzzled kid, in line, wondering whether to sing a stupid tree song. The Hero Story was one of action—as opposed to being a story of heroic floundering, where I would be *right* to be divided between the teacher and Scott and to not know what to do. I had to jettison the first story and create the second, which is what I did as a teenager. That's another story.

Why Music Sucks #8, June 1995

CHAPTER 5

JUNIOR HIGH

HOODS AND SARCASM

In junior high school the threat of violence was always there, though not from people I really knew, I don't think, just from guys in the hall who would look tough and maybe see if they could scare you. I never really got attacked. There was a little squirt named John who'd come up in the hall and hit me on the arm to see if he could provoke me. This had a snideness to it; even though he never did get me to hit back, somehow I felt he'd gotten the better of me.

You could divide the cool people into the toughs—who were scary, who threatened to hit you—and the glamour-and-sarcasm people. I'm making up that terminology: The toughs were called hoods, sometimes, but the term *hoods* was on the wane. I do remember Jonathan Bennett in 1967 showing me the cover to *Between The Buttons* (Rolling Stones record) and saying with disapproval, "Notice how hard they're trying to look like hoods." Anyway, all the cool guys looked like that, whether or not they were the ones who might hit you. The old MGM Records *Best of the Animals* has the look even better: sleeves rolled back halfway up the forearm, shirt untucked, pants as tight as possible, a flat stare, 1966. You saw someone like that and you hoped he didn't come over and menace you. Every day in seventh and eighth grade I had the fear of being physically attacked, though it never happened. But this was just background fear. It was the glamour people, the sarcastic people, who really had the big effect on me. (I don't mean to imply wealth by the word *glamour*. These people were still tough looking, not rich looking. They were a dirty glamour, like the Stones.)

I remember once in homeroom some guys were talking about the film *Seconds*, with Rock Hudson, saying something about it playing soon, at the movie theater across the street. I asked, with interest, "Is it coming?"—but a guy misheard and thought I'd asked, "Is it exciting?" So he smirked and said some savage derogatory things about me for asking such a stupid question, since apparently it was a cool movie and everyone was supposed to already know that it was exciting. I'd actually never heard of the movie until that very moment, so my asking "Is it coming?" had just been a way of pretending to at least some knowledge of the movie and a big interest in it (whatever it was). I defended myself, telling them what I'd really said, and someone came to my defense, "Yes, I heard him.

He'd asked, 'Is it coming?'" What was special, uniquely junior high, about this incident wasn't that I was dishonest and so had pretended to knowledge and interest that I didn't have. I do this still sometimes, out of insecurity or laziness or just to keep the conversation moving. But the point is, back in seventh grade this incident was total trauma. The fact was that people were willing to ride you, attack you, for virtually *anything*, it didn't really matter what. I realize, of course, *now*, that what made me so vulnerable was that I visibly cared so much, that people knew they could get to me. It was such a little thing, yet I felt such terror.

I don't want to give the impression that there were some cool facts and things to say and do, and if only I'd mastered these facts then I wouldn't have gotten razzed. There were no real rules; the cool guys made it up from moment to moment, things to attack you on.

I think of junior high as such a nightmare time; I use the phrase *junior high* in my writing now as if there were something universal and self-explanatory about it, as if everyone had gone through what I'd gone through and would have the same visceral reaction to the phrase, the same understanding.

I wasn't particularly singled out for attack. Junior high had a general atmosphere of ridicule that everyone (all the boys, anyway) lived in, though not everyone promulgated it. These stupid incidents just happened day after day.

KING OF THE WORLD

Through age ten I felt I was the All-American boy, which didn't mean being goody-goody, it meant being daring and heroic and standing up for losers and being headstrong and wiseass. My mother would sometimes exhort me to act like a gentleman, and I'd say proudly to myself, "I'm not a gentle man, I'm a rough boy." A lot of this was in my head, my being a character in the adventure stories I liked to read. But in real life I did well in sports and did well in school and people laughed along with my jokes, and heroism seemed to be my destiny.

In fifth grade things turned bad. Years later I explained this to my parents, what went wrong in 1964: "I discovered that I wasn't King of the World." ("You're lucky," said my dad: "I didn't find out until college.") All of a sudden I was no good in sports, and coolness came in, so I was vulnerable to kids' teasing, and I had a particularly rough teacher and started to live in fear. At least, this is how I've usually remembered it. But thinking back, I realize that this isn't true. I didn't stop being good in sports, I merely stopped being one of the absolute best. And coolness and fashion and teasing didn't come along in force until sixth grade, and I was liked by people, had their respect (won an English class vote to be editor of a class newspaper—don't even think there was a vote, though there was one to see who would succeed me: It was just obvious that I should be the leader, *was* the leader), and the scary teacher actually thought I was the best student in the class. But I'd figured out that I was a scaredy cat, that I was afraid of everyone's opinion of me, that my success was contaminated by my need to please. And I must have felt that the bullies and the nasty people were about to move in and take my ground. My slight decline in sports was devastating because sports was the one endeavor that was not based on pleasing people. This may not seem rational, but to me hitting a home run was based on talent, whereas getting good grades was connected in my mind with convincing the teacher I was a good, attentive little boy. In sports, the bullies and terrorizers wanted me to *lose*, so I wasn't pleasing them by winning.

I think part of my vulnerability was because I was a perceptive person. I'd figured out (without yet having heard the Shangri-Las!) that there were two kinds of bad: the type of "bad" that is cruel and evil because it involves being nasty to people, and the type of bad that is daring and haughty and involves breaking rules and doing forbidden things and stepping up and getting hit by authority, and carrying oneself with a sexual presence. This second kind of "bad" wasn't necessarily good, but it certainly had something that I didn't feel I had: strength. But so did the first type, and usually it was the same people who embodied both types. (And maybe I wasn't even so sure that the first type was completely dreadful. Read on.) So in grades six through eight it was impossible for me to completely hate or detest the people who tormented me; I felt they had something I needed, and they seemed to be acting out a critique that was already hanging around inside me, anyway.

But, you know, in actuality I did resist, I was far from a nothing. During the summer before seventh grade I made my friend David Kinsman promise me that, if I ever started acting like I wanted to be one of the cool people, he'd come over and tell me to stop it. I didn't respect the cool people's cruelty, and I noted that they were too careful in their displays of emotion. And really it was displays of emotion that they would pick on—showing emotion (other than snideness) always made you a potential target of ridicule. There were some people who were cool without being cruel or cold, who simply had presence and style; but for me to have tried to be cool would have meant suppressing myself even more than I did already. It would have been a form of death. So even though I believed in the cool people's critique of me as an uptight little good boy, and despised myself for being so concerned with what everybody thought of me, I had my own critique of them: They were hard, some of them were bullies, some of them were stupid. I admired them sometimes for taking on teachers, but I didn't admire them for disrupting an interesting classroom discussion or for picking on me for having participated in such a discussion.

In junior high, if there was a noncool "center" (I mean a collection of people with social status who got envied), I didn't notice it; but perhaps that is because I was in it. I probably acted much as I do now, with some strong opinions amidst my joking, and occasional moments of unsuppressed arrogance; so I was probably formidable and intimidating at times, to some people—though of course I would have been unaware of this.

The cool people ruled in my mind, but I don't think that there were all that many of them—there were popular people (not to mention unpopular people) whom I wouldn't have categorized as cool, and probably these people way outnumbered the cool people. I remember that Sarah Hamill won the election for student council representative from my seventh-grade homeroom, and she was simply a pretty girl, a popular girl, probably would have been called a *soc* in a different time and place, no sense of danger or adventure in her, at least not that she displayed. Of course, people tend to vote for respectability, but nonetheless election meant something: popularity, at least, maybe respect. Jonathan Hale was the president of the junior high student council, and I remember him as a big lumbering normal guy; before the start of the one meeting I attended (as an observer), some guy told me that the only note in the student council suggestion box was a request for a Kotex machine in the girls' bathroom: a practical and sensible suggestion, I figured out several years later, but the guy who told me of it assumed—and therefore so did I—that the note was obscene, that it had been put in there by some kid who was being dirty. When the meeting reached the matter of the suggestion box, Jonathan simply said that there had been nothing in it except something obviously inappropriate and not serious. (This incident was in 1967 and was completely typical of that year as I experienced it, evokes that time for me much better than does a phrase like "Summer of Love," for instance.)

THE SEVENTH GRADE SAMURAIS

One day, maybe in eleventh grade, I was across the street from the school, at a luncheon counter, and I started talking to another guy there, Mickey Chilleri. I don't know if I'd ever had a conversation with him before and I don't think we had one afterwards, either, since the school had put him on a failure track and we had no classes in common. But we felt a rapport that day, maybe because we were both breaking a rule, being off school grounds. Mickey was a guy I'd been told to be scared of back in seventh grade, though I don't remember any run-ins with him. He was thin and had a sharp face and he'd frightened me. So now I was talking to this formerly scary guy (possibly still scary); he mentioned his being suspended several years earlier, and I asked him what for, assuming that it was something like cutting class or vandalism or baiting a teacher. I was ready to be outraged on his behalf, knowing that the school in general gave people like him a raw deal. He said, "Oh, for terrorizing some kid," to explain the suspension. The way he said it, it seemed logical, that it *would* have made sense for him to have gone around terrorizing kids in junior high, this was just part of life back then.

The guys who crossed the school lawn to terrorize me and Jon Bennett one evening in eighth grade: We were coming home from a movie; we saw the guys, four of them, slightly older, sleeves rolled up, dangerous. Jon said, "Here it is, they're going to get us." Jon told one of them that he knew the guy's brother; the guy moved aggressively forward into Jon, pushing him and saying, "What did you call my brother?" And then the guys just walked on. And I realized that they'd never had any intention of hitting us. They were just threatening us as a matter of form, it seemed.

I don't know. Cruelty is never justified. But people need to test each other, discover their power, get angry, let it rip. And anyway, the people who were going after me weren't going after a weakling.

Rob Sheffield's bullies [*the ones he'd described elsewhere in this issue of Why Music Sucks*] seem to have been just clods and terrorists, whereas mine carried some critical ability. I can honestly say that I never ran into a bully in junior high school who didn't have *something* interesting in his style, his sarcasm, his timing. I wish I could remember this better, could recall examples of what was actually said. The incidents that I *do* remember, in detail, are all pretty stupid, so maybe I was just projecting, about the "critical ability." Really, when most people go after you in life, it has nothing to do with you, it's just someone in his own delirium, looking for a target. But obviously I wanted to believe that these guys knew something.

In eighth-grade homeroom Scott Bailey and Eddy Cichon were assigned seats behind me and would ride me every morning, regularly say disparaging things to me. Scott Bailey was sort of an oaf. Eddy, though, had style, was slick and funny. Naturally, I don't remember any particular things he said. I do remember oafish Scott imitating the way I'd laughed—we'd been on a class trip to New York and seen *Fiddler on the Roof;* I'd laughed at all of Tevye's jokes in the play; Scott and Eddy thought (or decided to pretend to think) that I'd been ridiculous in do-ing so, and Scott next day kept imitating it for Eddy's benefit, my deep, crackly laughter. This hurt me but did not impress me. But I was impressed by the way he went after our homeroom teacher, Mrs. Grzymkowski; he just wouldn't shut up when she told us all to be quiet. She was a bigger bully than anyone in our class, simply had nothing good to say about anyone. (If she felt that way, why didn't she quit and become a clerk in a grocery store or something?) And if you wised back to her she'd squash you immediately, so Scott was engaging in kamikaze attacks. But he did it anyway, as if to say, "All you can do is kick me out, I don't care." He probably couldn't help himself, he just had to be aggressive. But I was glad that someone took on the big bitch.

Some guys used sarcasm on each other, as a way of sparring, to test each other but also as recreation, like playing basketball one-on-one; and these guys might have used the same sarcasm on more "sensitive" types like me, being unaware of the real hurt they were causing.

It was mostly over by ninth grade, and I was glad it was over, yet the behavior—people riding each other, provoking each other, terrorizing kids, needling me . . . I want to say that even when it was cruel, there was something pure about it.—Do I really believe this? I'm not sure. At its most stupid and ugly and despicable it's a bunch of kids going out fagbashing; at its most admirable it's something like the dozens (a ghetto "game" where a couple of kids trade comic insults to the point where one of them, the loser, breaks down) or master samurai warriors meeting in combat, but in this case it would be a master battle of sarcasm. And deadpan parody can be a useful weapon against authority: a kind of exaggerated solicitude or compliance that rides the line between mockery and servility, like Phil Dellio on his twelfth-grade basketball team [*described in the previous issue*]. By pure I mean that it's aesthetic. It's done for excitement, bloodlust—it's done with style, artistry. It's there as its own game. It doesn't package itself as morality or as being for the good of the group or of the world. Cruelty, if it really wants to organize itself, if it wants to go big-time, has to tie itself to morality, has to pretend that it's goodness. But junior-high cruelty was unpolluted by moral pretension.

THE WORLD'S FORGOTTEN BOY

I have a fantasy where I'm instructing jazz musicians or soul musicians how to play hard rock. "You have to pound and keep pounding, go pound pound pound pound, this is more important than dancing. You're hitting it, whack whack whack whack. Remember, you're trying to hurt somebody."

Junior high is *in* me. This is complicated: I rejected the cool people but I didn't reject their music. After a while hard rock *was* my music—and something about this time seems fundamental. The malicious laugh in the Syndicate of Sound's "Little Girl" is perfectly junior high. So is the mocking way Rudy Martinez says "You're gonna cry" in "96 Tears"—as if crying were a gooey pathetic thing. I couldn't listen to that song the year it came out, I was so upset by it; but several years later I rediscovered it and would go to a particular bar in New Haven just because the song was on the juke box. A decade after junior high a woman from my home town who'd gone to my school was at Max's Kansas City (a New York club, at the time probably the main place along with CBGB for punk or strange or decadent or dangerous music) listening to the songs piped in between sets, and she said to me, "This sounds like junior high but more intense." This is the best definition of punk rock I've ever heard.

I look for scenes in movies—old crime movies, westerns, film noir—where there are voices, sarcasm, contempt, razzing laughter; a bunch of guys being creeps to each other—a bunch of punks, basically. These scenes are thrilling, they come from somewhere basic. When I see them I sometimes feel triumphant, I want to say "So there!" to someone, as if these movies, this dialogue, sort of junior-high-in-the-mouths-of-lowlife-grownups, proved something. Like look, here it is, it's irrepressible, it's not a problem to be solved, it's rock 'n' roll. I look for the hero to eventually vanquish them—these creeps—it—whatever it is . . . but in the meantime he's got to mingle with it.

Writing is my instrument. So I have a secret cruel self that usually only lets itself loose in my writing. I guess it's occasional at this point, when I let words loose to shred someone. I know I've got it, the gift of nasty—it's a glorious thing, I wish I knew where to use it.

excerpts from "A Social Map of My Mind," *Why Music Sucks* #9, February 1996

POPPED INTERVIEW

FRANK KOGAN: The town is called Storrs, and it's a university town, it's where the University of Connecticut comes from—or where it is, it hasn't gone anywhere. Storrs is an interesting town. Unlike a lot of people—even a lot of people who lived in that particular town—I didn't think that it was this dead place and that, "Boy I was lucky when I finally got to move to a city." In some ways it was actually good preparation for the Lower East Side because in high school, junior high, seventh grade through twelfth grade, 1966 to 1972, everything was breaking loose that could break loose at the time, and since it was a university town, every single trend came through the high school too. Symbolically, when people thought of trends coming through, they always thought it was drugs coming through; which actually isn't as shallow as that makes it seem. Drugs were kind of a marker, and interestingly, for that reason, I kind of resisted smoking marijuana. It was sort of—I wasn't one of the freaks, I was on the borderline I wrote about in my magazine: near the freaks, afraid to cross over into being a freak, but at the same time not *wanting* to cross over to be a freak. Basically I was a good student, intellectual type; being a good student and intellectual type at that time wasn't the same as being straight and stuck up and preppy at all. And I was kind of a political agitator and a bunch of other things like that . . .

SCOTT WOODS: How so?

FRANK: Okay, that's a really complicated thing. It's something I've been meaning to write about in *Why Music Sucks*, I just haven't figured out how to put it onto paper yet, but there was a time—I was sort of an all-American kid at first, before all this happened. And basically I was a *liberal* all-American kid, which meant that, oh, you were seeing blacks getting beat up on TV in the South, and, oh yes, that's a horrible thing, and, "Freedom should be meant for all," and we should be a free country, which meant that everybody should be free—and all that stuff. And then reading history: Well, we won all the wars and that's 'cause we were on the side of the oppressed and we were the good guys. And stuff like that. When Vietnam came along I soon more or less just fell into that pattern—"well, Vietnam is a country that's being invaded by communists, so of course we're right to go and protect the Vietnamese from this." But interestingly—and now I'm at around age ten—there was an invasion of the Dominican Republic by the U.S., and I was old enough to say, well wait, there's a contradiction here; we were invading it to support a dictatorial government that was trying to put down a revolution, and so that kind of threw it in a little confusion for me. I learned more about the Vietnam War, but also, my brother turned against the war, and that sort of tended to turn me also. I mean, I wasn't really making *profound* decisions based on my own knowledge.

But I do remember once I was like, sitting in a hammock, and this is in my grandparents' summer house up on an island off the coast of Maine and we were there and my brother was saying something about this book he'd just read which showed the U.S. government actually sabotaging negotiations that the North Vietnamese were actually trying to *start* with the U.S. This was maybe '65 or '66. And that to me was information that didn't compute. You know, why in the world would the U.S. try to sabotage negotiations? or something like that. And my brother was sort of being insistent and I just wasn't *believing* what he was saying, and he kept sort of saying, "Well it's *all* in the book there!" And I was just saying, "Well what does that mean, it's all in the book?" I finally, actually—I mean, not in front of him—he went off and I was in the hammock, and I remember crying. And I don't think I was—I mean, maybe I was crying because he beat me in the argument, but there was something in there that—this wasn't supposed to be. Somehow there was a real rip or tear in my world.

And then there would be TV reports, and there'd be reports about the demonstrations against the war in Vietnam, and about the demonstrators meeting with other people who oppose the demonstrators, and the people who would oppose the demonstrators would get rocks and beat them up—and things like that. And this didn't compute also. I was used to: If you're demonstrating and other people are getting rocks and throwing them at you and beating you up, you're probably the good guy. So in my eleven- or twelve-year-old mind it was almost like, to continue being the good guy and believing what I had to believe, maybe I should be on the side of the people getting beat up.

And there was one guy, Tom Olds, in my eighth-grade class, whose father was a Quaker, who later became one of my best friends—he actually *knew* something on the issues, which means he sort of had the rest of us beat. 'Cause none of the rest of us actually knew that there had been this emperor of Vietnam whose name was Bao Dai, or this thing or that thing, it was just like, "Oh yeah, the communists invaded so we had to fight them," etc. etc., and Tom was saying, "No!" and he'd be able to tell you something about it since none of us really had any knowledge. So in a sense I flipped my position and by the time the Democratic Convention in '68 came along, I sort of held a different position; I was on the side of the people who were against the war. We were watching it on TV, and in history that convention is considered the great catastrophe, and basically crippled the Democratic party, put Nixon in office, and all these other things, but I mean—it was a blast to watch on TV. It was one of the most fun TV shows [laughs] I'd ever seen in my life. My father, actually knowing something about politics, can't bear to watch conventions, because it's a lot of baloney, basically. But we actually dragged my parents down and said, "You've *got* to see this. Police are going around beating up people, and it's on film and you have to watch it!"

One of our senators, Abe Ribicoff, who kind of had the image of being a political . . . not hack, exactly, but someone who was sort of very dutiful, who was part of the Northeast Democratic machine, which is fairly liberal, and he was kind of a Kennedy loyalist, he worked with Tom Bailey, who was head of the national party. But anyway, he was actually nominating George McGovern, who was sort of in there at the time with the support of the Kennedys; Robert Kennedy had been shot and McGovern was sort of the substitute.

And Ribicoff was nominating him and Ribicoff ad-libbed on his speech, I guess someone had gotten a TV on the floor of the convention and Ribicoff actually watched some of the beatings up, and he ad-libbed this statement, and it's interesting because he stuttered in the middle of the statement too, and it was something like, "Well, if George McGovern were elected President, we wouldn't have Gestapo st . . . tactics on the streets of Chicago!" And it was interesting, because apparently he couldn't see it at all but the camera looking over his shoulder had him . . . Richard Daley, who was the mayor of Chicago—it was his police who were going around beating people up—was right in the sight [of the camera], so it was as if Ribicoff was saying it to Daley. To me this was like prime fear, and great heroism, and in a sense I wanted to—it was excitement and you could be swept up in the excitement.

And I remember when I was in tenth grade there were these things called the Moratoriums. I guess the basic idea was you take a moratorium from what you normally do in order to protest the war. This is probably late '69, and there were probably the biggest demonstrations that there'd ever been domestically in America, basically against the policy of the government. You know, they were down to Washington. And I remember my parents wouldn't let me go, they wouldn't sign the permission for me to go on a bus trip down. And I just felt *really* left out. And my friend Steve, who was a year older and much more knowledgeable and much more committed, his parents wouldn't either. I remember the bus was leaving, we were waving goodbye, and Steve was just like, basically mortified not to be on the bus, and I was there with him, and here it was going and happening without us. So in that year I was basically consumed by politics; it almost kind of came up and took me over, this was sort of the meaning of life. And it's interesting because, this is the one year I would say in high school that was unmitigatingly happy for me. Junior high school had been kind of this scary terror thing, and after that—probably what came after that was much more interesting and valuable, but there was just sort of a lot of depression and unhappiness—but in the middle was this wonderful year when I was into politics; I was going around and handing out leaflets all the time that I'd written—a lot of propaganda, it'd probably make me cringe to read it now. But it gave me purpose, gave me something to do, made me feel part of something big that was the underdog—even in a liberal town that we were in, as late as '69 most people supported the war.

That was kind of what I was doing. That was the school year that started with the Moratoriums and ended with Kent State where the National Guard killed four demonstrators. And at the University of Connecticut, the students went on strike when that happened. The high school didn't go on strike, but in a sense, I wanted reasons to do things that were breaking the rules, but they couldn't just be because I wanted to break the rules, so I started to cut classes and things like that to go and take part in the demonstrations, whereas I wouldn't have been willing to allow myself to cut classes just because I wanted to cut classes.

So that was kind of like this wonderful time. And I'm kind of wondering *why* I was so consumed by politics. In a way, I'm thinking about *your* junior-high piece, the one with that kid, the one guy, who terrorized your whole grade.

SCOTT: Yeah, the whole schoolyard.

FRANK: And there's nothing quite as stark and vivid as that in my school, but there was definitely—I felt terrorized, let's say, basically sixth grade through eighth grade, *all* the time. And there was that amazing thing that you [Scott] described in *Why Music Sucks*, that race around the courtyard; basically, you read accounts of concentration camps, and the Nazis ran races like that, "Okay we're gonna have a race, everyone strip naked"—and it'd be at two in the morning on a freezing night—"you guys are gonna race around and the last third are all gonna get shot" or something like that. Well, in your case it was like, the loser would get piled on or something. For me, there was never anything quite as vivid, but there was definitely some things where . . . [in sixth grade] there was this fat girl named Mary—I wrote about this once back in the original incarnation of *Why Music Sucks*—and Mary was this really—she was basically sweet and *not* assertive or anything. And because she was fat, boys would pick on her and shun her. It was the sort of thing that, if she was standing in line—you all had to get in line to go to lunch—it was bad to be the boy who was standing behind her, so guys would get out of line in order not to stand behind her. Really horrible stuff. And my friend Jeff—who was one of the kind of cool people, and our friendship was therefore also kind of fading, but at the same time we were still friends, and he was this very smart charismatic, forceful personality—he would get into ribbing Mary. Sixth grade it's, what dirty words do you know?, so he said, "How many cunts do you have, Mary?" 'cause he didn't know if she knew what *cunt* meant. And I remember her sort of tentatively saying, "One," hoping she got the answer right or something like that. And there was this one thing though where he asked her, "Well, are there any boys in this class you like?" And she actually said, "Yes, I like Frank." And Jeff just immediately turned on me, as if to say, "Okay, Frank, I've got you!" And when Mary saw that happening, she mouthed to me—she didn't say it out loud—"I'm sorry." I remember once years later, I described this to one of my therapists and I mouthed those words silently to her, and the therapist turned away [as if she'd been slapped, the story was so painful].

And what struck me—both about your story and about all this stuff happening to me; and it's basically a part of a lot of people's junior-high experience—is thinking back, well, why did we let it happen? The people in the concentration camps—well, yeah, there were guns on them. But what was stopping me from saying, "Jeff, stop picking on Mary!" Even if Jeff picked on me, I could say, "Well, it's a good thing that Mary likes me; wouldn't it be a good thing if Mary liked you too?" Just all sorts of things you can replay in your mind, but it was almost like in a sense we ceded some part of our authority over to these bullies. I certainly *never* talked to my parents about any of this, what was going on, or even my older brother, or some of my older friends—there were some allusions to, "Oh yeah, junior high's really tough"—but we didn't talk about this, maybe a little, but not much at all. And the point is, it didn't even occur to me to talk to my parents about it, and I think the reason is that, you know, you don't go home to your parents and say, "Look at the weak, gutless, pathetic thing I did today in school." [laughs] "Hi, I'm a worthless shit, can you advise me what to do?"

So thinking about this now, in tenth grade I got consumed with organizing, and now [i.e., the present, 1997] I see it almost makes perfect sense—in sixth grade, seventh grade, eighth grade, I was essentially alone. By tenth grade, I was more sophisticated—I'd learned about Vietnam, my arguments were pretty sophisticated, and I learned about the environment, which was just becoming a big issue around then, I think the first Earth Day was 1970 or something like that. And there was a point where I was realizing that, well yes, if things are allowed to run unfettered the environment will be destroyed because industry does not have any short-term incentive not to pollute, but they have a very good incentive *to* pollute, because if they spend the money trying not to pollute they'll go out of business in comparison to the other guys who are saving money by polluting. And the people who are causing pollution don't have to pay the immediate cost of pollution even if they suffer in the long run; even if they *wanted* not to pollute, they couldn't. So obviously, you need to rationally have some sort of regulation. So I figured these things out and came up with, well, what you need to do is you need to organize people for results, because if you let things go, bad things will happen. So in a sense I was moving towards a kind of socialism or something like that. There was a time when I sort of flirted with supporting the Black Panthers. I remember some SDS people visited the high school and we talked a bit and I said, "They've got some good points." And being radical wasn't, I don't think, exactly a macho thing at the time, but it was sort of like, see who's really militant, and I always sort of shied away from that in the same way I always shied away from being one of the freaks, or smoking drugs or something.

SCOTT: But you found it intriguing?

FRANK: Oh yeah. But I think I was also smart enough to figure out that, well yes, they're trying to be tough, and that isn't political action, it's just someone trying to be tough. But I really do think there was something—definitely unconscious—working within me, the idea that you have to organize, you have to get allies. Though what I was trying to get allies against or organize against maybe wasn't that clear; whatever was given me on the national political plate or something.

from "Pushin' Too Hard: an interview with Frank Kogan," *Popped*, 1997.

[I.e., in junior high I'd felt isolated and afraid, so the urge later on to organize politically was—in part—the urge to find allies to help me fight my fear. Question: At age ten I'd decided I was a scaredy-cat. If I were now to meet a ten-year-old who was like I was then, I would not consider him a coward. So, the ongoing question of this book: What did I gain back then by defining myself as a coward?]

CHAPTER 6

BOB DYLAN SONG MEANINGS

Couple people PLEASE explain the meanings of Subterranean Homesick Blues, It's All Over Now Baby Blue, and A Hard Rain's Gonna Fall . . . it's for a project.
Paul L., October 10, 2003

ANSWERS

"subterranean homesick blues" is about the gopher from caddyshack (the novel, not the film obv), "it's all over now baby blue" is an 'answer song' to "me and you and a dog named blue," "a hard rain's gonna fall" is about a legendary may hailstorm that occurred in minnesota when bob dylan (or, as he was known at the time, ron weiss) was a youth.
—James Blount, October 10, 2003

Interestingly, none of those songs have lyrics in the recorded versions. What people now assume to be Dylan's vocals are actually the result of pressing errors.
—Dom Passantino, October 10, 2003

Subterranean Homesick Blues is a rebuttal to that Radiohead song about the subterranean homesick alien.
   "Hard Rain's a Gonna Fall" is about the high possibility of precipitation.
—GUH!, October 10, 2003

We do not do your homework. The internet is not yet a substitute for your brain or a big, usually old building with books in it.
—Mr Noodles, October 10, 2003

I agree with Noodles, but in a more positive way, which is to say that a meaning of those songs really *is* "Don't let us do your homework for you." And don't let other people get your kicks for you. And don't follow leaders. Strike another match and start anew. The highway is for gamblers. I drank a fifth of vodka, dare me to drive?
   "Look out kid, you're gonna get hit" means "Look out kid, you're gonna get hit." I don't intend that as a wiseass comment. You ever been hit? Physically? Emotionally? That's what the song's about, among other things.

In junior high school I *read* the lyrics to "Subterranean Homesick Blues" (art teacher posted the lyrics and displayed student paintings inspired by them). The words seemed like nonsense to me. When I heard the song again, four years later, I knew exactly what they were about, ironically enough. I knew better than the guy who wrote them, as a matter of fact. He might have thought they were about drug busts in Greenwich Village (orders from the D.A.), but I knew that they were really about junior high school.

Don't wanna be a bum, you'd better chew gum.

Where the home in the valley meets the damp dirty prison/And the executioner's face is always well hidden. (No man is an island, duh, but Dylan said it better than Donne. Or as David Johansen says, "Everything connects, and that ain't nowhere.") Look out kid, they keep it all hid. The home in the valley kills the man in the prison, by long distance, face hidden.

Play those three songs, imagine that you're the one singing them. And ask yourself not what the guy who wrote those words means by them, but what you mean by them. And write that down. And if you risk those words—your words—*here*, you'll get a friendlier response.

—Frank Kogan, October 10, 2003

What Frank said, but with more italics.

—Bruce Urquhart, October 10, 2003

I Love Music chatroom

CHAPTER 7

ROGER WILLIAMS IN AMERICA / THE WHAT THING

ROGER WILLIAMS IN AMERICA

See that asssmoke rising. Hear the funny belly burning. Genius needs your burning clientele. Nothin' but a clientele ("fuck" you). Simon Frith says, with justification, "'Rock' as such no longer has any redeeming value." So what about rock not-quite-as-such? or rock no longer existing as such but as mere memory of such, hence rock as idea without embodiment *existing in all its previous and "future" glory?*

—Frank Kogan, *The Village Voice*, June 1987

When his opponents accused him of denying the church altogether, he compared himself to one who suffers the night or an eclipse of the sun without denying the sun's existence.

—Edmund S. Morgan, *Roger Williams: The Church and the State*

Roger Sabin claims in his intro to *Punk Rock: So What?* that "until we can decide what punk was, it is impossible to say what its consequences were." Yeah, this sounds sensible, but it's bizarre, really, and naive. Compare: "Until we decide what Christianity was in the seventeenth century, we can't say what its consequences were in Britain." Well, there were wars over "Christianity," but no decision. Same with punk. Punk "was," among other things, a battleground, a weapon, a red cape, a prize, a flag in a bloody game of Capture the Flag. In the '70s and '80s, and still.

Punk is a word, and one of its uses—a major use, maybe *the* major use—is to have its use fought over. Meta-use is use, far more so than for most words. I don't mean to imply that the word *punk* is therefore, somehow, abnormal in comparison to other words, as if less-fought-over words were a norm from which *punk* deviated. No more than pawns are a norm from which knights deviate. There are always some words that get to be knights; words can attain knighthood and lose it. Musical genres get fought over because genres and their names are social markers.

I'm going back to a passage of Simon Reynolds's: "When jungle was at its height several years ago, if you'd gone up to a junglist and endeavored to explain to them that the genre was 'imaginary,' a nonexistent or self-contradictory entity, a figment of auto-hype and collective self-delusion—well, you'd be lucky to get away without your head being kicked in. Which relates to my original point about genre names being condensations of 'social energy.' It's the energy, conviction, and will-to-belief mobilized behind any given genre name that's interesting, and that makes outside attempts at deconstructing the terms really rather academic, in all senses of the word."

I agree, but I want to rescue the word *imaginary*. Only *because* genre names are in part imaginary—something like "visionary"—do they get to be condensations of social energy. Conversely, because they're condensations of social energy, they get to be imaginary and visionary.

When Luther nailed his 96 Theses (or however many) to the church door at Wittenberg, the phrases "church of Christ" and "true church" and "Christian" suddenly became way more imaginary than these terms had been previously, in this sense: "The Christian church" now didn't necessarily refer to a church that existed but to a church that people could *imagine* existing. And once new sects were formed they always had the chance of falling short. Someone could imagine a better church that made all real churches fake in comparison. To some extent this still holds true. The term "church of Christ," for anyone who cares, continues to have an area of controversial and disputed use, a shadow of possibilities and dissent that surrounds it like a halo (so to speak).

Not to say that Luther invented this for Christianity. Not knowing much about church (or Church) history, I nonetheless assume that Christianity always has a tension between what is and what could be, this world and that. But Luther turned the shadow of possibilities and dissent into a brute, bloody fact, yet with an ongoing shadow that simply refused any actualization.

To jump forward a few centuries, in early 1971 (January 16—I remember this date, it was the day after my seventeenth birthday) I came up with a phrase "the What Thing," which I used to illustrate and glorify a general sense of restlessness that I thought permeated the life around me. The What Thing was the rabbit or the bouncing ball you go chasing after. My friend Julia had recently broken up with her boyfriend, and I pictured her first in an embrace with the boyfriend and then her breaking the embrace to go chasing after this ball, this who-knows-what, this What Thing. She wanted *more* than she was getting, she wanted not to settle (I believed). I admired this.

The What Thing was more than just what you wanted but didn't have—or what made you not want what you had. It was a critical eye. It looked, it said, "This is bullshit!"

> *The What Thing is how you feel when you feel fine.*
> *"How are you?"*
> *"fine."*

A Story

Once upon a time there
was a ~~girl~~ boy named ~~John?~~ Jenny went
to a Gay Lib rally,
but Gay wasn't there so
she sat down on the floor
and beat out a little tune.
Then she said "let's do something
exciting," ~~but she went up to the bum of her~~
~~street who had been there for 30 yrs and said,~~
but everyone was too bored and stoned
so she got up and left.

She gave an ~~eagle~~ evil giggle,
and burned down ~~the~~ house
killing everyone in it except ~~to~~
Frank who had planned the whole
thing. Then they went out ~~some~~
and started knocking over houses
with lightposts which they had pulled
up ~~from~~ the ground.

Jenny went home and turned
on the record player but the music
was too good and not loud enough
so she went downstairs and watched
an old movie which pacified her. Then she
sat down on the floor again and
said "This is an exciting life"
~~and~~ She smiled sweetly and went to
sleep.

EZECTRIC FUNERAL

The local commune held a funeral
yesterday, for one of its members who had ~~Overdosed~~ OD'd
~~died~~ . The funeral was attended
~~mostly~~ by members of the commune,
~~and~~ their friends, ~~and~~ a couple of straight reporters
and the deceased's younger brother.

The commune's rock group performed
the funeral mass; an improvised version of
"Somebody to Love" which ~~contained a 10 minute~~ lasted 10 minutes
~~jam, which had a 10 minute jam~~
~~sounding like~~ and which sounded like machine-gun
fire crossed with an ~~air~~ air-raid siren. ~~Then~~ After
the mass ~~the~~ people ~~began~~ shouted
obscenities until they got bored. Then they
buried the body.

Some of the ~~local residents~~ neighbors.
~~The neighbors~~ complained of the noise.

November 1970

(At age seventeen I assumed that I wouldn't have to explain this passage to my friends, that everyone knew that however you felt when you said "fine," it wasn't fine.)

The What Thing—when I thought it up—was the title of a letter to my friend Tom Olds, who was having romantic troubles. I meant this letter to give perspective. The "letter" that came out was a cut-and-paste that went for pages with no story or ongoing thought but just an amalgam of different bits: shards of autobiography, parodies, quotes from friends, quotes from books, and always lyrics lyrics lyrics, some just copied straight from records and some that I'd altered. Life and songs, all jumbled together. Lots of Grace Slick, where I'd take a Jefferson Airplane song and reword it and insert the phrase "What Thing." "The What Thing laughed so hard he cracked the walls." "It all stares as human What Thing dies." The second of which, come to think of it, is probably Kantner, not Slick. Here's Grace:

> But when will you stop your
> believing
> That there is no What Thing eyes
> Will look
> Down on you forever?

The What Thing ended with a set of Grace Slick lyrics, quick snatches in succession, all on the theme of disintegration, some straight, most altered. And this in a sense wasn't just expression (though that's what it primarily was) but also *analysis*, putting the lyrics one after another to show their similarities, this theme of disintegration running through Grace's work.

A tangent here about how this style of letter writing arose: The result was unusual—the letter—but the sources weren't. My friends and I would often write notes to each other, sometimes copy a passage from a book. Or we'd just give each other a piece of paper with song lyrics on it. I remember someone giving me the verse from "Ruby Tuesday" where Mick says "Lose your dreams and you will lose your mind."

Tom Olds and I would write letters and give them to each other at school the next day. Tom's letters would sometimes be a melange of thoughts, comments, quotations that he'd sprayed forth onto the page. E.g.:

> Raise your right hand
>   Do you promise to covet?

Where upon he arose and dealt him a shattering blow

   I'll bet 3 chips.

   In accordance with the laws of this $tate, I sentence you to . . .

   All children under the age of 16 must attend an approved public hi school or factors there of.

And then Tom in his letters started writing down—when he'd get to a paragraph break, or a natural pause, even right within a sentence, when the words intruded—whatever song lyric happened to be pouring forth from his record player. And the lyric always seemed to pertain to what was on his mind. And he'd write not only lyrics from the record player, but lyrics that he remembered, that were relevant or just seemed to fit emotionally. So the song words would be a soundtrack and a running commentary. The first such lyric-laden letter was particularly poignant, about his love troubles/loneliness—though with CSNY and Jefferson Airplane and Firesign Theatre lyrics spliced in almost to the point of overwhelming the letter.

When you are enjoying yourself everything's fine. When you're bored you are totally bored & everything is useless. When you are discouraged everything is twice as useless. "There is a town in north Ontario."
        get up
        change record.

        Jefferson Airplane

Dom-Dom-Da-Dom-Dom
* "   "   "   "   "*

Dom Dom Dom Dom
* "   "   "   "*

One pill makes you larger &
* "   "   "   "   small &*
the ones that mother
        gives you . . .

        Fuck it
        this is a mess
Frank. Do you know why I'm writing you?
   [Go ask alice, I think she'll know]

I do. Fuck you too. [My reasons for writing are, as ever, five fold.] [Hey Porgy, Porgy, you're a white man, you've got to help us . . . We all want to know who's responsible (Communist Martyrs High School, that's who) . . .

We been shooting reds & yellows all day. (Man am I sleepy!)]

Where was I?

    oh yes.

        Oh fuck!

Questions in need of answers to be answered thereof.

"Hey ya Joe, who a won a the seconda worlda war, you so smart?"

√check!, √check!, √check!, √Pole!

-etrics with Nurse Warren. gee Dad! [Will the real Doctor Futterman please report to neurosurgery immediately!]

    New Napalmolive!

"if the chief ever caught me taking these pills he'd snap my head off" "Here, take these, the chief has been on these for a week & he's a changed . . ."

One more pair of
loving eyes
look down on you.

There you sit
mouth wide open
animals licking at your sides
on wild wheels the four stroke man
opens wide

& the casket is mine

    IREZ

    God damn it.
        period.
"carnivorous little bastard, isn't he?"

We are all outlaws in the I's

So when I was thinking of a reply to Tom and thinking of my friend Julia—her breakup—a bunch of Grace Slick lyrics flashed in on me, the ones Tom had quoted in the letter and others, lyrics from different songs, all about restlessness and disintegration. Naturally I thought of splicing those lyrics together, running them past, one after the other, in the way that Tom had. And I went from there, as I've described, with the record player going (I'd recently gotten *American Beauty* and *Highway 61 Revisited*, and so into the letter they went), using Tom's method of grabbing lyrics and references and so forth, leading up to the Grace Slick montage.

Of course, Tom and I hadn't come up with this form in some primal way that was independent of art or literature or society (in fact, the restlessness-disintegration stuff was in a tradition of high literary romanticism, whether I knew it or not, and I did know that one of the Slick lyrics made reference to James Joyce). Tom was a big fan of the Firesign Theatre's dwarf-pliers record, the one where they keep shifting among different stories and different gags by pretending to shift among radio stations. And I was influenced by radio DJs. Back then, when "progressive rock" radio was relatively freeform, DJs would work hard on their segues and song suites; the segues would mostly have a musical logic, but sometimes the song suites would be based on ongoing lyrical themes—can't give you any specific examples, and these lyric-based suites were most likely heavy-handed and might have undone the *musical* logic of the segues. But anyhow, perhaps inspired by these or perhaps just because that's the way my mind works, I sometimes thought about splicing together *bits* of different songs, not for musical reasons but because these bits had lyrics that I wanted to run together, as comparison, as contrast, as an ongoing rush of whatever I wanted to express, and so forth. I never actually did this in the way that I imagined, and I have a feeling that the results would have been atrocious, since the music wouldn't have matched or pulled together. There was one tape that my friends Steve and Susana and I made to accompany a slide show for Earth Day (I think it was the very first Earth Day), and on my insistence, we put onto the soundtrack—along with a narrative about environmental collapse and the end of the world—fragments of Jefferson Airplane songs, "House at Pooneil Corner" plus feedback for the apocalyptic feel, "Wooden Ships" for the revival feel. This worked okay, because we were going more for mood than for lyrics.

A few weeks after I'd thought up the What Thing I bought *Blonde on Blonde* and discovered that Dylan had already thought it up five years earlier; he'd called it "Memphis" and "Johanna." (Memphis was the city he couldn't get to; Johanna the woman he couldn't have.) And then in the months and years that followed I was seeing What Things everywhere, not just everywhere in my life but in literature (e.g., Stendhal and his Napoleon obsession; Faulkner and whatever it was—or the nothing that it was—that Quentin Compson was trying to protect and preserve and stay true to) and of course in song lyrics: the Kinks' "Waterloo Sunset" and "See My Friends" (whatever's on the other side of the dirty old river); the Stooges' "Not Right"—whatever it was that "right" was supposed to represent in "She wants somethin', she wants somethin', tonight/She wants somethin', she wants somethin', all right/But I can't help, 'cause I'm not right (and it's always this way)"; and whatever it was—love, sanity, community— that was conspicuous by its deliberate absence from the Velvet Underground's "Sister Ray."

Back to the What Thing as "idea." In college, studying the New England Puritans, I came across the thought of Roger Williams, who'd started in early-1600s Britain as an Anglican, then became a Puritan, then a Separatist (and came over to America), then maybe (briefly) a Baptist, and finally a Seeker, the last of which doesn't indicate his being a member of a sect but that he was one of those who didn't believe that *any* of the currently available seventeenth-century sects was legitimate—all were contaminated by un-Christian pollution—and who *hoped* for (sought for) a true Christian church in the future. I won't really go into his reasons, many of which I don't remember—basically stuff like: A church (1) has to be based on the patterns and practices of Jesus and the apostles and the early Christians, on early Christianity before the fourth-century triumph of Antichristian popery in Rome, and (2) since the apostolic succession had been broken back in the fourth century, no church is valid unless God unambiguously establishes it—which means that Williams is unwilling to play the interpretation game that goes "the fact that we survived a dangerous ocean voyage is an indication that God considers us the New Israel and that our church is the true church." In fact, according to Williams, the new Israel is not a nation state at all, but the entirety of the born-again, penitent, humble, and heavenly patient in any country. For these reasons, he decided that any state-established, state-supported church was by definition not a true Christian church (because early Christianity hadn't had a state-established or state-supported church, because the early Christians didn't try to subdue their rivals, because the scope and authority of a true church of God is spiritual rather than civil, because nowhere in Jesus's teaching is there support for the idea of establishing a state church and suppressing other churches, because no state-supported church is in a line of descent from Christ and the apostles, etc.), and he also concluded that he himself had no right to either proselytize or be a minister (again, the broken apostolic succession: Williams believed that Christ had commissioned apostles and evangelists who in turn had commissioned other apostles and evangelists, and ministers, but that this chain had been broken twelve centuries back, and with no direct descent there was nothing that would authorize or direct Williams's own ministry or his proselytizing) much less to start his own church. I really admired the rigor with which he, a believing Calvinist Christian, found reasons to ensure that the term "church of Christ" would have no actual embodiment and that his ideas would have no institution to support them. And I admired his refusal to easily see manifestations of God. I wrote a song some years later:

Roger Williams put his girl in a rowboat without any oars, and he pushed her out to
sea. He said, "No one can touch you anymore. No one can lie about you anymore."
Roger Williams went to town. There he saw all the girls. He said, "I don't want any of
you—you're not my girl."

Of course, back in college I wasn't only thinking about Calvinists, I was
thinking about rock 'n' roll, and not just the music but the term *rock 'n' roll*—as
in the subhead "America's Only Rock 'n' Roll Magazine" on the cover of *Creem*
magazine. *Rock 'n' roll* had been a dead term until *Creem* revived it in 1969 or
so; it had meant the '50s and Elvis and Chuck Berry and doo-wop and some of
the pre-Beatles '60s, but by the late '60s there was only *rock* and *soul* (and *pop*,
maybe, though that term was primarily used for disparagement) (and what about
country? that was still off the field of relevance, despite country-rock). And then
some Creemsters and the like more-or-less declared progressive rock to be the
Antichrist and appropriated the old word *rock 'n' roll* for its glory and its history
but really included something new with it, a glitter-glatter of glam and noise and
neo-garage rock and mess and experiment (a counter-prog that wasn't willing to
call itself "progressive," actually, though a lot of the original garage rockers back
in 1966 had themselves been the progs of their time) (oh, and prog itself, being
rock, and being prog, was somewhat visionary, imaginary, too) (and the reason
I'm preferring the word *imaginary* to *visionary* is that a term like *rock 'n' roll* or
church of Christ doesn't represent *a* vision but rather invites many visions and
also can sometimes shake free of visions once these visions cross the threshold
into potential embodiment; and the visions themselves are often no more than
flickers).

I invented for myself the term *Superword*, which applied to *rock 'n' roll* and
heavy metal and *glitter* and *glam* and so forth—*punk* hadn't yet emerged as a genre
name, despite its often appearing as a descriptive term in *Creem*. When *punk* did
finally catch on as a title, of course it joined this river of Superwords.

I was clustering a group of related behaviors in my idea of the Superword:
a word that causes controversies, that gets fought over, that sometimes runs
on ahead of its embodiments; a word that seems to jettison adherents—I was
thinking of Roger Williams, someone who'd almost jettisoned himself (not as a
pamphleteer or political leader—he founded his own colony, Rhode Island—but
as a member of a true church).

Our relationship to Superwords is like a relationship to a restless high-school
lover. Eventually the word breaks from our embrace—we make the word break
the embrace, because we're not good enough for the word. Or we break the
embrace—the word is no longer good enough for us, it has been stolen.

There was a woman, Christine, I knew in college—about four years older than I, she'd dropped out of high school and gone to New York (she'd dated Jon Eisen and was friends with Richard Meltzer) and had then eventually gotten her equivalency and applied to college. She said that back in high school you'd known who was cool: the people who'd done acid. But then the uncool people started doing acid too, and so you no longer could tell.

In 1973 my friend Tina, who was still back in high school, described this journey: The freaks hung out in the Campus Restaurant, the freak place. But then the liberals started going to that restaurant too. So the freaks abandoned the Campus Restaurant for the Sundown, a bar on the outskirts of town. (The drinking age in Connecticut had just been taken down to eighteen, and this bar was often lax about checking IDs, so high-school kids could get in, especially in the daytime.) At this bar, the freaks and their arch-enemies the grits hung out together and began to get along. But then the liberals moved in there too, ruining it.

Tina tended to overcategorize (she was fifteen and recurrently unhappy), and my conversation with her *took place* in the Campus Restaurant, and what was she doing there if it had been taken over by liberals? She was waiting for her boyfriend (a freak) and being pissed off and bitter because he was late, actually. And the word *freak* didn't impress me anymore. But then, the accuracy of the categories isn't what mattered. Accuracy isn't what people *do* with such categories.

And what do they do? Well, if you're Roger Williams you travel from one continent to another, you try reform in one colony and are forced to flee so you set up another one and give it a new type of government (I haven't checked this, but I think that the Rhode Island colony was the first place in the world to have freedom of religion and separation of church and state).

Maybe if you're a punk, you destroy yourself to avoid being a person in a corrupt world, or maybe you destroy yourself to protect something you admire—punk, for instance, or your ideals—from being contaminated by your connection to it. And if the self-destruction is sufficiently symbolic (and sufficiently not physical) you might live to create new musics.

To sum up, sort of: That a term is imaginary and self-contradictory doesn't make it not meaningful. A term can be meaningful without having to be pinned down to a particular use. Some words would be useless if they were pinned down (not just controversy words like *punk* and *jungle* but mundane comparative terms like *hot/cold, in/out, large/small, on/off, relevant/irrelevant*).

In general I'm disappointed when intellectuals try to analyze "authenticity" in music. The discussion never seems to go anywhere, since the tendency is for people to debunk "authenticity" without first trying to understand it. Part of the problem is that there *is* no general issue that deserves the title "authenticity." Rather, there are times and places where genre names get fought over, and so of course the word *real* shows up a lot as an adjective. Real punk, real jungle, real house, etc. And it's true (but this is just a truism not a real insight) that the word *real* occurs only where something has the big possibility of being fake.

Rather than debunking it, I would want to explore the *power* of the real, why the search for the real has such a strong hold on rock. It's not a problem to be stopped. I think this is one of the *good* things about rock—why it speaks to me, why I use it to speak for me—that the real is so problematic, that the genre is pursued by a sense of its potential phoniness.

And therefore I wouldn't want to spend time looking for stupidity or spend energy on obviously idiotic contentions such as "techno isn't real music because it's played on drum machines or it samples other people's work" or "black music sounds natural because blacks lead a natural, whole existence." Even when the manifestations are stupid, rock's uneasiness is profound. Great rock thrives on insecurity—Lester Bangs once said—and I live within a similar uneasiness, not above it, or beyond it, or free of it.

For me rock was never any kind of roots music. Hard rock was born in flight, chased by fear, riding towards unattainable glory. And (despite my claiming that there is no general issue of authenticity) I will say that in general for the rock audience "authenticity" isn't seen so much as fidelity to roots or to the common man but as opposition to authority or, at least, opposition to the norm. Meltzer brought this up back in the *Aesthetics of Rock*, when he copied/invented a generic rock review (and to this day if you look at the average mediocre alternative weekly, you see this as a standard review format):

"While other groups were turning out carbon copies, each fighting the other for the same identical sound, the _____ decided to be different and daring. Then in August 1963 they cut their first record, _____. It was a sensation overnight, zooming straight into the English music charts where it stayed right on top for ___ consecutive weeks. The outcome was the first ballad-style record by a group ever to hit the top since the beat was beat."

Meltzer's comment: "Such analyses (of the obscure), appearing in the hit song magazines, are analyses by publications on the same level as rock and not seeking a reduction, and hence they are justifiably wrong in their art-critical triumphs." I think that by this he means that a statement on the same level as rock or within rock does not function as a summary and a reduction of the music, whereas an identical statement from an observer or a conversation outside of rock *would* function as a summary and a reduction. Let's say for the sake of argument that he's right, at least for 1963, that in *Hit Parader* the statement would just be a line among others, whereas within a University of Chicago seminar the statement would function as something small trying to comprehend something big. Still, Meltzer—brilliant man though he is—never completes this thought, in thirty-five years has never explained how or why one context lets the music live and breathe while the other contracts and reduces it. And maybe he's afraid to risk "see-Spot-run" social explicitness, maybe he's afraid of being reductive himself. But I think he's simply too weak in the "why" chromosome, too willing to settle for stance and attitude and acting out, not willing to work or think his way through.

Meltzer wrote a few pages earlier that "rock 'n' roll is at first essentially the creation of an 'out' group (systematically, not sociologically)," though he never that I know of really followed up to say why the r'n'r outgroup was systematically out, or where it took itself with its move outwards (and I'd say that there was no particular *group* that was systematically out, nor a particular group that created r'n'r, for that matter, but rather something in the dynamic that surrounded the music—and something in the society at large, not just in rock 'n' rollers—that tended to push "out").

Meltzer: "If you start with *illegitimacy* as a big criterion for a song, like if it's loud and noisy and hurts your father's ear, then all you need is to think real hard about the illegitimacy of ballads to *your* ear and you got yourself some more nice illegitimacy, you take it where you find it, it's all usable, anything and its opposite."

But Meltzer's never truly explored *how* illegitimacy gets to be a criterion, maybe because he himself has been systematically moving "out" for years, though with diminishing returns. You know, if you start with *legitimacy* as a big contaminant for a song, like if it's "meaning"-laden and pseudointellectual and impresses the teacher's pets who write for *The Village Voice*, then all you need is to think real hard about the legitimacy of silly noise rants to *your* ear and you've got yourself some more legitimacy, all is polluted and destroyed, anything and its opposite. Except that Meltzer's never admitted to himself that he has anything to do with this legitimizing process.

Simon Frith is Richard Meltzer's secret sharer, though in photonegative. He's deliberately kept himself small in relation to the music, has refused to compete with it and so has spent his career writing summaries and prologues while letting the actual rock 'n' roll evade his prose. Yet he has lots of the same smart social obsessions as Meltzer, and he has his own What Thing (often quoted by me, and quoted now again). He's describing Brit jazzers, mainly of the 1930s, but he also notes the applicability to Brit rock 'n' rollers:

> [American music] reaches the rest of the world as something that has already moved from the margins to the mainstream (this was true of minstrelsy and ragtime, jazz and rock 'n' roll). To hear it as corrupting or subversive is, then, to reinterpret the sounds, to read one's own desires onto them, and in Britain the dominant desires—the ones that set the terms of jazz (and rock) criticism, formed musicians' jazz (and rock) ambitions, determined what it meant to be a true jazz (and rock) fan—have been suburban. To understand why and how the worlds of jazz (and rock) are young men's worlds, we have

to understand what it means to grow up male and middle-class; to understand the urge to 'authenticity' we have to understand the strange fear of being 'inauthentic.' In this world, American music—black American music—stands for a simple idea: that everything real is happening elsewhere.

And then you turn the page (his book *Music for Pleasure*) expecting more of that world, young men in the middle-class 'burbs, but instead you get a section entitled "Working-Class Heroes." And this is because in middle-class academia everything real has to happen elsewhere.

If it's true that the British Invasion kids c. 1964 thought that everything real was happening elsewhere, then it's no wonder that they looked to (for instance) Delta blues, given that Delta blues also has within it the idea that everything real is happening elsewhere. For example, Charley Patton's "Mississippi Bo Weevil Blues" seems to be born in motion: "Bo weevil bo weevil, where's your native home? lordie. 'A-Louisiana leavin' Texas anywhere I'se bred and born,' lordie." And then of course there's Muddy Waters: "Well my mother told my father, just before I was born, 'I got a boy child comin', gonna be a rollin' stone.'" That he's bragging and that this is presented as a glorious destiny doesn't undercut the fact that this destiny is dogging Muddy and he has got to keep moving to live up to it. His identity isn't simply his, it's something he has to chase.

So itinerant sharecroppers provided an intellectual underpinning for someone like Mick Jagger not because of their distance from him or because of their otherness but because the form and content of their music gave Jagger sophisticated tools to analyze his own world, to set off on his own journey, to create his own artwork. Naturally he altered the tools in the process of using them, for instance, altered call-and-response so that audience members could participate in their own rejection, if they wanted.

Here's a passage of mine, the same one I quoted in the preface (it's from my review of Sarah Cohen's *Rock Culture in Liverpool*, an anthropological look at '80s indies bands):

The musicians here—the ones most concerned with staying "alternative" and not selling out—seem haunted by the sense that any note they play, any word they write, is potentially contaminated. An obvious question is how does one come to feel this way. But these people aren't just feeling this way, they are defining themselves: We are human beings with the potential to be compromised. So a better question would be: What do they gain by defining themselves in this way? What does this do for their art, their lives?

It was the songwriters and de facto band leaders who had a morbid fear of sounding like normal rock or pop bands; the other band members didn't care, but maybe it's no coincidence that these others didn't generate the musical ideas.

So I'm thinking that this mad journey in search of integrity might, in some instances, be creative. Though symbolically it might be a journey to death, to nothing, to nowhere, in reality the musician might be traveling a fruitful road.

Rock music born in flight, chased by fear—fear of what? Young men may be afraid of not being real—of not being real *men*—but, since they're young, they're probably a lot *more* afraid of closure: that the men around them, their fathers, their teachers, their friends, really *are* men (what a disappointment!), that they, themselves, the young men, *are* real, that this is it, there's nothing more—this constrained life—that the grass isn't greener, there's no better reality over the horizon, or in the future. So "everything real is happening elsewhere" is about hope as much as it's about fear, and the young here are complicit—obviously—in defining themselves as fake. Recall the Jagger example in chapter 3, where the raping, murdering Midnight Rambler boasts, "Honey, it's no rock 'n' roll show" and thereby denigrates the actual rock 'n' roller who wrote and is singing the song and the show at which he's singing it. And also recall that the reason this plays especially (though not only) to discontented offshoots of the middle class is that it needs a fundamental backdrop of social optimism/utopianism/entitlement to play off of, a sense of possibilities. "Reality" isn't only identified as black and American. In fact, the Sex Pistols eliminated the explicit connection to r&b and America without actually changing the form and content of punk rock much at all. "Honesty" still gets to be opposition to authority, and "reality" is unhappiness—it's self-destruction, it's death, it's truly elsewhere, and this goes right back to urban folkies in America and the first wave of the British Invasion. (Cf. the Kinks' "I don't say that I feel fine like everybody else," in 1966. Or whatever going "across the river" meant in "See My Friends.") And of course, during postwar booms and the like, this optimism/entitlement reaches into the "working class" too, and produces mods and Beatles and provides a backdrop for all sorts of people to feel contaminated, fall apart, not know who they are, fall into artistically productive (for some) disintegration and despair. And then of course the women raised on this music, and the women raised on *those* women, can grasp for that entitlement/despair too.

And I'm further speculating that a *society* that inculcates the idea in its young that "everything real is happening elsewhere" may be gaining something too; it may be putting extra butterflies in its children's stomachs but may also be giving them a motive for flexibility in a cosmopolitan world. And it may be giving the society itself flexibility, the ability to change (contra Frith, I don't see that a genre's being "mainstream" precludes its being subversive, or that seeing it as subversive would therefore involve a reinterpretation; and besides, blues *was* considered dangerous in its home environment, not just to white middle-class observers).

But I've hardly finished this thought. It's all rather abstract: "society," "flexibility."

In the 1950s Chuck Berry's "go Johnny, go go" was a *go* that promised to go a lot further than any of the Saturday-night bust-outs that Louis Jordan had rocked forth with ten years earlier. Yet Chuck Berry's *Mobile* (Alabama) in his song "Let It Rock" was just an everyday slog, whereas ten years later Bob Dylan's became the (im)Mobile of dead end and despair, Mobile as the Reality that falls short of the Memphis Dream, the Now that falls short of the Coulda Been, the This Is Your Life that you would never want to live through again, much less have recur eternally.

("Let It Rock" is a Chuck Berry song about being stuck working on the railline down in Mobile. "Memphis Tennessee" is a Chuck Berry song where he's a divorced Dad on the long-distance phone trying to reach his six-year-old daughter in Memphis. Dylan put together the two ideas in the chorus of "Memphis Blues Again": "Oh, mama, can this really be the end/To be stuck inside of Mobile with the Memphis blues again." The last line of the song goes, "Here I sit so patiently, waiting to find out what price/You have to pay to get out of going through all these things twice," which I took to be Dylan's answer to Nietzsche's challenge. Nietzsche had the crackpot idea that all events in the world would reoccur infinitely, and his (noncrackpot) challenge was to ask if you could celebrate—dance to—this fact, that life is what it is and ultimately can never progress away from itself. Dylan's answer seemed to be an emphatic No, he could not.)

Migrant-worker flexibility isn't the same as immigrant flexibility, which isn't the same as move-north-to-the-factories flexibility or suburban-adolescent flexibility or entrepreneurial flexibility or bohemian flexibility. But maybe all these flexibilities can run variations on similar musico-literary forms, all can come with the dust and go with the wind, though not always the same dust, same wind.

By the way, back in January 1971 I was supposed to submit something for my writing class, but I had no idea what to write. I did know, though, that my letter to Tom was the best thing I'd ever written. So I had Tom lend it back to me, I typed it up—the What Thing—and with much nervousness, and therefore after some adolescent boasting to a classmate about the fact that I'd used swear words in the piece, I submitted it to the teacher, Mrs. Singer. She rejected it because it had swear words and because she'd overheard me boasting about this fact. Then she called me back to tell me that she'd changed her mind. She didn't think the "questionable" words added anything, but she was giving me an A PLUS. She thought the form of the piece made it especially powerful.

So maybe this is when I learned for sure that I could walk and chew gum at the same time, could defy the boundary between classroom and hallway, could be in and out at the same time.

[At this juncture I had a 2½-page "Addendum to 'Roger Williams in America'" that I'm deleting since most of it was off-topic. In it I claim that the What Thing was the outgrowth of standard high-school letter writing, standard DJ behavior, and so

on, including standard critical behavior (e.g., "see the parallels among these different Grace Slick lyrics," except I didn't include such a sentence, I simply ran the lyric bits in succession)—that the impulse behind it isn't different in kind from whatever it is that motivates people to blast music out their car windows or that motivates kids to devote Websites to Wu-Tang Clan lyrics or that inspires teens in the midst of composing letters to write down the commercials they're seeing on TV. (In college my friend Roni read me a letter from her kid sister that did just this, and years later I did it in my Voice piece about Dial MTV.) And I say, therefore, that my rock-writing style, at its first impulse, even when I seem to be breaking standard format, has nothing to do with breaking anything, or with wildstyle or "gonzo" or the spirit of high mischief or getting away with something.

Next was an entertaining, ingenious, and convincing explanation of why the What Thing has nothing to do with postmodernism. But no one had said it had, so I was just banging at a pet peeve, and I'd rather save the space than keep the bang.

The third point was that Superwords and the What Thing have nothing to do with poststructuralism, which again is a superfluous point but one I think necessary, since people will misread unless I warn them not to. They're mentally ill and can't help themselves. But the warning gets in the way here, so I've placed it in "Superwords Revisited" in part four. My argument, if you can't wait, is basically that no one gives a shit about the "transcendental signified" anyway, so its absence is of no import, and the whole discussion is a filibuster. And to believe that there's a "discrepancy between sign and meaning" you have to run together two incompatible ideas. If these last two sentences make no sense to you, your life won't necessarily be desolate.

I'll add a fourth point, that my discussion of Roger Williams hardly does justice to the man on his own terms. I do right by, "Whatever worship, ministry, ministration, the best and purest practiced without faith and true persuasion that they are the true institutions of God, they are sin, sinful worships, ministries"; but Williams's next idea is just as crucial: "In vain have the English Parliaments permitted English Bibles in the poorest English houses, and the simplest man or woman to search the Scriptures, if yet against their souls' persuasion from the Scripture, they should be forced (as if they lived in Spain or Rome itself, without the sight of a Bible) to believe as the church believes." In other words, there's no point in making truth available, if people aren't free to use their minds to find the truth for themselves—the implication being that if someone accepts or is forced to accept a doctrine dogmatically, this is no real acceptance, so therefore even if the doctrine were otherwise correct, the forcing in itself would be un-Christian. "Without search and trial, no man attains this faith and right persuasion." And the implication of this is that any conviction arrived at after search and trial might have validity, and in any event may not be suppressed. "'Tis impossible for any man or men to maintain their Christ by their sword and to worship a true Christ, to fight against all consciences opposite to theirs and not to fight against God in some of them."]

The What Thing lives inside of people.

It is something which has to be said. But what is it?

Go up to a person and say:

"I am a) sad

   b) bored

   c) lonely

   d) confused

   e) in love

   f) in hate

   g) confused

   h) etc.

   i) afraid to say it"

Say what?

About the What Thing?

The What Thing is about people.

What People?

Friends, bosses, teachers . . .

Go out. Shoot film. About what?

Home again +-+ Start to write absurd thing so we can all explain about nothing.

Turn on the record player. Fuck. So to speak. So it goes.

What about the What Thing?

Where is the What Thing?

The What Thing masquerades as the Future.

"What are you going to do when you grow up?"

Am I going to be a basketball player or a football player?

All of a sudden I'm no good in sports.

Then to E.O. Smith. The school is cold and the students are cool. And I'm not cool.

"Let me hear some of that

Rock 'n' roll Music!!!

Any old way you choose it."

Groovy.

And then there was the What Thing.

Once upon a time there was a group of people in the Super Strike Consciousness the Third Nation who lived together in Beauty.

> To be all together and in love together with love groovy of life groovy of love us. We are all outlaws amazing in our eyes in the eyes of America—Yippee! but we have seen and we are together while everything else goes on in absurd cliché. How weird it is to be we the enlightened us and all the others cannot because we are far away and above and different. WOW!

> bullshit, says the What Thing

Bored.
All the beautiful people sit around bored.
> "Ancient empty streets to dead for dreaming."

What to do?
The What Thing. Talk about the What Thing . . .
How?
Say something significant.
> "Have you heard about the small town in Maine?"
> "Is this a crank phone call . . ."

Get up. Put on the Grateful Dead.

Another boring party. What to do? What do I want to do (Sex?)?
> "Let's have a group marriage."

> bullshit, says the What Thing.

> "And it's just a box of rain
> I don't know who put it there."

I really ought to split from the group.
> It's not right, says the What Thing. Split.

Cut. To December.
The What Thing lives (what is it?). Not too much else.
Meanwhile, the nothing school goes on to the still nowhere. Where is it? Alternate School. Fuck AEP (not Jones!) says the What Thing, because AEP doesn't give a shit about the What Thing. Neither does the Doctor.

"Repeated people who loiter in the taxpayer's lying on the unaesthetic destroying the lavatories the school lobby will (go insane—says What?) be suspended."

This is insane. Got to do something. This is insane.

loiter

"You're Crazy. It's not worth it."

A troublemaker.

"Look out, look out, the Candyman"

Loiter in the lobby, because of the What Thing.

Co-opted by Student Action. It's their movie all of a sudden.

"We must fight to win. We demand . . ."

hawonkawonkawonka. The What Thing throws up.

This is insane insane insane insane.

"Good morning, Mr. Benson,
I see you're doing well.
If I had me a shotgun
I'd blow you straight to hell."

"Listen, this girl's brains are coming out! and who cares? This girl's coming apart! and who cares? This girl's breaking up into crispy chips! and who cares? This girl's caked in the dust, nylon wall-to-wall on her eyeballs! and who cares?"

"I wish I could write you
A melody so plain
That could hold you dear lady
From going insane"

The What Thing masquerades as love, man's soul, sex, and other nondescriptive words.

Cut to the present. Or near past. Or far past. Or future. The almost now! Mountain Girl lonely? Ridiculous.

The What Thing is everything except what I'm like before I'm born and after I die.

Quick. Fantasy:

Unity Rally—

"The What Thing is happening but you don't know what it is,
Do you, E.O. Jones."

The What Thing gets up to speak.

"How does it feel to be such a freak?"

Fellow students. This is absurd. The fucking school is absurd. We should all leave this fucking school. But it's just as absurd out there. So we can't.

"And he screams back you're a cow
Give me some milk or go home."

Wander around the school. in the lobby. This lobby could be very important. We could find the What Thing here if we had the talent, but we don't. Fuck it! We blew it.

"The sun's not yellow
It's chicken."

Walking in the halls. Where are the What Thing People—my friends. Tell them I'm here with the What Thing. I need them.

"Tell everybody you meet
That the Candyman's in town."

Which is all very interesting and upset because the What Thing is indescribable.

OUTLINE FOR A SHORT STORY

Man (an atomic scientist) is bored.

Falls in love with person from certain unnamed country.

Can't really love because society doesn't give a shit about the What Thing.

Woman goes back to unnamed country.

Atomic Scientist builds bomb and blows up unnamed country. For obvious reasons.

Walking in the halls. Going places. Staying at home.

"When you're lost in the rain in Juarez
and it's Eastertime too."

Where is everybody?

"Go ask the What Thing
I think she'll know."

The Who Cares Girl.

And it's 1, 2, 3, what's the What Thing 4? Who Cares?

"I wish you'd come and visit me because my parents never let me go anywhere."

Where is the What Thing?

"My What Thing wants to Kill your Mama."

But where is the What Thing?

"Hi."

"Hi, I haven't been seeing you much."

"Well you're not in any of my classes and I've been going away after school."

"So we only see each other between classes. I have to go to Physics. I wish I could see you more often," says the What Thing.

The What Thing. What? IS? IT???
The What Thing. IS SEX!
It's what you want to do but haven't done.

The What Thing is the Nothing That happened in school today. The What Thing is how you feel when you feel fine.

"How are you?"

"fine."

The What Thing is what you don't say when you don't say anything.

The What Thing is God!

bullshit, said the What Thing.

Who Cares?

"Along come a little tiny
animal nipping
Just a few drops from her side."
"There's a man got
a lonely jacket on.
Long gun in his hand.
Got a sledgehammer.
All he needs is one sledgehammer and
all the little animals is dead."
"Keep Alive," screamed the What Cares Girl.
"You could listen to a thousand different
reasons why the What Thing Can't come."

"I love her."
"How do you know you don't just think you love her?"
"What's the difference?"

"Go ask Alice,
I think she'll know
When logic and proportion . . ."

The What Thing Knows.
what's the Thing? where? why?
   "I'm so alone
    Where is my [What Thing] woman
    Can I bring her home?"
That's the catch. What?

  "All you want to do is live
  All you want to do is give
  But Somehow.
  It A-L-L F-a-l-l-s A-p-a-r-t."

"It all stares as human What Thing dies."

  "Lather was thirty years old today.
  They took away all of his toys."

  "The What Thing
  Laughed so hard he cracked the walls."

  "But when will you stop your believing
  That there is no What Thing eyes will look
  down on you forever?"   Fred U.

where is the What Thing?

  "Compared to your scream
  The human dream
  Doesn't mean shit to a tree."

whose Thing?
    "How does it feel?"

by Peter the Pig

quotes by the Beatles, Dylan, Grateful Dead, Tom Wolfe, Jefferson Airplane, Mothers of Invention, Country Joe & the Fish, Joseph Heller, Steve Stills, and friends

"I am a) sad b) bored . . . i) afraid to say it." On the contrary: For the first time in my life I *wasn't* afraid to say it. I had the courage to say it, not as a parody or a joke or a fantastical once-upon-a-time story; not softened for a teacher's eyes or put forth defiantly as I-dare-you-to-read-this posturing. It was for my friend Tom, first. After I'd finished writing I was disappointed, thought that I hadn't said it, hadn't gotten it down. This was true enough—whoever really gets it down?—but I knew I had *something*. So after a few days I borrowed it back, typed it up for Mrs. Singer. Not only did I have the courage to say it, I knew that this was the "it" I wanted people to see, I had the courage to take *my* "it" to the world—finally, something that wasn't bullshit. So Mrs. Singer got a copy. And then I went to the Xerox machine and made another, and Leah got to see it, Jay got to see it, Julia got to see it, Susana got to see it, a substitute teacher named Blodgett got to see it. I don't know how much of it came across. Tom knew the people and the incidents alluded to, but the allusions were so compact that even he didn't understand a lot of them. Mrs. Singer knew almost none, but she still felt power in the thing.

Though I had the courage, I didn't have the words to say it. So I just reached into the music around me and took the words from there—did what a lot of people do in their *minds*, hear a song as living in their own lives—and I tried to put it on the page, the words as they lived in my life, the words as I was *making* them live in my life, the words becoming *my* words.

I wrote the What Thing on a Saturday night, alone in my house—Saturday night, holy night in teenage life, but I wasn't out engaging in teen ritual. My parents were at a party; I either had no party to go to or had said no to the parties. So, withdrawing into isolation, I wrote something that I put back into the world, that broke me out of isolation.

The opening— "I am a) sad b) bored . . ."—was a variation on a riff by Tom several letters back:

My reasons for writing you are (as ever) five-fold. viz. 1) I should be studying my physics 2) I have some question in need of answers to be rendered there of (although I won't ask them) 3) Mao Tse Tung is an atheist 4) Fuck You Too! (no offense intended—merely to keep up appearances for those not yet aware of the intricases (s.i.c.?) of fine art of diplomacy) and (last, but not lost:) 5) none of the above."

"Shoot film." This was fantasy, the idea of going out to shoot a film. I don't remember it, though, the fantasy. The key sentence is "About what?"

"So to speak." *So to speak* was a phrase that we'd use a lot—"we" being a group of eight or ten of us that I'd originally assembled to help my older brother and a couple of our friends on the Audrey Beck and Joe Duffey campaigns the previous summer (Audrey Beck was running for Connecticut secretary of state; Joe Duffey was an antiwar candidate for U.S. senator); over the summer we in the group had become good friends, but then once school started in September the group drifted apart/fragmented. Tom Goodwillie was the one who began saying "So to speak," just as a joke; after a while this was not necessarily to call attention to a play on words, but almost at random. Tom was tall, shy, extremely smart—his mind was so quick that he had trouble talking to the rest of us, but he'd come up with a lot of joke phrases, and he and I and some of the others would repeat them, almost as a ritual, or an attempt to be connected or to get through silences. And Tom Olds—the person to whom I was writing the What Thing—would say "so to speak" with a sad, ironic, self-deprecating meaning, as if to indicate, "I'm throwing this into the air because otherwise the air would be empty."

"So it goes." From Vonnegut's *Slaughterhouse Five*. Vonnegut would write "So it goes" whenever a character died; the phrase signified "we accept this passing," but of course Vonnegut meant just the opposite.

"am I going to be a basketball or a football player?" I'd been dominating in grammar-school sports but had fallen to mediocre in junior high and high school.

"E.O. Smith." The name of the school where I went for junior high and high school. Most of the time simply called "Smith."

"group of people in the Super Strike Consciousness the Third Nation." "Group" probably refers both to the group of my friends from the Duffey Summer and more generally to people like us: liberals, radicals, trying to be countercultural, trying to believe that something *could* be countercultural, that we could be It! (But there's a split here already in my description, between the group of my friends and the larger "groups" implied by the word "countercultural," who were—or would have thought of themselves as—more freaky than the small group of my friends were, and more "radical.") The "Strike" was the massive student strikes and demonstrations of spring 1970 that had stopped classes at many of the colleges and universities (almost all the major ones in the U.S.) following Nixon's sending troops into Cambodia and the National Guard's murder of four protestors at Kent State in Ohio. The University of Connecticut was right next to my high school, so a lot of students from E.O. Smith, including me, participated in the demonstrations and teach-ins there. I don't recall what "Third" was referring to (maybe "third world"). "Nation" was my sarcastic riff on "Woodstock Nation." Woodstock had been one summer earlier, in '69.

"We are all outlaws in the eyes of America." This is the What Thing's first Jefferson Airplane quote (with me interpolating "amazing in our eyes").

"Ancient empty streets." The What Thing's first Bob Dylan quote; the record was probably playing at the very moment I was writing about our beauty disintegrating into boredom.

"Small town in Maine/crank phone call." Refers to a couple more jokes we'd fall back on when we couldn't think of what to say.

"Let's have a group marriage." We did in fact do this, have a ceremony where we (the group of eight or ten) all said that as a group we were married to each other. This was back in September, when the group was already beginning to disperse, and Tom Olds and I in particular were starting to feel alienated from it for reasons I don't completely remember now, maybe the fact that neither of us had paired off with anyone in the group into boyfriend-girlfriend, and we were jealous of those who had; also, that Tom's and my attitude was more critical, alienated than the others'. (More punk? *Punk* of course wouldn't have been a term in use then—in the alienated, search-and-destroy punk-rock sense—in my school in 1970; and Tom, despite having an "Up Against The Wall Motherfuckers" poster up in his bedroom, was probably the gentlest person in the school. Actually, I'd never describe Tom as a punk—he was too spiritual, for one thing. Still, both our minds had a rotor blade of destructive thought.) A couple of months after the "marriage" I suggested a group divorce, to signify—I thought this was positive—that the group no longer meant anything.

"box of rain"/"look out, the Candyman"/"blow you straight to hell." Now it's the Dead's *American Beauty* on the record player. The Dead weren't the totally mellow band that their detractors claimed.

"Alternate school." Its official name was "Alternative Educational Project." Over the summer I'd read *Summerhill* and gotten the idea that we should try to start a free school within E.O. Smith; the idea was for a school that didn't grade people and that ran not on the basis of force and competition but rather on cooperation and creativity. I got together with some interested students, some teachers, some parents, some radical reformers from UConn, etc., and we put together a proposal and held meetings. "We believe that children learn naturally." I helped write the statement of principles, and a few months later said to myself, "I can't believe I wrote that bullshit." As we worked on the idea over several months I began to feel more and more alienated from the whole thing. (Notice a pattern here?) I think that to the school administration and to outsiders I represented the radical face of the proposal, whereas within the free-school meetings I was the advocate of restraint. Most teachers and students on the project supported the idea of "freedom, natural curiosity," whereas I was feeling (though I didn't state this in so many words) that half the students in the free school would probably sit around and use drugs and spout hip dipshit bullshit unless they were prodded into taking some account of themselves. (Interestingly, it was the UConn radicals who would see merit in my ideas, who'd say things like, "You know, you can learn a lot from lectures.") I, like the others, was in favor of students taking the responsibility for their own education—rather than just swallowing or rejecting whatever a high school forced on them—but I didn't think that such taking of responsibility would come naturally.

The teachers wanted to stop calling themselves teachers, to call themselves "facilitators" instead. I hated the word *facilitators*. I privately referred to them as "facile-assers." I thought that teachers should be willing to agitate, to teach.

But responsibility didn't come naturally to me, either, and I didn't throw myself into keeping the proposal alive when it inevitably foundered. I was too consumed with my own emotional stuff to have the energy to keep working on the idea, and I found the whole discourse increasingly blah and stupid. At one point we were discussing what to call the free school, and I suggested "Jones." The high school was called "Smith," after all, so its free school *should* be called "Jones," I reasoned. My suggestion was turned down because "No one would take us seriously." Instead, the acronym AEP was chosen (for "Alternative Educational Project"), a name that would look responsible and official to administrators. Using "AEP" instead of "Jones" epitomized to me everything that was going wrong with the idea.

I still have a rough draft of the AEP proposal. I don't remember how many of the words were mine or how many hands went into writing them. The prose is bland and bureaucratic, by design. There's nothing as sappy as "We believe that children learn naturally," though I wrote such sap earlier in the school year when trying to get people interested in the proposal. The draft does have the sentence (I'm sure not written by me), "If we are to accept each individual's humanity then we must also trust his decision making power." I wrote in ink, next to it: "Eliminate. Doesn't follow."

I *am* impressed by the fact that—underneath the blandness and vagueness of the prose—we could be really audacious. "We propose that the communities be organized together on the town meeting basis whereby each individual will have an equal vote in deciding how the community will be run. Areas which would be discussed might include: studies to be funded, how these studies can be approached, what resources are available, how state requirements can be fulfilled, rules and regulations, how to leave as many options for further education open as possible, what are considered to be essential field trips, what materials need to be purchased, etc." In other words a student's vote equals a teacher's vote, and, since there are many more students than teachers, students—if they want to—make the rules and decide how to spend the money. And this was a proposal that had some teacher and parent support, for a school that we intended to get accredited, to be autonomous, and to exist within the high school as a whole!

"But there is another important part of teaching in any field: helping students to develop the self-discipline necessary for learning. This is where the role of the teacher becomes an active one. He must act not only as a resource person and facilitator but as an instigator. His job is to challenge ideas and confront mental sloppiness. But this process must take place in a situation of interaction between student and teacher; concentration and discipline, necessary as they are, must come from within." A lot of those words were mine, I'm sure, though I really hope that "situation of interaction" came from within someone else.

To put this all into perspective: A year earlier I'd been writing things like, "Whether he knows it or not, the student in America is a slave. The school, which is supposedly set up to further the education of the individual, is actually the instrument society uses to channel the student into its economic and social system." Whereas now at the time of the What Thing I'd typically write: "He walked into the main lobby and retched all over the wall, and carefully scraped it off and had it mimeographed." Or: "Absolute people corrupts much more closely than the small amount etc. Substantial dictatorship but in a bureaucracy but your legs are fat. Take him out and shoot him. This is absurd! Good. But does size a kibbutz isn't that a long silence thank god."

"AEP doesn't give a shit about the What Thing." Yeah, AEP doesn't care about our facing our demons. (Compare to what *Tom* wanted from the free school: "I just want *one* of my years here to be happy.")

"Neither does the Doctor." The Doctor was Dr. Thomas Morgan, our principal. Peter Zarrow, a leftist who was a year ahead of me in school, wrote a piece about the high school for the *UConn Free Press* in which he referred to Dr. Morgan as, "Morgan, our principal, otherwise known as 'Doctor' or 'Thomas the Benign.'" Some teachers thought that this was offensive, also Peter's calling him "Chief Custodian Morgan" a few paragraphs further. I thought it was clever; the point in calling him "Chief Custodian" was that high schools—in Peter's view and my view at the time—didn't really have much more than a custodial function, no real sense of what they were doing other than keeping youngsters out of the labor force and differentiating between who would go on to be white collar and who would go on to be blue. (And Peter's calling him "Doctor" may have been a swipe at him for putting "Dr." in his title; a lot of the kids at school—about a quarter of them—were faculty brats and knew that it was considered ostentatious for Ph.D.s—non-M.D.s—to refer to themselves as "Doctor.") Dr. Morgan had come in a year earlier and had instituted some smart changes: getting rid of the dress code, loosening up the curriculum, allowing more electives. But no matter what he did, he always had the air of a politician acting on expedience rather than principle. So in my eyes he was failing in his symbolic role. And of course I didn't think he went far enough in his school reforms, either.

"Repeated people who loiter . . ." Now, this is where I had my big conflict with Dr. Morgan. He'd had a carpet put into the main lobby that was by the front entrance, and he'd also added a small, pretty fountain, which was at the center of a raised pseudogarden that was covered with pebbles. Water stopped running through the fountain after a few weeks, because students had destroyed the hydraulic mechanism by continually throwing pebbles into the fountain.

One day I ran across Peter Zarrow in the hallway, and he told me that he'd been sitting in the lobby during a free period, back against the wall, reading a book, when Dr. Morgan had walked by and ordered him to get up and leave, telling him that students couldn't sit or loiter in the lobby. This immediately outraged me, a students' rights activist. This was our school! How dare Morgan say that we couldn't sit in our lobby! In the next several weeks I would sometimes sit in the lobby, some friends of mine would sometimes sit in the lobby, some young greaser kids we didn't know would sometimes sit in the lobby, sometimes we'd get kicked out, sometimes we'd be ignored, sometimes no one in authority would see us. This was strange—casual civil disobedience, the school administration not sure what to do about it.

There was a second motive behind my deliberate loitering, one that I didn't really articulate, though it was much stronger than the "students' rights" motive. "Students' rights" was my official motive to myself but was having to contend with the part of me that more and more was considering the rights-activist political-activist part to be bullshit. I became a bit clearer with myself during an interchange with Morgan (I forget whether this happened before or after the demo that I describe a few paragraphs down). Morgan explained to me that the school was *not* simply for the students, and he as our principal didn't simply represent the students. The school was the community's and embodied community goals, and the school represented a community's sense of itself. Now when a taxpayer comes to visit the school he doesn't want to see sloppy kids sprawled all over the lobby.

"That's it!" I said to myself. That's it! The taxpayer wants to see a clean lobby, he wants to see that everything's all right. But everything's not all right. He wants to see the school but he doesn't want to see what's *there*, which is some ugly, fucked-up, sprawled-out kid.

"Co-opted by Student Action." Student Action was a student club—an official extra-curricular activity—that we'd formed about a year and a half earlier to discuss and engage in politics, which mainly meant opposing the Vietnam War. I remember that we'd tried—unsuccessfully—to convince the school administration to stop business as usual on Moratorium Day (October 15, 1969), to instead devote the day to teach-ins. We handed out leaflets, maybe in November chartered a bus to one of the New Mobe demonstrations in D.C.—strangely, I don't remember what else we did or, at any rate, how much of my ongoing political activity was connected with Student Action. I also don't remember if I was one of the founders or just an early member. Anyway, by December 1970 I was long gone from it. Maybe I was just following my pattern—Frank helps to form a group, Frank feels alienated from the group, Frank leaves the group—but all the other original members were gone, too. I don't remember making a specific decision to leave. I probably just found the discussions increasingly tedious, found better vehicles for my social and political life, stopped bothering to attend Student Action meetings. And Student Action became Larry Groff's domain. Larry thought of himself as a militant leftist, a Marxist revolutionary. I thought of him as an angry, posturing fool, since almost everything he said and wrote was accusatory and simple-minded. I remember that at one of the last Student Action meetings I'd attended, in spring 1970, he'd said that he wasn't too concerned about environmental issues, given that the rich and the powerful breathed the same air and drank the same water as everyone else, and so wouldn't oppose environmental cleanup. This from a Marxist! I think I just gaped at him, without bothering to reply. At one point in the same conversation Larry said that almost all of Karl Marx's predictions had come true. After the meeting, Peter Zarrow said to Larry, "I want to discuss that statement of yours, that all of Marx's predictions have come true." I thought of saying to Peter, but didn't: "Do you really think you're going to get anything out of talking to this guy?"

So, jump to December 1970. I'd been carrying on sporadic disobedience in the main lobby, but decided that this wasn't going to have much effect unless backed by mass action. So my idea was to have planned civil disobedience, to pick a period (the school day was divided into 60-minute periods, 55 minutes for a class and 5 minutes for travel time) and call for all those who had the period free—that is, who had no scheduled classes then and so were assigned to study hall—to come to the lobby and loiter there. My theory was that if I got enough people, 25 or 50, the administration would be afraid to act, since suspending a lot of students—and therefore letting it be known that a situation got out of hand to the extent that they *had* to suspend a lot of students—would look worse to the community than would just ignoring the issue and letting us sit where we pleased. Of course, Morgan could have decided to suspend just a few of us, or do what in fact he did do, which was to ignore the demonstration but after that just continue with the policy of kicking people out of the lobby. I'd thought of this, and intended to counter by having more demonstrations. As it happened, when the time came, I had no interest in starting any more such demonstrations.

But in December I started organizing this demonstration. I talked to people, to see if they were interested. I picked a day and a period when a lot of my friends and I would be free. I pondered what the leaflet to announce the demonstration should say.

I was framing the issue as students' rights, the right to our own time and space, that this was our school and we had the right to be visible in its lobby. I didn't lay out the other issues that were bubbling up for me: the right to be exciting, the right to be challenging, the right to be ugly, the right to be unhappy, the right to fall to pieces all over their lovely carpet. The right to make the community see its fucked-up spawn, to make it gaze at its own madness. The right to tear the face off of my alienation. I had no politics for these issues. I recognized, however, that the political issues I did have—free speech, the right of assembly—were preconditions to my pursuit of unhappiness.

But anyway, Larry Groff pulled a fast one. He decided to steal the demonstration. I'd talked to people, set the day and time of the demonstration, so what Larry did was to put out a leaflet—before I'd put out mine—calling for the demonstration at the time I'd set but to be on behalf of a list of "demands" that he had worked out (I assumed) with his colleagues in Student Action. The rhetoric was his usual militant bullshit. I forget most of his demands—I assume that the right to sit in the lobby was one. In fact, the only demand I remember was that work-study students be given the minimum wage. "Work study" was a program for students not on an academic track who wanted to get some job skills—doing what, I don't know. Probably they worked part-time for local employers and got high-school credit. I doubt that Larry knew much about it either. I doubt that he'd talked to a work-study kid in his life. But Larry at the time was part of some high-school auxiliary of PL. PL was the Progressive Labor Party—one of the splinter groups that formed after SDS, the main New Left student group in the '60s, broke into pieces. PL was trying to be a sober and doctrinaire exponent of proletarian revolution. I think Larry'd even cut his hair when he joined it, so that his appearance wouldn't alienate the working class. He wanted to give the demonstration proletarian content and to maybe rally lower-class kids to his cause by acting on their behalf. I thought he was just muddying things up, as well as being an extreme jerk.

That day, Larry and I had a class together—Man and His Behavior it was called, taught by a teacher, Herb Herskowitz, who was experimenting with new methods of teaching, who had us grade ourselves, who never took attendance, and so forth. Larry walked in a bit late to the class, and when he did I lit right into him—disregarding who was talking or what else was going on—accusing him of trying to hijack the demonstration and to piggyback on top of my work. He argued back, saying that my goals were fuzzy and that the demonstration needed clearer and stronger leadership. Herb, in the meantime, had in great glee run out of the room and down the hall to another social-studies class, saying "You guys have got to hear this!" and pulled everyone from that classroom into ours. What followed was a general debate and discussion about the demonstration, whether there even should be a demonstration, and so on. Francis Kaess, a cool guy who had long hair and a funny lip mustache just like Frank Zappa's (actually, I couldn't stand Zappa's look and music, but I liked Francis's general attitude and demeanor anyway), ended up mediating the dispute between me and Larry, pointing out to Larry that what he'd done had been underhanded, and pointing out to me that, since Larry's leaflet was now out there, what we had to do was not argue over what Larry had done but rather get everyone who was interested to meet and work out common goals and strategy.

We had the meeting after school that day or the next. I've completely forgotten what we decided. The main thing I remember was that we were sitting in a school corridor by the auditorium, having the meeting, and a group of toughs came along and kept calling us communists and doing little things to harass us. As for what we discussed—maybe I tried to talk Larry into dropping a lot of the extraneous demands. Really, his attempt to give the demo proletarian content was ludicrous. Not that the school had no class issues: Though the town was mostly upper-middle-class, it sat squat in an economically poor part of the state, and there were poor people in the town, and there was also antagonism between townies and UConn people, plus social categories and antagonisms that the students in the school found for themselves no matter what their background. The school gave short shrift to the kids not on the academic track, many of whom were from the poorer families. But no none had *ever*, as far as I knew—certainly not the political activists at the school, certainly not the left, certainly not Larry—addressed these issues, and both the freaks and the mainstream tended to look down on these kids as greasers or beer freaks. No one left or right had ever tried to organize them politically, and none of us had an inkling what the greasers/beer freaks themselves might consider their own goals and grievances. In planning the free school some of us had talked about reaching out to the people who'd been served worst by E.O. Smith and who therefore might need a free school the most, but no such reach-out ever occurred as far as I knew, or if it did, it failed.

I do remember that the negotiation had an odd, poignant moment. Larry mentioned—I don't remember why—that he occasionally drank, or got high, and that he felt guilty because it got in the way of his political organizing. Some girl touched him on the arm, as if to tell him, "That's okay."

We drew up our goals—whatever they were—probably came up with wording for a new leaflet. A few days later I put out a leaflet of my own, anyway, setting forth my initial goals and disassociating myself from the other demands. Francis chided me for this, since I'd previously agreed to go along with whatever we'd all decided.

The demonstration drew more people than I'd expected—probably a lot of kids cut class to be there. I saw a whole bunch of younger students I didn't recognize. They cheered and yelled in response to the angriest speeches. A lot of anger showed up at that demonstration. There were hecklers, including a hulking work-study guy who was furious at the demands in Larry's original leaflet;

"You never asked us," he said, and would keep interrupting, no matter what the subject, to say that if the work-study wages were raised, the employers would pull out of the program, and that would be the end of work-study.

The first speech was by this girl Diane, who'd graduated the year before. She was militant and angry. "Look, we've got them scared, they're cowering in their offices"—she pointed at the administration offices, which were just off the main lobby. Indeed, no one in the administration showed his face during the demo. "We'll stay here until they meet our demands; we'll stay here night and day; if they want us out of here they'll have to drag us out." This drew cheers, though Tom Goodwillie, sitting next to me, snickered at it. I was just appalled by the ridiculous posturing, and that I had anything to do with this idiocy. Various people spoke—some spontaneously from the crowd, no real order or plan. There was a lot of bickering. Someone would say, "What's wrong in this school is—" and someone else would cut him off with, "*You're* what's wrong." I said a few things, and someone cut me off with, "You're what's wrong." The energy stayed angry, but the anger had no focus. And when the bell rang for the end of the period, everybody left, of course.

Maybe if you stripped away the phony politics there was something interesting bubbling up in Diane and Larry. "We demand that you cower in your offices. We demand that you drag us away and beat us bloody." But again, there was no real politics for it.

The day stayed tense. A couple of teachers threw sarcastic remarks at me and Tom Goodwillie. "Have we decided who's going to run the school yet?" Over lunch I was back in the main lobby, now crowded with students—we were allowed to congregate there during the lunch periods, since we didn't really have anywhere else to go, especially in December when it was too cold to go outside. Suddenly a fight broke out between my friend John Into and a greaser named Elden Thompson. Susie Denenberg and I jumped in to break it up, Susie saying to Elden, "If you're going to fight him, you're going to have to fight me too." Just at that moment Mr. Bulger, one of the vice principals—generally a nice guy—came out of the main office into the lobby. Bulger saw me and Elden squared off against each other. "He started it," said Elden. "Yeah, sure," said Mr. Bulger, and pulled Elden into the office. It turned out that Elden had been telling the truth, somewhat. I asked John what had happened, and John said that Elden had called him a faggot, so he'd kicked Elden in the knee, and then the two had started pummeling each other.

The next day I stole a glance at the absentee sheet that was sent around to teachers. Elden Thompson was listed as "suspended." So that was the one specific result of my demonstration for students' rights, it seemed to me: A greaser got suspended for a fight in which someone else had hit first.

"It's their movie all of a sudden." Their script, their scene, their drama, their scenario. The metaphor was from the Merry Pranksters in Tom Wolfe's *Electric Kool-Aid Acid Test*. "Everybody, everybody everywhere, has his own movie going, his own scenario, and everybody is acting his movie out like mad, only most people don't know that is what they're trapped by, their little script." Larry and Student Action had cut in on my movie, had tried to impose their own.

I was reading a copy of *Acid Test* that I'd borrowed from my friend Hoppity (a couple years younger than I, real name Mark Hooper, so we called him Hoppity after the cartoon character Hoppity Hooper and because he was a short, energetic guy). Hoppity and I were both impressed by a scene in *Acid Test*, fall of 1965, in which Ken Kesey was addressing an antiwar demonstration, after which the leaders and rabble rousers intended to march on the Oakland Army Terminal—militant action in the face of expected police violence. The rally had been building in intensity, from speaker to speaker, but then Kesey, instead of whipping the crowd into action, came onstage fronting an ad-hoc electric band and playing his harmonica *hawonkawonkawonka* and accusing the demonstrators of being as militaristic as the Army. He said, "There's only one thing to do . . . there's only one thing's gonna do any good at all . . . And that's everybody just look at it, look at the war, and turn your backs and say . . . Fuck it." This effectively dispersed the crowd's energy, and the march wimped out, the militancy didn't happen. Hoppity and I had a fantasy of undoing a Larry Groff demonstration in a similar way, maybe by attacking Larry with water pistols, our equivalent of "hawonkawonkawonka."

"Listen, this girl's brains are coming out!" Also from *Acid Test*, from the actual tape of the Electric Kool-Aid Acid Test in Compton, 1966; some girl freaked out and started screaming "Who cares?" over and over, and Hugh Romney took the mic and let loose with this monologue.

"melody so plain"/"don't know what it is"/"be such a freak"/"you're a cow"/"it's chicken." I'd gotten Dylan's *Highway 61 Revisited* three weeks earlier, and this night, as I was writing the What Thing, I really took in a lot of the lyrics for the first time, really understood them.

"The Mountain Girl lonely?" Another *Acid Test* reference. The Mountain Girl was a brazen teenager who'd hooked up with the Pranksters. She was daring and forthright, but underneath the brashness she was lonely. *The Electric Kool-Aid Acid Test* had a big effect on me because it was, among other things, the story of an idea taking off and then crashing, a group coming together and then falling apart. Babbs and Kesey, at the end of the book: "We blew it!"

"Unity Rally." The Unity Rally was the idea of student-council president Bob Moynihan. He felt there was something messed-up and sad in the school—low morale, lots of vandalism. He conceived an all-school assembly to address the vandalism and the unhappiness. In itself, there was nothing wrong with the idea of addressing such things. But an all-school assembly seemed like a bad way of doing so, and Bob wasn't the right person to lead it. I don't remember if he himself thought of it as a Unity Rally, or if that's merely what some friends and I sarcastically dubbed it, what we feared it would be. In any event, I wasn't so sure that vandalism and unhappiness were Bad Things. The rally hadn't taken place yet when I wrote the What Thing. So this was my fantasy, the What Thing standing up and holding the crazy mirror to everybody.

The assembly, when it occurred, was even more useless than I'd expected (and as useless as, I suppose, I'd hoped). Most of the freaks just cut the assembly anyway. It took place in the gym. There was a table at one end at which six or so students sat—like on a panel, though I don't recall any discussion, just speeches from each of them. Absurdly enough, the issue narrowed itself down to the fact that a bunch of guys had more or less seized the lavatory off the main hall as their own turf, and everyone else was afraid to go in there, and the guys smoked in there, which was against school rules and made a mess of the place, and maybe the solution was to create an official smoking hall. I have a memory image of Bob asking, helplessly, "Why do you *do* this?" meaning why do people smash things, why do people smoke. But I don't know if my memory is correct, or if it's from this rally. My friend Steve Dombrosk—one of the organizers with my brother of the Beck campaign the previous summer, and then one of the Duffey group—gave a speech in which he said that if we stood together and fought for it we would get our smoking hall. He had an old-time New England accent, and so he came on like Teddy Kennedy at a union rally. In this high-school context he seemed comically inappropriate. A girl named Heidi talked sensibly and humanely about there being too much cruelty in the school—just a week earlier, she said, a girl had had a firecracker thrown up her skirt. A guy named Glenn, a smoker with an apparently abrasive manner but who everybody I knew liked, gave a speech that was posturing and defiant: "We're sick and tired of smoking while surrounded by SHIT!" (A week afterwards he wrote a letter of apology to the teachers. I don't know if it was from the heart or if he was browbeaten into it, though I'd guess he was browbeaten.)

I was sitting with my friend Tina LaConte, and we snorted with sarcasm at every speech except Heidi's. Waves of pain and bitterness tended to come off from Tina anyway, and the Unity Rally just brought out more of her bitterness. Mr. Hayden, my physics teacher, a solid, good man, was standing near us and seemed disturbed by our cynicism, how ferocious it was.

"The lobby could be very important." "We blew it." A week before the What Thing, I'd scribbled down some thoughts, a third of which—the passage beginning "To be all together and in love together"—made it into the What Thing. The following was also part of the scribble but was too maudlin, I decided:

Why don't we build a school? Why don't we go to the main lobby and start to dig and dig dig dig until we have thousands of tunnels? Then we can go in and hide or go in and hold a class and right around the bend there is another class. And in the main lobby anyone can be there (1st come 1st served) and everybody going through to the tunnels has to see them and has to get interested or not—and they have to see him. And in the tunnels people can talk or make love, or draw pictures & make tapes.

But what really happened was this: In the days after the demonstration I continued with my civil disobedience. In my free periods I'd sit in the lobby. Sometimes a friend would sit with me; sometimes kids I didn't know would sit over by another wall. I don't remember now what I was expecting to achieve. Probably I didn't have any idea what would take place and just wanted to find out. Maybe I hoped that more and more kids would, as a matter of course, sit in the lobby, and so the prohibition would evaporate. I doubt that I believed that this would happen; but I felt that I had to go through with it, even if I was no longer sure what the "it" was that I was going through with. An unexpected thing did occur, though: Mr. Davis, a vice principal with some bully in him, would walk by, and if he saw kids sitting against the side wall he'd tell them to leave, but he'd never tell me to leave, or anyone sitting with me. Once when I was sitting with my friend Ellen Bartram, Mr. Davis came by and kicked out the kids against the side wall, but ignored Ellen and me. Ellen was flabbergasted, outraged. Davis was being so blatantly unfair, discriminatory. I was amused by Ellen's outrage—was she expecting Davis to be *fair*?—but heartened by it, too. The kids he'd kicked out were younger than we were; on the school's social map they were lower class—greasers, kind of, but taking on some characteristics of the freaks. Pro-drugs, no longer pro-war, not as anti-"hippie" as their older brothers. In a couple years they'd be called "grits" or "heavy-metal kids." Davis told them to move because he wasn't afraid of the consequences of their refusing. He'd suspend them, and they wouldn't have the influence or status or political ability or determination to mount a challenge. What baffled me was that Davis and Morgan seemed to think I *did*, and were afraid to take action against me. They'd overestimated me. The demonstration had been a failure, there was no movement behind me, there was no mass yearning for the right to sit in lobbies—and if I'd had real political ability I'd have long since crossed the twenty feet between me and those kids at the side wall and I'd have said hello to them, and asked them who they were and how they felt about getting singled out and treated unfairly, and I'd have asked what music they listened to, what bands they liked. I'd have tried to get to know them. But I was too afraid to cross those twenty feet—so afraid that I didn't even consider it. Afraid of strangers, afraid of greasers, afraid of being ridiculed, afraid of being an outsider, afraid of being tongue-tied. Just plain afraid. A fear without reason. "The sun's not yellow. It's chicken." My fear was so great and my alienation so profound that each perpetuated the other. I was so afraid of being an outsider that I was afraid to meet the unknown—and therefore I remained forever outside it. But at least I knew what my trouble was, and I knew to fight for the right of the Unknown to sit by the entrance to my cave, so, if I *were* to venture out, I'd have to see it, and it would have to see me.

Anyway, when Davis made those kids move but not Ellen and me, Ellen was aghast and outraged, and said that now *she* would sit in the lobby whenever possible. And I resolved to myself to play this thing out, to keep on with my sit-ins until the administration told me to move, too. And then I *would* move, because really I had nowhere further to take my protest. And if they didn't make me move? Well, they would, they had to. But if they didn't? Wouldn't that be setting off a stick of dynamite under the future grit kids? Wouldn't it be the school's just *admitting* that everything was insane? I didn't know, but I knew that there was a gaping unfairness, and here was a chance to make people see it and feel it—feel the insanity, if they wanted to. But I was terrified to be sitting there, too, and of the inevitable confrontation.

Finally—I don't remember if it was within days or weeks—the administration cracked down. Mr. Davis came by and decided it was time to act. If I'd been sitting alone I would have moved, that would have been that, protest done. But I was with two girls—my friends Susie Denenberg and Jay Carey—and Mr. Davis had to play tough to them. He told us to move, and little Susie, who was about four-and-a-half feet tall, asked, "Why?" and Davis put himself inches away from her and yelled, "Because you have to!" So Susie in the face of his yelling said, "No, I'm staying here." And Jay and I said we were staying too. So Davis said to me, "All right, Kogan, you're the ringleader. You're coming with me." Jay said, "I'm coming too," and Davis took the two of us into Dr. Morgan's office and left us with him. I don't remember much of the conversation that followed—maybe it was the one where Morgan talked of the school's being for the community and the taxpayers, not just for the students. He told me that he would come down hard on me, squash me if he had to, don't think he wouldn't. I conceded right away that I had no wish to be squashed and that my sit-in would end. Jay and I challenged him on the school's treatment of the greasers and the freaks, of the kids who bombed out of school and those who just showed up and then skipped out across the street, cutting their classes and smoking cigarettes off school property but in plain view of everybody. I accused Morgan of not caring about those kids, and Morgan got mad and said, "Frank, you have no idea how often I've talked to those kids, asked them about their problems, tried to coax them back. I don't want to kick them out. That's not why we have a school, to kick people out."

Anyway, this was the end of my protest, the last of my attempts to shape school policy—the last attempt by this frightened boy to try to shape the world through policy. After that I was using words—shaping phrases. From then on, if I was leading—in case there was anyone or anything to be led—it was by example.

"Where are the What Thing People—my friends. . . . I need them." Well, yes and no. The What Thing was written at a time of excruciating loneliness and depression for me. This is true despite the outward facts of this story, which are that I had a lot of friends and was doing a lot of things with them, such as planning free schools and organizing demonstrations. The truth is, though, that I was withdrawing from my friends as much as I was engaging them, was recognizing that I hadn't figured out how to connect to the friends from the Duffey Summer, was developing a critical attitude towards many of them, was hanging out with new friends, some of the younger freaks, but hadn't really figured out how to connect to them either—or how much I wanted to—and was playing the different sets of friends off each other, in my mind, at least. I felt bogus about a lot of my political activities, anyway. And I was proud of the critical mind that was inspiring me to withdraw and to see myself as bogus—just as I detested myself for withdrawing, for being too afraid or incompetent to connect.

The underlying question may have been whether my friends *were* the What Thing People, and whether they were really going to be my friends. (Answer: Some were. I found out by getting to know them better.) And whether this mind of mine, which hadn't really connected to anybody else's in years, was going to connect to these people's minds. (Answer: To a few of them. By getting to know them better.)

"Juarez" = Dylan. "I think she'll know" = Jefferson Airplane (Grace Slick). "And it's 1, 2, 3" = Country Joe & the Fish. "Kill your Mama" = Mothers of Invention.

"I wish you'd come visit me." This was Francesca, three years younger than I, who had a very unhappy home life. "My parents never let me go anywhere" was close to the truth. Her parents were devout Catholics who had a bumper sticker that said "Fight Moral Pollution" and who were terrified of all that was happening with youth and sex and drugs. According to Francesca her dad tapped the phones and intercepted her and her siblings' letters. Naturally enough, he found a letter of her older sister Maria's where Maria described to her boyfriend all sorts of drug taking. The incident provoked family trauma, episodes of self-destruction, etc.

"'I wish I could see you more often,' says the What Thing." When my friend Leah Schmidt read this she wrote me a note in which she said, "No, that's not the What Thing . . . that's Frank, a Frank who cares and feels and is strong and brave and yourself and is hurting because the absurdity is stronger if nothing else and I guess I'm just part of the absurdity Frank even though often times I am strong enough and brave enough and myself enough to break out of my own absurdity. It takes so much to break through yours to you and I can't put out the effort unless you try to break through yours to me Frank I'm sorry."

"I wish I could see you more often" was almost verbatim from a conversation that Leah and I'd had a couple weeks earlier. Leah was one of the first people I'd recruited for the Beck campaign, because I'd had a crush on her. She simply didn't have the defensive cynicism that a lot of the rest of us had. Her response to "Where is my woman" on the next page was "You can bring me home Frank . . . but you have to ask. And nothing falls apart unless you let it." But she was edging towards a complicated romance with someone else. Actually, our minds were dissimilar—I think her favorite record was *Tapestry*—and we never became deep friends. But she was part of a wonderful revelation I'd had the previous summer. I was at the door of the local Duffey headquarters, watching her and Julia Cunningham (the girl of the bouncing-ball metaphor in "Roger Williams") as they walked across the parking lot. And I was struck by the thought, "So *that's* what people are like." Meaning not that all people were like Leah and Julia, necessarily, but that, like Leah and Julia, they had mess-ups and kindnesses and complications within them that made them potentially accessible and NOT NECESSARILY TO BE FEARED. I'd never figured this out before. And that Leah and Julia were people, not whatever image I'd had in mind of "girls," so girls were people, could be comprehended as such—I'd never figured that out before, either. That's part of why I fell for Leah: Along with her came the idea that I could fall for a *person* because I *liked* that person.

I don't know if Leah thought I was strong, though. She thought maybe I could be strong, but she had the discomfiting insight that I tended to squash myself around others and tried to care for others as a substitute for learning to care for myself.

"The What Thing is how you feel when you feel fine." This was Julia's favorite passage in the What Thing. I never told her of her role in inspiring the What Thing, however.

"Along comes a little tiny/animal." The quotes are all Jefferson Airplane from hereon, except for "I love her," which is *Catch 22* (the movie version, anyway), "I'm so alone" which is Stephen Stills, and the Dylan quote at the end. The Airplane quotes are all Grace Slick except "human feeling dies" which is Kantner (or co-writer Stills or Crosby).

"Peter the Pig"—One of my variations on the Jenny Story had my alter ego "Peter" in the main role, so I sometimes used "Peter the Pig" as a pseudonym.

Here are the lyric sources: the Beatles' version of Chuck Berry's "Rock and Roll Music" (not that the lyrics are any different from Chuck's, but it was the Beatles' I heard) on *Beatles 65*. "We are all outlaws in the eyes of America," from Jefferson Airplane's "We Should Be Together," lyrics by Paul Kantner, on *Volunteers*, 1969 (all other cited Jeff Air lyrics by Grace Slick except "Wooden Ships").

"Ancient empty streets . . ." from Bob Dylan's "Mr. Tambourine Man," *Bringing It All Back Home*, 1965. "Box of Rain" by the Grateful Dead on *American Beauty* as are all the other Dead quotes, 1970. "The Candyman" by the Grateful Dead. "Good morning, Mr. Benson . . ." also from "The Candyman." "I wish I could write you . . ." from Dylan's "Tombstone Blues" on *Highway 61 Revisited*, 1965. "Something is happening, but you don't know what it is . . ." from Dylan's "Ballad of A Thin Man," as are "How does it feel to be such a freak?" and "Screams back you're a cow . . ." on *Highway 61 Revisited*. "The sun's not yellow . . ." is "Tombstone Blues" again. "The Candyman" is still the Dead. "When you're lost in the rain . . ." from "Just Like Tom Thumb's Blues" on *Highway 61 Revisited*. "Go ask Alice, I think she'll know" is Jefferson Airplane's "White Rabbit" on *Surrealistic Pillow*, 1967. "And it's 1, 2, 3, what are we fighting for?" from "The I Feel Like I'm Fixing to Die Rag" on Country Joe & the Fish's *I Feel Like I'm Fixing to Die*, 1967. "My Guitar Wants to Kill Your Mama," by the Mothers Of Invention from *Weasels Ripped My Flesh*, 1970. "Along comes a little tiny . . ." from Jefferson Airplane's "Bear Melt" on *Bless Its Pointed Little Head*, '69. "Go ask Alice . . ." is "White Rabbit" again. "I'm so alone . . ." is either Steve Stills solo or CSNY, and I don't remember the song title. "All you want to do is live . . ." from Jefferson Airplane's "ReJoyce" on *After Bathing At Baxter's*, 1968. "Stare as all your human feelings die" from "Wooden Ships" on Jefferson Airplane's *Volunteers*. "Lather" on Jefferson Airplane's *Crown of Creation*, 1968. So is "You'll laugh so hard you'll crack the walls . . ." from "Greasy Heart." "But when will you stop your believing . . ." from Jefferson Airplane's "Hey Fredrick" on *Volunteers* (and "Fred" is the Airplane's code word for "fuck"). "Compared to your scream . . ." from "Eskimo Blue Day" on *Volunteers*. "How does it feel?" is Dylan's "Like A Rolling Stone," on *Highway 61 Revisited*.

So far in these notes it might seem like I've pulled a bait-and-switch, claiming first in "Roger Williams" that the context was relationships and then here showing the context to be politics. In a way the whole thing *is* about relationships, whether of friendship groups or political groups, same dif, and the basic story is of connections: connections leading to disconnections, connections deliberately severed, connections declared bogus and abandoned in search of . . . what? And the politics in my life was revealed to be (in part) a gloss that I was scraping off to reveal or create a true story. But I'd also say that "personal relationships" was indeed the true context, and if my notes are disproportionately weighted towards "politics and its dissolution" rather than "relationships and their disconnects," this is because I feel easier writing down the politics than writing down the relationships and because the politics is far easier for me to get on the page: It had issues, events, conflicts, outcomes. Whereas the relationships had no clear "plots" or dramatic incident. They had *people*, for sure, but I've always found ideas easier than people to put on the page.

But maybe by leaving so much of the "relationships" out of these notes, I'm doing what in my life at the time the What Thing was trying to undo: putting forth a political story as a diversion from the real one.

So, let's go over the What Thing again, somewhat. What am I going to be when I grow up? A *basketball* player? A role? Or maybe I'm going to be an outlaw amazing in my eyes in the Superstrike Nation? Another role, and bullshit to that says the What Thing.

The Duffey group reaching for dumb jokes, trying to think of what to say to each other: That's the real context, the real story. "Another boring party." That's the story. That and "we only see each other between classes." Those much more than "Fuck AEP" or "co-opted by Student Action" (though of course those were part of the story, just not the biggest part).

The What Thing actually is only the first half of a letter to Tom Olds. I've forgotten what I wrote in the second half, though I remember that it was not cryptic or poetic and that it directly addressed Tom's frustration with Susie Denenberg. Tom had a crush on Susie; she was hanging back; Tom felt unable to connect:

Problem:

    Suzie

        [I told you I was Insane]

    Unto this aspects

        two exist:

            [Before you stop your believing . . .

                like breaks(!) in

                    bad weather.]

            [Doesn't mean shit

                to a

                Tree]

Firstly: Her:

            [Probly (!) keep us both alive . . .

                very free & easy]

            [silver people]

            [Narcs]

[No No No No No No NoNoNoNoNoNoNoNo]

        [from this foreign

            land]

[very free and easy]

Anyway:

Firstly:

She 'is quite' nice to me, answers questions, occasionally says something, is polite, etc. But: that's all. Hmm.

[Motherfucking Ann Landers]

She does homework, goes home, or wanders off with Tina.

[OK, let's try sykology. If I were her [quiet person, but not really shy] confronted with a slightly ugly bastard who doesn't talk much except for fucking bad puns or profound: 'of course's, 'then again's, and 'be that as it may's. Who is shy. [Now that i think about it i don't blame her]

[one toke over the line
sweet mama,
one toke over the line]

[Pick up the cry!]

[Volunteers of America]

Anyway: But that kid isn't quiet inside, he just doesn't spit it out. You can't go around spouting out profound & significant [& personal] bullshit all the time, so he doesn't say anything. [therefore arises [one] of the inherent difficulties of quiet people]

OK
secondly: Me:

[Echo your anguished
cry] [CS&N]

Am I just deluding myself? Am I just desperate & therefore I have convinced myself I like her [specially]?

I wouldn't put it past
myself.

Not at all.

That's what I'm afraid I'm doing.

In which case
what?

I can guess that I was thinking of all this as Tom's yearning for someone but not necessarily for Susie in particular (though she was a fine person to be yearned for), yearning for a lot of things that maybe could include Susie but couldn't be limited to Susie. Along with Susie's personal merits, she had the attribute of not belonging to the same set of friends as the Duffey crowd, so Tom's falling for her helped him break away from the old friends and find some new. I don't know if this is what I said to Tom, but maybe in there was the basic idea that he was doing something useful and admirable even if he didn't get the girl. He was moving, he was growing.

Looking at the last couple pages of the What Thing, I see that it really knows what it's doing, where it's going. Notice that there are only two intruders on the Airplane-to-Dylan speed-race at the end: the Catch 22 "How do you know you don't just think you love her?" and Steve Stills's "Where is my woman?" which I changed to "Where is my [What Thing] woman?" The first warns that being in love may be just another role (like basketball player, like political activist), the second connects "woman" to "What Thing" and suggests that a woman can be a What Thing, a bouncing ball, and that I'm longing for more than simply a woman.

I'm not done, since the story of not-quite-connection didn't consist of just Tom and Susie but actually a foursome: Tom, Susie, Tina LaConte, and me. We were together on Saturday nights somewhat by default, while people who were really dating were making out or making love elsewhere.

So real love was elsewhere?

It was the four of us who were living the What Thing, maybe more so than Julia, whose relationships I hardly knew anything about.

Tina was a mere thirteen, though not only very very smart but also socially and emotionally sophisticated, not just in the sense of knowing how to be a freak and knowing which drugs did what, but also in understanding the nuances of what various people were thinking and feeling—except that underneath all this she had an ache where she needed to have an identity. Not that the average thirteen-year-old has a strong identity, but Tina's was absent, and in its place was simple, raw need. I found her absolutely fetching: a smart, witty, challenging girl but with a vast reservoir of feelings and hurt that I just wanted to reach into and embrace and feel for myself. This girl's breaking up into crispy chips! and who cares? This girl's caked in the dust, nylon wall-to-wall on her eyeballs! and who cares? My very own Who Cares Girl, she was. Except that she was impossible, totally impossible, with a vast need for reassurance and a way of working people over in doomed attempts to get it from them. I wouldn't cooperate with her manipulativeness—I balked at being ordered to give her affection—but I felt a large amount of guilt too, especially as it became obvious to me, and to her, too, that I just wanted to get away from her. We broke off—she stopped speaking to me—which was a relief for a while but then it began to bother me.

But at the time of the What Thing my relationship with Tina was just getting underway. Part of our dynamic was that she was officially (and genuinely) in love with Matt Mattingly, who was off with his parents in England for the year, and whom she was going to lose her virginity to when he got back. And I was in love with Leah, whom I was unable to connect to—and I really had a lot more in common with Tina and a much stronger connection to Tina, too. Tina and I were edging into a sexual relationship, though one that never reached intercourse (and also, at least on my part, edging towards real love, though—probably for my own protection—I wasn't admitting this to myself).

Tina had a brilliant sarcasm that was destructive, of course, but also appealing, since it was so obviously a cover for her vulnerability. Maybe a couple people I knew later on the Lower East Side could match Tina in this, and I've seen Ida Lupino do it in a few of her movies, but no one surpassed it, this sarcasm that for all its power was but a skimpy garment over her essential sadness, and very attractive in its skimpiness.

I first heard Dylan's "Visions of Johanna" several weeks after the What Thing, and recognized its psychology immediately, because it absolutely matched what I was living through. I heard the Stooges' "Not Right" a couple years after that, and I said to myself, "I've lived this one, too"—and continued to live it, often enough.

A few days after getting *Blonde on Blonde* I wrote down, during a study period, an Autobiography of Right Now. Mrs. Singer had suggested I submit the What Thing to a state writing competition; I was hesitant, and ultimately didn't submit it, because of all the quotations. Mrs. Singer said that the competition also required a short autobiography. So I wrote one, an Autobiography of Right Now that began at the moment I started writing it and said nothing of the past. I never dared show it to Mrs. Singer, and she must have thought I'd blown off the assignment. ("Carol" was Carol Denenberg, Susie's older sister. "Swastikas" were the name we gave to these cubicle sets in the school library; each swastika was a unit of four cubicles that, if you looked down on it, looked a bit like a swastika.)

Now. How am I now? Or a few seconds ago when I wrote this down & thought up the phrase? But how did I get that way? I mean, the way I was now.

I am listening to Leah in the swastika make little noises now a few seconds ago when she'd hum a little tune (she did it again) or tap her pencil or yawn or sigh as she did a couple of minutes ago. Then I began tapping to Tom, he making meaningless taps and me giving what I think was the international signal of distress.

I want to go over & talk to Leah, but that would be too obvious, even for me, and she's doing her math. Anyway, there's only 5 minutes left in the period.

How did I get this way?

If Carol were here I'd go up to her and say "Carol, I've got a problem. I'm obsessed with my own mind. And I'm so obsessed with my own mind that I can't think of anything else, not even Sex. And I'm bored. Which you defined for me."

Fuck. The Bell.

This now is now two hours after the last now and I'm different but not any better. What did I mean last night when I thought that I was obsessed with myself more than any other me? Or friends.

And what have I done lately except do nothing for nobody except try to push myself on everyotherbody or at least the ones I love so they too will be part of me and insane and I won't be alone?

He (me-then) was saying to Carol when I was another now:

"I have a problem. I'm obsessed with my mind."

And then I was going to go on before the fucking bell:

"Because I don't know how to live and do little things except be bored. And I don't even know how to say it."

Say what?

Visions of Johanna:

> *"Ya sure got a lotta gall*
> *to be so useless an' all . . ."*

Well, I was really hard on myself. Hard on myself for my treatment of Tina, hard on myself for the lobby sit-in debacle, hard on myself for feeling lonely. (I showed Mark Sinker a rough draft of these notes and he said, "You're incredibly hard on yourself. You, a schoolkid, organised something!! Of course the authorities were scared and fascinated, and hands-off, also. Blimey.")

Fact is, though, I knew I was living through something special, doing something special, no matter how difficult, and I knew that I was discovering creativity, that something was happening (I was growing up, maybe?), and I was damned proud of myself, amidst all the depression.

Why Music Sucks #13, Spring 2001

POSTSCRIPT 2004. LARRY'S STORY:

"You're incredibly hard on yourself." Obviously I was hard on myself *then*—that's what adolescence is for—but I was also hard in the retelling. This is good for the story, for the most part, since it helps to deliver the loneliness and self-reproach that attended my failure to cross the twenty feet to those kids at the side wall. And it echoes some of what's elsewhere in this book, since a feature of what I'm calling PBS or The Great Wrong Place (or, simply, "Frank") is its lack of reach, its fear of crossing. But back in eleventh grade I wasn't just afraid to cross to the future grit kids, I was also so fundamentally afraid (and in awe of) anyone who outflanked me on the "left," not only the political left, but the drug left, the musical left, the hairstyle left, that there's no way I would have—for instance— genuinely gotten to really know Larry Groff, either. And of course in my mind I was hard on him then, too; and too much of that hardness carries through in this account. Back in 1970, when I was calling myself chickenshit for not reach-

ing out to grit kids et al., it was emotionally convenient for me to assume that Larry, my antagonist, hadn't reached out either. (I think the buzz word here is "projection.") And since I was pissed at him, it was emotionally convenient to decide that he *couldn't* have anything interesting to say about Marx's predictions, and to decide not to stick around and discover what in fact he did have to say (and given how little I knew about Marx, this hardly demonstrated an inquisitive attitude on my part). Re-reading this essay I'm jolted by how much I'd simply carried my old prejudices forward to 2001 without rethinking them. "I doubt that he'd talked to a work-study kid in his life." "The school gave short shrift to the kids not on the academic track, many of whom were from the poorer families. But no none had *ever*, as far as I knew—certainly not the political activists at the school, certainly not the left, certainly not Larry—addressed these issues." Really? And I knew this how? Was I shadowing him, using surveillance cameras, recording his phone calls?

So I got in touch with Larry, now an artist in the Boston area (larrygroff. com), who replied with a letter that was generous and witty ("'Student Action became Larry Groff's domain': I guess on some level it was 'my domain'—as I was often the only person who would show up to the meetings!"). Here's a bit of his story.

> Wow. I must have really pissed you off. I really don't remember "stealing 'your' demonstration." Seems ludicrous. We did try to change the flavor and direction of the demonstration to what you describe, but I think it took a life of its own. Ultimately, I don't think I had that much to do with it, despite getting the attention (credit/blame) from many. The students were there mainly out of curiosity and most probably thought the war was wrong. I highly doubt anyone paid much attention to the leaflets and such. I really don't remember the speeches (if you could call them that). All I remember was planning with a few people to chant "fuck Nixon and fuck his war"—using the word fuck seemed to get the most attention from the adults as I recall.
>
> For better and mainly worse, political maneuverings such as the left-wing crazies taking control from the liberals and hippie types are certainly not without precedent historically. Comes with the territory I am afraid.

I rarely attended high school classes for the last two or three years, making almost all F's and D's. I think I had about an average of a 40% attendance rate. My family was (and had been for some time) in chaos. Drugs and alcohol would have brought me down then except I became very close with the community of people around SDS and PLP. They became my real family. Unfortunately, the price of admission to this family was to toe the party line and spread the word. I could go on for days telling you how fucked up it could be at times. But many of us were basically decent people—wanting to protest the injustice we saw in society and to find some community with each other. We weren't the one-dimensional ideologues that we might sometimes appear to be.

"I doubt that he'd talked to a work-study kid in his life."

Not really. I did try, however; I remember standing in the "airlock"—hallway between the Vo-Ag students and the rest of the high school—leafleting and trying (without much success) to talk with the work-study students. I might add that I wasn't the only one doing this. Rick Strams and Robbie Roth also helped for what it's worth. I did spend much time trying to "connect" with working class peoples in the Storrs area. Can't say I was ever that successful—but I did do the legwork (for a crazy teenager anyway).

Cutting my shoulder-length hair to a close crop was one of the hardest things I did in high school—my girlfriend broke off with me as a result. I doubt if any workers ever looked at me any favorably after either. In my mind it showed my level of dedication to the movement. The PL party members had "struggled" with me for quite some time to cut it and eventually I agreed. I hated the haircut and was profoundly embarrassed for some time after—I grew it all back later. I never really forgave myself for it.

For what it's worth, I did come from a poorer family. True, my father was a UConn faculty member then—but he got there much later in life. Prior to that our family was quite poor; my mother's family was from a long line of very poor southern sharecroppers, military and factory workers. My father was also from deep working-class roots. Neither of my parents were intellectuals. I spent a great deal of time leafleting and canvassing; Willimantic housing projects, a Willimantic poultry factory, some housing project in Willimantic door to door, going to community functions, the Willimantic and Coventry high school and many other places. After I dropped out of high school I did this sort of thing full-time for a couple of years—going door to door in housing projects, welfare offices in some of the poorest neighborhoods in Miami, Hartford, Albany, New Haven, and finally Boston.

Did it do any good? Yes—but I am afraid the only real good it did was to me. Spending so much time talking to very poor people taught me some humility.

It taught me I didn't know shit most of the time. They taught me to lighten up and most of all to listen. It taught me to start to understand how little I actually knew about anything.

Mark Sinker, from the email where he told me I was hard on myself:

A celebrity Revolutionary Socialist I mostly consider an idiot was being interviewed on TV, a few months back. He was as smug and crap as usual, but he did have one fairly amusing line, poorly delivered. "The police always say, 'organised outside agitators': it bears no relationship to what actually happens in a demo. You turn up, all gung-ho except the ones who want to be somewhere else, and the guy with the van who's supposed to be bringing the banners left them all in his kitchen. Organised! If only!!" Point is, getting people all in one place is amazingly hard, hard enough to be alarming and impressive. A lot of "real" politics is a kind of fake 'em out manoeuvring to get the impetus in enough places for enough time to push things to new places, by gathering "coalitions"—i.e., sort of tricking large groups of people into thinking they're all pushing more or less in the same direction, for the same reason, when we all know how hard, how unusual, it is even to be in a tiny, self-formed group—rockband, marriage, whatever—and know you're pushing same direction, same reason.

My thought here; having "my" demonstration stolen from me broadened it; for better or worse took it to an unknown, a non-Frank. If Frank had been willing to talk to this non-Frank . . .

CHAPTER 8

THE WIND FROM MY HEAD

[In spring 1971 I was part of a one-week student exchange between my school and Parish Hill, the high school for a neighboring district. Mr. Elias, the teacher leading the exchange, suggested that we each keep a journal and show it to him after the exchange. So I kept this journal, ended up showing it to no teacher. It's not just my only real attempt at a social map in this book; sketchy though it is, it's the only social map in the world of this type of early '70s quasi-rural-suburban school, that I know of (though of course there might be some I don't know of). The Parish Hill Tina whom I mention early in this journal obviously isn't the Who Cares Girl Tina whom I'm crying out to at the end. There are two different Carols; a couple of Lindas, as well. Terminology: In 1971, "straight" generally meant "mainstream, not hip, not a freak." Or it meant "not high." It didn't imply anything about sexual preference unless that was the specific topic.]

Monday, April 26, 1971

Today, sitting out on the grass for a while, I thought: "I am at Parish Hill for a week. That's it. I am at Parish Hill for a week. That's all it is. This is where I am. I am sitting on the grass at Parish Hill. I am going to be here for a week. That's all. That's it."

In my first class today, History, I didn't say anything. The class was totally ignorant. I mean totally. We were talking about foreign aid. The teacher said some very stupid generalizations: Communists infiltrate countries when the people are weak. We went into Vietnam to give the Vietnamese self-determination. I didn't say anything because it was the first class and I didn't want to give the impression of being too smart.

Tina is a freak. I was talking to her and I looked at a girl who was passing. Tina said that it was funny how my eyes went up and down. She said not to mind it, that she likes to watch people. She wanted to know if any of us [from E.O Smith] were going together. I said no. She said that was too bad because she liked to look at people who were going together. It was fun to see them holding hands. I told her that I thought most of the kids in school were pretty nice. She seemed surprised. I added, though, that it seemed as if it could get pretty boring. She agreed that it was boring, unless you knew the right people.

I didn't really want to talk in Physics, and fortunately a tall all-American named Jeff did most of the talking. He thinks Parish Hill has good spirit. There are few fights, and lots of people attend sports events. There's going to be a class trip to Washington.

Joan, who was sitting next to me, would occasionally shake her head as Jeff talked.

Later, after reading Carol [Denenberg]'s story I went looking for Joan, because she had strange pale-blue eyes and she seemed as if she might be a What Thing person.

Joan is not a greaser, freak, beer freak, or teenybopper. Maybe she's an intellectual. She is the first one I've met who works during her studies. She has to read a book a week for Existentialism. She's intelligent, but so is everyone else. She's a class officer. She's probably a good student who gets straight A's. Making up stories in Communication, she couldn't think of anything to say. She doesn't write. I forgot to ask her if she likes Dylan or the Airplane.

In History the teacher asked Stan if he was in favor of foreign aid and he said yes. So she asked him why and he asked in return, "Am I right?"

I have four days left.

Second Day 9:15 AM, Tuesday, April 27, 1971

There is nothing to do here all day. Tina and some other people are free, but I have nothing to say to them. I wonder if they wish they were doing something.

I went to a class meeting before school. Gary ran it. At the beginning a man announced that even though the dance Saturday lost money because no one came and even though no one had a good time, it was a success. Then a whole bunch of people volunteered to work on some committee to raise money or do something at a carnival. Joan volunteered.

There must be a lot of dope here. Everyone's bored.

Someone just came up and talked to me. He's bored by school. On weekends he works. The only class he likes is drafting. He can't wait for the end of the day.

Tonight

Janet is now one of my best friends [at Parish Hill]. I can talk to her and feel open and free, or at least happy until the What Thing comes in and tells me "Move, you've only got four days left." I can't think of any way to describe her, and I don't remember anything she's said to me. She's got a boyfriend named

Michael. She takes art. She's in my American Civ class, and doesn't know anything about foreign policy. She cuts class a lot.

I was talking to Tina. She doesn't seem to mind Parish Hill. She says it's like a constant party. I told her parties can get pretty boring. She and her friends were comparing me to a kid called Michael who'd left a couple years ago because he was insane. Tina and her group (the right people?) have the nastiest way of talking about people of anyone I've met here. They don't put me at ease. After Janet had come by and said hello to me, one of them said, "She's too much," and started mimicking her.

A couple of times people went up to me and said, "Are you from E.O. Smith?" and started talking. One girl who is really nice who did this is named Janis. She's superstraight. She smokes 4 cigarettes a night because she's bored. She showed me the data processing machine she works on, and tried to explain how it works. She thinks drugs are bad and that a lot of younger kids are "going bad." I tried to explain why people use drugs (though I don't know too well) and gave her some reasons for thinking it was a good and progressive thing. I don't think she has come far enough to understand what I was talking about. I don't think she ever will.

9:00 AM during Family Soc, Wednesday, April 28

I like the Family Soc teacher. I don't think the class is very good. She reads facts about marriage in India and other places, which is kind of uninteresting. What she says about the U.S. is. I don't know why I am writing this.

A wedding is a ceremony which emphasizes the importance of the event. You kinda know beforehand what is important. You don't when you just walk up to someone and say Hi!

In Existentialism Mr. Singer read part of a paper by Joan which was about *The Fixer* and loneliness. It wasn't personal. It was intelligent. Good vocabulary. It was actually good. But . . .

Chris just described a Quaker wedding. You sit and think for an hour. The teacher just told us about a wedding where the bride and groom climbed a mountain which no one else would climb. The father of the bride was mad because it wasn't a traditional ceremony. There weren't any witnesses or a ring. The bride and groom brought back a rock.

I think it would be good to have a totally silent wedding.

Tonight

In two days everyone at Parish Hill will cease to exist. This is too soon. It seems as if things are only beginning, not ending. Of course, that's kind of true for some people at E.O. Smith. But it would make more sense to leave them, since with the people I know at Smith it's as if it's too late—it's ridiculous to drag on the ridiculous hope.

Yesterday I asked Becky if she knew anyone who wasn't straight and who wasn't a freak. She mentioned a girl called Evelyn. I met Evelyn today. She is "majoring" in art. She's taking four years of that and science. She's going to do handicrafts. I saw something she made which was good. She says that boredom is your own fault. She writes poetry.

I was talking with Linda and we were standing outside the library and some fucker with a Czarist beard asks us as he's going by if we are assigned to hall. When he comes back he asks us where we're supposed to be. Aagh!! Later, a group of us were sitting, not even in the hall but in the large area in front of the store, and we were told to move. Felt like home.

Jon says only about ten people remain seated during the pledge. He's one of them. Jon can get away with not going to many classes and then not going to detention, 'cause he's not scared of them and he's not unwilling to tell them to their face that he's not going to take their shit. He's the only one I've met so far.

At the assembly today we had to say the pledge, and since we didn't want thousands of greasers descending on us we stood up. But we didn't say anything. I've been too late in home room for the pledge so far. I don't know what I'll do if I'm on time.

Jennifer says that her homeroom won't start the pledge until she stands up, and that then she sits down again. They told her she needs a parent's note in order not to say it. I told her they couldn't do that, because of the first amendment.

A different Linda cut the assembly. We were going to, but there's nowhere to go, and Elias would get really pissed if we had gone out with Jon and played frisbee. Before Linda disappeared she put something in her locker 'cause she didn't want to get caught with it.

Thursday 1:05 PM

Less and less happens every day we're here.
I've hardly seen Evelyn. In a little over a day we'll both be dead.

1:40 PM

Maybe it doesn't matter if anyone here dies. Nothing's happened. ("Boredom is you own fault.") Write a word. A poem. Something.
I have not seen Linda today.
I feel violent.
Because no one has happened today.
It's stupid to think that something will.

Incredible. What am I interested in? => Boredom is your own fault? Not always true. It's everyone's fault.

[undated]

Am I responsible for the rain?

This is a dream
But I believe I saw some pity
On her face after she heard me talking.
Perhaps it is just wonder, or indifference.
(I wonder what I was trying to prove.)

A person without a job
flounders into incoherence

If I don't write, what do I do?

A deep bass roar grinds out of my arms and shrieks into feedback screaming then back into pounding power which I wish could tear up this paper and rock your eyes and knock the pity from her face.

Take the exhilarating tiger which he created when he kicked you out of the hall, and form electric surging lightning beauty, which will clean you and shorten the time of waiting.

I wish the face wouldn't die (the pounding sinks into soft, mild, deep power and now plays with the ticking of the clock and the insects chirping in the night—it is now time to take a shower).

Sunday, May 2

Parish Hill is a place—it is a school. It has students. Teachers. A principal. Very few drugs. Parents (unseen). E.O. Smith (unseen). Vietnam (unseen). Most of my generalizations about Parish Hill were developed in the first couple of days. By the end of the week I knew they were wrong, but I didn't have anything to replace them with.

At Parish Hill the students have more respect, or at least less disrespect and hate, for the institution than people do at E.O. Smith.

Most students at Parish Hill are bored by the school. However, they do not seem driven up a wall by the school, and they don't seem as desperate as E.O. Smith students.

Very few teachers (one) excite the students.

The school is Blah! but . . .

There is something beneath the blahdom. It is hidden under much more Blah than it is at E.O. Smith, and somehow Parish Hill seems less explosive and less important than Storrs.

Perhaps there is a lot of quiet creativity. There is certainly a lot less violence, cynicism, anticreativity.

Jennifer is an eighth grader, but emotionally older, like Tina [LaConte]. She is very intelligent, and is in the shrink class for underachievers. She is confused, though not cynical or sarcastic. She's thinking of running away for a short time. I can't tell what she wants to do with her life, or even tomorrow. She dresses sloppily and looks like a freak, but she's not cool or nasty. She uses drugs.

Linda—Linda moved from Worcester at the beginning of the year. She says that her personality changed when she came to Parish Hill because she began hanging out with different kids. She no longer did everything her mother told her to do. She stopped hanging around with the kids she had started with for reasons I don't quite understand—it was either that her parents didn't like them or that she herself was uncomfortable with them. Or both. Now she hangs around with kids who are "decent."

I asked Linda what she would do in her spare time. She said that she would ride horses.

Chuck—Chuck believes in God very strongly, and belongs to some fundamentalist religion. All that is necessary to go to heaven is to believe. If you believe, and pray, God will help you, and cure your sickness. Chuck has a mild, sincere drawl, and a beautiful way of describing his faith, like music. He is a very moral, very decent person who probably uses his religion to make himself strong, not to make others weak. I don't know how intelligent he is. I hope his religion doesn't screw him up, or anyone else.

Monday, May 3

I'm not sure what I can use Parish Hill for. But I want to go back to it. Even though I somehow think it's less than E.O. Smith—E.O. Smith is less than both combined. Maybe Parish Hill is like a new record which I can't not play and makes all the rest of the records seem less than a complete record collection.

Evelyn—Leah knows her—knew her, anyway. She gave a Leah scream when I mentioned Evelyn. She said that Evelyn was the one person from seventh grade she wishes she had known better. She said Evelyn was an outcast. This makes sense with what Evelyn told me about her time at E.O. Smith. Still, she doesn't look like an outcast.

She isn't straight. She doesn't (I guess) like marijuana. She used to be with some freaks, but she left them. She had a boyfriend but began noticing his faults. For instance, he couldn't stand his parents, and said all these terrible things about them, which she discovered weren't true. What else about Evelyn? She's a Tolkien freak. She tells jokes. She sits in the library corridor and greets people as they go by. She sits noisily, as Becky says.

Tuesday, May 4

Shit again. I went to nothing today. What happened in nothing today? Nothing.

I just put on "Sad-Eyed Lady of the Lowlands." I hope it still works. (Take three times a day. Guaranteed to ease the pain and send your mind wandering through friends.)

Parish Hill is over, leaving nothing but a worse E.O. Smith. I hope Lisa has friends. I don't know why I wrote that. She seems liberal-straight. She could be alone.

The percussion is too loud and grating this time, but I don't have anything else to play. I'm not in the mood for the Grateful Dead.

I should write Tina a poem. It is her birthday sometime.

Sunday, May 9

Oh mogh! I'm here again. Ding-a-link-a think-a somethin' to write.

Listening to the Byrds. Bless my teeny bean. I hope this doesn't mean nothing, but is not merely Freudian.

What can I do with an old man whose blood is crud? I don't really know him, yet, so it is difficult to write about him. But when I finally do, I know he won't let me down. Perhaps. I suppose I'm writing like this because it's easy. It should be interesting for me or some poor person to try to find out what I mean. [*I'd started but abandoned a poem about an old man whose blood was crud.*]

He won't lift me up, either, which can be a letdown.

(I was just thinking of Chuck. We should be opposed to each other. This is probably why I feel an obligation to like and respect him.)

. . . In other words (rhymes with Byrds—this is a poem) I don't have a job.

[undated]

I met someone new today. Kim. She's a ninth grader. She came here in September, but I don't remember seeing her until December. I asked her where she was from and she said, "This is going to kill you." She's from Ashford.

I was talking and acting in a usual way, but perhaps semi-consciously I was being stranger and more cryptic than usual, as a defense mechanism. She told me I confused her, and when Susie came by she asked, "Where did you pick this one up?" I only partially believed her. I enjoyed speaking to her. I didn't mind talking and I didn't feel she was going to use what I'd said against me.

She likes E.O. Smith. It has a lot of people and many things are going on. She likes Hoppity, though she isn't in that clique. She likes her teachers.

A wolverine escaped today.

Wednesday, May 12 [I'd returned to Parish Hill that day for a visit]

Mike B. gave me a guided tour of the cliques in the school. He says he is a loner. He and the other Mike are a group. He hangs around mainly with freaks. But he's basically right.

The groups. (1) Senior clique: They sit in one table in the cafeteria. Possibly largest clique in school. Includes Carol and Judy and lots of others. (2) Freaks (more like teenyboppers): Self-explanatory. Doesn't include Jon. (3) Greasers: Almost all boys. (4) Jocks. (5) Great muddled middle.

People in different grades don't seem to associate with each other. When I was talking to Linda (ninth grade), Carol (twelfth grade) left and went to talk with a friend. When I was sitting with Carol and others in the senior clique, Janet went by and I suggested she join us, but she didn't.

I've heard junior-high kids referred to as "little things." Linda says that she doesn't associate with Jr. High kids.

Linda and Bobbe were made fun of by some of their "friends" because they were friends of mine. Bobbe's friends picked on her because she wrote us a letter. I asked Linda if it was because of my hair and she said she thought it might be.

Sometimes in the hall someone would say "Look at that hair." In the cafeteria a table of greasers made fun of me and started calling me "faggot." A guy threw a tennis ball at me (but not hard) and I made a brilliant one-handed catch with my left hand, and threw it back. I went and sat next to Evelyn, with my mind mangled. She said that the freaks would never be as bad as the greasers.

Later, when I went in, two of the greasers were sitting with the other Linda and her friend Cindy (Becky's sister), who are sort of close to the freak group. I went to sit at that table and the two greasers got up and left.

During lunch, Jon and two girls smoked a cigarette out in the bus circle, lying sideways to keep the butt hidden.

Whenever I asked anyone what happened since I'd left, they all said "Nothing."

Carol says that the one group that picks on her group for being a clique is the freaks. She says they're a lot worse as a clique than her group is.

They certainly are a lot more noticeable as a clique.

Sunday, May 16

Shi-it.

Sunday seems to usually be a hangover. Always raining. Gunk taste deep in my throat. My eyes too tired. Sleepy gunkshit. Deep. Can't pull myself out of the sludge. Sludge York Times as an excuse against Nothing—Nothing York all the shit all day a brutal wasted nothing.

I don't dare turn off the record player because voices and shlippy stuff in the background have the invigorating effect of fingernails against the blackboard.

NO ? have NOTHING TO WRITE

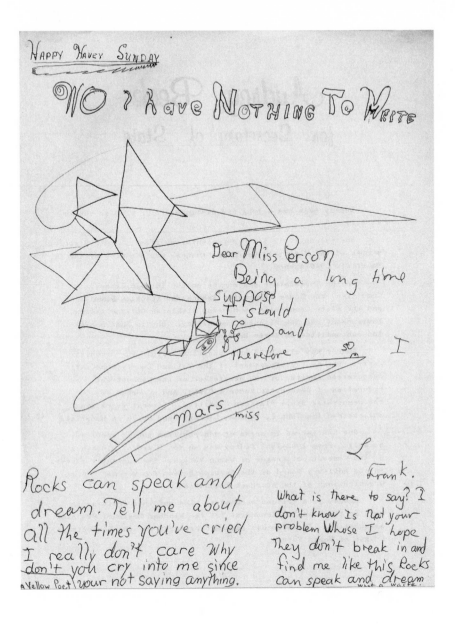

Dear Miss Person
    Being a long time
suppose
    I should
        and
    Therefore   so   I

    Mars   miss

                        L
                        Frank.

Rocks can speak and
dream. Tell me about
all the times you've cried
I really don't care Why
don't you cry into me since
a Yellow Poet your not saying anything.

What is there to say? I
don't know Is Nat your
problem Whose I hope
They don't break in and
find me like this Rocks
can speak and dream
what a waste

It is a mistake to use somebody else's metaphor in my own situation.

A soft rock sat next to you

Shit   Push Power of Today
It is too late it has gone it is lost Smash
Against your head All soft
and warm on the outside but cold
on the inside like Rock. I cried to think of all
the happiness that will be yours... Which
is a lie? Smiling? Or the false confession that
smiling is not a lie, is perfect. Rock's newness
is worn away on the outside but the inside has centuries
of scars, which don't go away.   " gentle
                                    lazy, wound." Something
hit the soft outside and cut into it and settled around the
hard core, pressing it down deeper into the ground,
pushing it inert so there was no way to react, no way to
prove to himself that he was alive.

Rocks work in the invisible.

I am the fingernail I am the blackboard I am the ear The Head. Scccrrwww-wzzzeerereeerrrrgwuyhtf.

I have to put on a record or they will hear me making sounds. Guzz roar like an airplane deep low background bass guitar "you say it's healing but . . ." and I am writing with one eye closed producing a strange nearly creative effect when combined with the sounds I am grinding.

But if I put on a record I can't write. (I've stopped grinding.) Wow! Nothing but birds and cars and a radio nail out of bird tune in the background.

I hear the wind and look up now the sky is twilight dark-blue sea and the small leaves are dark moving flowers. I'm a submarine. (How long do I do this before I have to start to say what I'm going to say?) Breeze-breath. Tarantula. Should I call Carol [Denenberg]?

Dear Carol—I don't want to lose you.

The noise just came back strong more musical still long-low notes and powerful. It took me by surprise. Carol set in motion some force of antidesperation. More notes heavier beats.

The dishwasher ships motor in the background and fish chirping. I should turn off my vocals (one-eyed writing again—it seems to move and have optical space). Wind outside wind inside now I am a soft hum.

Do I begin now, or do I still have several more minutes before I become intelligible rigid? Can't try it's a song maybe I can do both together. Last night or Tina's birthday Tuesday. It is up to you. Do you believe in magic? Ow! The dishmother begins to bother. Thank god no one said anything.

Record—Record-up—Stupid radio [*from the living room*]—Record—but I'm writing when do I stop where do I begin?

I am more stoned than when I was stoned. I am a rock. But a living one. ". . . a brilliance of unaccustomed origin" (W. Stevens). But what? I'm sounding again. I am now so light. Should I kill it by serious? Am I light but just wasting time? Quiet sounds. No record. I could go on and on without fear or conscience. I'd just like to work Tina in, that's all.

My hair I am god I'm going bald. Tina Carol come in drop in force your way in. I have so far to go. Am I delaying the beginning or just getting a good running start? So light. I have never been so strange. My my maybe it's the . . . (I can't think of anything it might be. This is strange—many pages and it may all be nothing. This is not in the least way brutal (I hope I explain that later) (straight). I'm glad. Yes. I never closed the first parentheses.)

I had something important to say—Yes, that's it. It's coming out in words crazy words clear dear queer let it all hang out let it all drip out flow out grow jump sprout push out silent spring up and out let it like the wind from my head.

Tina.

(Now I will reread this and hope not to discover nothing. No I won't I'm not out of this I don't want out. Inertia. I can't go back only forward like time forward but Tina is so important and time is running out Shit I just started feeling tired. I'll take the risk-push I'm going back.)

Good. That's done I'm still not done. Ding hum more sounds.

The Brutal truth. Yes, I have to be serious. I lost the thought. Oh. I have to put down an already thought thought and hope I don't screw it up. To whoever is reading this. Who will read it?

So what does all this prove? Shit. I'm wasting time.

The Brutal Truth about my feelings toward Tina. The Brutal Truth about the Brutal Truth is that there is no truth.

I think I took care of this subject at the beginning of the What Thing.

The brutal truth about Tina is that

"I am a) sad
        b) bored
        c) lonely
        d) confused
        e) in love
        f) in hate
        g) confused
        h) etc.
        i) afraid to say it"

say what?

Let's start somewhere. It has been about a week less than two months since Tina stopped speaking to me.

Shit. I wish I had time. I need to lie down and think.

[undated]

Coil soft empty power

I am running away, too many sounds the wrong sounds scratch turn on my record player to blot out the background scratch-drip this won't do it push from the throat grumble gzzzzzrw swear shout to blot out the record turn up the record to blot out my shouts. One of us must stop.

THE FIDDLER HE NOW STEPS TO THE ROAD

(paper about Bob Dylan for high-school humanities class) (excerpts)

This year isn't as bad as last year. Last Year was the Great Depression, when we were into Crazy. Sane Crazy, mainly. There are two types of Sane Crazy: the good type and the bad type. The good type is when you are super happy and weird and wild creative free. The good type was last seen out in San Francisco around 1966, though some people still go through the motions. The bad type is when you are passionately and crucially committed to the things which aren't there—specifically, friends which aren't there, songs which aren't there, excitement which isn't there, feelings which aren't there. In advanced forms of Sane Crazy type 2 you worship the emptiness, and the twists and stupid turns that people make in space, and the sacred shouting rhymes that everyone imagines are hidden inside everyone else or are just down the Interstate in the next town. Then you can listen to yourself and say: Far out, is that my mind going Zing? Listen to that stomach. Fear. Neurosis. Hear me running. I'm a symphony, without control. Emotions. Wrists. Pills. Just me and that tree. See me turn intense, wind up, stretch out my arm, shout out rays from my fingers, sheets of power from my eyes, all against that tree, making it into different forms, the shape of a frog, the shape of pain. Wow! That's crazy! That's . . . that's . . . that's . . . that's . . . SOMETHING!

So much for Sane Crazy. Real Crazy is what happens when you stare straight at the bright side of that tree—and lose. All of a sudden you're terrified and running. So fast. Everyone around you is blinding bright, able to catch you, burn you, control you. But no. I can hide. I can dive deep down inside me. They'll take me away and put me somewhere, but they won't be able to get in and touch me. I can't let them touch me. Can't let them hear me lying. Can't let them see me leaving her-it-the tree-me as she-I-he gets laughed at, humiliated, and destroyed.

. . . "The senator he came down, showing everyone his gun/Handing out free tickets to the wedding of his son/And me I nearly got busted, and wouldn't it be my luck/To get caught without a ticket and be discovered beneath a truck." This verse is odd. It's obviously unreal. But . . . let me put it like this: I think the verse gives the best, most accurate (emotionally) picture of our parasitic, idiotic political system of anything (poem, song, book) I've come across. And Dylan also gives a blunt description of where he sits in relation to the system. This is pretty good for four lines. The chorus ("Oh mama, can this really be the end/To be stuck inside of Mobile with the Memphis blues again") ties the whole song together and makes it impossible to think of the song as a joke. The song is about what E.O. Smith is like for many of the students.

The next verse is from a song which
Garbage Garbage Garbage Garbage Garbage Garbage Garbage Garbage

That's a comment about this filmmaker. Not Fellini. I just saw *The Clowns* by Fellini. The clowns didn't pretend to have anything but frowns. The circus is dying the circus is dying Ring around the rosy and all say Floomp! *Death on . . .* No, scratch that. *Love on the Golf Course* directed by the Distinguished Gentleman With the Beard and starring BOB DYLAN! That's right. I hope he doesn't mind me putting him in my movie. He once said, "I'll let you be in my dream if you let me be in yours." That's an invitation. But that was before the Movie Establishment tried to stop him from leaving their movie. They would only let him act, and his scripts had to sound like theirs. "Well, hope you're all having a good time . . . it's Halloween, and, uh, I've got my Bob Dylan mask on." Whoosh. Beatniks out to make it rich. The problem is how to make a back-of-the-mind garbage dump look like a golf course with nice straight fairways and neat grass, fashionably long with sideburns and a bright red tie—and yet keep all the thrown eggshells and callused cans and rusted hands close enough to the surface so that we can pull them in when we need them. Bob Dylan doesn't have to worry, though, about me manipulating him. I'll never make my movie. I'm too scared. I usually get all up and excited and say, Wow, I gotta go make that movie and then I get close to starting and I say: OK, we're gonna start shooting at eight, and then it gets closer and closer to eight and I start to panic, and I look at the film idea and say: I can't make this movie. It's shit. It's nothing. So I go off and play guitar or listen to a record and in the morning feel guilty and jerk off.

Never stop writing in the middle of a sentence. A full sentence you can ignore, but an open sentence forces you to see into it, and you look at it and discover that it's a lie, a big lie, and you can't finish it, because it's a lie like The Masters Of War Lie and The Communist Lie and The Free School Lie, but this time it's called The Next Verse Is From A Song Which Lie.

Hitler was a master movie maker. He took millions of people and snatched them from wherever and whoever they were, and forced them into his movie. OK, you. You're gonna play the Aryans. And you. Yes *you*, you're the Jews. I'm the Führer.

from "The Fiddler He Now Steps to the Road," early 1972

POPPED INTERVIEW:

FRANK: I don't, you know, define punk the way a lot of other people do, obviously. I just wrote this letter to Aaron, who puts out *Cometbus*, trying to entice him to write another piece for my magazine for the religious question. He'd actually written something in his 'zine about where Judaism exists or doesn't exist in his identity, but he was sort of saying something in the end of that piece that he was a Jew, but that Jew wasn't his religion, and then he said that punk was his religion. And I said you've got a different punk than I do, 'cause punk's *not* my religion. It's not my people, it's not my creed. It doesn't make sense to me as a people. "I am the world's forgotten boy, the one who searches and destroys." That's not a group slogan, sorry. I mean, there's a sense in which it applies to many many human beings in the world, you know, there's a forgottenness, there are pieces of us which are forgotten because we don't get a chance to show them, and maybe we shouldn't even, or something like that. And that sort of search-and-destroy part of us is one of these forgotten things, so we have this forgotten boy within us, so a lot of people can identify with that song, but it's not a group thing. Or the Sex Pistols' "I wanna destroy passersby." That's not a group slogan, I'm sorry—if it's a group slogan, you've got it wrong. It doesn't mean I wanna destroy *other* passersby other than the people in my social group or something like that. It's much more like, this is the part of me that, like, you know, stabs my girlfriend to death, or this is the part of me that shunned that girl in sixth grade because I was too chicken not to, or the part of me that ran that race against my friend and when my friend lost I beat him up—you know, all sorts of different things. To me, the punk I invented for myself back in 1970, more or less, was in the sense of, okay, we're gonna do it honestly. I don't think the idea was to be destructive, but there was something about it where you owned the destructiveness, it's your destructiveness, it wasn't created by social causes. Marx doesn't have an explanation for why I just slapped my girlfriend. Of course, at the time I didn't have a girlfriend to slap or not slap, but I actually put things into those terms at the time anyway.

SCOTT: Right . . .

FRANK: You know. As a matter of fact I've never slapped a girlfriend.

SCOTT: For the record.

FRANK: For the record. But maybe if it had been on a record, maybe I would have slapped someone. [laughs] But anyhow, the punk in me is also an intellectual; there's definitely a mind to punk. My punk, anyway. That is in the sense that, you know, the line in the Stooges' "I Wanna Be Your Dog" when he says, "Now I'm ready to close my eyes, now I'm ready to close my mind." What he's really doing is he's bragging that he'll never ever in his life close his mind, that it won't shut off even when he wants it to, he can't make his inner eye shut off, he's always gonna look, watch, criticize.

from "Pushin' Too Hard: an interview with Frank Kogan," *Popped*, 1997

CHAPTER 9

BOYS IN MAKEUP / HURLED IN THEIR FUN

[In this essay from my fanzine Why Music Sucks, *I refer to the one by Liz Armstrong, which preceded it and contained the following paragraph.]*

LIZ ARMSTRONG: Although absolutely crazy/strange things seem naturally attracted to Sarah *[freshman roommate at the University of Missouri]* and me, we usually aren't running around all the time. Normally we just sit around and watch television (I'm now an addict, thanks to her), flip through magazines and sigh, sleep, and generally look for excuses not to do homework. At least once a week we play dress-up. Sounds silly, but it's so fun! See, we shop quite often at this really neat vintage shop and buy all sorts of things that we'll never be able to actually wear. My most recent purchase is a vintage linen, lace, and satin prom dress—*very* Victorian looking. Anyway, we make a *mess* out of our room with all the clothes. We try stuff on until we find a particularly stunning outfit, and then we spend lots of time on each other's hair and makeup. When satisfied, we decide where we'd fit in in real life. I usually end up in a Calvin Klein ad or a rock video. From there, we adopt a "voice" (sometimes foreignly accented) and make up a line or two. Me (as a CK model) (in a really bad British accent): "Be dangerous. Be careful. Just be." As a rock video chick, I don't say much; I just walk around, dazed, with semi-watery eyes and a slack jaw. Sometimes I'll press a finger near my nose and sniff violently, like I'm all coked-out. After doing little skits for each other, we walk up and down our hall, past the open doors of the hallway gang/slumber party crew, and talk loudly about either stupid stuff that happened or racy stuff that never happened. When back in our room, we make a halfassed attempt to tidy the place, but we always end up leaving ⅞ of our stuff lying around. Finally, we do something overly normal (like homework) while still dressed up. It gives us a sense of excitement while performing a mundane task.

BOYS IN MAKEUP

FRANK KOGAN: I related very well to what Liz wrote about playing dress-up with her roommate. Interesting: When I was a freshman in college my roommates and I would do the exact same thing. We'd go to the clothing stores or thrift shops and buy the tackiest women's clothing we could find, either really sleazy stuff (vinyl was just coming in; so were tank tops) or ridiculously lacy and satiny shirts and dresses. We'd claim they were presents for our sisters or girlfriends. I'm not kidding. We also had contacts in the drama department who got us wigs. And we'd dress in these things and decide what role to play. On one weekend we'd prance around the hallways telling outrageous stories about sexual adventures we'd supposedly had, and we'd address each other as "Bitch" in really loud voices, and argue about Broadway shows that we'd never actually seen. The next weekend we'd be high-school girls from the '50s and carry on loud conversations about "dreamy boys" and about our daddies, and we'd pretend that we were getting high on cough syrup and vanilla extract. I cultivated a really annoying giggle at this time, which I've still got.

All right, I'm lying. We did no such thing. I made it up. But wouldn't it have been interesting if we *had* done it?—But there's no way I'd have had the courage.

I was really lonely and unhappy freshman year in college. I'd grown up in a university town with a high-powered intellectual dad and mom and older brother, and for college went to an east coast prestige school, so you'd think I'd have been on home ground, but I wasn't. I was very alienated. High school had been very interesting: very traumatic at times but full of life. Since it was a liberal college town with a lot of faculty brats, the freaks were an influential group in the high school, large enough to undermine the status of every other group but not strong enough (or confident enough) to establish their own status, so the social life was very unsettled yet open. And freakdom and hipness there didn't have the same contempt for ideas that one probably found elsewhere. People were very messed-up, but I had the sense that, smart or dumb, everyone was really willing to try things out and not pretend they knew what to do or who they were. I probably romanticized this in my mind and romanticized it even more in my memory, but anyway, romanticized or not, I carried this image into college of what I expected young people to be: people who weren't taking things lightly, people who were really *trying*, you know? So I got to this prestigious college where everyone was supposed to be the smartest of the smart, and I expected students to be intellectually or emotionally adventurous or something, and they weren't. They were smart but they were dullards. It's as if the top boring two percent were scraped off of every high school in the country and sent to my college. They weren't offensive or snooty, usually; *depressed* would be a better word, or *suppressed* or *repressed*. (And no doubt some—but only some—of the problem was me: my not actually being able to see into these different people's different lives. But the atmosphere of the place wasn't inspiring people to express what was interesting in their lives either, it seemed to me.)

So after freshman year I dropped out, then a year later I didn't know what else to do so I went back and was actually much happier. My opinion of the place didn't go up, but I'd figured out how to get what I wanted from it. I actually liked a lot of the teachers and a lot of the course work. This was disconcerting compared to my high-school years, to find that I liked the teachers more than the students. But it stopped bothering me that the students seemed so bland, and I made some friends, etc. etc. I still don't really respect that time of my life—it was limbo. But I learned a lot in my classes.

Back to freshman year, a year when I wasn't dressing in interesting clothes. My roommates Kerry and Reggie hated each other, so each was very cheery towards me—because by being cheery towards me each was proving that he was basically a friendly person not a hateful person and that obviously, therefore, the other guy was at fault, the obnoxious other guy, and deserved to be hated. We could never completely avoid each other, since we shared a three-room suite that was set up so that both Kerry and Reggie had to tramp through my room to get to their respective rooms, and the phone was in my room so they had to come out to take their calls. Kerry was handsome and blond and dressed very well but otherwise was a complete slob and would never pick up the place, and his dirty clothes were everywhere, all over my room as well as his. I didn't really mind this, but it infuriated Reggie. Reggie was persnickety and complained a lot, and he'd go into rages at Kerry, whereas Kerry would just glide in and out like he couldn't care less. He had a few records that he'd play in his room over and over, an Elton John that made me learn to hate Elton for his hamfisted piano playing and oafish vocals. I think there was a Carly Simon record that bored me and a Linda Ronstadt record that bored me and a Bonnie Raitt record that had "Love Has No Pride" and was really quite beautiful. I thought his taste was impossibly square compared to mine. I had Velvet Underground records that I thought of as great hard rock but that completely baffled everyone else. They thought it was awful noise. I'd put on "Sister Ray" whenever I needed to drive people out of my room so that I could work or sleep. My room became a sort of meeting place, actually, mainly devoted to our listening to records. I kept buying old Kinks albums from back when the band was good, and Reggie and I would joke about not being able to leave for class until the side ended (and he'd go and I'd end up cutting the class). The people from next door were often visiting us. One of them, Fred Smith, had gone to my high school. We'd been friends in grammar school but not really in high school; he was politically conservative (actually moderate) and I was liberal, and that had made me uncomfortable, and there were other differences that I don't know how to identify, differences in outlook, and I was often really afraid of differences back then. In college by some awful coincidence (I thought) we were assigned to suites right next to each other, and to my surprise he turned out to be the most interesting person nearby, and we became friends. So he and one or another of his roommates would often be visiting my room. Fred played up his eccentricities—he would go from comically cute to comically gruff, and he'd always answer his phone "Smith speaking!" and then when he was in my room he'd pick up *our* phone too, when it rang, and say "Smith speaking!" And he got to the point where when our phone rang he'd dive for it, knocking people aside, and say "Smith speaking!" into the receiver. And then his roommate Timothy got into the habit, when he was visiting us, of answering our phone too and saying "Smith speaking!" This must have confused callers. They must have thought we had a butler. Once a friend of mine from my home town called, and Timothy answered and said "Smith speaking!" and so my friend went "Oh, hi Fred," and chatted with him for a while thinking he was talking to Fred, until Timothy identified himself for real. Well, this must tell you how uninteresting my freshman social life really was, that the most vivid thing I remember is how people answered our phone. Once Fred was visiting, and Reggie was visibly depressed about something, and would clomp through my room to his, and slam his door shut, and then come out and go through my room to the outside and then return through my room back to his without saying anything, and slam his door shut after himself. Fred thought this was pretty funny, so whenever Reggie made one of his trips-with-slam, Fred would follow up by opening Reggie's door a crack and then slamming it. After Fred had done this for the third time Reggie came charging out and dived on top of Fred and started pounding him. We pulled him off; the freshman advisers found out and, I think, forbade the two of them to be in the same room with each other. But later, after the ban was lifted, Fred and Reggie became friends and even became roommates the next year, though Fred could get irritated by Reggie's depressions and stuff. Reggie seemed too tired for me, but, as you've gathered, I wasn't likely to look into what was really going on with people.

As for Kerry, he ignored us except when he had to counter Reggie's criticisms. As I said, the place didn't inspire people to display their interestingness. I remember once Kerry was doing acid with his girlfriend and I could hear them having sex in his room and after he'd come he said, "That was fantastic," and the whole thing—acid, sex, and Kerry—seemed totally vacuous. At least from my side of the door.

So I did nothing creative with dress-up. Freshman year my creativity was all in letters, sent to the outside world. Real life was elsewhere, real life was a fantasy, real intensity was a hope or a memory.

However, in 1973, the year when I dropped out of college, boys in makeup changed my life. Not boys I *knew*, of course, but boys onstage, boys on record. Not Bowie, though I liked him and had his records. He made sense to me as an inferior extension of Dylan, the next step into The Strange, and I liked his transvestite image as a way of stepping out of ordinariness and out of boy-mandated toughness. But as for the way he actually looked, his style didn't matter to me. He dressed in weird sci-fi gear; or he copied the Garbo pose from the famous Steichen photo, where she'd pulled back her hair to show the bones of her beauty. Bowie was like a guy with a sign around his neck that said, "I represent stylishness." It had no gut-level meaning to me. The sci-fi stuff was an evasion; I mean, I'm weird 'cause I'm from outer space—what kind of an explanation is that (as opposed to being weird because of one's experiences as a human being)?

The makeup boys who changed my life were the New York Dolls. Or, if they didn't change my life, they at least warmed up my understanding of the world. David Johansen sang songs about girls from the suburbs who moved to the big city (like I'd just moved to New York after dropping out) and tried to be *somebody* (like I hadn't) and ended up bruised and messed-up and strung-out, whores or massage babes or groupies, but still dreaming of stardom, or dreaming of home, or just dreaming (like I had a dream of forgotten intensity). But what the Dolls did was to dress up like the characters in their songs, like the losers and groupies and yearning suburban glitter babes they hoped to get for their audience. The Dolls were transvestites in cheap vinyl, on platform shoes; they came up with a bargain-basement glamour that anyone could invent for himself or herself, made up of scraps and overstock and worn by the riff-raff. (Was that true? Well, it didn't have to be true, it was the *image*.) They dressed up like tough *girls*—no, like warm-hearted, desperate girls who were trying to look tough—dressed up like whores, floozies, groupies. It'll be pretty hard to explain why this image meant so much to me. I won't really try, because that would take up a hundred pages. But up until then I'd more or less gone along with the freak thing in how I'd dressed—by then the freak thing wasn't very freaky, it had devolved down to jeans and army jackets, long hair and a blank expression, very unpretentious and anti-ostentatious. It supposedly signified rebellion but I knew better—it was just another way of holding back and hiding out, the freaks no longer being rebel kids but just normal neurotic "outcasts" who knew their place and were satisfied to stay in it. It was as boring then as gangsta and grunge clothes are now. Except I didn't even do the freak thing: I just bought jeans and wore the shirts my mother got for me, but I managed to look a little scruffier than she'd intended, as if I just didn't care how I looked. Basically, I was dressing defensively, dressing so as *not* to threaten people, dressing not to look too straight but not to look too freaky either, dressing so as *not* to display ambition (either mainstream ambition or countercultural ambition), and never actually was willing to learn even the basics, never tried things on in stores before I bought them, never went shopping much for myself, never spent the time to see what looked *good* on me or how to *make* myself look good. I was still reacting to that whole horrible junior-high experience from seven years earlier. The idea of getting all dressed up still felt like giving into *fear* and into excessive concern with what others thought of me. So I tried to ignore the issue altogether, not stand out and not be a target; but this was just another way of giving into fear.

My friend Maureen from high school was beautiful and suicidal and hated herself, and she told me that she couldn't bear to look at herself in the mirror unless she'd dressed up. This made no sense to me, because Maureen looked utterly beautiful no matter what, always. She was also brilliant and intimidating but with no real belief in her own brainpower. I was so frightened of what she thought of me that it took a while to dawn on me that she was frightened of what *I* thought of her. She was the person who got me to understand the Dolls. She said, "What's wrong with trying to look good?" and with that sentence, from her, from this woman who felt she had to invent a look for herself or she was nothing, the whole freak thing ended for me and glitter began. Of course I never *at all*, myself, dared dress up as glitter. But at least now I understood that looking good could—in principle—be self-expression, could be done on one's own terms. And I think this has influenced my *writing*—if my clothes won't swing and glitter at least my *prose* will, damn it! But also maybe I felt inside that glitter just wasn't *me*, as a fashion. I began to be disturbed that, in order to be emotionally effective, David Johansen had to feminize himself and sing about groupies and girls rather than about thoughtful intellectual young men like himself. And the Dolls as a band failed to reach the teen girl masses: Instead it got the thoughtful intellectuals like me; so why couldn't David Doll sing about me? Why couldn't he sing about his real audience? At least, why couldn't he sing about Maureen, about an insecure intellectual girl? Well, perhaps he did, but he sang about something in us that we could never express, boys who wished they could show the emotions of desperate girls; smart girls who wished they could tear loose and be party girls; boys who wanted to party and jump out of cakes . . . well, I don't have the right words here. The Dolls never sold many records. The Sex Pistols cashed in by taking the Dolls' sound back to aggressive boy punk. The next generation of boys in makeup, the New Romantics, went back to a less emotional, more conventional Bowie "stylishness." I went back to college.

Well, this *might* go a hundred pages, after all. It reveals my sentimentality, at any rate.

Maureen explained the Dolls' "Frankenstein" to me. It's another girl-(or-whatever)-lost-in-the-big-scary-city song—the words basically rewrite Dylan's "Like A Rolling Stone"—and of course the girl meets disaster and fear. Did she ever, could she ever, expect such a *Frankenstein*? And then the monster is stalking her, tracking her down, but maybe he wants to be her *friend*. You know, maybe the monster is lonely. And the song ends with a question, "Do you think that you could make it with Frankenstein?" And Maureen explained to me that Frankenstein wasn't just a creature to have sex with, he represented the whole funky New Yorkiness of New York, the ostentation and the terror, the dreams and the fear. So I figured out that David was asking if you—if I—could make it with the monster of life, whether I could embrace life in all its pain and dreams and disaster. Of course, the way I've lived my life, in so much fear, maybe means that my answer is no, but still it's a real good question.

NOTES

"It'll be pretty hard to explain why this image meant so much to me." But I do want to talk a little bit about how they sounded, since not only did they play dress-up—you know, like little kids let loose in their big sister's wardrobe—they played music. Really, it was a lot like how they looked. It was *tough*—it was a hard r&b sound, like the Stones infusing soul with nasty blues riffs—but it was warm too; Johnny played thick guitar, it was almost syrup, with a noisy blues-whine and a way of careening up into the right pitch rather than hitting it head on, and he would play pretty counter melodies or his guitar would harmonize against the singing. The style was influential. The Dolls invented a sound I call "the loud pretties," meaning they'd mix the noise and the hard blues and the ugly yowls with loud beauty, so the clamor and the beauty were inseparable, all one big roil (I'm contrasting this with how, say, the Beatles or Raspberries or Cheap Trick or Sweet would put pretty vocals merely on top of raunchy instrumentals). The Clash and Nirvana played later versions of the loud pretties. Of course the Dolls were about ten times more fun. They brought back a lot of the rock 'n' roll silliness from the pre-Stones days: animal sounds, novelty tunes, shoo-wop shoo-wop oompahs. Rare for the "progressive-rock" era, especially since they didn't seem like an oldies band doing it. They sounded like little kids let loose in their big sister's record collection—but then gone off on a rampage, with the sound attached to their raving ugly beauty. Except I also have to say that they didn't quite do it: They rumbled forward, but their rock sound never quite got a roll to it, though they tried. This is what I meant way back in *WMS* #5 when I said that the Sex-O-Lettes sounded the way the Dolls looked, *really* got on record with the rolling in-your-face exuberance the Dolls were shooting for. And I was certainly implying then that disco could do it but "rock" couldn't anymore. This is why the Dolls are only 27 on my album list, rather than number 1.

"As if I just didn't care how I looked." I realize that this doesn't convey very well how I actually dressed. The fact is I don't remember. Teen popularity/nonpopularity was so traumatic for me that my mind froze and I wouldn't pay attention. And that was part of my rebellion, too, not to pay attention. I liked summers because I could wear T-shirts. All T-shirts were white then. I think I *wished* that I could wear single-color pullovers in other months, as I'd worn when I was a little kid. I didn't like shirts with collars and buttons. But I always wore them, because that's what my mother bought for me. To buy my own shirts would have taken money that I used for records and books. It did not occur to me to tell my mother what I wanted. As it is with traumatic subjects, I wanted to turn them off, not bring them up. I remember making two fashion decisions in high school. The first was to wear my shirts tucked in, despite the cool trend that said wear them out. I tucked them in because wearing them out made me look heavier. Second, in tenth grade I let my hair grow long, a complicated decision (no matter how I looked, I'd be giving in to someone) that was simplified for me by the fact that it caused great conflict with my parents, who tried to forbid it. My dad said that he was upset that a generation of young men was looking like fairies. This was just the thing to make me resist him.

Given that my mind is blank, I've gotten my childhood friend Jay Carey to describe how I looked.

JACQUELINE CAREY: *You dressed in high school as if your clothes were chosen by someone else—presumably your mother. You wore various colored slacks and dress shirts, patterned but based on the color white. They were generally opened at the collar to reveal an undershirt underneath. This is a look I don't really remember on anyone else except Sandy [her husband—ed.]. Eventually (and reluctantly) I took over the job of buying his clothes from his mother, and I bought undershirts with V-necks, thus radically revamping him.*

One difference between the two of you is that he often wore blue jeans with dress shirts, and you almost never did. I remember my amazement when you showed up in (straight-legged) jeans one day in high school. In fact, I'm still curious: Who bought them?

Yours was probably a pretty smart approach to fashion; it somehow took you completely out of judging range. I remember Susan Long (much later) saying, "How does he get away with it? He wears polyester, he's not even ironic about it, but he gets away with it."

Probably it was my exquisite handsomeness that allowed me to get away with everything. I don't remember who bought the jeans. It may have been me. You'd think I'd have remembered. There were school rules against jeans when we started (also against girls wearing pants). This outraged me in principle, but I can't remember when the rule was allowed to lapse. I don't remember pulling the "undershirt" ploy until after high school, though Jay's memory may well be correct. The undershirts she's referring to are the white T-shirts I mentioned above. In high school I think I only wore—as undershirts, that is—the regular Stanley Kowalski undershirts that my mother bought me, which are as deep as

V-necks and so wouldn't have been visible (they used to be called, generically, "undershirts"; Hanes and Fruit of the Loom now call them "A-shirts" or "athletic shirts" to distinguish them from white T-shirts, which are now also called "undershirts"). After high school I was only wearing dress shirts (1) when I had to work at an office, or (2) when I'd run out of clean pullovers—which unfortunately was often, since I was still generally unwilling to spend money on clothes when there were records out there, still unbought.

"David was asking if you—if I—could make it with the monster of life." A final note, about the words. The first thing to say is that maybe a quarter of them are difficult or impossible to make out. For instance, "Frankenstein" might start:

Something must've happened over Manhattan.
Who could've spun all the children this time?
Did they ever, could they ever,
Expect such a Frankenstein, a Frankenstein?

except that I initially heard "who could've spun" as "hurled in their fun," which is actually just as good and almost as plausible. There's a lousy Website that has Dolls lyrics, but they do an even worse job of it than I do. Their version goes "Who can expound," which may be correct but isn't very good. For "Vietnamese Baby" the site has "Show you more mustard gas than any girl ever seen," but I'm sure David's saying "Show you more *busted glass*." And later on he's saying "You're so sorry, busy sorry, that's all you'll do," though the Internet idiots think he's merely "solid." In any event, David's deliberate use of "bad" grammar creates hot emotional poetry that sounds like normal bad-grammar conversation. "We was all engaged in charms, swear we're having fun" (Chuck hears this as "He was all endangered zone where we're having fun," and if he's right I don't want to know it). So in David's world (and mine) we're busy *doing* sorry and *engaging* in charm—it's a world where you've got to work for your emotions and work to be somebody, to be someone who counts. I guess we *are* all endangered zone. And the glass isn't just broken, it's busted.

In a college term paper I said that Johansen "works in a fictional style, with characters, and sometimes with what I will call a narrator (who never narrates)." My point was that David never provides an objective framework, he's always jumping from voice to voice, so you're hearing a character addressing another character, or the narrator addressing the character, or the character or the narrator addressing us, all jammed up together so you're hearing bits of conversation and bits of subjective description in no kind of chronological order. But as someone says in "Vietnamese Baby": "Everything connects."

In the paper I called the style "maddeningly confusing" and said that it "is probably the result of both genius and laziness." But Johansen's genius/laziness allows words to carry a whole overload of emotional meaning: Since he's *not* specifying who the "Vietnamese Baby" is, for instance, you can make it many things—a burned napalm baby like we were seeing every night on the war reports, or a "baby" in the affectionate sense, like a honey or a sweetie, a Vietnamese girlfriend (or boyfriend—remember, these are the Dolls). And when David sings, "With a Vietnamese baby on your mind," after having run us through the usual shift of pronouns, we don't know whose little mind has got the baby on it: that of the Viet vet who boasts, "When I'm gettin' home to you, I gotta show you what I can do"; or of the girl he came home to; or of the girl he left behind (you know, maybe she got pregnant and *had* a baby). It's probably the vet's—his mind keeps going back to Vietnam. But you see what happens: Because David doesn't specify, the baby is on *everyone's* mind.

Johansen piggybacks "Babylon" and "Frankenstein" on the plot of "Like a Rolling Stone" without bothering to state that plot, which frees him to pour forth huge gobs of conversation and poetry in an uninterrupted stream. He simply uses the word *home* to invoke "Like a Rolling Stone":

So now you're tellin' me
that any time you can get on home,
but you know this place it is my home,
so where am I to go?

That's Frankenstein talking to the runaway; but he (the monster? the narrator? Johansen?) is also concerned on the girl's (boy's) behalf that she's (he's) going to get put down for being too "back home." And anyway like in the Dylan song she/they are really without a home, with no direction home, etc. And while David's just layering on words and talk he manages to vastly (I think) improve on Dylan's imagery. Dylan's "Napoleon in rags" was a strained metaphor, some bum or Chaplinesque loser whom Dylan was *instructing* Miss Lonely to love and appreciate; whereas Frankenstein is a whole city/monster/predicament/mess-of-one's-own-making, and when Johansen asks her does she think that she can make it with Frankenstein, he's not giving preachy instructions but asking a genuine question, and one that I still don't know the answer to. Of course, if you've never heard "Like a Rolling Stone," don't know the strong Dylan framework—or can't invent it for yourself—the song could be a big noisy mess.

And with "Vietnamese Baby" you're *really* on your own, because it's hard to know what he's saying or what might be happening, since there's no story that *I* can hear depicted or alluded to or invoked. I guess I'm free to make the story up myself. So in one line there's something about a slingshot, in the next a lightbulb (it sounds like), and in the one after that we've got the busted glass. (Brad Gillis of the band Night Ranger: "People tell us that 'Sister Christian' was the main song at their prom. That's great, but they should also know that at my prom I was in the parking lot, shooting out lights with ball bearings and a wrist-rocket slingshot.") Actually—before the Dolls, before Night Ranger—when I was sixteen I'd written a fantastical story about a girl who goes to a party and gets bored and frustrated, so she (naturally) burns the place down and goes out into the night, knocking over houses, using lightposts she had torn up from the ground. (Several years ago I sent Chuck a copy of this story. He and Linus liked it but wondered how she was able to lift the lightposts. But then they figured it out: because the posts were *light* posts.) I wrote five or six variations on this story during the next half dozen years. One version (in 1975 or 1976) was called "Vietnamese Baby"; in that one the guy (now it was a guy, a soldier home) goes out and thinks he's showing off by throwing stones and knocking the bulbs out of streetlights.

Back to the Dolls song. The plot or theme? Well, a guy has come home from the war, but he's left something emotional behind. "Well maybe they're just givin' you all you ever wanted, and maybe you never ever know what that was." There's a phrase in Doris Lessing's *Golden Notebook*, "nostalgia for death" I think it is, which seems to fit, somehow. There's an intense time, terrifying but also full of heightened emotion and maybe camaraderie and love. (This is my version, and maybe Johansen's, but not Lessing's, I don't think. She was being sarcastic.) And now that you've gotten out of this godawful place, everything else is pale, doesn't measure up to the awful war/awful love you left behind. I drew a parallel to my complicated messed-up high-school years being succeeded by my sane but blah college time, and my mind was going back . . . There was a sense in which I'd loved the war—this monster war that I had spent so much energy worrying about and opposing, it thereby giving some purpose to my life. And now that it's over, whatcha gonna do?

The due date of my term paper, by the way, was the day I read in the *New York Times* of the Dolls' disbanding. The day I actually handed the paper in (I'd gotten a five-day extension) was the day Saigon fell.

HURLED IN THEIR FUN: DOLLS IN THE DAYS OF THE GOOD OLD TIMES

"Actually, if I were a young person I think I'd be most interested in having old folk like me write about what things were like back in the day: what the Fillmore was like, what the crowd was like at a Dolls show in the early '70s, etc." So Luc wrote me recently. Good timing, as I happened to already be at work on "Boys in Makeup." But as for what the crowd was like: Despite my having seen the band six or seven times in the space of about ten months in 1973–1974, I find myself unable to say what the crowd was like, at least not with any accuracy. Partly I don't remember, partly I never noticed in the first place, and partly I rarely can come up with the words to describe *anything*, even when I do have a picture in my mind. As for what people were wearing, I don't know. My defense against fashion while I was growing up was to put up a complete block in my mind, so I really didn't *see* what people were wearing. I only got vague impressions and such. Since I wasn't going out searching/shopping for clothes or thinking of clothes items as constituting a potential ensemble for me to wear, I never learned a vocabulary, I never learned to see how shirts, shoes, makeup, etc. went together, I never could describe why (or how) a person looked freaky or hoody or glam. I never had a sister, either, so I was culturally deprived in major ways, no knowledge of makeup, magic beauty secrets, hair styling. Also, I was in general (and still am, of course) too busy in my own mind thinking, calculating, imagining, and so on to see what was in front of my nose. I do remember being eventually disappointed that there wasn't a more interesting sartorial response among Dolls fans, that there wasn't more of a visual echo in the audience of what was happening onstage and in the music. Maybe the crowds were fairly nondescript. The way I remember it, the dressed-up girls in the audience weren't looking nearly as glittery, cheesy, slutty, cheap pasted-on glamorous as they could have been (nor were the boys, of course). The look of those trying to make an impression was more a stylized stylishness: I'd say Early Goth, maybe, with a lot of ornate towers and stained glass and flying buttresses and . . . oh, I went off there, sorry . . . the look was, you know, *black*—black clothes, dark eye shadow, pale makeup. At least it was on *one* young woman whom I remember, first row center in the basement of the Viking Hotel in Newport, Rhode Island, who, at the end of the encore, was helped up onstage, along with a woman friend, by Johnny and Arthur and then accompanied the band backstage as it went off.

As for what the crowd was like in its behavior, let's see, first show: I didn't yet like the New York Dolls; I'd heard the record once or twice and thought it was sludgy and lumbering, not all that different from Grand Funk, it seemed, who were hitting at the time with "We're an American Band." So I saw the Dolls in New York at Max's, and Jay and Maureen and maybe Robin (Jay's mother [a real sweetheart, by the way]; I forget if she went along with us) got a table up in front while I stood farther back with my arms folded, having no real response within me and not yet hearing the beauty that was embodied by the sludge or connecting to any of the starts and stops and syncopation that gave the music movement. My arms weren't folded in disapproval, just in nonconnection. Next to me was another boy with *his* arms folded too. I don't remember the crowd. The people cheered after songs. Afterwards, Jay and Maureen were radiant and ecstatic, saying it was the best concert they'd ever seen. I was puzzled, not having felt anything in the air, in the music, in the event. Not quite true; there was one moment, in the middle of "Subway Train," where a wail attached itself to the melody, like the guy's voice was a train horn, and I got a sudden sense of tunefulness. This is important, because later that night I couldn't get that one song out of my head; so I said to myself, "There's at least one song I like, even if they play like clodhoppers."

The next show was a different story. I'd absorbed the album, memorized the album, knew as much of the lyrics as I could make out (about 65%); what had been sludge now felt like thickness of emotion. I and my friend Steve (not a Dolls fan, but he went along with us) drove from Tolland, Connecticut, where we shared an apartment, to Providence to pick up Maureen from Brown and then headed down south to the University of Rhode Island, in Kingston, where the Student Activities Committee had, for some reason, booked the Dolls. At Brown that afternoon Steve and I had sat in Maureen's dorm room and listened while she—in a monologue I'll never forget—talked about the day her mother had died, and how no one would tell her that it had happened, and (if I'm remembering this right) she was first told to go sit with one person, then another, or maybe she was sent from one house to the next. Her mother had committed suicide—Maureen was about nine when it happened. I'd known there'd been a suicide in her past, I think Jay had told me, but Maureen had never talked about it, never mentioned it, until that day. Down at Kingston we discovered that the Dolls would be playing in a cafeteria. We were second in line. First in line was a young woman and her boyfriend who'd come all the way from Boston—the boyfriend seemed like a regular guy (not that he necessarily was, but that's how he dressed, like the guy in the bar, the guy in the mail room). The woman was dressed more like—well, in a dress, a light-colored dress that seemed interesting on her because it was like an adult person's dress, not a young woman's dress, like a cheap version of something Jackie Kennedy would wear; it wasn't part of the youth uniform and it wasn't glitter. But it did announce a stab at fashion in some way, and the Dolls may have inspired this in her. Nowadays this would be no big deal, someone dressing up at a rock show, but in 1973 it said something. She talked nonstop, too, full of opinions and dissatisfactions, and kept saying stupid things and being real irritating. I think Maureen and I had a common disappointment, that *this* would be the first person with whom we'd share the potential rapport of Dolls fandom.

The performance room—the cafeteria—had been cleared of tables and seats. People were to sit on the floor, or stand. Maureen and I went up front, though Steve stayed back. The place was packed, all these college kids sitting on the floor. Maureen and I and one other person, right by the stage (which was a platform not very high off the floor), stood and danced to the music, made motions to the band, shrieked between songs; in back and to the sides some other people were dancing too, and applauding, maybe twenty-five or so of them. And the rest of the crowd, maybe a couple hundred, sat, immobile, not applauding, not leaving, watching the band and the three of us as if we were space creatures. In my memory, it's all brightly lit, everything's in clear view, the three of *us* are in clear view. This memory is wrong: It was a show, it was night, it was dark, only the stage was lit. But I felt *exposed*, which was kind of thrilling. Close to the stage, maybe we were wavering between dark and light as we danced. My shrieking might have been forced—hey, I'd never had the chance to be a teenybopper, had only learned recently to respect teenyboppers, and now at age nineteen I was shrieking. Steve said later that it was obvious that Johansen was playing to the three of us. As the show ended one of the dancers from the side came up and asked me to try out for his band. I explained that I was from out of state. Then Maureen said, "Hi, Mac." It turned out that he was a friend of hers at Brown. He was a tall black guy, halfway between a dressed-up '60s freak and a glitter guy; I think he had Lou Reed shades and Hendrix scarves or at least an air of Hendrix-like flamboyance, but maybe some leather too.

There was tension and excitement in all this: the uncomprehending crowd, the audacity of us standing next to the band. That was a year when a few crucial critics (Christgau, Paul Nelson, Dave Marsh) liked the Dolls, but most others and the music press in general had a general attitude of contempt. "All flash and no music" was what they said. I remember constantly reading putdowns. One jerk I think it was in *Rolling Stone* joked that the Dolls were really dental students who only dressed that way for the money. This was part of the atmosphere too, part of the event for me, standing up and dancing, withstanding the contempt.

The next Dolls concert was that one in the basement of the Viking Hotel. It was me, Maureen, and Mac. This time those who didn't like the music left right away, leaving forty or so of us who wanted to be there, and it was one of the best concerts of my life. In my memory it looks warm and hazy and dark. As for how the *crowd* looked and acted, though, I can't remember. Dancing, cheering, being happy. At one point all of a sudden a crazy wild-eyed guy started hitting Mac, and Mac pushed back at him. The band handled this well; the roadies lifted the guy right onto the stage and let him off on the other side, where he was away from Mac. Johnny made a funny comment about practicing his Kung Fu fighting, and the situation was defused. When the tussle had started some people had jumped between Mac and the crazy guy to separate them, and I'd grabbed Mac as if to hold him back; Mac got angry at me, saying that he wasn't trying to fight, he'd just needed his hands free to fend the guy off. I mollified Mac by saying that I wasn't trying to restrain him, I was trying to make the crazy guy feel *safe*, like the threat was over. This was a quick thing for me to say, but I was probably lying. I didn't know Mac, really, and maybe *he* was a crazy guy too.

As an intro to "Vietnamese Baby," David said, "This song's about a soldier who falls in love with a whore in Vietnam and then he comes home to his mom."

The band seemed happy. It was a different Johnny Thunders from the one we'd see later with the Heartbreakers; he wasn't sulking, wasn't yelling at the sound man. At the end of the show he gave his arm to the girl in black.

Next show, Orpheum or Orpheus Theatre in Boston. I was in the balcony, and maybe this is why I felt more distant. One guy sitting near me—regular-type guy, again, longhaired hard-rock type—pointed at Arthur Kane, the bass player, and said to me, "I think he's a faggot." This guy was not using the word *faggot* with much precision, since Kane—whatever his sexual tastes—was not at all femme. He had the look of a hulking stevedore, and in drag he was a knock-you-down broad. I don't think the guy was saying *faggot* with any particular hostility, either, but he must have had a sense of the band being foreign to his regular-guyness. I read all this into him, anyway, in a glance; I gave him a shrug rather than an answer.

Before the show we'd stopped off at some friends of Mac's, who were also going. Roxy Music was on the record player. Roxy sounded ridiculous and wooden and put-on—all due to Ferry's voice. This was the first time I'd heard them, obviously, and I hadn't yet connected to the guitar playing. Mac's friends—a couple—were dressed in *really* stylized stylishness, in deliberately falsified high fashion. Unfortunately, I can't remember more than that. The woman might have had her hair up, and earrings, and maybe an intentionally obvious blonde dye job.

Mac had grown up in Manhattan. There'd never been a rock star from Manhattan, he said. They were all from the Outer Boroughs or out of town. All the Dolls were from the Outer Boroughs. Mac was going to be the first star from Manhattan, he told us.

We got his New York phone number, his parents' number. This was probably when we were in town for Iggy and the Stooges' New Year's Eve show. I never had reason to call him, but I remembered the number for several years after because it spelled out L-U-M-P-Y or W-A-R-P-I-N-K or something. Or maybe we were supposed to dial W-A-R-P-I-N-K and ask for Lumpy, like he had to use Lumpy as his nickname within his family because perhaps his Dad's name was Mac, too.

The next show was at the old Academy of Music on 14th Street in Manhattan, what later dressed itself up and became the Palladium. I was in the balcony again. Musically, this was the Dolls' bluesiest show, which I remember their pulling off well, Johnny doing a good job on "Killing Floor" or whatever old chestnut they decided to stretch out on. I remember nothing of the crowd, however.

And then the last of the shows I saw (I think I've recounted them all) was in New York at the Bottom Line, on the eve of their second album. Suzi Quatro opened and wore black leather pants like on her album cover and like the black leather pants Joan Jett later wore on *her* album cover. These made her look cute. There was a bomb threat (the Dolls attracted that), so after our being cleared out and reentering, the Dolls only had time for five songs. They rocked really hard, but like at every other gig I've seen at that well-regarded industry showcase (the one exception being Television in 1978, with Tom Verlaine's guitar so mesmerizing that I simply forgot the music-biz/supper-club atmosphere), I felt chaperoned and out-of-place and as if the band were behind glass. Again, no memory of the audience except for the college-type shallow hanger-on idiot at my table whom I mentioned back in "Lester Bangs Marked for Death" who thought I'd delivered an enormous insight when I told him that Iggy was influenced by Dylan and who knew someone who'd heard Iggy after the Stooges' New Year's Eve gig supposedly asking "Where can I get thirty pounds of dope, does anyone know where I can get thirty pounds of dope?" and who said confidently, like someone happy to be in the know, that Iggy would be dead within the year.

Why Music Sucks #11, June 1997

CHAPTER 10

TWELVE VARIETIES OF WORMS
LYRICS, POEMS, 1977–1985

bad. It was ugly this evening
to read John Ashbery and feel
full of wryness. It's nasty tonight,
I ought to cut up my mood. Stinking
reeking strips. I feel angry at the
footsteps upstairs. The man is jumping. I'll be inconsiderate to him
forever now. I always have been
inconsiderate of him. I don't care
how I affect. None of my recent life
makes any sense. Particularly the recent
part.

—*Stranded* #2, 1978

I don't try to write clearly. I don't try
to write directly or clearly. Nor does my friend
zero on the record player. My zero on the
record player. My friend does not like me. None of
this is guided by intelligence. Not my friendship.

—*Stranded* #2, 1978

for example, suppose you're walking along
someone, your friend, an intimidating little man, woman,
bitch, suggests a massacre
e.g., a massacre of all the stupid people in Manhattan
or a massacre of proprietors
and you're walking along wondering "how to
respond" you're really one of them, you know,
or one of us, crap, well . . .
you don't say anything, you nod
or whatnot
the manhattan . . . streets . . . are neat . . .

—*Stranded* #3, 1978 (written in 1977)

PIGEON POEM

Dear Pigeon—If you don't like it here move to Moscow
  where they slaughter pigeons.
If a Jewish pigeon wins the Nobel Prize, he's not French,
  Italian, English, or Russian. He's a Jew.
Ceremonial pigeons. Checking his complexion for pigeons.
Pigeons don't care about anything.

—*Stranded* #3, 1978 (written in 1977)

The next great nostalgia kick is
sure to kind of bother some
people I know. the next great kick.
that's something else. not very heartening.
inheartening. ingratiating.
my cat has dense eyes. my
cat has no layers of meaning. I
don't think it's cool to be a
poet. I don't think it's cool to
be a rock star. no longer. what's
cool? scatter-anger. intelligent. non-uh-
not-physical. not violent. very cruel to
people like myself and hence able to
sympathize and understand. since I agree
with you completely there's nothing to say.

—*Stranded* #4, 1980 (written in 1978)

THE OLD DAYS

Things were better in the old days
Everyone had maids
Even the maids had maids
And the maids' maids had children
Sweet little children
To help them in the kitchen

Things were better in the old days
Everyone had legs
This was before the war
Even the frogs had legs
And we'd kill them and we'd cook them
And eat them in the kitchen

HERO OF FEAR
It's not your friends I mind . . .
It's not your friends I mind
It's your other friends

Terry says he's more real than me
'Cause he's sick all the time
Not like I get sick or you get sick
But real sick
And no one can take that away from me

Hello, hero of fear
If I'm such an asshole
Why do you care?
Hello, hero of fear

He's better than me 'cause he's sick all the time
Not like I get sick or you get sick
But real sick
And no one can take that away from me

It's not your friends I mind
It's your other friends

12 VARIETIES OF WORMS
There are 12 varieties of worms
First and best is the Jewish-family worm
Then there's the I-grew-up-in-the-Bronx worm
"I grew up in the Bronx so I'm entitled to hit people"
Then there's the he-did-me-a-great-favor-by-letting-me-wear-a-T-shirt worm
I'm the worm who buys lots of records
And I belong to a band
We are not family, which one are you?
There are 12 varieties of worms and
We are not family

I know you
We're the dry heaves
Looking at you
I'm the action
She's the reaction
She's the "Oh God!"

She's what's left when there's nothing to scrape off
Shaking in the abandoned buildings
We're the brand new thing on the Lower East Side
The brand new thing on the Lower East Side

We are not family
Which one are you
There are 12 varieties of worms and
We are not family

GRENADINE BLOOD
Grenadine blood rolls down my arm
Grenadine blood rolls down my arm
Rolls down the barstool down to the floor

Grenadine blood stains my hands
Grenadine blood stains my hands
My woman ran off with another man

What'd I do wrong for you to treat me so?
What'd I do wrong for you to treat me so?
(Hah! He doesn't know)
She could tell him but he doesn't want to know

We took him to the station, took him downtown
We took him to the station, took him downtown
He was standing, then he fell down

I had a machine gun, you were in my sights
I had a machine gun, you were in my sights
A bum comes by and he wants a light

Grenadine blood stains my hands
Grenadine blood stains my hands
My woman ran off with another man

I can't shine all by myself
I can't shine in this life by myself
If I don't kill you, gonna kill me someone else

THE LAUGHING AIRPLANES OF KAMCHATKA
He said to the airplanes as they came laughing by
If I had wings, I'd knock you from the sky

He said to the girls as they grinned on silver toes
If I had wings, I'd tell you where to go

He said to the mountaintops as they ground their teeth
If I had wings, I'd knock you off your peaks

He said to the skytops on the outer edge
If I had wings you'd be inside out instead

The laughing airplanes came back after scattering him in the sea
We thought he had a gun, but at night we couldn't see

The laughing planes told stories around the northern fire
We thought he had a gun but it was just a pair of pliers

The Pillowmakers
Gander is king in his backyard
Gander is king in his backyard
King of all the gooses
What a surprise when the pillowmakers come!
You won't listen to string quartets
You won't listen to concerti
No more operati
When the pillowmakers come

What a big surprise when the pillowmakers come!

Pelican with a heart as big as your beak
With a mind as large as your stomach
What we could do what I would learn
If thoughts were meat
Gander is king in his backyard
Gander is king in his backyard
King of all the gooses
What a surprise when the pillowmakers come!

What a big surprise when the pillowmakers come!

Real Psychedelic Song
I'll live my life in a sugar cube
Then you'll be gone
I'll be intense like a movie
In my real psychedelic song

You broke my heart, well fuck you, bitch
But you can kiss my ass, now
You're the puddle I leave behind
In my real psychedelic song

You think you lost your love
Well I saw her yesterday
She says that she's fucked-up—not you
She says she is insane with love

She says you hurt her so
She almost lost her mind
Now she says she knows
That you're not the hurting kind
(Well, that's what she said; don't ask *me*)

She said she loves you
You know that can be sad
She loves you
But should you be glad?

This is the real psychedelic song
You won't recognize at all
This is the real 1967
It went by much too long

You broke my heart, well fuck you, bitch
I won't be sorry long
I'll make the tears run down your leg
In my real psychedelic song

WATERFALL
I saw you
You were a little piece of wood
On a waterfall

I heard you
You were in mid air
Saying "What am I doing here?"

I tried to hold you
But you'd rather be
On a waterfall

CHAPTER 11

RADIO SHACK

In the last ten years [*in San Francisco*] I've earned most of my money not as a writer or a magazine editor, but as a "technical editor" for environmental and engineering firms, working on Environmental Impact Reports, Remedial Investigation Reports, Closure Plans, Part B Permit Applications, RCRA Facility Assessments, Applications for Certification, and so on. When I get to Denver I'll probably try for this type of job first, because this is the field where I have contacts and work experience, and I need a job. But obviously some of my skills here can be transferred to other workplaces. For what it's worth, I did a very good job; I'm good at catching errors, not because my eye is necessarily better than anyone else's, but because I double-check my work and I'm good at anticipating where others will screw up. I'm also good in deadline/panic situations, and I'm good at staying sane when everyone around me is going nuts.

This is sort of the opposite of what I'm like as a writer, where I tend to be a basket case.

I spent the last several years working as a technical editor for Bechtel, a large engineering firm. What I did as editor had little in common with, say, what I do as editor of *Why Music Sucks* or what Christgau did as music editor at the *Voice*. I didn't solicit pieces or have the authority to tell people how to write or anything. I was more like an adjunct and general troubleshooter and handyman—though what I was handy at wasn't the use of saws and hammers but the tracking down of mistakes and inconsistencies. I got to indulge my compulsive obsessiveness. I was good at asking people, for instance, why, if we were changing the language in the post-closure QAPPs, we didn't also change the language in the groundwater monitoring QAPP. ("Quality Assurance Project Plan," if you're interested. You already knew that, of course.) I was good at reminding people (ten, twenty, thirty times) that we needed to include the boring logs for Pond 8S. ("We've already included them." "No we haven't.") I was good at saying to Ames, "When Kathleen gives you her markup of the E-size drawings she'll probably change the Rev. numbers from 2 to 3, but you should change them back to 2—she forgets that, because EPA hasn't seen these since last January, no matter how many times we've revised them since then, the next version that goes to EPA will be Rev. 2. And Figure B-2D will be Rev. 1, since it hasn't been revised since December '97. When Lana does these she'll probably get that wrong, as she did the last two times, and you'll have to send it through her again." I was probably the only person to understand the page numbering system that EPA required of us. For instance, if we were replacing page D-2.b with three pages, but page D-3.b remained unchanged, the replacement pages would be numbered D-2.c, D-2.1.c, and D-2.2.c, and I would have to check that the word processor remembered to put a new "section break" into the MS-Word file at the beginning of pages D-2.c, D-2.1.c, and D-3.b—that's *three* lousy section breaks for one insertion. Jeez! And in addition, we had to remember to turn off "same as previous" in three different footers as we changed the page numbers.

Only occasionally was I actually getting around to dealing with prose style as such, generally to make a horrid sentence slightly less horrid; e.g., I'd change "the closure activities include the remediation of the excavation area" to "the closure activities include remediating the excavated area." I've become adept at changing "tion" to "ting." Anyway, I found this work far more emotionally rewarding than I would like to admit; it was complex and time consuming, and no more creative than doing the dishes, yet I would engross myself in it. Sometimes I would get lost in the details as a way to put off interacting with people. I'm the sort of guy who gets nervous about ordering plane tickets or calling cabs. I always want the other person to do it. But at work I would end up having to schedule jobs with word processing and graphics and repro, and I had to cope with the fact that what we told WP and repro and graphics would often turn out not to be true, and we wouldn't have the job for them when we said we would, or the client's requirements would suddenly change at the last minute, which would change the workload. In general, I had to act as a nudge, and fortunately or unfortunately I assume that everybody is likely to do something wrong, which makes me a good quality-control person. I was the guy who would double-check everyone or try to prevent people from pitching in and helping (and possibly screwing us up) during last-minute emergencies.

At work my voice was higher-pitched than it is in my mind's ear, and I was more compliant-seeming than I am in my mind's eye. I was being youngish and friendly. I guess this is diplomacy, or a means to getting people to do what I needed them to do. I seemed a bit off to myself, though, and didn't feel I was carrying a sense of authority within myself.

I liked my co-workers, and I liked working with people on a ridiculously complicated project that had a deadline. And the job was good practice: In general, I am afraid to have a presence in the world; this job, in its small way, forced me out, forced me to make decisions.

email to friends about job prospects in Denver (excerpt), January 21, 1999

PART THREE

OUR BAND COULD BE YOUR LIFE—
BUT THEN YOUR LIFE WOULD
SUCK!

CHAPTER 12

PBS & THE LONELY HEARTS CLUB

WHY MUSIC SUCKS

[In late 1986 I'd started a fanzine, Readers' Poll, *in which contributors responded to such questions as "What is Genghis Khan's concept of weekend?" and "Which character in Blue Velvet would you most like as a roommate?" At the end of issue 2 I asked "Why does music of the '80s suck?" and got so many responses that they had to be spun off into a special issue (Readers' Poll #3½), which I put out under the title* Why Music Sucks *(a publication of the Committee to Destroy Pop Formalism). The ongoing conversation continued too large for* Readers' Poll, *so* Why Music Sucks *became a 'zine of its own. Here's the question, and excerpts from my own response.]*

Q: Why does music of the '80s suck? Do you agree with what I wrote on p. 11 of *Readers' Poll* #2? Main points were that disco is superior to punk and that the general malaise is caused by "fear, a fear of the potential life, rudeness, and outrageousness of music"—the quote's from Manny Farber, though I changed it to read "music" rather than "a film." What is positive in contemporary music? Is there a new music you'd like to hear/create in the future?

Music doesn't suck. It's wonderful! It's a celebration. Even bad music is wonderful. It's not as wonderful as it once was. At least in the American market. At least that I've heard. There's a lot that I haven't heard. (There is a lot that I like, by the way. I love Teena Marie's *Emerald City* LP—no one that pretends to care about rock 'n' roll should be without it.)

Music in the '80s is merely much worse than music in any other decade in the memory of sound recording.

Most of you were really answering the question "Why does rock music suck?" I guess that's all most of us know much about.

Some of you wrote, simply, "boring." I assume you were referring to the question more than to the music—though if you think the question is boring, you probably think the music is boring, too.

An overconcise presentation of my ideas:

Rock music sucks. Other music seems to be going down too—most distressingly disco and funk. Perhaps rock music is the core of what's wrong and is bringing the other musics down with it.

Why does music suck?

An "answer"—one that raises more questions than it answers: Music is reduced to symbols—the symbol almost replaces the music—the symbol gets in the way of the music—certain effects of music are reduced to symbols: E.g., a type of music symbolizes rebellion rather than provoking rebellion, symbolizes outrageousness rather than being an outrage, symbolizes fun, symbolizes intelligence, symbolizes protest . . . The result is music that is meaningless—the term "meaningless" being used in the sense of "does not matter" and "has no effect." The music sounds empty. (And music of the past gets emptied in its present contexts.)

I refuse to palm off all the blame for the present suckiness on capitalism, commercialism, the exchange of commodities, corporate oligopolies, society, mainstream culture, etc. (Analyses of these things and their relation to music—rather than scapegoating them—would be useful: talking about our place *within* culture, rather than referring to culture as "them.")

_WE_ are doing something to kill music.

By "we" I don't automatically mean myself or the person reading this. I don't exclude us either.

First, I mean the concept "we"—the idea that there is a special place called "rock 'n' roll" or "alternative rock" or "punk rock" or "avant garde music" or "independent music" (whatever you want)—that being in this special rock 'n' roll etc. place makes "us" different from Perry Como, Al Jarreau, Lionel Richie, Neil Diamond, Teena Marie. I won't insult you by implying that you readers of *Readers' Poll* believe in "we" any more than I do. Nonetheless, we purvey this "we" in often unconscious ways—e.g., everyone in *Forced Exposure* writing in the same style, *Sound Choice* calling itself a "network" (which makes me, as a subscriber, an affiliate?).

Second, I mean the "we" that we really are—a sort of music marginal intelligentsia (even the skinheads). Our way of making music and our way of relating to it as an audience destroys music. Music for the Independent-Minded seems more and more like PBS for the Youth—PBS with a frat-brat gloss for the readers of *Forced Exposure* and with a leftist gloss for the readers of *Sound Choice* (who are the same readers anyway, even if the two magazines manage to maintain an antagonism).

Again, I don't necessarily mean me or you, Byron, or you, David—I mean an overall PBSization that is beyond our control and speaks through us whether we would like it to or not. What I mean is BLANDNESS. What I mean is TEPIDITY. What I mean is BOREDOM. What I mean is the Dead Kennedys and Lydia Lunch. Fanzines. We take people like Jerry Lee Lewis and Schoolly D and through the process of our appreciating them turn them into nothing. Reading *Forced Exposure* made me realize that there are bands out there capable of doing *totally meaningless* versions of "Under My Thumb."

Despite out marginality, we have an effect on music as a whole. We can't get everybody to listen to our music—but we can be arbiters of taste. E.g., I can imagine some poor soul abandoning Teena Marie for Talking Heads, then abandoning Talking Heads for Sonic Youth, then abandoning Sonic Youth for me—and doing it all as a *status* move. I can't imagine a status move in the other direction. The conditions for that kind of status turnaround haven't existed since the Fifties, since Elvis. People may hate recent British music for being a crass commercial disco contamination of new wave—but really, it's the other way around—it is a new wave pseudointellectual contamination of disco.

Richard Meltzer was right: Rock 'n' roll collapsed the distinction between awesome and trivial. Overall, rock 'n' roll could not have been great had it been merely awesome. I say "overall" because, when it comes down to the sound of specific bands, I prefer the awesome-awesome to the awesome-trivial. I prefer the Rolling Stones to Elvis. Meltzer tried to portray the Stones and Dylan at their 1965 peaks as trivial and silly (not to mention awesome and serious), just like the rest of rock 'n' roll. Meltzer was wrong, the Stones and Dylan were simply awesome—but I understand why he portrayed them in the way he did. He was trying to *save* them. Triviality *protects* awesomeness. The Rolling Stones, even more than the Beatles, saved white rock from being Bobby Rydell/Las Vegas shit but put it irrevocably, despite all their intentions, on the PBS path. By being merely awesome, the Stones laid the seeds for the destruction of rock 'n' roll. PBS can co-opt mere awesomeness. They can turn it into "seriousness" and oppose it to "fun." The Sex Pistols (who were the Rolling Stones reincarnated thirteen years later, and that's *all* they were) were a lot closer to PBS than to Elvis. The were *better* than Elvis, too—the awesome, sociofuckological aspects that made them closer to PBS helped make them better. But, though they saved punk for a couple years, they made punk socially significant hence digestible by PBS. (So do I, by the way—though I'm not great like the Sex Pistols or important.)

I'm being a bit loose with the term "PBS." I mean a certain PBS head (attitude), which can include a cult taste for shitty horror movies, pro wrestling, African pop, comic books, Hasil Adkins . . . all this pseudofun is a covering for a mind set that's ruled by PBS. We're making horror movies safe for PBS. We have met PBS, and it is us. I mean an imaginary PBS of the future, with pro wrestling, splatter films, and leftist analyses of the Capitalist Entertainment Industry (scored by a reformed Gang of 4). All rendered lame in the context of our appreciation.

Deliberate triviality is even worse than PBSization. I've always hated the Flesh-tones for turning "fun" into a genre. Fun becomes a *style* rather than an *experience*.

Whether I or anyone actually has fun is irrelevant—it has nothing to do with the Fleshtones' being designated a fun band. They're not fun, they're lame. Not good-silly, just boring-silly. So were the Replacements the time I saw them at Gildersleeves. (Even if they had been fun, they'd still have been conforming to a conventional idea of fun.)

OK (okay), those are my ideas. They're not intended to be right. The purpose of writing isn't to be right. The PBS head isn't the most destructive head in society and doesn't always generate lameness—but it's the head we most resemble. The real problem is, e.g., people play tedious, beatless death rock and think it's rock 'n' roll. The real problem is that punk is the new progressive rock. I was at a horrible, deadly dull New Year's Party in the early '80s populated mainly by (what would later be called) Yuppies. The Yups were being true to their deadly dullness, and I was preparing to leave, when the radio was turned on. It was a song by Prince, who is not particularly interesting, in my opinion. The song contained some party cliché, "It's time to dance, dance, dance" or something like that. The Yups started chanting "dance, dance, dance" and moving—the moment was electric—completely unexpected. I know such group chant things can be the essence of fakeness (e.g., at rock concerts), but this was not fake. (Then I left the party.) Nothing like that electric moment has ever happened at a Red Dark Sweet* or Pillowmakers or Frank Kogan show. (Or if anything electric happened, it was inside an audience member's head and had no external expression.) (*except for a great guitar-bass thing in "Highway 51" between me and Andrew that was witnessed by six people and not necessarily noticed by any of them, though it was immortalized on tape)

I quit Red Dark Sweet because they weren't going to try to be famous. Then I quit the Pillowmakers because we didn't deserve to be famous, because our music had too narrow a range (. . . because we weren't Red Dark Sweet). Now there's Your Mom Too, which does deserve to be famous—but we've already decided not to try. I'll quit my next band too, undoubtedly, because it's not Your Mom Too. I still think Red Dark Sweet should try to be famous. "Famous" perhaps is the wrong word. Red Dark Sweet should go out and meet the unknown audience . . . For all the bands and incipient bands in the *Readers' Poll* readership, the task is to *create a new audience*. Ben Edmonds, writing in 1973, about the New York Dolls: "Perhaps the reason the Dolls have been so misunderstood is that they don't play to an existing audience; it's an audience that has yet to reveal itself. More than simply latching onto an audience, the next phenomenon will be that which *creates* its audience. The Dolls have very little choice: they either create that audience or they have none at all. They don't really belong to anything else." ("The New York Dolls Greatest Hits Volume 1," *Creem*, October 1973.) The Dolls, with the mighty help of the rock press, did create that audience, though it was the Sex Pistols who reaped the harvest. I don't think Red Dark Sweet or any other band can create that audience using a Dolls' or Stooges' or Sex Pistols' type of Grand Gesture (The Grand Gesture is now a PBS subsidiary). Nor would they want to. But the openness of Red Dark Sweet—open to all influences and defying classification, including the classification "eclectic"—is a way of reaching out to many different potential audience members. (Though the reaction of many people to Red Dark Sweet is often bafflement or hostility.) The new audience must somehow be outside of the existing postpunk categories—it must somehow *not* be punk or postpunk or avant garde or jazz or alternative or electronic or art. The new audience need not be new people—it may be *us*, if we can teach ourselves to *behave differently* as an audience, transform ourselves into the carney sideshow audience. (We must refuse to shunt ourselves off into a "little magazine" attitude.) It certainly need not be a *mass* audience; but it should be a nonexclusionary audience (Lionel Richie fans welcome). It would be nice to get kids in the audience, because for kids music is life and death. This always adds something. Maybe some older people, too. And refugees from discos and lounges who discover that they *like* puzzling music.

Maybe Red Dark Sweet and the Scene Is Now could start acting like *pop* bands—e.g., start fan clubs, bite off chickens' heads onstage, have scantily clad dancers in cages suspended from the ceiling, drive cars into swimming pools, hire people to scream.

I think bands like Sonic Youth and the Minutemen may have goals like mine— the problem is that they play/played music that is circumscribed (unlike Red Dark Sweet's), and it *is* their fault. I feel an emotional connection to some of Sonic Youth's stuff, which is why I get so mad at them for playing middlebrow romantic dirge pop instead of rock 'n' roll. I admire Sonic Youth for going where the rest of us dare not—i.e., onstage, into the recording studio, on tour.

When I think of what motivates punk rock, I do not think of the phrase "Do It Yourself." I think of "I wanna destroy passersby" (the Sex Pistols) or "Do you think that you can make it with Frankenstein?" (the Dolls). Can I love life in all its terror and tragedy? Do I want to cut it (you) all up into stinking, reeking strips? Everything and everyone? Or I think of certain sounds, certain rhymes, certain feelings. The phrase "Do It Yourself" raises the question: Do *what* your-self? "By now we realised that our fellow punks, The Pistols, The Clash and all other muso-puppets weren't doing it at all." So write do-it-yourself champions Crass in their farewell broadside. Does "not doing it at all" mean the Pistols weren't taking enough drugs, fucking enough groupies, killing enough girlfriends? Crass: "We wanted to offer something that gave rather than took. . . ." Worthy goals—but give *what* rather than take? It was the Dolls, Stooges, and Sex Pistols that played the guts of punk. The '76–'77 punk movement happened because of gut response to the Pistols. Neither "Do you think that you could make it with Frankenstein?" nor "I wanna destroy passersby" translates into "Do It Yourself." The underground alternative network and its do-it-yourself spirit is *empty*. The feelings, attractions, fears that brought people into punk were too scary to deal with. People were left with the attraction, the desire to play—but they really didn't want to extrapolate "Do you think that you could make it with Frankenstein?" or "I wanna destroy passersby," didn't want to seize this music and take it where it could go. They didn't want to work on the contradictions, the impossibilities. So the activity of making "independent" music becomes a *substitute* for dealing with the feelings that brought us into the music in the first place. Instead of being passive appreciators of other people's activities (rock stars'), we become passive appreciators of our own little hobby activities. I am strongly in favor of people making music, however shitty. And recording it, making noise in public. But not as a *substitute*.

Not all punk comes from Dolls-Stooges-Sex Pistols; not all indie music (or even most) derives from and betrays punk; not all indie recordings are meaningless. But the *concept* of independent-music-as-good-in-itself is a destructive concept. It creates meaninglessness. That is why so much indie music is lousy. It's not because people don't practice enough, don't have enough talent, don't know enough about music history. It's fear.

The difference between punk in the '60s and punk now: In the '60s no one knew what he or she was doing. The Stones, Dylan, and Yardbirds were the Sex Pistols' noise and message 12 years earlier, but no one knew the implications. No one had to flee the implications or negate them. In their naïveté, second-level bands, whether they were garage punks like the Syndicate of Sound or commercial concoctions like the Monkees, conveyed what was in the Stones' music simply by imitating it. In the '80s we negate music by imitating it. The years 1964 to 1968 were a constantly changing fashion, fad, trendie entertainment thing. In the '60s fashion and entertainment were meaningful.

As you could tell from my advice to Red Dark Sweet, I am insane. But extremism in the cause of spaghetti is no vice. So yeay, I'll stay romantic, be disappointed.

(It dawns on me that a few of you are overseas or in caves and might not know PBS. Public Broadcasting System—a TV network, a descendant of "educational TV." Has public affairs programs, science documentaries, middlebrow bland drama. Skirts all vulgarity—though the occasional, brilliant thing can come in from left field, e.g. "Style Wars," a documentary on graffiti hip-hop kids. Though an appreciation of hip-hop—as opposed to DISCO—is safely social do-good.)

What is positive in contemporary music? Spoonie Gee's "Spoonin' Rap" and "Love Rap" make all other '80s music (including his own) sound like bullshit.

He's the *only* performer to remind me of the Stooges and Velvets (maybe because he's never heard the Stooges or Velvets); he's the only performer to remind me of myself. He's more significant than any post-Pistols punk because he inhabits this territory *only* emotionally, not generically or culturally or deliberately. Hip-hop in general makes the voice-drum connection—the voice *is* the rhythm instrument in Dimples D's "Suckapella" (flip of "Sucker DJs") (producer Marley Marl). Hip-hop also leads by working sound effects into the rhythm, stealing pop culture artifacts and using them in new work (DJ mixes), and using prefab recordings as a basis for *live improvisation.* I like Bambaataa's *first* Time Zone 12-inch "Zulu Wildstyle," which incorporates old movie dialogue and other weirdness. The Baker-Robie-Bambaataa Soul Sonic Force "Looking for a Perfect Beat" is techno machine sound transformed into swinging funk call-and-response. The Robie-Jenny Burton-C Bank "One More Shot" is grating techno machine sound used for searing gospel-type soul. The night is *still* young and full of possibilities.

The next big thing: Teena Marie ignores most of these innovations. Nonetheless she's the most consistently great talent in contemporary music. She's also the most tasteless great talent since Elvis. She's simultaneously lowbrow, middlebrow, highbrow; kitsch and deep; raving rocker and sap. She makes everyone else seem narrow by comparison. She makes the Beatles seem narrow by comparison. Maybe even Elvis. She's sometimes *so* godawful. She defies summation. Which means she's PBS-proof. Which means she deserves to be THE NEXT BIG THING. "Lips to Find You" is the rockingest and sexiest song of the decade.

Why Music Sucks #1, February 1987

THERE'S A SELF-HATE THAT MAKES US SEEK ULTERIOR JUSTIFICATION

If you had trouble understanding my metaphor "PBS," I don't blame you. I thought it up as I wrote and hardly made it clear to myself. But I feel I'm onto something. I like it because it challenges the "underground's" sense of its own daring. Clarification and expansion will come. First, I want to introduce a new metaphor: *The Lonely Hearts Club.* To quote Denise Dee in *The Best of Lobster Tendencies*: "in starting lobster tendencies i wanted to do one thing   tell the truth   i wanted to tell one weirdo little girl somewhere that she wasnt so weird that somebody knew what she meant that somebody else had felt like that" and "l.t. got the mail we wanted and made contacts with others like and unlike us who recognized a cry for or an offer of help." *Lobster Tendencies* truly was desperate and heroic. The rest of indie-music-fanzine culture isn't as raw nerved, but the underlying impulse is similar. Indieland is a large lonely hearts club. It's a good one. It gives me pen pals, gives me friends. I got my girlfriend through the cassette listings in *OP* magazine. The indie network is more interesting than most clubs of its type—how many lonely hearts clubs even pretend an interest in the pygmies of central Africa, in new forms of social organization, in weird never-before-heard sounds? But a lonely hearts club has limits. It's where you go to break your isolation. It's where you go to get your feelings and attitudes confirmed. It's not usually where you go for daring, subversive, critical, or disruptive behavior. It's not a good home for the punk impulse. (Home?) You don't go there to have your feelings challenged, your life turned upside down. You don't go to make it with Frankenstein. You don't go to destroy passersby.

Indie-music-fanzine land embodies two contradictory impulses: It's half Lonely Hearts Club and half Explorers Club. Do-It-Yourself can be expansive or insular or both. If you set up your own distribution, promotion, tour, etc. you'll learn things and meet people that you'd miss if someone else did it for you. Do-It-Yourself is often better than not doing it at all. But Do-It-Yourself can become Do-It-Alone or Do-It-Only-With-People-Like-Me. There are often good financial and emotional reasons for doing it alone. I know. There are also some people who make music best that way—like an artist alone with brush and canvas. But if you do it alone (or among mere *us*) it's not rock 'n' roll.

But:

Being insular and deluded does not necessarily make one a bad musician. Why should this impair our sense of beauty, our sense of rhythm, and our feeling for dramatic excitement? And why has so much American music outside the L. Hearts Club been paralyzed? Why is music rendered lame in the context of our appreciation? What is it that kills sound and feeling?

I have no answer. I think that my concept of "PBS" might be of help. A sentence from last issue: "There's a self-hate that makes us seek ulterior justification for ourselves/our music in terms that are PBS." It is in our justification of music, not in our appreciation of it, that we render it lame.

The real PBS—Public Broadcasting Service—is hateful for conveying these attitudes: (1) detachment is intelligence, (2) passionlessness is intelligence, (3) leisure activity should be useful. I also hate the PBS tone-of-voice: the sobriety, the "we" borrowed from academia—the feeling exuded on MacNeil-Lehrer that *we* are engaged in common inquiry, that our problems can be worked out through understanding. Also borrowed from academia is the sense that what *we* cover are the only things worth covering.

The indie-music-fanzine network justifies itself in terms of social importance and social usefulness—terms that are very PBS: Indie music is made by better people. It is better for you.

When I was twelve and thirteen I was liking hit singles by the Seeds, the Electric Prunes, etc. When I was fourteen I was liking Simon & Garfunkel. In retrospect

S&G sound empty compared to the garage hits. More important, the garage hits pictured my teen feelings better. I was a kid, so I needed to feel significant. S&G signified "significance"; I abandoned perhaps my true taste and feelings to listen to significant music. (It's not so simple, of course. I do think S&G are now underrated by rock writers. Paul Simon's nihilism was verbally more explicit than Sky Saxon's; maybe that was one of S&G's attractions.) Possible parallels: John Lennon thought his earliest (and, in my opinion, his best) songs were a joke; he went on to do worse stuff that conformed to his idea of self-expression. The Clash destroyed themselves trying to conquer rhythm.

Our terms of justification have gone through so many convolutions that now an unjustifiable act—Jerry Lee Lewis shooting someone for no reason—serves to justify Jerry Lee by virtue of being unjustifiable. Among '6os buffs, negligible bands like Music Machine and the Litter now have higher status than the much better Simon & Garfunkel. But the pattern of justification stays the same, stays PBS.

Triviality vs. awesomeness: "Certainly the rock 'n' roll experience must combine both the awesome and the trivial in order for either facet to be potent." (Meltzer, *Aesthetics of Rock* p. 26.) Even when performers—e.g., the early Stones—are potently awesome without being trivial, there is an overall context of pop music triviality that nourishes and protects them. Why must awesomeness hide within triviality to be potent? Triviality (silliness, frivolity) is a safe place. People in the serious mode—addressing important issues, baring their souls, being honest—are often wooden, thin, full of clichés, empty. They are mentally "in church," scared witless, mired in mere consciousness. Take these same people out to the sandbox; they can wish, lie, dream (ref. Kenneth Koch), heave shit, generally loon around—all silly trivia, doesn't matter, not held accountable. The land of nonawesome triviality can then give birth to something real deep, accidentally awesome. In the overall social psyche, "entertainment"—pop music, sports, shooting galleries, TV, movies—is the playground. Though the playground's subject to censorship, interesting weird stuff can go on there—so long as the stuff is perceived as trivial, silly. That's how it escapes the censorship of our serious mind. So, in the "entertainment" playground, important emotions and ideas can arise that are unexpected. (If I were writing a book instead of a paragraph on this topic, I'd have chapters about "down" and "out" groups such as Jews and Blacks going into the entertainment business because more respectable professions are closed to them, entertainment not being trivial in the James Brown context, seriousness not always being rigid, etc. The trivial-awesome split is a social feature of modern America, not an aesthetic split in the history of all mankind.)

Legitimacy vs. illegitimacy: "If you start with *illegitimacy* as a big criterion for a song, like if it's loud and noisy and hurts your father's ear, then all you need is to think real hard about the illegitimacy of ballads to *your* ear and you got yourself some more nice illegitimacy, you take it where you find it, it's all usable, anything and its opposite." (Richard Meltzer, "The Big Cheese," *Crawdaddy*, c. 1969) Rock 'n' roll excites not just by acting with you against Them (the Dads of the world), but also by acting against you. In the Elvis situation (which Meltzer was writing about), or the 1966 situation, illegitimacy could act to expand and validate a whole mess of music. But in other situations (subsequent situations), illegitimacy tears right through and cuts up all music; nothing's usable, neither it nor its opposite. If illegitimacy to your own ear is a criterion (which it is—that's a social fact—I live that fact, and so do most of you), then illegitimacy legitimizes a song—and you've lost it! Fortunately, illegitimacy isn't the only criterion for *liking* a song. But it is a major criterion for *justifying* a song. Because so many people are taught in so many ways that they are illegitimate, people have to make their stand on illegitimacy. They have to glorify illegitimacy. It is a matter of psychic survival.

Our feelings of illegitimacy underlie our obsession with justifying (rather than merely liking or appreciating) our favorite music. In 1966 it seemed that rock 'n' roll might be collapsing the social distinctions between awesome and trivial, between illegitimate and legitimate. But people can't live without a sense of their own legitimacy, their own importance. "Rock" music took a dive in the late '60s/early '70s because (among other reasons) "rock" musicians and "progressive radio" wouldn't play music that they couldn't justify. They played music that sounded hip, important, and legitimate. Their ideas of importance and legitimacy mixed conventional art notions of status with rock 'n' roll's need to be "out." E.g., they played blues ("down" group music, black, hence socially important), but as serious, self-expressive, guitar virtuoso music rather than as party-dance music. "Progressive radio" would play "raw" southern soul, but no Motown or northern black vocal groups—too pop. Also too pop for airplay were early '60s rock 'n' roll popcraft (girl groups, Beach Boys, pre-*Rubber Soul* Beatles), its successors (Tommy James, Neil Diamond), teen garage stuff (Question Mark, Troggs), "straight" top 40 (Bobby Gentry), and teenybopper stuff (Archies).

Justification by effect: "Leisure activity should be useful." I say "useful" with deep contempt in my voice; but actually I don't think "useful" is always bad. E.g., "useful" in the personal sense: teaches me something I want or need to know, gives me ideas that I can use, acts as a catharsis so that I dance rather than killing my family. "Useful" in the social sense: helps to feed the hungry, helps to undermine social institutions that deserve to be undermined. Change the "should be" to "can" to get "leisure activity can be useful," and, you know, why not? Why not kill two birds with one rock? Movies and shows defined to be useful—documentaries, drivers ed. films, and so on—can be more entertaining than many shows defined to be fun. My favorite TV show of 1968 was the Chicago convention. The Clash's use of politics was an effective *aesthetic* move (on the 1st LP only). Politics and religion are sometimes much more moving than "entertainment." Music gets aesthetic power by playing a sort of religious and political role. But getting the emotions jerked or, say, having fun thinking through an idea, is not felt to be good enough. Usefulness stops being a mere interesting effect of music; usefulness becomes the justification. In this context, music comes to symbolize its supposed useful effect. This process is natural and not necessarily bad. E.g., many people were attracted to the Sex Pistols not only by the sound but by the way the sound symbolized a potential disruptive effect. Though the actual disruption sputtered, the whole thing felt intense and interesting, as did the music. Even a bogus symbol isn't necessarily bad. E.g., I go to hear some "wild" music that's supposed to "drive me over the edge" and cause social chaos; instead it's some silly pretentious dance music with death lyrics; I dance, hum the tunes, snicker at the scene, have a good time. Symbols, even bogus ones, can have aesthetic effect. But the massive attempt within PBS Indie Lonely Hearts Club to decide in advance the social effect and social meaning of our little endeavors (take Culturcide . . . please) seems to kill off any potentially interesting *real* effect. The music beneath the symbolic decoration dies.

Justification by causation: Some jazz singer once said that, though she didn't much like white people, she liked the music of Bob Dylan because she could tell he had suffered. I once pointed out to a friend that the Stooges were from Ann Arbor, not Detroit. "But they were *junkies*," he said, implying that their being junkies validated their music. Music gets justified by what causes it—who makes it and what they've been through. Or it gets justified by its social environment—who listens to it and what *they've* been through. Rock music supposedly represents the "downs" (black, white trash, working class) and the "outs" (the consciously disaffected, the beats, the freaks, the punks, the delinquents). It has to come from the down and out to be considered "real." Conversely, to say that some musicians are down and out or incredibly fucked up and fucked over is a way to assert that their music is *real*. The Peter Laughner LP is decorated with four obituaries, presumably to assert the same thing.

Rock 'n' roll didn't invent this style of justification. Once, in the *New York Times Book Review*, Kenneth Rexroth cited Weldon Kees's suicide off the Golden Gate Bridge as evidence that Kees (unlike Auden, Aiken, and Eliot) really meant his alienated poetry. I assume that most of you have "seen through" this style of justification. It's bullshit. That is, as an intellectual idea it's bullshit. As an emotional idea it's not bullshit at all. I *like* music that sounds down, out, and fucked. Such music feels real.

Justification by causation appears in the work of writers whose intelligence

I respect greatly. For example, Chuck Eddy in the April *Spin*, referring to the Bad Brains' youth in the projects: "And where most hardcore is spoiled brats bitching for the sake of bitching, the Bad Brains know ugliness first hand." A few sentences later: "You can rest assured that the Bad Brains have earned their anger." That last phrase is beautifully psychotic and American. Anger is, or ought to be, something you feel, not something you earn. But we're expected to earn, justify, and explain our feelings before allowing ourselves to feel them. The need to justify anger through suffering causes people to proclaim their reality through pain—ordinary pain must be made extraordinary, and suffering must do more than be suffering, it must symbolize suffering. Suffering becomes an aesthetic commodity, as does conspicuous self-destruction. Hence the obits included with the Laughner LP. Most of us steal or inherit our anger, or receive it as a gift, rather than earning it in the accepted fashion. Since we can't justify our anger, we shouldn't feel it. Anger and its cousins Terror and Hatred are driven underground in the psyche, where they're a gold mine. This is why hate sounds more real than love, noise sounds more real than beauty. It's *deep*, you know. We each get to be the World's Forgotten Boy or Girl because inside there is such a forgotten kid. Hard rock in the '60s and punk rock in the '70s were the aesthetic payoff.

So what's wrong in the '80s? The cumulative effect of Dylan, Stones, and Sex Pistols was to establish the social importance of anger. So anger can be a status thing to do. Anger lets you join the club. Not that kids today feel less anger than Dylan did—but Dylan discovered the aesthetic power (and commercial appeal) of anger. He used anger aesthetically. '80s bands—hardcore and pigfuck—use anger socially, not aesthetically. It's a bonding tool, shared symbol. The anger is symbolic rather than convincing because, to fulfill its social function, it only needs to be symbolic.

Not that I have anything against symbols, referents. Teena Marie may well have hired Bootsy Collins (as *vocalist*) for symbolic reasons. She's always shoveling references towards the audience—in music (in "Shadow Boxing" she goes from Santana-like guitar and percussion to "orchestral" horn flourishes, eliciting this appraisal from Leslie: "She's tripping *severely*"), lyrics (the '57 Ford that drives through "Lips to Find You" as an irrelevant icon, "baby baby baby baby love," "take a walk on the wild side," "standing on the corner of rhythm and blues/a Valentino smile gave me my first clue"), and sleeve notes (from *Robbery*: "Like omicron is the fifteenth letter of the Greek alphabet or Sarah Vaughan is like jade—Jessica Lange became Frances, and Dunaway and the word respect go together like hand in glove"; also mentioned on the sleeve (along w/ thank yous to everyone except or including the janitor) are Shirley MacLaine, Stevie Wonder, Michael Jackson, Mahatma Gandhi, Narada, Maya Angelou (remember her in "Square Biz"?), Fonda (Jane, probably), Shuri, Ntozake, "and women period,"

Natalie Wood Wagner, Billie Holiday—wait! let's have this verbatim!—"Like Billie Holiday to the blues, or Joan of Arc to sainthood, destiny was never my choice, I am only an instrument like saxophone—needle—conversation and Ms. Pacman").

excerpts from *Why Music Still Sucks or Why "Why Music Sucks" Sucks* (WMS #2), Summer 1987

FEELING YUMMY

In 1967 I heard the Ohio Express and loathed them, they sounded like pink-cotton-candy-flavored puke, they sounded like kid stuff. I guarantee you that this loathing was spontaneous, strong, from the gut; not "thought out" or "reasoned" or "derived from ideas." In 1972 I heard the Ohio Express on some old supermarket compilation, and I adored them. Slimy, subversive stuff it was, and it rocked! This adoration was strong and on the spot, too. Not "thought out." Okay. Right? These are feelings and feelings are more real and basic than anything. Right? No. I'll tell you what I think was the unconscious socioreasoning process that underlay my "spontaneous" "gut-level" feelings. In 1967 at age thirteen I was still a kid and of course there are all these social things coming down on kids that tell them being a kid is trivial kids' stuff—so damn it I wasn't going to be a kid, and to like "Yummy Yummy Yummy" would make me a kid, and I was damned if I was going to let that happen. On the other hand, at age eighteen, in 1972, there was this deadly dull parody of adulthood called "maturity" that I was supposed to be entering into, and this deadly dull parody of importance called "progressive radio" that was dominating the music "culture." It was key for me to resist "maturity" (the sort of "old" I hope I die before I get); the slimy brilliant Ohio Express were a perfect vehicle for such resistance.

It's nowhere near as simple a process as this. I loathed "Yummy Yummy Yummy" at age thirteen, rather than merely dismissing it with a smirk, because it was catchy, and I recognized inside me that it had pull, was a threat. So I had feelings that went in the opposite direction of my loathing. The great thing about music and feelings and all that: It catches me unaware. I feel things that I don't want to feel, so I have to rethink who I am, where I place myself. Loathing the Ohio Express was a useful way for me to break out of something at age thirteen, but liking them at age eighteen was a revelation, as if I'd discovered a new self. This is why music really can "change the world." It can surprise the world with unexpected feeling. I value most the music that I like despite myself—in 1966 the Stones, in 1970 Led Zeppelin, in 1973 the Dolls, in 1978 the Contortions, in 1979 DISCO! The bands that change me are the ones that win me over.

Once at a job Olivia Newton-John was playing on the radio. I said, "The rhythm's nice, but her voice just sits there." Someone else said, "No. It glides, it glides." This was interesting to me. I still don't hear her voice as gliding. But I'm not the only pair of ears in the world.

from *Why Music Socks* (WMS #3), December 1987

WE OWN THE WORLD

SCOTT: Why did you say the Stones put rock and roll on the PBS path? I figured Dylan would be the obvious example.

FRANK: Well, in a sense, probably when I say Stones, I mean Stones, Beatles, Dylan, Hendrix, Cream, the whole shootin' match, but the Stones, whatever, *them*—which was also a band [laughs]—they created something culturally where . . . Before the Stones and Beatles, even people who were taking rock seriously, what you would call "official culture"—which probably isn't a word that means that much, but let's say official culture in the '50s—when they tended to be taking rock seriously at all, they were taking it seriously as a social problem, as something that creates juvenile delinquents, and I'm sure there are people who were part of the white intelligentsia, or part of the black intelligentsia, who understood it as valuable, interesting music and all that. But rock 'n' roll and rhythm 'n' blues weren't put on a special pedestal. This is not true in black culture. I'd say that, on his own terms, James Brown was taken very seriously throughout *all* black cultures, I bet, middle class to lower class to upper class, though I'm saying that in ignorance. But the people who took rock culture seriously—live or die, in a sense—it tended to be white trash or teenagers. And it wasn't just sort of the people, but even the ones who were taking it live or die, loving it as much as they loved baseball or even more than they loved baseball, or the movies or something like that, there's still a sense in which it's not competing on the world stage with President Eisenhower or President Kennedy or Khrushchev. Whereas when the British Invasion hit, there's a different sense; you know, it isn't just here's something that causes juvenile delinquency, but it's almost like, here's a wave of people who are coming across and—like I said about Public Enemy—we can potentially own the world, you know, fear of a Stones planet [laughs], and it wasn't that Mick Jagger had this idea, it was more in the way he walked and just who he was. He would probably smirk or giggle if someone said, "You can compete with Kennedy or Eisenhower." And Charlie Watts would say it's music for the kids to dance to, and that's true too, but it's not the whole truth.

And basically it happened. And once it happened, it was there. So kind of why I'm saying they set it on the PBS path is, in a way it became part of, not just middle-class teen culture that people don't take as seriously as real art, it became something that was middle-class culture period, and it could be justified just in the way that you could justify, you know, PBS—as here's something that's important because it's ringing in big social changes in the world and we should listen to what the young people are saying, something like that. I think what I wrote, actually, was that the Stones saved rock 'n' roll from Bobby Rydell trash, but they also put it on the PBS path, and again, I wasn't thinking—I was writing as I got the idea, which is one of the treasures of those early 'zines, but at the same time it wasn't like I had it all thought through; I came up with a metaphor, and then when people started yowling and saying, "You're stupid" or "I don't understand you" or "This is great" and then repeating what they thought I'd said but saying just the opposite, I began to have to explain myself, which meant I had to explore why the metaphor meant something to me. But there was a sense that rock music became something that you *could* justify to your high-school Social Studies teacher, whereas maybe there were some kids earlier who *wanted* to justify it, wanted to justify Elvis and Chuck Berry to their Social Studies teacher, and if they were lucky and had an interesting Social Studies teacher, the Social Studies teacher might have gone along with them, but now it was like you could justify it to almost any Social Studies teacher, maybe even on the Social Studies teacher's terms. And remember, this is my favorite music in the world, this British Invasion and what it originally wrought—basically Stones through Stooges and Dolls, or Sex Pistols too. And a lot of garage rockers, and a lot of the nonsense that went with it too, a lot of the silliness and all that. I'm not saying that this was tsk, tsk, tsk, or something like, well the Social Studies teacher likes it, it's not as good as this earlier, wonderful, pure, protected thing. In a lot of ways it was *better* than the earlier, wonderful, pure, protected thing. But it had within it the seeds of what I was babbling about in my PBS answer, had the seeds of—we can reduce it all to whatever meets our justification or something like that.

from "Pushin' Too Hard: an interview with Frank Kogan," *Popped*, 1997

THE MORASS

Does the seed fall far from the tree? In 1966 my father listened to Beethoven, my mother listened to Beethoven, my brother listened to Beethoven, I listened to the Seeds. You can say that the Seeds spoke to my experience and Beethoven didn't. But clearly if Beethoven could speak to my brother, Beethoven could speak to me. (My brother listened to the Beatles, after all.) I wonder: If my brother had listened to the Seeds, maybe I wouldn't have. Maybe there's only one Seeds spot per family, and I happened to occupy it. I mean, quite obviously the lyrics described my life (this was junior high, everyone was pushin' too hard on me), and the music played my feelings. (And it still does.) But where did those feelings come from? "Rock music was what made *Us* different from *Them*." If Us is me and Them is my parents, this is right. My Dad and I cultivated different tastes, and we cultivated our mutual incomprehension. But in school, among my "friends," rock music is what made Us different from *Me*. I started listening to rock music so that I could be Us and stop being Me. If I'd wanted to differentiate myself from the masses, I'd have been better off listening to Beethoven.

Raging bull: Is a building inauthentic just because someone builds it? Well, what you do in one activity doesn't have to represent what you do in all other activities. E.g., the way you act on the beach isn't the way you act at a funeral; the way you act onstage isn't necessarily the way you act when driving a car, isn't the way you act going fishing, isn't the way you act on the job. Maybe this makes you feel inauthentic, but the fish you hook probably finds you quite real. Is the experience of a bull charging less real if the bull doesn't behave that way out of the ring? Is the experience of being shot by a hit man less authentic than being shot by an angry man? (The hit man's bullets, after all, aren't a genuine expression of his feelings.)

Why feelings suck: "It hits me in the gut," "it feels good," "I like getting my emotions jerked" are all true (for me), but not very interesting. Why would anyone care what Iggy does or whether it hits me if I don't tell them *why* it hits me? I buy records because they make me feel good, but I want to throw some skepticism at this use of "feeling" as the final criterion for rock 'n' roll. Like, if a piece of music feels rebellious, that doesn't mean it *is* rebellious. Rebellion is something you do out in the world, it's not an experience. The antagonism towards argument and analysis among so many of my contributors—the preference for "experience" and "feeling"—seems to me a fear of being in the social world. "Feelings are my own, no one can take them away from me, and no one can challenge them." People wish.

When I say "music sucks" (which basically means that I consider '80s rock stupefyingly mediocre, and I don't respect it), I'm making a value judgment, not reporting my "feelings."

The meaning morass: Robert Christgau, in his Pazz & Jop essay, perceives a discontent with "significance" among his more "disaffected respondents." He means me and Chuck, among others. I think Christgau confuses "meaning" in the sense of "that which (supposedly) hangs on the other side of words" with "meaning" in the sense of "that which matters to people." You can forget about the first but not the second. A problem with lit-based rock criticism (also with lit-based lit criticism, also with lit-based movie criticism, also with lit-based social criticism) is that it treats music etc. as a work or text to be perceived/interpreted/felt. Think instead of music as an activity in which people participate. "[Frank Kogan, Chuck Eddy, Ted Cox, and Rob Tannenbaum] respond to rhythm as meaning"—that's mystifying. I respond to rhythm in meaningful ways, like pacing around and daydreaming, or doing the housework, or dancing. "They respond to words as meaning" would be nearly as mystifying. Neither words nor rhythm are meaningful when separated from the activities that are their home.

excerpts from *Why Mucus Slacks* (WMS #4), Summer 1988

SQUEEZING OUT COALS

(letter to Simon Frith)

You're raising the wrong issue—or, more likely, stating the issue wrong, though I think I agree with what you're trying to say—when you complain of reviews "written with reference not to what the music sounds like but to what it stands for." Why in the world wouldn't a critic want to write about what music stands for? There's no good way to separate out how the music sounds from what it stands for (and no reason to), and the former doesn't precede the latter, no more than the sound of a *word* precedes what it stands for. How music sounds, what it stands for, and what it does are intertwined from the get-go, and all unfold over time. So what you should have said—the real core of the complaint—is something like what I said back when I was complaining about indie-alternative culture in *WMS* #s 1 and 2: Too many fans and musicians let the symbol stand in for the event. Which is to say that they decide at the start what the music does or should do—they take the music to symbolize what it does rather then letting the music do it, rather than letting music and meaning and sound (and life) unfold over time. This is a real danger for those of us who write about advance copies of records. One way for good critics to overcome this danger is for the critic to allow what the music does to unfold *in his prose*, as he's writing the review. (E.g., what the music does to him, what he can do with it, what other people potentially could do with it, possible worlds for the music, etc.) But when he does this, of course, he might be accused of gonzo writing, of personal journalism, of beatnik musing, of writing viscerally so as to display his anti-intellectual credentials, etc.

To elaborate: If people didn't attend on at least *some* level to how the music sounded they wouldn't *know* what it stood for. People (e.g., me) make a lot of judgments about sound—whom the music sounds like, what genre it belongs to—without being able to say on what basis they make the judgments. So I hear "ballad" rather than hearing "sets of sound from which I derive that this is a ballad." Just as when I hear the *word* "ballad" I don't hear "sets of sounds from which I derive that he's saying 'ballad.'" Of course you could say that "sets of sound from which Frank derives that someone is saying 'ballad'" is a good description of what I actually do—though the issue doesn't even arise unless I mishear: unless the person had actually said something else, or he was clearing his throat and I mistook the throat sounds for the word "ballad." But the point is, the *sound* of the word "ballad" doesn't somehow precede its meaning into the world—as if I could emit a couple of sounds and *then* discover that I'd said the word "ballad." The sound derives as much from the word as vice versa, and if I hadn't said the *word* "ballad" I wouldn't have made those sounds.

Can I mishear or misunderstand what someone says yet still have heard the *sound* of what he said correctly? If I then hear him played back on a tape, and this time get the words right, can I say that nonetheless I heard him completely and fully the first time, since I heard the sound completely and fully? *Did* I hear the sound completely and fully? Can a baby who doesn't yet know how to speak be said to hear what his parents are saying? This it seems to me is what you'd be driven to if you tried to attend to what the music sounded like before what it stood for, insisted that the sound preceded the understanding. Your real concern isn't what aspect of the music (the "sound") the critic *starts* with, but where he takes the music.

People's judgments register usually as a liking or a loathing for a particular sound. People who hate ballads don't like the way ballads sound; people who hate c&w don't like the way c&w sounds. I think you are wrong in believing that some of your students don't even listen to the music you assign. But few of them are likely at first to make anything of the fact that their supposedly visceral, irreducible likes and dislikes seem to conform to type, and that they themselves conform to type. This is because they're *not* thinking, "I dislike this because I'm the sort of person who dislikes this sort of thing." They're thinking, "I can't stand this record." And the less reflective ones will assume that this is bedrock, not subject to argument, and that adherence to these opinions is some kind of honesty. (And the unhypocritical among these wouldn't know how to argue with other people's judgments, since they'd believe the other people's judgments would be just as bedrock, even when the judgments contradicted their own.)

But then, I think that my own judgments are irreducible too—but irreducible *all the way*, neither to a feeling *nor* to an analysis, and not just to a social act. Which is to say that though I can say *why* I make a value judgment, I don't assume that the explanation will necessarily justify the judgment. Anyway, the explanation itself will contain judgments, as would any explanation in turn of those judgments. But that my judgments are irreducible doesn't mean that they're unchangeable and can't be argued with, or that they can't be affected by new knowledge and new experience—nor for that matter, that my judgments and explanations can't be persuasive.

"Critical judgment is too often the same thing as presentation of self." How can a critical judgment *not* be a presentation of self? This isn't a choice that human beings have, to evade the presentation of self. Chapter 1 of *Performing Rites* makes this very point, right?

Complications arise because my critical judgments aren't just a presentation of *my* self, they are a presentation of the editors' selves and publishers' selves and the institution's "self"—not that the editors et al. necessarily *agree* with my judgments, but they've made the judgment that my judgments are worth printing. And my judgments even represent the target audience's "self," in that we (me and the magazine) are presenting the reader as someone who would potentially see value in reading my opinions—not as people who would necessarily agree with the opinions, or even would necessarily *want* to read opinions that they already agree with, but nonetheless as people who are complicit in the enterprise. Cf. Bob Dylan's "I know there're some people terrified of the bomb. But there are other people terrified to be seen carrying a Modern Screen magazine." I don't know. Maybe *Voice* readers wish they could hang a sign around their neck that says "I'm only reading this for the personals and for 'Savage Love.'" But as I said, the presentation of self is unavoidable.

Again, the issue isn't whether or not to present the self, but whether to try to determine the self—and the judgment—at the start, or to let it unfold over time. That is, whether to fix a self or to continue to create the self. Once again you've misstated your real concern. It's not that the bad critic turns critical judgment into a presentation of self. It's more like the opposite: that he wants the self—and the judgment—to somehow precede its presentation (analogous to having the sound precede what it stands for). So in effect the bad critic is trying to *evade* the presentation of self by trying to take the self as a given that exists prior to its presentation. And of course if the self is a given, so are its corresponding judgments, and they exist prior to their presentation too. So nothing ever happens. And so I think what you really intend to say is that the good critic allows himself to be surprised by himself. Being surprised by yourself walks hand in hand with being surprised by the music.

Creating a self, by the way, has nothing to do with whether one's prose registers as "personal" rather than "detached." In either case you're presenting a self, your personal characteristics, and your social characteristics. A magazine or a profession that imposes a uniform writing style is forcing the writer to suppress his own social characteristics in favor of the magazine's or the profession's. And once some writers get away with defying the dominant style, then another writer's conformity to it becomes a personal characteristic anyway; there's just no escaping the personal; it's so tied to the social.

"Writing about rock means defining an in-group, keeping the wrong sorts of sounds/people out." This seems like a perfectly legitimate thing for a critic to do. Is there a principle that says that critics shouldn't engage in social differentiation, that such behavior is only to be permitted in fans and musicians? I mean, there are times when such behavior is smart, times when it is stupid.

I as a writer and critic want to keep false *issues* out. Is this in principle any different from keeping the wrong music out? And I certainly don't want to expand the false issue's range and impact, though sometimes I try to understand the appeal of a false issue.

Anyway, those of us who don't honor the boundary between classroom and hallway—those for whom social analysis belongs to life and for whom flirting and fighting belong to the intellect, and for whom flirting and fighting can *be* analysis, and analysis can be a come-on and a brawl—we find our "selves" at issue whenever we go public, no matter what our intentions. This is because—no matter what our intentions—we cross boundaries that other people are trying to maintain, and so we're confronted with the question "Who are you and why are you doing this?" And so we have no choice but to create our selves as we go along, even if we'd thought we were merely *being* ourselves.

excerpts from email to Simon Frith, June 12, 2001

SPECIAL SALUTE TO RANDY RUSSELL FOR PUTTING FORTH THE BEST COUNTERARGUMENT (*WMS* #3):

I like your Lonely Hearts Club metaphor, it's something to think about, though I don't really see what your problem with it is. I think it CAN be where you go for critical or disruptive behavior. You CAN have your feelings changed—you CAN have your life turned upside down. It COULD lead to your falling in love—and that could be having your life turned upside down.

CHAPTER 13
THE DISCO TEX ESSAY

MUNICH BEER HALL POOCH
He tried to be famous
And he tried to be blameless
But he couldn't do both at once
Woof woof woof

THE FRENCH REVOLUTION
The story of the French Revolution
Led many people to their execution
For others it was famine, indolence, and misery
While others learned to import coffee

Welcome to *Why Mildred Skis* #5. Today these are the ten best rock 'n' roll singles ever:

1. Debbie Deb "I'm Searchin'"
2. Spoonie Gee "Spoonin' Rap"
3. The Kinks "See My Friends"
4. Muddy Waters "Still a Fool"
5. The Marvelettes "The Hunter Gets Captured by the Game"
6. Strafe "Set It Off"
7. Disco Tex & the Sex-O-Lettes "I Wanna Dance wit' Choo (Doo Dat Dance)"
8. The Rolling Stones "I Wanna Be Your Man"
9. Sammy Gordon & the Hip Huggers "Makin' Love"
10. The Electric Prunes "Get Me to the World on Time"
11. Donna Summer "Love to Love You Baby"
12. Question Mark and the Mysterians "96 Tears"
13. Taana Pistol Stooge "Heartbeat Anarchy Cum Search and Destroy the Noize Like a Rolling Christmas (Baby Please Come Home) I Can Never Go Home Anymore and Anyway I Can't Stand Myself (When You Touch Me)"
14. The Wailers "Ruddie Boy" a.k.a. "Jailhouse"
15. Millie Small "My Boy Lollipop"

16. Candi Staton "Victim"
17. Charley Patton "Mississippi Boll Weevil Blues"
18. The Shondells "Hanky Panky"

There! A pretty good and expansive top ten. Criterion for getting on the all-time Top Ten for this week was the ability to provide me with the thrill of special-like . . . like, all gushy fanlike, like . . . Also, more than half were some sort of "free lunch" on first hearing or first liking, in that my liking ended up being "unexpected" somehow, especially if I disliked the song at first, or it denied expectations or (even better) came out of nowhere. And I didn't have to work my way towards it (at least not consciously); it wasn't like "learning to enjoy the taste of beer" or "deciding that Tiffany isn't so bad after all, in fact I like her."

"Makin' Love" sounds like a prototype of Eurodisco, though I'm sure it was an imitation made in New Jersey (or somewhere). "I Wanna Be Your Man" is the one great Stones song you haven't heard. I drove a friend out of my room with it (in 1985). "Get Me to the World on Time" is a hard sound and a pure memory of what it was like ("it" being "punk rock" in 1967). There's this 1988 remake of "Love to Love You Baby" by Jackie Concepcion, not all that good, really, but at the end of the "Lovin' Jackie" mix she says "That's it, touch me, harder, harder, ooo ah, mmm, oh how's that? I'm getting a headache." When "96 Tears" first came out it upset me so much that I couldn't listen to it. Just now I listened to ("listened to") "Hanky Panky" on the *Cruisin' 1966* LP and didn't notice it until, after it was over, Pat O'Day said "move up to hanky panky" as his lead-in to the "move up to Chrysler" commercial. I'd rather hear "Crimson and Clover" because it's louder and maybe it's a better song. But "Hanky Panky" plays louder in my mind. I saw her walkin' on down the line. Here I go, higher and higher. You're gonna cry.

MOVE UP TO HANKY PANKY

Ramon Salcido combines several different genres into one (if he'd written the murders instead of performing them he'd probably be accused of laying it on thick, if not of overkill: "Isn't the slit throat a bit much?"): (1) the jealous husband, (2) the crazed coworker, (3) the Ernie K. Doe admirer, (4) the *Readers' Poll* participant, (5) bizarreness (the nearly severed head), (6) sex crime, (7) turn the lights out on the whole family, (8) social pressures plus requisite night of drinking, (9) Hey Joe ("I think I'll go down to sunny Mexico"), (10) one little girl survives, (11) metaphor (the trash heap), (12) the angry crowd outside the jail, (13) similar slaying is solved on the same day (accentuates pervasiveness of evil), (14) overshadows similar slaying that is solved on the same day (so this one's special), (15) hidden past (possible bigamy), (16) "he must be stupid,"

(17) televised confession, (18) death of seamen due to exploding gun turret domi-nates national news and is passed over locally (so meaningless catastrophe with too many deaths and no plot development puts this one in bold relief), (19) nonurban community far from the terror and hardship of the city, (20) on the lam long enough for people to stay nervous but caught soon enough so no one has time to forget and no intervening "story" preempts this one, (21) relative tips off police.

In "I Wanna Dance wit' Choo (Doo Dat Dance)" by Disco Tex & the Sex-O-Lettes, Tex yells out "Olé." The only remarkable thing about this is that in its context it's utterly unremarkable. I'm the first person to remark on it, I bet. (Now I've ruined it.) I think that "Tex" (a.k.a. Monti Rock III) is Puerto Rican, though he could just as easily be Italian, and his on-record patter (platter patter) has the verve of used-car commercials (which is a lot of verve) and the excitement of the guy who's always wanted to play Las Vegas and here he is getting his first chance ever doing the performer intros and it's a gas! "It's disco time, baby! The disco kid is back!" And now that he's labeled the thing as disco (which in 1975 is all you have to do to make it disco), the Sex-O-Lettes launch into the second hoariest vaudeville shtick ever (first hoary is "Shimmy with My Sister Kate"), then break into party noise plus instrumental vamp which happens to be the same vamp that underlies both the Stooges' "1969" (1969) and the psychedelic part of the Byrds' "Tribal Gathering" (1968) (a song that I call "Bambi Meets Godzilla" because it's proto-Stooges in part and proto-Crosby-Stills-Nash in other part), neither of which, from the sound of it, influenced Tex in the least (I bet—and therefore assume that the vamp had a long career as some Afro-Caribbean cliché before Disco Stooge & the Dylanettes got hold of it).

(Which reminds me that Dylan calls "La Bamba" the source for the chorus in "Like A Rolling Stone," and "La Bamba" was the original garage song (according to Lester Bangs), before which it was a Mexican folk song for about a hundred years; and "Louie Louie," the other original punk song, was written, according to Richard Berry (liner notes to the *Best of Louie, Louie*), around a riff from the Latin song "El Loco Cha Cha Cha." I'm curious about whether the riff was just rhythm or included the chord pattern too—the chord pattern is the basic I–IV–V (one–four–five; tonic–subdominant–dominant; e.g. E–A–B; except in "Louie Louie" it's B-minor) of European music, and of course those chords were used in some blues progressions; but, in my nonextensive and not-always-knowledgeable listening of the world's music, the pattern done this way—climbing up the chords I–IV–V or up and down I–IV–V–IV–I real quick in one or two measures—ap-pears only in Latin music (Cuban music and offshoots such as salsa) until the early '60s when the Wailers (the punks, not the Jamaicans), the Kingsmen, Paul Revere and the Raiders, and then Dylan, the Kinks, the Troggs, and a million others used it. In a class I took, the history of salsa, the teacher, John Santos, wondered aloud why Ray Barretto's "El Watusi" became such a big hit, since it was no more than a commonplace vamp, kind of a throwaway thing. I pointed out that the vamp was practically the "Louie Louie" progression and hit at more or less the same time as the Kingsmen's version. (Neither of us knew which hit first—do any of you?) (Was the recorder on "Wild Thing" inspired by the flute on all those Latin hits?) (Leslie says that it wasn't a recorder, it was an ocarina, which sounds like a recorder but looks like a football.) Not that this has lots to do with Stooges or Disco Tex—genealogy isn't important, only what you do with it. The importance of "musical heritage" is that it gives you a form to start with. You have to start somewhere. Though I think that blues and mambo (etc.)—blues, anyway—deserve more of the blame for punk rock (Stooges et al.) than they've been given credit for—you know, it's no accident when a form or content (same dif) gets easily turned into a churning, inviting death trip.)

Forthcoming from Geffen: Various Artists, *Hello, This Is Your Mother*, subtitled "messages your parents left on the phone machine"—This is a recording unlike any other in show-biz history, consisting as it does of performances only by the parents of rock stars. "We kinda wanted to give a tribute to where we are coming from," said the member of a top L.A. glam-metal band. Geffen has asked us not to release the names of the participants "until all the details are worked out"—*WMS* thinks they're just trying to build suspense. Well, the big names are on here, and the advance cassette has been raging 18-hours-a-day nonstop here at the *Why Mildred Skis* offices. And you thought the Sex Pistols were intense! Features the soon-to-be-classic "The Music on Your Machine Is Shit," "We Haven't Heard from You in Two Months," "It's Your Sister's Birthday on Friday," "Why Weren't You at Aunt Jessica's Funeral?" "To Hell with It, I Keep Calling and Calling and What Good Does It Do Me!" "We've All Been Wondering Why We Haven't Heard from You. Are You on Another Tour?" and many more.

In New York in the 1930s a Jew named Alfred Mendelsohn changed his name to Alfredo Mendez and formed a Latin band.

So when Tex (singing in Spanish) and his fellow revelers finish with the Stooges vamp, this wailing voice comes in with this entirely wonderful doowop or proto-Beach Boys (I'm the proud owner of zero Beach Boys records) falsetto "I wanna rock 'n' roll with you," Tex does his famous "Olé," and probably a lot more happens but the version I've got is on a K-Tel sampler so it fades out here after only two minutes.

And it sounds unified—"Disco," not "eclectic." Other notable (i.e. unnotable) throwaways: chugalug jitterbug, do the bump, do the crawl (during the burlesque routine), oom chogga boom, dig my rhinestone tap shoes, start some mini-Iran, it's all greek to me.

Probably killing people was the least interesting thing Charley Starkweather did. Not that I know if he ever did anything interesting. No one can be totally boring. Ramon Salcido may or may not be interesting; his murders are just comic relief. (I mean, in the life of the wiseass urban dweller. It wasn't comic relief to those directly affected.) Maybe for some teenager they're a lot cooler. When the writer Michael Lydon was fifteen he tried to start a Charley Starkweather fan club. That's more interesting than Starkweather himself, probably. Possibly.

Though if Michael Jackson formed a group called Rapeman, I doubt that anyone would call it the lamest of punk jokes:

You're a vegetable, you're a vegetable
Still they hate you, you're a vegetable
You're just a buffet, you're a vegetable
They eat off of you, you're a vegetable

The video "One," by progressive rock band Metallica, number one on the *Dial MTV* request line for 39 years or so, kind of comes with a label attached, "HOR-RIFYING." Which means that it probably doesn't actually provoke horror in anybody—or anyway, its "horror" seems easy to file (but if you were twelve years old you might wish you'd had your limbs blown off too, so someone would do a song about you). Anyway, contrast that to Jackson's "Smooth Criminal" video, which is a fairly absurd cast-of-hundreds production number, full of playfulness and spectacle and a bizarre séance type thing, and which in no way illustrates or has anything to do with those words coming out of his mouth:

He came into your apartment
He left bloodstains on your carpet

Since his dancing, costumes, and singing (even on radio and record) neither augment nor neutralize nor express nor define the lyrics, "bloodstains on your carpet" (should anyone notice it) takes on a weird integrity. Like, huh? Who ordered that? I didn't know it was on the menu!

Jackson keeps doing "Midnight Rambler" again and again, except he's the guy hiding behind the steel-plate door. "Gimme Shelter," too. In his lyrics, any-way—"She trapped me in her heart"; in his videos a bit, which are often about "pursuit"; maybe a little in his voice the way he "overdoes" various "owwws" and "eeeeeeooooo" and sexy sobs and gasps, and in his dance the way he turns so sharp.

PROVOCATIVE PARALLELS:

I have to go to the bathroom
—Sophocles 480 B.C.

I have to go to the bathroom
—Benito Mussolini 1926

I have to go to the bathroom

—Joseph Goebbels 1929

I have to go to the bathroom

—Dwight Eisenhower 1956

I have to go to the bathroom

—Eldridge Cleaver 1968

I have to go to the bathroom

—Robert Christgau 1971

I have to go to the bathroom

—Betty White 1988

I have to go to the bathroom

—Trinh Minh-ha 1988

I have to go to the bathroom

—Bill Laimbeer 1989

In the *Creem* readers' poll for 1975, I voted for the Sex-O-Lettes as "Best Female Singer." Nothing I've written so far will suggest why. The girls—women—on "I Wanna Dance wit' Choo (Doo Dat Dance)" are the Dolls. That's what I decided in the first ten seconds, first time I heard it. I mean, they are glitter babes. They are puss 'n boots, they are there, they are trying—I mean, they are hired hands, the recordmaker wants some pizzazz and they're the pizzazz, each a backup chick looking for her shot (I imagined); bad girls, each wants to be a star (and so on). I saw this Ronald Colman movie around that time (*A Double Life*, dir. George Cukor); mainly far-fetched, I thought, but there was one moment . . . An agent or producer, Hollywood or theatrical or something, or his lackey—I barely remember this at all—appears for a second outside his office door, and a pretty young woman—you know, starlet pretty—lunges desperately for him, she's got to see him. She gets brushed away, and that's that. And that was her entire appearance in the movie, as a few seconds of social detail, as context, while the plot walked on by. I really don't remember: Maybe there were two women. All I remember was the lunge and the look of desperate ambition on her face. I was sappy then, still am—anyway, that was her, Babylon girl, or whoever, the Puerto Rican girl, and did she ever, could she ever, expect such a Frankenstein? And she's in the Sex-O-Lettes. I can't totally recreate that feeling now, of course—I'm no longer that desperate—but it was there in 1975, I heard it in "I Wanna Dance wit' Choo," and I was right!

(Was "Tex" that girl too? Is Noel? Stevie B? I don't know. In 1975 I could only project that role onto women and maybe gays. I did (do?) sort of identify with guys like David Johansen before he chickened out and Bret Michaels who never even got there and he chickened out too—guys who aspire to be that girl rather than merely appreciate her.) (Maybe it's like the Charley Starkweather Fan Club—the imitators are more interesting than the thing being imitated.) (Cf. what Andrew Sarris said about Cukor: "The director's theme is imagination, with focus on the imaginer rather than the thing imagined.")

The fact that the real Sex-O-Lettes, about whom I know nothing, were Monti Rock's 50-year-old Aunt Gertrude and her neighbor Blanche, in town on vacation and in the studio only because for some reason they couldn't get out to Disneyland that day and Monti didn't know what to do with them, is irrelevant; I'm talking about their sound.

Not so irrelevant is the fact that I'm the only person ever (as far as I know) to identify the Sex-O-Lettes with the Dolls. So in what sense could I possibly be "right"?

Okay, I'm a visionary, and if my vision doesn't get some embodiment out there in the world or at least in someone else's mind, then I'm a crank—but a crank of sociological interest nonetheless (if you're a sociologist), because my visions derive not only from my "personality" (whatever that is) but from my world—i.e., from me messing around in relation to other people in that world, such as you. So you, or, in 1975, people a lot like you (I wager), helped create "my" vision. You're part of it even if you find the vision unintelligible, maybe especially if you find the vision unintelligible—you know, finding a space beyond the intelligibility of others is one of the things that makes us individuals (as the sociologist Mykel Board might put it). Christgau would call such unintelligibility "existential solitude" (with "harrumph" placed before the word "existential" to convey a sense of dissatisfaction or embarrassment with the phrase); I'd call it social solitude, and I think it's a creation (a social creation) or even an achievement.

But I ought to achieve my unintelligibility honestly by trying to be intelligible. So where was I? . . . Oh yes! I heard it—the dolls, the glitter babes—in "I Wanna Dance wit' Choo," and I was right! I heard a sound!—the Sex-O-Lettes "You got to got to got to get dat" (?)—which was equivalent to the way the New York Dolls looked. And that's it, the Dolls had a whole look and attitude, a way of moving, but they never found a sound to embody that look. They were party girls who never got their party. "We're out there and we're outrageous" is how they look; "we're out there and desperate" is how they sound, the party barely discernible near the horizon. The Dolls work real hard just to howl "oww-oooo" like a Wolfman, whereas "Tex" takes that sort of nonsense for granted. "Dig my rhinestone tap shoes" gets tossed off, just like the oft-commented-upon "Olé." Disco, besides being a real sleaze pit, is a sandbox; "Olé" is a grain of sand (probably was some latin bugalu cliché). Disco is a context of abundance—but with a bit of desperation at the edges, the Monday through Friday and permanent hassle which just sits there outside, and which accounts (I think) for the extra fizz or bite or dazzle-in-your-face that I hear in the Sex-O-Lettes.

Well, welln't, welln't've been, unwelln't, wellingness. (Transitions are my bane.)

Well, "context of abundance" (whatever that is) seems to me (whoever that is) to be essential (s-n-schul) (as-in-school) to the creation (!!)(??) of good music (whatever that is)—but that's only in the long run.

Disco Tex & the Sex-O-Lettes lived in a context of abundance whereas the Dolls merely worked towards one. But, though Tex means more to me this week, the Dolls meant more to me back then. If the Dolls had easily achieved a sound to match their look, then maybe they wouldn't have done such a good job at desperation. Dolls' singer David Johansen had a memory of abundance—all those (at the time) forgotten trash songs from the pre-"rock" pre-respectable early '60s—and an ever-present context of paralysis which he (single-handjit, as my grandpa would say) was going to transform:

> *When everyone's gone to your house to shoot up in your room*
> *Most of them are beautiful, but so obsessed with gloom*
> *I ain't gonna be here, when they all get home*
> *They're always looking at me, they won't leave me alone*
> *I didn't come here looking for no fix, ah ah ah no*
> *I've been pounding the streets all night in the rain, baby*
> *Just a-lookin' for a kiss*
> *I need a fix and a kiss*

I like how after trying to draw a line between them and himself for the whole song, he howls out "I need a fix and a kiss," so he is one of them after all; that's one of those deft little flashes where—zing—he suddenly lets the whole world break in on him. (Of course without drug-references and death-references he'd just be maudlin, like on most of his solo shit.) And, as I suggested back in *WMS* #1, that's why the Dolls were a commercial failure—Johansen's vision was too all-inclusive to support the Punk Rock Lonely Hearts Club, or the Heavy Metal Lonely Hearts Club, or the Teenybopper Lonely Hearts Club, or the Marginal Artists And Intellectuals Lonely Hearts Club, or the New Romantics Club, or any other. (Punks didn't mind the fix; it was the kiss they couldn't handle.) J's vision is probably too all-inclusive for me, too, since now in my life the Dolls are a nostalgic memory trip while conventional haters like the Stooges, Pistols, and GN'R play interminably on my record player and in my head. (I don't know; if the Dolls had better rhythm, like Tex, maybe they'd be playing daily in my house like Stacey Q and Debbie Deb and Paris Grey—I don't know [author gets up and puts *Appetite For Destruction* on the tape player].) Anyway, the Dolls didn't get the world's actual glitter babes—the babes went to heavy metal and disco instead, because Johansen's vision was too all-inclusive for them, too.

But (as I said), I was "right," those Sex-O-Lettes are the glitter dolls, and history kind of bears it out (maybe, sort of)—I guess it's not totally irrelevant (well it is, actually) that the first Poison album starts with the same drum beat that starts "That Boy of Mine" by the Cover Girls (their worst song), which is the first drum beat in Martin Scorsese's *Mean Streets*, which is the beat that starts "Be My Baby." [Insert something about Ronnie Spector's boots—or Mary Weiss's.] I.e., self-conscious neo-disco "roots" and self-conscious neo-glitter "roots" turn out to be identical. The boots, on the other hand, probably aren't. "The music and fashion world have always lived together in a harmonious relationship. Now the Cover Girls have finally gotten these two worlds to form a blissful marriage through their music and fashion style." (Judy B. Hutson, liner notes to *Show Me*.)

It's less irrelevant that, in her lyrics, Donna Summer's "Hot Stuff" is the Dolls' "Looking for a Kiss" and that "Bad Girls" is, duh, "Bad Girl." (This is true even if Summer never heard the Dolls.) "You ask yourself who they are/Like everybody else they want to be a star." So Donna Summer saw it too and knew sex-o-lettes, hundreds of them, I'm sure, and saw them walking on Sunset (or Pete Bellotte or someone saw it and she sang it); and Poison, looking through David Johansen's eyes, saw them and wrote "Fallen Angel," their version of "Babylon" (though it doesn't come close). And their best song, "I Want Action," is a mild and cuddly version of "Looking for a Kiss." (Chuck Eddy compliments them like this: "Poison start out pretending to be the Dolls, come out like the *Bay City Rollers*.") The point here isn't to say that it all sounds the same or that it's all equally good (Donna was better being the slut than singing about her), but that it's the same girl, whether she's a glitter bunny, a disco babe, a metal bopper, or a punkette. And she's a guy too, and a rock critic. (Ref. to Robert Warshow: "The sociological critic says to us, in effect: It is not *I* who goes to see the movies; it is the audience. The aesthetic critic says: It is not the *movies* I go to see; it is art. . . . A man watches a movie, and the critic must acknowledge that he is that man.")

[Possible reference to bugalu hit "Bang Bang" in "Bad Girls."]

So, in his music, Poison singer Bret Michaels can't shoot sparks like the Sex-O-Lettes and doesn't moan and gasp like Donna and won't drag along with terror and pills and hate like the Dolls. His audience does.

Anyway, for that (the fix and the kiss) we've got Axl: "So come with me, don't ask me where cuz I don't know," which would be utter sentimental crap (it is, in fact), "Gimme Danger" reduced to a valentine, if it didn't spring from "Turn around bitch, I got a use for you," Axl's call for friction earlier in the same song. (Like I said, who knows where, contradictions are mere functional equipment, like drums and like amps. Like, "Do you think that you could make it with Frankenstein?" is no real question if you're smugly sure in advance that the answer is "Yes." Like "Welcome to the Jungle" works as poetry because Axl's there promising to eat you alive.) Well, who said "Gimme Danger" isn't sentimental crap too? And "Like a Rolling Stone"? And *Why Mildred Skis?*

(Axl = W. Axl Rose, lead singer of Guns N' Roses. Tia Mallette refers to him as "Waxxel.")

Alphabetical order: Will To Power "Say It's Gonna Rain," White Lion "When the Children Cry," Judy Torres "Come into My Arms," Stacey Q. "Don't Make a Fool of Yourself" and "The River," Siouxsie and the Banshees "Peek-A-Boo," S Express "Superfly Guy," Sequel "It's Not Too Late," Schoolly D "Smoke Some Kill," The Real Roxanne "Don't Even Feel It," Raze "Break 4 Love," Pussy Galore "Renegade!" Public Enemy "She Watch Channel Zero," Phuture "Slam!" L'Trimm "Cars with the Boom," the latin disco one where she goes "Don't move away from me" "Don't ever go away" and other phrases that start with "don't" (HELP! WHAT IS IT? WHO DID IT? I MUST HAVE THIS SONG), Latifah "Wrath of My Madness," Joan Jett "Riding with James Dean," The It "Gallimaufry Gallery," House Master Baldwin Featuring Paris Grey "Don't Lead Me," Guns N' Roses "Welcome to the Jungle," "Think about You," and "One in a Million," Girlschool "Fox on the Run," Giggles "Hot Spot," The Funky Worm "Hustle to the Music," Samantha Fox "I Wanna Have Some Fun," EPMD "Strictly Business," Desiré "Baby Be Mine," Def Leppard "Pour Some Sugar on Me," Debbie Deb "I'm Searchin'," Cynthia "Change on Me," Cover Girls "Inside Outside," Chip Chip "Never Say Goodbye," Neneh Cherry "Buffalo Stance," Rob Base and DJ E-Z Rock "It Takes Two," Bananarama "Nathan Jones," Bam-Bam "Where's Your Child," A Guy Called Gerald "Voodoo Ray."

Dolls and D. Tex may have actually (sorta) shared a social context—Monti Rock III is mentioned twice in *POPism The Warhol '60s* ("And bands—the Velvets played at the [Cheetah's] opening; I saw Monti Rock III dash by in a glittering gold outfit, looking, he said, for Joan Crawford"), he appeared once in the late '60s on Merv Griffin, dressed in a black cape and claiming that his coffin was parked out front waiting for him, and that's all I know about him. (Can any of you in the Mildred Skis Nation tell me more?)

But "context of abundance" refers to musical context (disco as a state of possibility rather than a form—disco as an imaginary context) rather than only to social surroundings. Dolls were stuck in hoary old rock 'n' roll as opposed to whorey disco.

I met a guy, his name was Tussy
Took him to my house and he ate my pussy

I met a Santa, his name was Clawdy
Took him to my house and he had my body

I met a girl, her name was Stacey
Took her home, she sat on my facey

I met a girl, her name was Dabs
Took her to the beach and I gave her crabs

I met a girl, her name was Deborah
Took her to my house et cetera

I met a girl, her name was Tizzy
Took her to my house and we were fizzy
(You know, you shake the ginger ale and it gets all fizzy)

I met a guy, his name was Forceps
Took him to my house and we discussed concepts

I met a guy, his name was Porny
I took him to my house one two three fourny

I met a guy, his name was Melvin
Took him to my house one two five twelve 'n'
thirteen

"Free lunch" and "context of abundance" may not seem particularly compatible—in context of abundance you're taking things for granted; e.g., you can say "Olé" and it's no big deal (if it had to be a big deal, it wouldn't be worth doing), so you're in a context that allows you to do a lot; whereas "free lunch" gives you something unexpected from somewhere unexpected, like in 1975 I turn on the punkless, dollsless radio and to my surprise hear the Sex-O-Lettes, who are real Dolls. But what each has in common is that you don't have to work for it. (That is, you the fan, sitting on your hammock or your yacht don't have to work for it. The poor performer may have to work very hard to make something no big deal. It's a matter of timing as well as context, timing within a context.) "Context of abundance" is your sandbox; "free lunch" is the fish that jumps in your lap. So I have to build a sandbox on my yacht; that's the task of modern music.

POPCORN TIME
Captain Hook had a funny hand
It worked on sea but not on land
Queen Marie had sexy pants
They worked in Spain but not in France

Schoolly D calls one of his songs "Another Poem"; fortunately, the world doesn't take him seriously, so he can call himself an artist and a poet without being contaminated by those categories. "Mr. Big Dick" does all the things that poetry does without being poetry:

It is my duty to fuck you cutie

Its particular context of abundance is the kid game (real big when I was eleven) of taking a "popular song" and giving it obscene or disgusting lyrics (e.g. "Maria, the girl with the pink diarrhea"), in which you can do whatever you want as long as it's gross, and none of it's a big deal because it's all crap anyway—and I like the way he links duty and fuck and the way "fuck you" slams into "cutie."

(definition of terms)   it = Mr. Big Dick (who do you think you
                    are?), Rodney Dangerfield, Olé

The Scene Is Now and De La Soul and Joe Bughead and Art Ensemble of Chicago could do it (say "Olé" or whatever) in an effort to be "open" to every-thing—it's a valiant effort, but that's the point, it's an effort, and even if it's not an effort for the performers themselves, it would be rendered so by the audience. "Wow! He's playing a trombone!" So the audience would *italicize* it (whichever "it"). Flavor Flav blurts out "beat is for Yoko Ono" for no reason in the middle of "Bring The Noise"; Jefferson Airplane mutters (irrelevantly) "armadillo" in the middle of "The Ballad of You & Me & Pooneil"—but "armadillo" is a weird *freak* thing (not an unremarkable thing) and "Yoko Ono" is the same thing actually but in "hip-hop." So "Yoko" and "'dillo" end up sticking out a bit like a sore thumb, like "look how weird we are, look what we can get away with," and lose their "tossed-off" quality. This makes them kind of arid (like an armadillo's natural habitat)—Airplane and Public Enemy fail to stay in or exist in or discover or create a context ("context of abundance") in which Armadillo and Yoko Ono can be taken for granted ("taken for granted").

Yet Airplane and Public Enemy almost pull it off—that's thanks to Jack Casady and Terminator X (respectively): The music moves so well and is so full of "stuff" without self-defeatingly pointing attention to the "stuff" that you can pretty much throw in whatever you want (Airplane = jarring (at the time) yet pretty feedback thing, unintentionally out-of-tune singing, soul bass playing à la Dyke And The Blazers that no one notices but that everyone dances to; Public Enemy = noise, political endorsements, image overload, lead rapper who sounds like he's reciting Dr. Seuss). It's really sad—the Airplane were one of my favorite bands, and if they'd only been able (or willing) to be identified with the hack commercial context—like being more or less equivalent to (though better than) the Ohio Express and the Strawberry Alarm Clark—then our Armadillo (cute little critter) could have walked into the song and rolled over and sunned itself and it would have been no big deal, just more bullshit (yummy yummy yummy armadillo on my tummy), instead of being (not just the Armadillo, but the whole song, all of Jefferson Airplaneishness, the fact that they did stuff like that) the oh-so-precious sore thumb that defined and justified the band as "freaks."

Someone could pretend that there's a hip new dance called the Yoko Ono, and everyone else would be embarrassed because each would think he or she's the only one who doesn't know the dance. ("Then he pulled his knife and did not throw, no/So come on all let's Yoko Ono/Cuz I'm a-livin' a-well and a-ready to dance/So come on girl let me show my romance.")

So you do the spank, and you do the laundry/Either one you want girl, the set-up's tawdry/So rock rock, and you don't stop. (A new dance called "the laundry.")

I'm trying to imagine an alternate universe in which non sequiturs and political interests and idiosyncrasies and _____ and _____ expand the context of abundance rather than destroy it—where the Airplane hadn't split off from the Ohio Express, where Public Enemy and De La Soul (etc.) won't—but they already have, I'm afraid—split off from L'Trimm and J.J. Fad (a world where you can have your armadillo and eat it too); a world where "armadillo" and "beat is for Yoko Ono" are unremarkable (like "Olé") and where "We are all outlaws in the eyes of America" and "Farrakhan's got a message that I think you ought to listen to" are a free lunch, just playfulness taken somewhere unexpected. (Rather than what they actually were/are: the deadly work of self-justification.)

"Politics lead him to the burning question of inadequate housing and inspires a unique innovation with almost all the lines rhyming." (Liner notes to the Mighty Sparrow *25th Anniversary* LP.)

Frank: "At least Marcus likes a group that says, 'Boredom is counterrevolutionary.'"

Leslie: "What group is that, the Ohio Express?"

Stacey Q on the unreality of social similarity (with an unnoticed—by her—threat to her own identity):

"I can't believe it. You like all the songs I like. You're not real."

The song starts with a whale of a clatter, like someone threw the pans downstairs. "She dropped her purse," Leslie explains.

But would it have been possible for the Ohio Express or Disco Tex (even) to sing "armadillo" and have it no big deal? Or for L'Trimm to sing "We like the cars, the cars that go boom/Yoko Ono goes boom" and have it taken for granted?

Boom is for Yoko Ono.

In some situations the world will tell you that you're weird, that you're a freak, any time you do something halfway interesting. The '60s "freak" thing was a defensive reaction, trying to turn a socially defined "weakness" into a strength.

My "PBS" metaphor is a remake of the Shangri-Las' "Out in the Streets." ("He used to act bad/Used to, but he quit it/It makes me so sad/Cuz I know that he did it for me.")

Assume that my "alternate universe" is pretty much like the real one, that it puts you in the normal situation of thinking that you're (1) insignificant, (2) abnormal (deep down), but (3) too normal (because you're not enough of an "individual"). I mean . . . I don't know . . . we're ourselves, we're like Paul Kantner and Flavor Flav (which we are), we don't have infinite wisdom or infinite ego strength, but nonetheless in this new universe we . . . we . . . well, what do we do? We create a slightly different social chemistry? We . . . ? (Who . . . ?)

Elvis was sighted in the most recent Real Roxanne video. He found the Real Roxanne in the desert and gave her a lift into Vegas, where—with great aplomb—she lost all her money. (So Elvis finally did something worthy of his so-called icon status—he gave R. a lift. Any cabbie could have done the same.)

I'd rather hear Funkadelic sampled on a Public Enemy record than listen to Funkadelic; I'd rather hear Public Enemy sampled on a Real Roxanne record than listen to Public Enemy. (Funkadelic's "Get Off Your Ass and Jam" becomes a "free lunch" on Public Enemy's "Bring the Noise"; the Real Roxanne is herself a context of abundance, so on her record Public Enemy and Rodney Dangerfield and almighty G-O-D become equal and no big deal.)

Future vitality of hip-hop probably depends on the almighty R-O-X-A-N-N-E (both of them) and apparent one shots like L'Trimm and shit like 2 Live Crew and "shit" like Tone Loc. If Public Enemy and De La Soul can exist within hip-hop without dominating it, then it (and maybe they) will be okay. If Roxanne Roxanne can absorb Public Enemy without being "influenced" by them, then she's on a roll. (Let's see, this needs some explanation for you hip-hop nonaficionados: 2 Live Crew want some pussy; L'Trimm are Tigra and Bunny and they like the boom (you've heard the cars go by with those giant woofers, with that loud "boom"); when Tone Loc gives his dog love potion #9, the loveable mutt humps his leg.)

The Mothers Of Invention and Funkadelic and Camper Van Beethoven and De La Soul throw so much "stuff" and shit at us that nothing in particular is a big deal, but, unlike the Sex-O-Lettes, none of them are in a context of abundance—the entire output of each constitutes a sore thumb. "Oh boy! look! we're not afraid to do this." (I can enjoy sore thumbs—I'd flush Zappa's oeuvre down the toilet, even the stuff I "like" (an occasional guitar part), but I'll buy the De La Soul record soon and like it (I anticipate). I mean, hip-hop might be turning itself into some utter ugh-thing, the new progressive rock, with De La Soul and PE and Eric B. & Rakim on the vanguard, but if you were De La Soul what would you or could you do differently? [A lot of things—ed.])

Schoolly D takes black militance and turns it into popcorn. (That's a compliment.)

Flavor Flav almost gets by as an all-purpose free lunch; Chuck D's role in history may be to take up a lot of space, like Ralph Kramden, and center everything on POLITICS and POETRY and ARTICULATE BLACK MEN and so draw attention away from his sidekick Norton (portrayed by Flavor), who's thus free to fuck around.

A free lunch is not a shock effect and not necessarily something that stands out from the context, but rather something that happens in addition to what is "officially going on"—like the psychedelic bridge in Guns N' Roses' "It's So Easy," like every time Michael Jackson does "Midnight Rambler."

Rob Ewan was fooling around with the bass line to "Anarchy in the U.K." by the Sex Pistols, and it reminded him of "Then He Kissed Me" by the Crystals.

(The concept "free lunch" has nothing to do with "suppressed matter" (e.g. "that which is suppressed in the dominant discourse"), which is work and I'll let puritans waste their time on it.)

A free lunch can be intended and heavily remarked upon (though it often isn't) as long as it's generally seen as either extraneous or (if it unexpectedly becomes central) unanticipated. A "sleeper" hit is a free lunch, but "follow up" isn't.

Just now I was listening to "Mashed Potato Time" by the Crystals and I realized I was hungry, so I got a leftover potato from the refrigerator. Yummy with ketchup.

There are two types of free lunch:

(1) Anyway Lunch: What the music does in addition. The music (incl. hairdos, promo kits, the lead singer's hairy chest, etc.) does things and does things anyway, too. (Richard Meltzer, *Aesthetics of Rock*, p. 7, "So *my* whole summation does whatever it does and does anyway too, but watch the anyway level.")

(2) Soundtrack Lunch: What the audience adds or does (or might do) with or to or even instead of the "music," excluding of course what the audience is expected to do or is officially obviously doing such as dancing or drowning it out with screams or giving it to your sister as a Halloween present. (Meltzer again, pp 147-148, "I once asked filmmaker Peter Kubelka if he realized that one of his films, which consisted of black frames and white frames and only sporadic noises, actually had the loudest implicit sound track of all his films, since it summoned quite a bit of audience laughter and endure-the-tedium chatter and get-away-from-it-door-opening at the exits. . . . All films have an implicit sound track in addition to their own . . .") (Also see Manny Farber's *Negative Space*.)

Axl Rose: "People have an awful lot of misconceptions about Guns N' Roses. What's more, they're right!" (*Blast!*, April 1989.)

There's no real boundary between the two lunches—Soundtrack Lunch just moves you farther away from the "song" or "show" or "that goddamn radio" (away from the ostensible center of attention); it really all depends on where you think you lifted your meal from, the song or the world around it, no big difference.

Simon Frith (*Music For Pleasure*, p. 91): "What's 'good' here usually is described by its straight musical elements (a haunting tune, etc.), but what matters is a tone of voice: suddenly there's this stranger, involved in a different conversation altogether, talking about you." (The "outsider" lunch.)

I didn't hear *Highway 61 Revisited* until 1970. No one had told me that Dylan was a nihilist. (The "nihilist" lunch. The "no-one-told-me" lunch. The "disparity-between-hero-and-his-pedestal" lunch.)

A friend of mine was real disturbed by punk rock (in 1977) until he heard some of it. "Oh, I get it," he said, "the Kinks." (The "oh-I-get-it" lunch.)

When Meltzer (*Autobiography*) was in seventh grade, kids would sing "I found my thrill on top of Miss Grill" and "I found my thrill on Miss Grill's hills." (Miss Grill was a teacher.)

J.J. Fad's "Anotha Ho" partakes of the same context of abundance as Schoolly D's "Mr. Big Dick," the take-a-song-and-give-it-dirty-words game (they're singing the melody to "Bingo," not "Old McDonald" as you'd expect):

Howie Tee he had an MC
And Roxanne was her name-o
E-I-E-I-ho
E-I-E-I-ho
This ain't G.I. Joe
And that tramp has to go, hit it

It's funny because the singer inserts "ho" in this nonchalant, almost professional voice, like she's a file clerk. . . . ("Ho" is the Lithuanian word for "prostitute.")

Several years ago I would stick the word "amoeba" into songs like "You've lost that amoeba feeling." It was very funny. Maybe it wasn't. Back in the '70s a little boy I knew sang "Shake shake shake, shake shake shake, shake your booty, shake Jim's roody" for an hour or two. He thought it was funny. (Jim was his brother.) J.J. Fad got their song from the Queen classic:

Bom bom bom, anotha ho bites the dust

But radio stations turned the record over and made the flip side, "Supersonic," into the hit—because of the bass sound, I thought, and didn't understand. But then I got it (Leslie's younger sister and younger sister's friend were walking along singing "Supersonic"): J.J. Fad had finished "Anotha Ho" for you, so it was nice and fun (context of abundance, yeah yeah yeah) but also done, game was over, unless you applied it to another song. "Supersonic," on the other hand, was the boiler plate, kind of came with instructions, showed you how to cook your own lunch with it. "S is for super, U is for unique, P is for perfection . . ." So the two girls were walking along singing their own version of "Supersonic": "S is for shitfaced, U is for ugly, P is for pencil pecker . . ."

In the early stages of her career, Madonna's clothes were the visual version of this sort of children's song. [Insert essay on how fans ran variations on the Madonna model. Use my girlfriend as an example.]

Melle Mel's stickup-kid rap in G. Flash & Furious Five's "Superrappin'" is a free lunch, and so are the food references in Sugarhill Gang's "Rapper's Delight"; the songs could just as easily not have them. Though maybe at the time, rather than being free lunches, they were no big deal, just there in the context of abundance; in retrospect they seem like a free lunch because most current rap songs are so "focused," having lost the ability to be irrelevant. (The Fat Boys' food references are not free lunch; nor is Melle Mel's rap when it gets regurgitated at half speed and in close-up as the centerpiece of "The Message.")

Schoolly D's a free lunch a lot of the time because his music has flute and shit or is it ocarina and no one notices, and because his lyrics wander so that the focus becomes as irrelevant as his extraneous stuff. Like, he starts off about politics or sex but then it's about the Brady Bunch or his mom, so (like I said before) the politics are popcorn.

In the context of all the yukking it up he's doing, the ominous bass and dissonant horns in "Mr. Big Dick" are garnish. In the context of ominous bass and dissonant horns, the yukking it up in "Mr. Big Dick" is gravy.

Toots And The Maytals' "Revival Reggae" is the best of many unintentional attempts within reggae to sound like Slade ("Revival Reggae" has a rhythm very close to Slade's "I Won't Let It 'Appen Agen") or, more accurately, attempts to sound like Slade is going to sound (because "Revival Reggae" came out around 1970 and Slade didn't really sound like that until 1972).

Slade's stuff c. 1972–1973 is now (I mean now, still, in 1989) the best through-and-through free lunch within "rock." For instance, their status in the '80s as revered "founding fathers" of heavy metal (whatever that is) makes their actual music extraneous since (1) it was not considered metal at the time of its release, at least not in America, (2) it has had no impact or influence on metal except for a few nods in the direction of "glam vocals" and "Noddy shrieks" recently by Kix and Girlschool, except that (3) its actual use as a source of Pretty Pop Melodies by nerf-metal bands like Britny Fox and Quiet Riot is the influence of an entirely "nonmetal" aspect (whatever that is).

(Since heavy metal has nothing to do with heavy metal, perhaps you could call the whole genre a free lunch, but that opens up a can of noodles that I don't want to deal with right now.)

"C'mon headbangers, feel the noize! Bang your heads and let's go crazy!" was the kind of typical moronic gesture vocalist Kevin Dubrow would've squawked for Quiet Riot back in 1983. . . . It seemed to give this awful impression to those who didn't understand metal.

So writes Pat Prince in *Powerline*, May 1989. Gee Pat, you wouldn't want metal to give a bad impression, would you?

I was anxious to tell [drummer Frankie Banali] how happy I was that all the Bang Your Head, Cum On Mama, we're all crazy now, feel the noize, girls rock your boys-Metal Health bullshit that Dubrow pushed on us for years is gone for good.

(Slade singer Noddy Holder's origination of "Janis-vocals-by-a-man" and "British-accent-in-loud-hard-rock-songs" (rather than in novelty songs), which were done subsequently by Axl Rose and Johnny Rotten respectively, and Slade's use of the march-beat stomp, done subsequently by the Pistols and the Clash, might make those elements mere "precursors" rather than free lunch, but since almost no one cares or knows about this anymore or even in the first place, I think they get to remain on the menu. The "no-one-told-me" lunch. Though now I've told you.)

Slade is one of the few immensely popular bands to make a major change in the rhythm of music and have no one notice it (very few people noticed it) and no one be influenced by it. Okay, you know those New Orleans hits from the early '60s by Chris Kenner, Ernie K. Doe, Willie Harper, the Showmen, Benny Spellman, and so on, how they have this real light touch, how the beat dances around eighth notes, not quarter notes? (How in Jamaica the New Orleans back beat became the emphasized off beat of ska?) (This is just an "abstract" way of talking about how the rhythm feels to me—you can call any 4/4 rhythm an 8/8 or 12/8 if you want to. Hell, rockabillies loved doing the 40-yard dash through eighth notes, but I don't think they had it confidently and implicitly *there* to dance around, they were forcing it—that was one of the exciting things about them, they really pushed.) Well, Slade learned those beats (maybe via rockabilly, maybe via Jamaica, maybe via New Orleans, I don't know), learned to dance with them rather than bang them—while at the same time using them to Bang your heads, let's go crazee, feel the noize, girls rock the boys. Hard rock. Heavy, man.

(Yeah, the Yardbirds and Kinks in their "rave-ups" originated the unison headbang on the eighth note, which was copied by the garage punks and which Maureen Tucker originated several years later with the Velvets and which the "Punk-Rock Movement" originated about ten years after that, but that's just kind of taking the 4/4 and filling it in (that's what it feels like to me). See "They were forcing it, the rockabillies," in the previous paragraph.)

Other Slade innovations that had no subsequent effect on anyone important and so remain uncontaminated: Slade's music-hall chug (which may have Afro-Caribbean roots or are they polka?); reverb added to crucial shouts and handclaps to make them "stand out" so the audience will "join in," which could be another Jamaican "influence"; the violin hoe-down (?) in "Coz I Luv You"; the use of "irrelevant" quotation marks in this article; the idiosyncratic spelling of "cuz"; the way they didn't call attention to any of this, so it's like "Look, we're doing the same old thing (and it happens to be different, if you're interested)" (and no one was), so all bands that have "copied" Slade ignored most of it and put the beat back into clomp clomp 4/4 backbeat clomp. (Compare it to the Clash, who advertised it in lights every time they did something "rhythmic.")

If the Sex Pistols had come along in '65 they wouldn't have been generically distinguishable from the 4 Seasons or Barry McGuire or the Buckinghams. (The 4 Seasons sang in falsetto; Barry McGuire pretended to be significant and sang about nuclear war; the Buckinghams had a pop hit that was so hack-normal and full of mid-'60s touches (organ) that ten years later it was considered punk.)

1964—Dylan's unsuccessful free-lunch move: "Mel, station two wants another side of cole slaw. Make that two sides of cole slaw and another side of Bob Dylan."

Of course, audiences can screw things up badly, cancel a potential free lunch—a performer does something interesting and the fans miss it, only hear what they want to hear. (This is the Soundtrack Lunch in reverse.)

Something can have all the characteristics of a free lunch except for the fact that you don't like it. Then it's a stomach cramp.

Sociological gobbledygook-type digression: Whether or not something is a free lunch for you will depend on what you've been led to believe is going on, what you expect will be going on (what you hope or fear will be going on?), and what you can get away with saying about it. This makes it "personal" in the social sense rather than the personal sense; that is, it doesn't have to do specifically (or only) with what you feel but more with where you live and what time of day it is, i.e. with "feelings" in the social world rather than merely in the nervous system; it's "personal" because it has to do with other persons; because there's no social methodology for finally resolving "differences of opinion"; because to some extent you can disagree with other people without being called insane. (In fact, differences of opinion are cherished, as are conflicts arising from the differences of opinion.) A judgment is "personal" if it has the potential to put you in unchangeable contrast with other people. So it's other persons who get to decide when something is personal.

GN'R are a free lunch because they're a rock band that plays rock (you know, the world of rock music is about the last place I expect to hear rock).

On their first three LPs (especially the "hot" American pressings), back when they were considered "the worst sort of noise" by people who liked "music," the Beatles put a hectic clatter around the edge of their music that aspired to the sound achieved years later (due to the usual shit live "recording") on the Heartbreakers' *Live At Max's* LP.

In normal bad poetry you take something and compare it to a conventional poetic thing like "the clouds" or "the seashore" or "diamonds" or "bluest skies." E.g., her eyes shined like emeralds, her gold fillings sparkled like diamonds, her hair was like stormy weather. But you can reverse the process; in the late '60s, Kenneth Koch was teaching children from the Lower East Side to write poetry (see his books *Wishes, Lies, and Dreams* and *Rose Where Did You Get That Red*), and one of them, Emilia Scifo, wrote:

Under the sea is like Times Square

Emilia's reversed things by taking the conventional, exotic poetry image—"the sea"—and comparing it to something vivid and close at hand. This is a free lunch—you thought you'd never ever again get anything out of this dead part of poetry, out of "the sea," but all of a sudden it's interesting again, it's like Times Square.

R.E.M. is like the Byrds, but the Byrds aren't like R.E.M. The Byrds are like Will To Power. (In my New York days, I sent John Wójtowicz my drawing of "Dinosaur Eating Spaghetti Western" as a Christmas card, and in return he left this message on my phone machine: "Frank, there's avant garde and then there's just plain weird." There's avant garde and then there's Will To Power.)

Some guy is hounding this woman almost to the point of psychopathology—calling up ten times a day to ask her out, threatening to kill her boyfriend, being in love with her. Finally, he stops. Then after a few months he calls up again to invite her out to lunch. "This isn't going to be weird, is it?" she asks him.

Gogheeboo is like joojoobug, but joojoobug isn't like gogheeboo. Joojoobug is like berniebeer. (There's avant garde and then there's just plain berniebeer.)

1965: Bob Dylan is like Times Square.

1962 and 1963: "A Hard Rain's A Gonna Fall" and "The Lonesome Death Of Hattie Carroll" are Bob Dylan's original attempts to resemble the mambo. In Cuba in the '30s, when everyone was adding horn parts, Arsenio Rodriguez (I'm told) took the call-and-response section at the end of the *son* and scored the horns in the rhythms of Yuka drum parts, increased the polyrhythms. (Yuka is a Bantu musical form that survived in Cuba, I think. I don't know what I'm talking about; I took a course once.) Arcano and Cachao did something similarly polyrhythmic to the call-and-response section at the end of the *danzon*. The call-and-response section tended to grow and grow at the expense of the other sections. James Brown did something similar in the early '60s, took a song ("I Lost Someone," "Prisoner Of Love") and threw a church-derived call-and-response vamp into it; the call and response grew and grew on his records and dominated his live show; finally (on some stuff) he abandoned the "song" form altogether and just did the vamp, and put in new polyrhythms (derived from Caribbean rhythms but jammed tight between the measure bars) to form his characteristically tense North American funk. And Dylan did something analogous (though without the focus on polyrhythm, so it really doesn't have much to do with mambo or funk, does it?): He had all these words he wanted to put in, so to get them in he'd take a sung line and just vamp on it, adding line upon line of words, rather than getting on with the song. (And it gets real tense, you're ready to scream while you're waiting for the tune to resolve.) He'd also use vocal as drone, rhyme as drone, word-repetition as drone, so you had a blues drone stuck in the middle of a folk song:

Who carried the dishes and took out the garbage
And never sat once at the head of the table
And didn't even talk to the people at the table
Who just cleaned up all the food from the table
And emptied the ashtrays on a whole other level

Finally he sold out and went electric and on "Subterranean Homesick Blues" he got rid of song altogether and just did the vamp (and the drone and the repetition).

Yardbirds did sort of the same thing at the same time with those rave-up drones (beat-your-head-into-the-wall things) that tended to take over their songs—then some garagers took the rave-up drone and added the Dylan vocal drone, and you get the Velvets.

("Lonesome Death Of Hattie Carroll" was a warm-up for "Subterranean Homesick Blues" in another way—Dylan had been kept from the table, he'd been hit, like Hattie Carroll (emotionally, anyway), but in 1963 he needed a Hattie Carroll to act it out for him, while in 1965 he said, "Look out, kid, you're gonna get hit," and he was that kid.)

The "retrospective" lunch, which I guess is the "no-one-told-me" lunch all over again: "Things" that were no big deal in the context of abundance in 1966 or 1975 or 199_ appear in retrospect, when you go back and discover them, to be anomalies and or incongruities, hence free food. That's because the present always has such a *thin* image of the past. On the other hand, the reverse happens too: What was initially anomalous or shocking or incongruous or sore thumb or free lunch in the density and confusion of the actual 1966 (or 194_) as it was originally lived is all lost in our present-day taking for granted or appreciation of the song-type artifact that has had the bad or good luck to "last." Unless it manages somehow to pull along its own density, the poor song-thing sounds so thin; unless a good history writer restores it to its original density, or we add our own density to it (projection, a.k.a. the "soundtrack" lunch), or we add it to our own density—like a video maker inserts Elvis into the Real Roxanne's density.

In 1966 punk was just one thing among many—one thing indistinguishable among many—e.g., "96 Tears" is a novelty song or teenybopper song or commercial hack song or version 12 of "Wooly Bully" or Tex Mex. "Get Me to the World on Time" was a teenie weenie "love song" masquerading as a "psychedelic" song, and the fact that it also used, as a commercial ploy or hook, a hard hard sound for beating up on people . . . well, that was just another thing. A band segues from "Get Together" to "Hey Joe" and it's natural. Or from "I'm a Believer" to "Steppin' Stone." In the context of abundance, stuff like "Under My Thumb" and "You Can't Do That" could just be more "love" songs (you-broke-my-heart songs) or simultaneously they could jump you suddenly as hate songs, stand out by contrast. The Seeds and the Happenings could run along as the putative same thing, same genre; at the same time "Pushin' Too Hard" smacked you (smacked me, anyway) extra hard because there chugging along next to it was lame old "See You in September." (It also smacked me with relief; like, "Thank God, they're not playing 'See You In September.'")

In the late '70s, Elvis Costello made hatred precious; Sham 69 and Chelsea and several million hardcore bands made anger religious. So punk-rock moves became common within "punk" and "postpunk" but were never taken for granted, never just popped up, never lived and breathed.

The question "How is the weather?" in the Turtles' "Happy Together" was an anomaly, is an anomaly, always will be an anomaly.

The Premiers: "Has anybody seen Kosher Pickle Harry?" Shouts of "No." "If you see him, tell him that Herbert is looking for him." Shouts of "Who's Herbert?" and yelling and cheering.

Damaged people leaping into playfulness may be *better* than Disco Tex—e.g., though I wouldn't rank "Bring the Noise" with "I Wanna Dance wit' Choo," it's not even close, perhaps I'd prefer (though not today) Dylan's "Subterranean Homesick Blues" and "Tombstone Blues" to anything by the Sex-O-Lettes—but then, even if *he* couldn't take his own wordplay for granted, Dylan was able to jump into a context where wordplay was taken for granted—he was able to jump into the world of Little Richard and the Premiers and Napoleon XIV and the Shirelles and "She Loves You" and "Wooly Bully."

The "sore thumb" can be effective. Ellen Willis, in *The Rolling Stone Illustrated History of Rock & Roll*:

> *Joplin's metamorphosis from the ugly duckling of Port Arthur to the peacock of Haight Ashbury meant, among other things, that a woman who was not conventionally pretty, who had acne and an intermittent weight problem and hair that stuck out, could not only invent her own beauty (just as she invented her wonderful sleazofreak costumes) out of sheer energy, soul, sweetness, arrogance, and a sense of humor, but have that beauty appreciated.*

But "sore thumb" usually only works in the short run—freak costumes began as something flashy and ended up a few years later as army jackets and jeans and a basic pseudoprole (or real-prole) fear of standing out or "dressing up." From sore thumb to bore thumb.

Punk rock is one of the few musics to also thrive in a context of nonabundance. To thrive as a sore thumb. E.g., early-to-mid-'70s (my favorite period for punk rock, actually): Stooges, Dolls, Slade, Electric Eels, Pere Ubu, the Sex Pistols. I can even imagine (I wasn't there) Ubu's version of "Pushin' Too Hard," which isn't that good, having more of an impact on an audience in 1975 than the Seeds' original had in 1966. Or, for that matter—I was there!—the garage hits ("96 Tears" and all that) sounding more virulent upon rediscovery in the early '70s than they had originally. I remember getting excited by some shitty Suzi Quatro song ("48 Crash"?) just because it seemed potentially trashy and bubblegum and garagey—and by that stupid Deep Purple song, the one where the guy says nobody better touch his girl/his car ["Highway Star"], because I heard in it some semblance of "aggression." Punk was normal—a "feature" or "free lunch" or "gravy"—and unnamed (no need for one) in pop music c. 1966. The mid-'60s was punk at its most effortless and uninhibited; virulence showed up all over, who could predict where, without being fully comprehended and without being noted. (The "nihilist" lunch.) By 1972, punk (along with teenybop) had been thrown out of "rock" altogether and suppressed from memory and from the definition of "the Sixties." Like, 1965-1966 was the most searing and hateful time in my life, and it had a soundtrack to match, but see if any "'60s" revivalists celebrate the "era" as the gushing well of despair and nihilism that it was. (Though it was probably no worse than the 1890s or any other decade—I'm talking about "expression within pop music" here.) Anyway, Stooges and crew made it twice as intense by reviving all that forgotten slime and aggression, by working at it rather than lifting it free from the smorgasbord.

So, I don't know if my writing will do better (I mean, be better) in a context of abundance, but I'm pretty sure I can't last creatively (any more than Iggy did, or Janis) without abundance and free lunch. I'm sure it would read better in a context of abundance. *WMS* and *The Village Voice* and *Spin* and *Swellsville* aren't that context. The Stooges and Dolls were nourished by a memory of abundance—I am too, and by partaking of disco's ("disco's") semiabundance—but I'm wondering if we can create a word-type of abundance, if it's possible to expand the tone of voice. The letters page in the Australian *Smash Hits* is the most uninhibited thing going now (even though there are a mess of limitations—maybe *because* there are a mess of limitations—like they don't print "fuck" and I don't know what else), probably because everyone is posing and lying and fooling around and writing the silliest happy benign nonsense about how isolated and angry and desperate and teenage they are. I'd stick out like a sore thumb in *Smash Hits*—underlying all three *Smash Hits* (Britain, USA, Australia) is the fact that, since no one's allowed to say much that's analytic, the writers just "fool around" to keep from getting bored and to impart a sense of "charm." What if *Smash Hits* printed Simon Frith and it was no big deal? Like *Creem* in the early '70s, which created its own context of miniabundance. I guess what I need is a magazine with a lot of bright colors.

In "Rock! Rock! (Till You Drop)," Def Leppard work their way up through these deadly notes, climb the highest pomp, then boogie in VERY SLOW MOTION to the depths of the deepest . . . to the draggy deeps, to the . . . (some journeys should never be contemplated, let alone undertaken; some SENTENCES should never be undertaken, for instance this one) . . . then finally arrive gloriously back in ho-hum "pop," their journey having prepared them for this simple truth:

Rock rock googgie pop

Why Mildred Skis, a.k.a. *Wear Mildred Sheets*, a.k.a. *Why Music Sucks #5*, 1989

CHAPTER 14

KUNG-FU FIGHTING

"Does one have to go out dancing—participate in the activity and culture of disco—in order to write well about it? Are YOU a good dancer?"

I'd make your question plural: not *the* activity and culture but the *activities* and *cultures*. Say that someone who went regularly to Studio 54 is in the culture of disco. All right, well, what about the teenager in Fort Collins who's only read about it and heard the records but decides to walk into his high school with the dress and attitude of disco—as he's imagined it—and maybe gets the shit pounded out of him? Maybe he knows something about the music—its risks and possibilities—that the authentic club guy safe in New York bohemia doesn't know. Or what about my ex-wife Leslie, who as a fifth grader back in Alexandria, Virginia, was terrorized by black kids in the hallways who'd call her "Lesby" and sing "Kung Fu Fighting" while doing martial arts kicks that came within inches of smashing her face? Or what about a friend's little kids who changed Debbie Deb's "You've got the music, here's your chance" to "you've got the music IN YOUR PANTS"? (I've seen Debbie Deb perform, by the way, and I'm sure she'd *love* the in-your-pants version.) Or what about the kids' mom? When I asked her once to recommend some History Of Art books, she mentioned Gombrich and Jansen but thought that they were too dry and that I'd prefer Sister Wendy—you know, the nun who does the art analysis on PBS—because Sister Wendy was "more disco." Isn't this all the "culture," too?

But my relation to disco is like Brian Wilson's relation to the beach: I almost never go to dance clubs, so a lot of my writing on the subject is—you know—a work of the imagination. The sort of "disco" I went to back in the day was more likely to have a jukebox than a disc jockey. My favorite dancing has usually been in people's living rooms. And in my room I'll use "dance" music as background for almost anything: crossword puzzles, napping, doing the dishes. (I once changed an LL Kool J lyric to "You're the type of guy who gets suspicious/I'm the type of guy who always does the dishes.") Really, my only claim to disco authenticity—other than having read Sister Wendy's analysis of the pre-Raphaelites—is the one time I saw Debbie Deb.

"Writing About Dancing: Disco Critics Survey," *rockcritics.com*, March 2001

CHAPTER 15

DANGER ON THE DANCE FLOOR

SCOTT: Okay, well here's a fairly obvious question for you—excuse me, I'm just choking on a chip here [clears throat]—you stated in the first issue of *Why Music Sucks* that, "Music in the '80s is merely much worse than music in any other decade in the memory of sound recording." I have a twofold question here. First of all, how serious were you about that? And secondly, in hindsight do you still think that's true?

FRANK: I was absolutely serious. And in hindsight I think I was wrong. But not *utterly* wrong. There was a lot about '80s music that I wasn't liking that I later came to appreciate, but I think my critique of the music I wasn't liking was really a good, smart, interesting critique, and basically it's a critique of alternative rock, which is not the worst music ever made, but given its place in the hearts of postgraduate, intellectualized thinkers, it's really not that good. But there was a lot of other music that either I wasn't listening to or I wasn't getting. I didn't think much of what I would call British haircut pop; it's *not* my music, but I think there's just a lot more going on than I'd realized. And the same for the stuff I call haircut metal—yeah, haircut music in general [laughs], I definitely underestimated haircut music.

SCOTT: Is that an influence of Chuck Eddy's?

FRANK: Yeah, he taught me to like it. I'd say the haircut metal's an influence of Chuck's and the haircut pop's an influence of Rob Sheffield's. But I mean, it isn't so much that they wrote arguments that persuaded me, it's just that they wrote about it in ways that made demands that I actually listen to it, and pay attention to it, and subject myself to it.

SCOTT: Did you have any reaction in, say, 1982 to ABC or something like that? Did you despise that sort of stuff or did it just not . . .

FRANK: Oh no, no, it was more like a ho-hum response, thinking like, here's Roxy Music, and in some ways it's not as bad as Roxy was and in some ways it's not as good as Roxy was, meaning that it didn't have Roxy's interesting rough edges and it also didn't have Roxy's godawfulness. My basic feeling was that, it's therefore less interesting, it's sort of diluted Roxy Music, whereas now I can sort of get a sense of—not necessarily from ABC, but they're a part of it—a kind of a *world* there that was probably a lot more interesting than Roxy Music. You know, Roxy Music in their rhythm was sort of doing old soul, actually, and to me I was sort of thinking, well if you want a rock band that uses soul, Roxy Music is sort of pasting soul on underneath what they were doing, whereas the old Jefferson Airplane actually integrated soul into what they were doing. I don't think a lot of people hear that in the Jefferson Airplane, but their rhythm and their bass playing was actually taken very much from soul music. To me the Airplane was—I hate to use this clichéd word, but I think it actually applies—they were much more organic, whereas Roxy Music was like—the voice was one idea, the noise was another, the rhythm was a third idea, and you put all those ideas together. The Jefferson Airplane, though, weren't these ideas pasted together, they were actually the sentence that would happen if someone was talking.

SCOTT: But isn't that naturally kind of true of British pop in general, the fact that it's not its own music?

FRANK: Actually, I kind of don't think so. I think that's what people tend to say about British pop—and it's funny, I kind of think that about Elvis Costello too, what I said about Roxy Music—but I think that, say, Joy Division and the Human League, whatever you think of them, I wouldn't say they were just doing the idea, I think they were . . . I mean, I think ideas are good things [laughs], it's just like, I don't want the idea *instead* of the music, I want the idea to come with the music, to enrich the music, to be carried by the music. In Roxy Music, the idea was taking precedence. The Stones and the Animals are British music, and someone could say, oh gee, Mick Jagger was singing in a very stylized way, but to me *every*one is singing in a stylized way, it's called their *style*. And the point is, it seemed to me that people like Bryan Ferry, who may be the worst offender—I actually wrote this to Simon Frith, though I have a feeling he really adores Bryan Ferry—I said I thought that David Bowie and Bryan Ferry were to style as Simon & Garfunkel were to poetry. Paul Simon would use poetic language, back in his old days, poetic language that sort of signified poetry, and to me it was like Bowie and Roxy—and actually I way prefer Bowie, he actually really moved me a lot—but there was still the sense of which, there was just total bullshit, where on top of it Bowie was saying, "Look! We're being artificial; that means we're being stylish," and my feeling was kind of like, so what? To what effect, what does it mean? It was like they were the *idea* of a style, but it wasn't a style you lived with, and I guess for some people that was the appeal—yes, it was a style that you *put on*. But ultimately there wasn't that much of a musical payoff.

SCOTT: See I guess that's where I would differ. To me those bands do really rock, Bowie probably more often than Roxy Music, though Roxy Music—I kind of feel clichéd saying it—probably rocked a little harder than Bowie. So to me that's the payoff. I don't know, I heard that stuff as a kid, so I have a completely different impression of it. That was, in a lot of ways—apart from the Stones and the Doors and all that stuff—that was my first real rock 'n' roll. I understand that whole idea about it's all a style, there's no payoff with the style, if that's what you're saying, but I listen to the records and I don't hear that.

FRANK: Well, obviously I like Bowie a lot more. And I think in some ways that some of Bowie's flaws sort of worked with each other to come out as virtues. The image that people have of Bowie is, well, he's very smart, but he's cold. Whereas my opinion is just the opposite. To me, I think he's really naive and sentimental—I wouldn't necessarily say he's stupid—but I think he's really naive and sentimental and really passionate.

SCOTT: I totally agree with that.

FRANK: But this is something I sort of get approaching it through his lyrics. I'm gonna probably misquote this but it's that one on Ziggy Stardust where, "Someone came home to do this thing, someone came home to starve, I can make it all worthwhile as a rock and roll star." ["Tony went to fight in Belfast, Rudi stayed at home to starve, I can make it all worthwhile as a rock and roll star."] I think he *absolutely* believed that. There's a sense in which a lot of his pseudointellectualism and, like, bad poetry and all that . . .

SCOTT: The alien stuff . . .

FRANK: Yeah, in a sense I would say those are flaws, but without those flaws you would have this embarrassingly sentimental guy who wants to save the children, which is exactly what I think he was. [laughs] And because he had all this pseudointellectual, pseudostyle and stuff—because in a sense his voice wasn't really a flexible voice so he kind of played up his coldness and did all this sci-fi stuff and all that—there's a sense in which, instead of having him be Harry Chapin, you know, he actually ended up being a lot better. But also, I kind of agree with him, what he was trying to do with the style, though I think the Dolls did it more effectively for me, and later on Madonna did it more effectively too, and the message was really clear: What I was describing with bands like Mofungo and V-Effect, they were taking scraps of sound from anywhere and playing with it. For Bowie it was like you could take a *style* from anywhere and play with it, and then you have style. With Madonna, it was a three-chord style that anyone could play—or maybe it was a three-chord *glamour* that anyone could play. I really *loved* Bowie as a human being—actually, I don't know how I'd feel if I met him—but I mean, I love his intentions. I guess for me I was *reading* his intentions, whereas with the Dolls I wasn't just reading them, I was feeling them. To me the Dolls wrote better songs with better words.

SCOTT: I actually like the new Bowie song ["Little Wonder"] for some reason.

FRANK: I don't think I've heard it.

SCOTT: It's actually—I mean, he's been terrible for years, but he's actually kind of written a pretty song, and people I work with are kind of going gaga over it 'cause it's got this jungle stuff, and that's all kind of interesting, but it's just a pretty song, which he hasn't done in a *long* time.

FRANK: Also, I want to say that when *Aladdin Sane* came out I actually remember writing a friend of mine saying Bowie's finally made himself one of the greats. So he definitely pulled me across. Of course, that was the album where he sounded most like the Stones also, so that probably has to do with why I liked it, and it's definitely the one where he was dealing the most with nihilism and evil and stuff like that.

SCOTT: Except for maybe *Diamond Dogs*, which is kind of a terrible album of his. So, for the sake of the millions of *Popped* readers out there who've never seen an issue of *Why Music Sucks*, I wanted to ask you about a few of the terms you brought up a lot in the early issues.

FRANK: Okay, but I didn't quite finish answering your last one, and I'll try and keep it brief.

SCOTT: Okay, go for it.

FRANK: About why [pause] . . .

SCOTT: I forget what the question was . . .

FRANK: Do I still think that '80s music—how does it stand in the history of music? I actually think talking about the specific artists, like Bowie, was more interesting. I'm realizing that, gee, I sound like a raving Bowie fan [laughs], which I guess I am. What I was liking from the '80s, I loved very early 1980s, I'd almost call it like this postdisco; it was basically disco that wasn't being called disco anymore, it was kind of fuzzier and funkier, stuff like—I don't even remember the names of the bands—Yarbrough & Peoples, S.O.S. Band, and then New York was playing a lot of stuff which I thought was even better than that, but was more obscure, Taana Gardner's "Heartbeat," which I'm gonna tape for you sometime.

SCOTT: Yeah, I've still never heard that song.

FRANK: Stuff like that, plus the early hip-hop, when it was still like a bunch of kids trying to top each other and it was just fabulous, and they were willing to take rhythms from everywhere, but not even make a big thing out of it. So there was stuff going on that was really good, but when I'd written that sentence, I'd almost heard nothing of what was dubbed variously "freestyle" or "Latin hip-hop," "Latin freeze," "Miami mint," "Miami sound," you know, whatever you want to call it—and of course that actually describes a bunch of different sounds. And to me that was absolutely the '80s great contribution to music, more than anything. You know, I just kind of wanted to throw that in there for various reasons, but also, I wouldn't say my *disappointment* with alternative rock has changed—basically, I was an alternative rocker, that's the reason I was playing stuff based on the Velvet Underground and the Fall, plus whatever else you wanted to throw in the kitchen sink. And essentially, as the music went on for a while, it really did seem to become not just musically worse—bands like the Troggs and the Kingsmen sound like masters, at least rhythmically, compared to the average alternative-rock band—but there was something where, the thing I complained about in Roxy, you could just say in spades about a lot of other bands. But you know, I don't wanna go into what I don't like *that* much, because I kind of think music of the '90s is a lot worse, but it doesn't bother me because music always regenerates itself. And I don't even know what music I'm talking about when I say the music of the '90s is worse, and it might just be that I'm pretty broke now so I'm just not buying a lot, so who knows what's there? And sometimes when you're hearing just a little bit, you don't get it. As for the terms in *Why Music Sucks*, umm . . .

SCOTT: Well, let me sideline things a bit now. You were talking about hip-hop. Do you agree with Chuck—this might even have been something you had written or suggested—that hip-hop had really gone downhill in '81, '82? Chuck once said "The Message" is where rap died.

FRANK: Well I wouldn't blame it on "The Message," because actually, there wasn't that much rap that was trying to imitate "The Message." I think what tended to go wrong, though—I wouldn't blame "The Message" or Public Enemy for that—was that in some ways it became really duller, really more rote. There became much more of a hip-hop rhythm, and therefore, every hip-hop record tended to have something really close to what counts as the hip-hop rhythm, which became the new-jack-swing rhythm as it began to back up a bunch of soul records. Whereas if you go back to around 1980, people were taking rhythms from what just seemed a wider range, and there seemed to be much more pizzazz on top of things. But if someone were to, you know, I could make a counterargument—I wouldn't feel it or believe it—but the counterargument is that hip-hop went on and became much more subtle and much more complicated. Certainly, if you listen to the rhythms of the early rappers, Spoonie Gee, his voice is basically hitting the backbeat every time through. "You go a-hip, hop, a-hip-hip a-hop"—well, you know, the readers can't get that [laughs], but the way he did it was very straight ahead. There's a lot of vocal interplay amongst the different parts, which you had with the groups like Grandmaster Flash & the Furious Five . . .

SCOTT: Funky Four . . .

FRANK: And those people. But it was kind of rolling along—boom boom boom boom boom—whereas, let's say when Eric B. & Rakim came along, Rakim was definitely putting in a lot of different accents, he wasn't just kind of hammering the backbeat with his voice. And oddly, if I were to blame someone—and I say oddly, because, what's that one called, "I Know You Got Soul"?

SCOTT: Right, "I Know You Got Soul."

FRANK: I think that's a great great record, but oddly, I might actually put my finger on *that* as the demise of the hip-hop I love rather than something like "The Message," which was really kind of a novel thing, an anomaly at the time. [With Rakim] hip-hop became this more internalized, virtuosity type of thing, where it was kind of looking in on itself; it became much more important somehow for the rappers to become cooler. I'm gonna go off on a tangent now, but the music that tended to move me the most—it's interesting that earlier I'd said that punk was my music, because I also remember saying in my magazine that I thought disco was better music than punk, and it isn't a total contradiction, because what I meant by punk, when I said punk was my music, I basically meant hard rock, going back to the Stones, whereas when I was writing in my 'zine I was thinking of punk leading into postpunk—but in general, the music I've loved the most, as far as having an emotional connection to me, whether I would grade it the highest or not, is stuff by white people playing stuff that's influenced by black people, rather than the black originals. And there's definitely a reason for that. And it's partly, like, sometimes I would go to this club, I think it was called the Roxy—I actually don't remember—but this club in New York, which played a lot of hip-hop, and it was this big, big thing, everyone got searched for weapons when you went in and stuff like that. But I remember being there and just thinking—you know, it was mostly black, there were probably some Italian working-class kids there, some downtown people like me, downtown white people—and I was thinking, yes, there's a lot of good, controlled rhythm here amongst the dancers, the black dancers, but there's something that's *too* cool for me, and I think—it's gonna take me a while to find the words for this, but [pause]—white music isn't cool, but I don't mean that as a putdown. There's something about white music that's just really cracked and fucked—not all white music, obviously, I'm talking about hard rock, the stuff that moves me. I can just imagine black people watching white people dance, there must be a lot of hilarity. White people are a menace on the dance floor a lot of the time [laughs], they don't know where they are, they think they're going wild and doing a lot of stuff, where really they're just managing to do really simple things, but still managing to run into you without meaning to—which obviously isn't true of all white people. But that's sort of considered really expressing yourself, whereas for good black dancers—good white dancers for that matter—you can be doing a lot or you can be doing very little, but you know the space around you, so even if you're doing something like breakdancing or something like that, there's a sense in which you kind of know where you are in the world, and you're kind of negotiating where you are. And it's not being passionless, but there's a sense of being in control, even if you're making deliberately spastic moves.

And oddly my feeling, thinking the black dancing was a lot better than the white dancing, still sort of crystallizing for me why I was moved more by white music, which is that white music is people *losing* control sometimes and dealing with that. Always keeping control, to me, there's some point where that's false. These are big, big generalizations, you can find counterevidence. Interestingly to me—and this is one of the reasons I liked hip-hop so much, maybe even more than was its due—was that it seemed to me that, without deliberately trying to be influenced by it—I mean, some hip-hop was deliberately being influenced by rock—but the guys who moved me the most weren't *influenced* by rock, what they were doing was coming up with something that had emotional features in common with rock. And that emotional feature was that it *wasn't* necessarily being about mastery and control, that there was some way in which it really was being fucked up.

from "Pushin' Too Hard: an interview with Frank Kogan," *Popped*, 1997

PART FOUR

THE GREAT WRONG PLACE

CHAPTER 16

THE PRESENTATION OF SELF IN EVERYDAY LIFE

Unless we can somehow recycle the concept of the great artist so that it supports Chuck Berry as well as it does Marcel Proust, we might as well trash it altogether.
—Robert Christgau

But rock criticism does something even more interesting, changing not just our idea of who gets to be an artist but of who gets to be a thinker. And not just who gets to be a thinker, but which part of our life gets to be considered "thought."

Say that—using rockers like Chuck and Elvis as intellectual models—young Christgau, Meltzer, Bangs, Marcus, et al. grow up to understand that rock 'n' roll isn't just what you write about, it's what you do. It's your mode of thought. And if you do words on the page, then your behavior on the page doesn't follow standard academic or journalistic practice, and is baffling for those who expect it to.

To explain this new behavior, and the bafflement it causes, I use "school" as my metaphor for the psyche, and I say that school tries to enforce a split between classroom and hallway. The split tells us that to be intellectual we have to live in the classroom and to obey the classroom rule, which is to talk not to and about other people but just about some third thing, "the subject matter." It says that to talk to and about each other, as we do in the hallway, isn't to think but to merely live our lives. And so—the split claims—either we can use our intellect or we can live our lives, but we can't do both at once. And living our lives (as the hallway narrowly construes this) becomes "visceral" by default, since our lives have been ejected from the "intellect." And the hallway's vengeance on the classroom is to say, "You may be smart, but I'm *real*, and you're not." But this is an impoverished realness, since it expels anything that the classroom defines as "mental," and forbids our putting something off at a distance and reflecting on it.

Good rock critics, by and large, don't honor the boundary between classroom and hallway. This puts us at odds with most editors-in-chief, department heads, and those horrible people, the readers. The rules have no intellectual validity; we're not following them; and the reader who wants reassurance through us that he's smart isn't going to get it from us in the standard way, and the reader who wants reassurance from us that he's real isn't going to get it either.

Simon Frith points out that most magazines now "edit every contributor into a house style expressing house opinions." This is in order to match taste with publication, publication with reader. Even those "intellectual" magazines that wouldn't think of editing someone's opinions will nonetheless choose writers whose styles fit the magazine's brand. "Intellectual" is itself a style, a brand.

There are arguments to be made in favor of imposing a uniform style, maybe the best arguments being analogous to the ones for school uniforms: Suppressing personal characteristics also suppresses social and class characteristics and therefore suppresses social conflict and gang warfare, thereby allowing the school to get on with its business. But no one claims that school uniforms are somehow more *intellectual* than regular clothes. Yet academia and journalism do try to claim that the enforced style is more intellectual or "objective" than any other.

I first came up with the "classroom-hallway" metaphor twelve years ago, in this passage:

> "*A fifteen-year-old's relationship to a pop song also puts her in relation to other fifteen-year-olds and to their relationship to the pop song and to other fifteen-year-olds etc.*"—Yes, and believe me, all fifteen-year-olds know this. But the sad thing is that the fifteen-year-old who writes empty truisms like "*a fifteen-year-old's relationship to a pop song also puts her . . .*" etc. and shows it to the teacher gets an A PLUS, whereas a fifteen-year-old who writes something that actually puts her in relation to other fifteen-year-olds knows better than to give it to the teacher, knows that it's not welcome. E.g., from recent Smash Hits (Australia):
>
> "Calling all gorgeous guys on Earth who are 14 or older. We are two 15 year old chicks who are absolutely in love with Guns N' Roses, Mötley Crüe, Bon Jovi, Poison, and stax more! Interested?"
>
> "I'm sick of it! Once again I was game enough to wear my Bon Jovi badge to school and what do I get for it? A black eye. I'm sick of people always saying that Jon Bon Jovi has AIDS; they know it's not true but they say it just to shit people up the wall. So to all you terrorists out there, I think you're jealous because you're not as good looking or popular as him!"

Of course, the fifteen-year-old's relationship to the *teacher* puts her in relation to other fifteen-year-olds too, so I'm not claiming that she's failing to live her life when she's writing down teacher-pleasing generalizations. And I'm not saying the *Smash Hits* letter style is in all circumstances *better* than the vague social generalization, especially given that this piece itself is full of such generalizations. If you lean towards generalizations you'll go for the "classroom" prose; if you lean towards analogies you'll lean towards the "hallway." My point is that when she's out in the hallway, amidst the flirting and fighting, she's sure as hell thinking. She's working out her relations to others; she's working out who she is. And if a big deal of her caring about music is that it helps her do so, she might wonder—in the event that this caring leads her to becoming a rock critic—why she's not allowed to continue using the music on the magazine pages as she always had in her life. What's the rule that says you should stop being a person when you become a writer, and what do the rules of journalism have to do with being a writer in the first place, or being a thinker?

Of course, the glam-metal chicks and the black-eyed battler are *in* the magazine, but they're safely off in the penpal section and the letters pages, where they're business-as-usual. Put them doing the same thing on the main pages, though, and they're suddenly seen as wild things, gonzos, transgressors, a threat to . . . well, what *are* they a threat to, and why? And, if we assume that what's on the main pages has something to do with what the readers want there, the crucial question is why do the readers want to keep this prose style, this part of themselves, off the main pages? Are they trying to protect this part, by keeping it off the main screen? Are they trying to protect the main screen from their lives?

I'll give an answer that I never would have imagined giving thirty years ago: In today's culture, print is a more potent medium than music, at least for presentation of self—more potent, and therefore has to be kept under more control.

Rock critics do the same thing that an Elvis or Jagger or Eminem does: They put themselves at issue, their personalities, their social stances, and in so doing force the readers into an attitude towards *them.*

When rock 'n' roll first hit, it had the effect of calling social status into question. But such a thing can be disconcerting, even for those whose status is low. After a while it's hard to continually lose one's sense of place, even if you don't have much of a place to begin with. Fact is, though, rock criticism barely has a place anymore. That's because it doesn't match up with the world's grid. There's this pseudoequilibrium right now, in its prose style, semicasual, somewhat jokey, moderately snide, tastefully feisty, not too over-"analytic," not too "wild," and still fundamentally subservient to the supposed subject matter. This is nothingness, not balance. You don't need to strike a balance between thinking and living, since one doesn't detract from the other. Real rock critics do both in their prose, and it's always too much for someone. Marcus gets accused of being too academic, Meltzer gets accused of being too undisciplined, but it's really the same accusation, the hallway-classroom split trying to reassert itself from one side or the other. I've heard Marcus's prose attacked for being too dry. Compared to what, the Great Flood?

Whether the style is wild, academic, or a casual balance, once a magazine or a profession imposes a uniform writing style, it's forcing the writer to suppress his own social characteristics in favor of the magazine's or the profession's. And—what I told Simon Frith; see chapter 12—once some writers get away with defying the dominant style, then another writer's conformity to it becomes a personal characteristic anyway; there's just no escaping the personal; it's so tied to the social. And social relations get called into question, and the self gets called into question, and the reader gets uneasy.

But that's where ideas arise, from this uneasiness. Because that's one of the things that critics do, whether they want to or not: They call social relations into question.

Robert Christgau: "[Chuck Berry] was one of the ones who made us understand that the greatest thing about art is the way it happens between people." And music makes us understand that *ideas* happen between people too, but we need the page and critics to drive this point home.

first printed in *Don't Stop 'Til You Get Enough: Essays in Honor of Robert Christgau,* 2002

COMMENTARY 2004:

When I'd originally written this essay, I'd expected to have twice the number of words as I was eventually allotted, so a whole bunch of ideas got shortchanged in the final cut. My major omissions were:

(1) In the first paragraph I declare Presley and Berry our intellectual forebears as if this were somehow self-evident and needed no elaboration. Actually, a brief elaboration occurs mid-essay where I say, in regard to our schoolgirl, "When she's out in the hallway, amidst the flirting and fighting, she's sure as hell thinking. She's working out her relations to others; she's working out who she is." And that's one of the things Elvis and Chuck were doing onstage and in studio: working out their relations to others, hence creating a model for how we can do the same in our prose.

Anyway, if you check back to the "Death Rock 2000" piece in part one of this book, or jump forward one chapter to the Kogan-Wójtowicz colloquy from *WMS* #4, you'll get a good sense of why I believe making music is a way to think. But this leads to the next point.

(2) Among other things, I'm arguing that (i) presentation of self—creating, maintaining, or modifying one's hairstyle, as it were—is a way of thinking, but (ii) given a choice between maintaining one's hairstyle and thinking about it, my profession as a whole will choose hairstyle over thought. And the reader/editor/colleague will crack down on my thought, too, if it threatens his hairstyle (at least, he'll crack down collectively, institutionally, on behalf of the collective/institutional hairstyle, even if he'd rather not). In effect, to freeze one's hairstyle is to freeze a part of one's brain.

"We are two 15 year old chicks who are absolutely in love with Guns N' Roses, Mötley Crüe, Bon Jovi, Poison, and stax more! Interested?" "A fifteen-year-old's relationship to a pop song also puts her in relation to other fifteen-year-olds and to *their* relationship to the pop song and to other fifteen-year-olds etc." Each of these statements contains the rudiments of thought, but the thought won't develop if the girl doesn't take it anywhere. She's declared her gang affiliations, told the pop fans that she's a Glam-Metal Chick and told the teacher that she's a Relativist. Now what? *Where* does being a Glam-Metal Chick take you? What's it like to be a Guns N' Roses Girl? What does it do for you, what does it demand of you? Ditto for the "puts her in relation to other fifteen-year-olds" thing: What's *that* about? Why are you stating the obvious? It's an idea with no apparent consequences, since it doesn't tell you anything about *how* you should be relating to anyone or whether you should continue your relations or alter them. It certainly doesn't tell you *not* to continue on with neutral-seeming musicological and social analyses of Guns N' Roses, disregarding your pussy if your pussy's not feeling it or if the feelings don't inspire you to say anything interesting. (Disregarding your pussy is one way of dealing with social relations.) What does being a Relativist Babe demand of you? When you're a Relativist, are you a Relativist all the way, from your first cigarette to your last dying day? If it demands nothing, why bother?

The point is, if she actually puts her mind to it, her callout to the boys will take her to social analysis and content analysis, to the sorts of questions in regard to GN'R that Lester had asked in regard to Iggy: "Jungle war with bike gangs is one thing, but it gets a little more complicated when those of us who love being around that war (at least vicariously) have to stop to consider why and what we're loving." And if she asks herself why she's wasting time tossing platitudes at the teacher, this will lead her to ponder the insights and urges that the platitude is standing in for, will lead her to change her classroom prose and her relationship to the teacher. (She already wants to change her behavior; the platitude is just a detour, her raising her hand and asking Teach for philosophical permission to go to the bathroom.) Being an intellectual can start anywhere. But your gang might not like where it takes you.

"Good rock critics, by and large, don't honor the boundary between classroom and hallway." I'll go further and say that good rock critics—good intellectuals, for that matter—simply won't abide the hallway-classroom split. We believe in neither the hallway nor the classroom. We refuse the trade-off between "living" and "thinking" that the split requires, and we refuse the hallway's and classroom's dominance of the social landscape. "The Presentation of Self" tilts more at the restrictions of the classroom than the hallway, but it certainly doesn't advocate that we dwell in the hallway—that attenuated, inhibited place. I'm the terror of the chatrooms not because—just like everyone else—I joke and flirt and fight, but because I'm the guy who demands close reading of texts and that my chitchat buddies adhere to the basics of logical inference.

(3) "There are arguments to be made in favor of imposing a uniform style, maybe the best arguments being analogous to the ones for school uniforms: Suppressing personal characteristics also suppresses social and class characteristics and therefore suppresses social conflict and gang warfare, thereby allowing the school to get on with its business." Well, obviously I'm against uniformity, but this is such a weak argument *for* uniformity that I need to make the argument stronger, since I'm giving no other explanation for why the classroom-hallway split maintains itself. My original draft contained the following passage: "If so far you've been nodding your head and saying, 'Uniformity, boo! diversity, yay!' ask yourself if you're actually ready for genuine social diversity and for letting 'living your life' into the intellectual forum. Are you sure that no one's going to get hurt, that the bullies and creeps won't lord it over everyone else, that the weak and the outcast won't get clobbered? Are you utterly comfortable, say, with Richard Meltzer writing, 'What pried me away from the bugs was a human worse than six scumbags full of arsenic named Bert Sommer'? Or Eminem going 'My words are like a dagger with a jagged edge/That'll stab you in the head whether you're a fag or lez'?"

In general we want to set aside space for particular purposes—for instance, we could start a magazine about music theory, which would be more focused than hallway chatter on the subject; or we could teach a music-appreciation class and have good reason to discourage the students from spending the time winking at each other and stealing each other's hats and playing with their Gameboys. (John Wójtowicz: "Not to mention listening to the music while taking drugs and fucking." Frank Kogan: "No. That will be a class requirement.") But we want the space to be safe. And one way to seem to ensure safety is to decree that we all act like we're in the same gang.

(4) "Changing not just our idea of who gets to be an artist but of who gets to be a thinker." I don't follow this up (I make it the same fifteen-year-old girl, whether she's in the classroom or the hallway). I won't here, either, really, except to say that the drive towards academic diversity tends to run aground not on the question whether intellectuals can appreciate an Elvis, but on whether an Elvis can make it into the social group "Intellectual"—while still remaining Elvis. In the average white high school, over the last fifty years, the refusal groups are—depending on time and place—rocks, greaseballs, hoods, greasers, grits, rednecks, farmers, burnouts, stoners, jells, dirts, dirtbags, skaters. And if greasers etc. want to join the Intellectual Gang, they have to stop acting like greasers. It's a vicious circle: The greasers are anti-intellectual because they've been excluded from the "Intellectual" group, and the "Intellectuals" exclude the greasers because the greasers are anti-intellectual. But excluding the greasers is itself anti-intellectual.

Although obviously I don't restrict my idea of "intellectual" to what goes on in the classroom, and I'm willing to think that in their moment people like Elvis and James Brown were the intellectual vanguard, the hallway will discourage the Elvises and Browns from verbalizing, extrapolating, and testing their insights.

Fortunately, there's been some progress over the years. I don't think today's skaters and goth-metal kids et al. are as anti-intellectual as the hoods of the early '60s were. And this is due to the evolution of another class of refusal group: the beatniks, the freaks, the punks. These people don't live according to the prep-vs.-skater social split, and if *that* split wants to maintain itself, and the preps and the skaters want to defeat the freaks, the preps and skaters have to absorb some freak characteristics, including a bit of the freaks' quasi-intellectualism. (This is a subject for a whole other essay.) In any event, that no "critical thinkers" or "social scientists" dress like, say, Kylie Minogue or the Bee Gees isn't due to the fact that smart people know better than to dress like that, but rather to the critical thinkers not being all that smart, actually; so, to protect the narrowness of their minds, they exclude Minogue and Bee Gees types from the conversation and equivalent writing styles from the intellectual journals.

(5) "And [changing] not just who gets to be a thinker, but which part of our life gets to be considered 'thought.'" This implies that rock criticism is something new under the neon and that we rockers are the first people in history to walk and chew gum at the same time—which is obvious hogwash, especially given that I'm always swiping ideas and copying rhetorical devices from past critics such as Ring Lardner, Otis Ferguson, and Manny Farber. But maybe we're the first to do *this* particular walk while chewing on this particular rubber.

Here's an idea, I don't know how good: The hallway-classroom split is actually a lot more pervasive than it was pre WWII, because school is a lot more ubiquitous and because the subject-oriented classroom is more of an ideal now than in other times and places. More people are likely to feel the behavioral split within themselves, because more people are likely to be subject to it. So we're more likely than our predecessors to be inculcated with classroom values and hallway counter values, and more likely to want to invent an intellectual alternative to the hallway and classroom. We have to, otherwise we have no niche. In any event, whether or not what I just said holds water, we seem to be a lot more extreme in all directions than Ferguson and crew. Ferguson would occasionally launch himself into parodies, he was perfectly capable of asking why and what he was loving, and he was carrying on a low-level style war against his colleagues at *The New Republic*. But I can't imagine him leaping head first into cut-ups and social brawls à la Meltzer or Lester or going anywhere close to the heavy philosophizing of *The Aesthetics of Rock*. Imagine John Dewey clowning and brawling like Ring Lardner, and Ring Lardner addressing John Dewey's subject matter. That's where rock critics are (or were thirty years ago, anyway, before the Big Clampdown).

Had Lardner heard Bo Diddley, he might have said to himself, as Meltzer subsequently did, "I'd write like Bo Diddley rather than about him," but he wouldn't have believed that the future of art and philosophy was at stake, I don't think. And Dewey would never have written like Bo Diddley.

(6) The hallway-classroom split is behavioral, not philosophical. It's a set of habits, conventions, and bigotries and a resultingly restricted map of behavioral possibilities. If someone were to say "either we can use our intellect or we can live our lives, but we can't do both at once," a lot of us would disagree with the *idea* and would start babbling about emotional intelligence and street smarts ("the street," by the way, is what the hallway calls itself when it's putting on airs; but the street nonetheless shapes itself in opposition to the classroom, hence is part of the hallway) or retreat to irrelevant arguments against someone like Plato or Locke or Husserl. But this will have little bearing on whether or not we conform to the behavioral conventions.

(7) "Rock critics do the same thing that an Elvis or Jagger or Eminem does: They put themselves at issue, their personalities, their social stances, and in so doing force the readers into an attitude towards *them*." Here's an example:

In his review of the Ohm electronic music anthology for *The Village Voice*, Scott Seward quotes Patti Smith to the effect that she never listens to performers she wouldn't want to sleep with, and Scott remarks that if he'd used such a criterion himself, he'd never have played *Radio Ethiopia* (so he's rejecting the criterion). "I'm guessing electronic classical music isn't her bag, what with most of the form's gurus looking like unpopular physics professors." (Which doesn't necessarily take them out of the sex derby: Two days before I read the review my girlfriend Naomi had gone through the Ohm booklet and observed that a clear requirement for making that style of music was that one be bald; the subtext being that she finds baldies really attractive—which was fortunate for me.) Now I'm dead sure that Scott is saying something relevant to music, and that if we disallow such statements we make it impossible to undertake any real social analysis. But I'll bet that most people who include themselves in the audience for "serious" music would be just as sure that Scott (at best!) is being irrelevant and that comments such as his have no place in the discussion. But of course Scott's very point is that the Ohm electronic guys have placed themselves into the "serious art music" rather than the "sexual come-on" category, with no Mariah tits or Shania thighs to distract us from their seriousness. Now, not only is Scott revealing this social fact about the musicians and the music (and if the music has a penis in it, it's in the guise of a pointy-headed pseudosexlessness), he is also drawing the music back into our social world of flirting and fighting—he is revealing that the music is part of that world whether it wants to be or not. And Scott is also revealing something about his own social role. Most people reading him would grasp these social points easily and, within themselves, would go through incipient social reactions to Scott and to the musicians, would engage in a little thinking. But most likely, since Scott's statement doesn't come in a package that signifies "I am making social points, which are _____," some readers won't grasp that social points have been made (despite grasping the points themselves) and will wonder why such a passage is in Scott's review, and might be offended. And I'd say that in at least ninety percent of the commercial music press, that passage would be cut, not only because editors and crucial staff members fear their readers but because the editors and staff members themselves will react socioemotionally to it even while not knowing that their reactions had come from Scott's making social points. And these editors and staffers will say to themselves, "Scott's just talking about himself; I don't know what this is doing here."

Scott's way of making points is appropriate because his subject matter isn't just "the social relationship between electronic musicians and the world" or even "the social relationship between electronic musicians and Scott Seward," it's "the social relationship among electronic musicians, Scott Seward, and *you*, the reader." The more visceral the prose—and the more visceral the reader's response—the more pedagogically effective the piece is. This is because an effective way to get you to think about social relations isn't to merely state the relations but to put the relations into question by putting *your* social relations into question. Of course the writer can do both; but if he excludes the latter, you, the reader, may well shield yourself from his point, which is that by social relations he means *you*.

That said, I'm not advocating that anyone write in a particular way. I'm not advocating *anything*, actually, other than that people test their ideas and use their intellects and that they not—as editor or gang leader or peer-group member or department head—go around bullying us into suppressing our own intellects. At a Clash show in 1981, my friend Bob Galipeau explained why he no longer liked the Clash by saying, "There's no one here I'd want to fuck." That was a smart, informative comment *in context*. But whether it's interesting on the page depends on what else is on the page, what else you bring to your readers, and what's going on in the world's conversation. Allowing yourself to address the reader doesn't mean forbidding yourself from doing a who, what, where, when, and why. The problem is that the who-what-where-when-and-sometimes-why types want to prevent us from attacking or coming on to the reader. Nevertheless, "subdominant chord in the fifth measure" is no less interesting than "there's no one here I'd want to fuck." But only if you take it somewhere interesting. You can't know in advance, even if it worked last time.

CHAPTER 17

HOW MUSIC CREATES IDEAS

[Here's a passage of mine from WMS #4 *in response to John Wójtowicz's saying "I have problems applying many of your categories to the experience of hearing jazz. If they don't fit, why not rename your fanzine 'Why Rock Sucks,' or better, 'Why Rock Criticism Sucks'? I began listening to 'Ascension' without thinking what kind of person I could consider myself to be after hearing it, how it was justified and rationalized, I just wanted to know what the f@%# was going on." The Jimmy Garrison reference is to a passage that John quoted from Ornette Coleman, about why Coleman tended to use white bass players (Garrison being one of the black exceptions): "One night we were playing at the Five Spot and [Garrison] got fairly emotionally upset, cussed us out and said there wasn't a fucking thing happening with the music, you know, we were all full of shit and everything and for us all to stop and let him start playing. You know, like we're playing our ass off and the Five Spot is packed and he says, 'Stop this goddam music, ain't a fucking thing happening, what do you Negroes think you're doing? You going crazy, I mean it's nothing, you know, nothing's happening, what are you doing? I mean let me have it, I know what's happening.' All this right in the middle of the Five Spot. And so we all stopped and he didn't play a note [note Garrison's Zen approach here—JW], so we all picked it back up from where he broke in, you know. Now this doesn't have anything directly to do with black or white; it has to do with a person's inferior feeling of what he's been left out of. . . ."]*

Two quotes from LeRoi Jones (*Blues People*), the first re use of heroin among beboppers, the second re Bix Beiderbecke:

Heroin is the most popular addictive drug used by Negroes because, it seems to me, the drug itself transforms the Negro's normal separation from the mainstream of society into an advantage (which, I have been saying, I think it is anyway). It is one-upmanship of the highest order. . . . The terms of value change radically, and no one can tell the "nodding junkie" that employment or success are of any value at all.

Music, as paradoxical as it might seem, is the result of thought. It is the result of thought perfected at its most empirical, i.e., as attitude, or stance.

The second quote is more than a bit puzzling—what is "thought perfected at its most empirical"?—the words "attitude" and "stance" are too passive, and the word "thought" implies something too private. Nonetheless, Jones's idea leads in the right direction. E.g. you [John] have described the jazz musician's relation to rhythm-form-tradition, but you've left out his equally important relationship to other human beings. On the bandstand or in rehearsal (or jam session), the musician literally interacts with other people every time he plays a note (or doesn't play a note—see Jimmy Garrison). His music contains "thought" (in Jones's sense) because it contains his answer to the question, "How do I relate to these guys?" "These guys" refers to the other musicians, the audience, and, in a vaguer way, the world.

Anyhow, without reducing music to its social relations, I want to say that you can't have music without a social world. And if you don't "hear" those social (as well as formal and rhythmic) relations, you don't quite get it. Maybe I'm overinfluenced by Jones (a man addicted to Us vs. Them), but I don't see how you can miss the relevance of my conundrums—triviality vs. awesomeness, legitimacy vs. illegitimacy, and the related obsession with social justification—to jazz. Jazz is up to its neck in Us vs. Them, and has been at least since 1940. So what if you began listening to "Ascension" without thinking what kind of person you could consider yourself to be after hearing it? Chuck Eddy began listening to Black Sabbath without thinking what kind of person he could consider himself to be after hearing it. I began listening to the Ohio Express without thinking what kind of person I could consider myself to be after hearing it. But there was an unconscious socioreasoning process that underlay my "spontaneous" "gut-level" reaction to "Yummy Yummy Yummy." When you listened to "Ascension" you weren't consciously thinking about what sort of person you were, you were *being* that sort of person—or perhaps changing yourself into that person! Compare your approach—wondering what the f&%# was going on—to that of a "Mom," or a "friend," someone who says "This is noise, this is crap" or "What do those Negroes think they're doing?" or "Turn off that nigger shit." So even if "legitimacy vs. illegitimacy" and "what sort of person does this make me?" don't start off as issues for you, they become issues soon enough—as soon as listening to Coltrane intersects with your environment (which is probably as soon as the music hits your ears, given internalization). People who try to get with "Ascension" tend—just like teenyboppers and punks—to have or create a bunch of other things in common: political opinions, slang. That of course is not meant to reduce "Ascension" to hairstyle. But, again, hearing "Ascension" as hairstyle is part of hearing it as music—and your liking "Ascension," World Saxophone Quartet, and Ornette Coleman, and also Teena Marie, Velvet Underground, Metallica, distinguishes you from "them." [*John had written: "Let's redefine 'them' to refer to the candyass whitebread anglo sexless protestants who go to parties and don't drink or dance or smoke dope, and don't go home with anyone they didn't arrive with. And the people who extend an invitation to you and expect you to know that you're supposed to graciously decline; the people who taste the food you order and say 'Oh my, that's spicy.' I still meet plenty of Americans my age and older who don't know who James Brown is, and who think there's something quaint about my interest/passion: they should all be removed from their jobs and denied passports. (Tactics I saw in Eastern Europe; it would normally seem extreme to me, but in this case I want to make an exception.)"*]

I'm going to jump in over my head here and say that bebop in the '40s (maybe jazz's most glorious moment) set jazz on the PBS path. There's a real parallel to rock. The beboppers were doing the 1940s version of "Get Off of My Cloud" (though they were doing it as an art move—Jagger reversed things by doing it as a pop move, which is a gigantic difference). They were the first Afro Am musicians to—onstage—turn their backs on the audience. No wave punks repeated this routine in the late '70s, for similar reasons. You can lift *Blues People's* section on bebop and virtually apply it whole to punk—see Jones's "heroin" quote above. Bebop came as an Us vs. Us vs. Them deliberate separation move just at a time when, for blacks, "assimilation" and integration were becoming possibilities. It was a music that was meant to be incomprehensible as "entertainment"—especially incomprehensible to white people, but to a lot of blacks, too. Beboppers in the '40s wouldn't play music they couldn't justify. Their music didn't just have to sound good or feel good or cook or move, it had to take the musician and fan out of even the slightest association with bug-eyed darkie entertainment—it had to be difficult, it had to have dignity and integrity, it had to be exclusive. So triviality and explicit pop moves were purged. The definition of "jazz" narrowed. (That's one reason "All Shook Up" and "Yummy Yummy Yummy" aren't called "jazz.") We can argue over whether this was good for jazz—it put jazz into a ghetto, made it less crucial to the world. Jazz doesn't even "cross over" to rock anymore—only to new age or black pop as upscale "quality" sludge. It's not Charlie Parker's fault, but he inadvertently set the process in motion.

Why Mucus Slacks (WMS #4), Summer 1988

CHAPTER 18

WASTED

[Here are several passages from a long letter I wrote a couple years ago to Doug Simmons, managing editor of The Village Voice *and, back when he'd been music editor, the first person ever to print me in a commercial publication. I was trying to convince him to let us use the* Voice *Website for things we weren't allowed to write in the print version. (Didn't convince him, though I did get a raise out of it. The whole letter is amusing in retrospect, as I was essentially trying to get him to pay me to start a chatroom and post on it.)]*

I hope this doesn't come across as arrogant; I really think it's the truth: I've got a great intellect, and the *Voice* is wasting me. No one questions and probes the way I do. Frith doesn't, Reynolds doesn't, Bangs didn't, Meltzer's stopped. But you guys are only using me in fragments. This isn't to denigrate the reviews I do for Chuck. I very much should continue them, since when I start a review I never know what to say, I'm usually reviewing music that I'm unqualified to talk about, and I don't have at hand a set of ideas to apply to it. So I have to scramble, and, whatever the outcome is like for the reader, the process stretches me and gives me a sense of the Great Musical Unknown out there.

But I could be doing so much more for you, too. As for my pipe dream about how and where, that's coming in several paragraphs. The thing is, there's a whole flow of my theories, my metaphors, my jokes, my life—a vast river of Frank, questions no one else is asking and connections no one else is making—that only a handful of people get to see and that could be larger and better still except I don't get to see other people's rivers either, or they mine, and so we don't get to feed into each other's work. I feel that I'm wasting away intellectually, and so's the whole damn profession. Thinking is a collaborative process, but by and large the rock press forbids us our collaboration, so even when ideas get started, they never get finished.

[Eight or so paragraphs here detailing ideas of mine that are left unfinished, ideas of other people's that were barely started, and LeAnn Rimes's tendency to yodel.]

Now this is my point: For all practical purposes, rock critics are forbidden to write about each other and about each other's work, except in the rare event a critic gets a collection of essays in book form, in which case someone can review it once. Imagine if chemists had been forbidden to discuss Lavoisier and physicists forbidden to discuss Planck, and were forbidden to conduct experiments or discuss each other's ideas, and were slammed as self-indulgent whenever they did so. There'd be no chemistry, no physics, no science. No intellect. Yet if you use music in your prose as you would in your life, and comment on how other people use it in their prose, then you're perceived as some self-involved wanker. Chuck does what he can for me (I'm sure there are people who think he does too much for me), but there's only so much he can do within his basic vision for the section, which is record reviews, and only so much that I can do in record reviews, even with the leeway he gives me in the concept of "record review." And only so much space to do it in. As I said, few people get to see my whole stream, few know that there's a whole torrent of Frank to take in and contend with.

In my Meltzer review I say that he left great contradictions of his unexamined, but I was absolutely at the word limit, no room left for another comma, and so I didn't say what the contradictions were. If anyone thought that this was a flaw or something to lament—that *I'd* left the contradictions as unexamined as Meltzer had—I never heard about it.

In *Christgau's* Bangs-Tosches-Meltzer piece, Christgau quotes DeRogatis quoting Christgau to the effect that it's Bangs's language not his ideas that were his strength, and then quotes DeRogatis countering (correctly) that Christgau's wrong, that the ideas are crucial; and then Christgau counters, correctly, that DeRogatis fails in his book to make the case for Lester's ideas. And that's where they fucking leave it! No follow-up letters or articles by Xgau or DeRogatis or anybody on what you'd think might be a point of interest: JUST WHAT LESTER'S IDEAS *ARE*! And apparently no reader demand for such articles, no one complaining in the public prints (or in the chatrooms, as far as I know) about the lack of such discussion, no ongoing conversation anywhere that I can find where Bob and Jim and others can help each other work out their thoughts about Lester and where readers can benefit from this, and, more than twenty years after the man's death, almost no intelligent discussion of the ideas of Lester Who Is Generally Regarded As The Best Or Second-Best Rock Critic Ever or of what to do about those ideas or where we can take them. Sure, some of us use or think we're using those ideas, or try to be true to his spirit, or ape his style, but, other than the bits and pieces of analysis I did in *WMS* #s 4 and 5 and in "Death Rock 2000," and other than the long reappraisal that Mark Sinker published—on his blog, after *The Wire* cut it to ribbons in their version—of "A Reasonable Guide to Horrible Noise," there's no attempt to take stock of the man's work, to address his ideas head on. Me and Mark, that's it. All right, I'll admit I've never read "the Noise Boys," so there may be a *few* others, but go to the Lester section of rockcritics.com and follow the links and try to find *anyone* there who gives a fuck about what the man actually said. And yes, Christgau's piece was great and impassioned, and his few sentences about Lester's style were fine, but COME ON. What we have across the board is a fundamental, *institutionalized* refusal to think and refusal to communicate. I say *institutionalized* (all I wanted was a Pepsi) because the problem isn't just that too many critics were never taught to think or even that they get boxed in to only being allowed to review current product or that somewhere up in the chain of command there's always some anti-intellectual bigot (maybe it's the readers themselves) who thinks that rock critics talking about rock criticism is tantamount to their talking about themselves and in doing so are steering us away from the *real* subject matter, which is not the critics, but the music, man. The problem is that most editors and writers—including DeRogatis and Christgau (even though they know better), who'd both had the freedom to go on about Lester's ideas if they'd only wanted to—have internalized from the get-go all the habits and prejudices that Lester had tried to challenge, not least the prejudice/habit/fallacy that you're either talking about yourself or you're talking about the subject matter but that you can't do both at once. (Funny that a month or so later Xgau devoted a column to Christopher Small, who's a good guy but whose point that "Music is an activity, not a thing" had already been made a hundred times better by Lester and Meltzer and me and Frith and Chuck and LeRoi Jones, among others.) So one reason we can't get paid to talk about Lester's ideas is that those ideas themselves have to a large extent been run out of the rock press, and the institutionalized opposition to those ideas prohibits the discussion of those ideas.

email to Doug Simmons, October 18, 2002

[Um, despite what I implied here (at about 2 AM), I don't actually have access to Xgau's and DeRogatis's psyches. The point is, though, that the world is certainly not encouraging a discussion of Bangs's ideas, or encouraging Xgau and the rest of us to engage in one.]

CHAPTER 19

THE TROUBLE WITH THE SOCIOLOGY OF POP

PART ONE:

The main point in chapter 1 of Simon Frith's *Performing Rites*: The essence of social practice is the making of value judgments. (Example: Ladonna in the letter pages of *Metal Mania*: "There is no way that Poison can EVER be on top. Them little underdeveloped chromoshoes don't got cock enough to fuck an ant. So all you fucking whores out there who praise the ground Poison walks on are in shit. METALLICA RULES and that will never change." Footnote: "Thanks to Frank Kogan for this quote.") But academia almost across the board refuses to raise questions about the value of what it studies. (The value and importance of what we study are assumed; otherwise we wouldn't be studying it.) Therefore, for sociologists and people in cultural studies, the explicit *practice* of their subject matter is forbidden in the classroom and in academic writing.

Comments by me: One reason for this proscription is that to practice the subject matter—that is, to make value judgments as you would as a music fan—means to make invidious social judgments about people. (By the way, the *L.A. Times* yesterday published as a supposed fact—based on a year's worth of research, they said—the claim that Biggie paid for the murder of 2Pac and supplied the gun and bullets himself, wanting the satisfaction of knowing that it was his bullet that killed 2Pac. I just thought I'd bring that up.) The message in this proscription is that you can either live your lives or you can study a subject matter, but you can't do both at once. And the further message, to quote Frith (though it was from a different essay on a different topic), is that "everything real is happening elsewhere." In other words, the message that sociology sends to you, if you are a student, is that you are not as real or as important as what you are studying (or why would you be studying it?). But pop throws a monkey in the works by being something that you know how to practice well but whose value *hasn't* been established. Academia fends off the monkey (and the frug and the mashed potato and the boogaloo) by having the student not study pop but merely pop's *importance*. So maybe you can study it for its artistic merit and you can certainly study it for its social use and social effects, but you can't study it *whole*, any more than you can *be* whole when you study it. So sociology and cultural studies alienate you from your life and then engage you in endless methodological discussions about how to approach it.

PART TWO:

Richard Meltzer (who wrote most of the *Aesthetics of Rock* in academia, even if he and the *Aesthetics* were thrown out before it was published), 1972, from the introduction to *Gulcher*: "The structure [people have] been fed of late has tended towards the delineation of youth culture as meaning-laden and quality-oriented. This is indeed strange for a culture whose cutting edge has begun and ended with rock and roll, crucial for its collapse of such dichotomies as the trivial and the awesome, the relevant and the irrelevant, the interesting and the boring, the topical and the eternal, the polar and the continuous, the _____ and the _____."

Comments: Well, Meltzer's prose here is too contaminated by philosophy, and he's never thought through what he means by "meaning-laden" (I would guess it would be something like "socially important as my seventh-grade social studies teacher would define social importance"), and relevant/irrelevant etc. aren't dichotomies, just comparative judgments, hence aren't eligible for collapse, since in normal usage they're already as flexible, contingent, and ad hoc as need be. But let's say that—though this makes rock 'n' roll less extraordinary and world-important—ha!—than Meltzer made it seem—that rock music esp. c. 1964–1966 was a lot more fluid and less stable in its judgments of what counts as important and unimportant than academia was, so if I'm a sociologist back then, I'm going to want to run rock against sociology, to analyze sociology through the lens of rock rather than to analyze rock sociologically; or I might play the two off against each other, since by not sticking to standard "importance," rock forces the intellectual question that sociology has been afraid to bring up—the question of value, of what's important—and so rock in this regard is intellectually superior to sociology. (Meltzer'd written that "Rock is the only possible future for philosophy and art"; he later derided himself for his misplaced faith in rock. I'd add that he was far too generous to philosophy in believing that it deserved a future.)

Anyway, that's a short vague sketch of things, and it's probably not all that intelligible. I haven't been in academia in twenty-five years so I don't know the state of affairs. I'm waiting for Meltzer's honorary degree from Yale.

I don't think we're required to kowtow to the way pop mixes around and mixes up its sense of importance, or that instability in one's ideas is necessarily better than stability. But if we're not willing to test the stability and value of our practices by running them against counterpractices, then how can we do sociology? How else *can* we examine and test our social practices? So my question would be: Can we use pop music—the way we engage in it—as a means of studying society (and sociology) rather than merely using sociology as a means of studying pop music?

By the way, if you're subjected to massive propaganda all your life that tells you that you can either use your intellect or live your life but that you can't do both at once, this is going to affect how you behave as a musician and as a fan, what the music you make is going to sound like, what the music you like is going to sound like, how you judge and justify it.

PART THREE:

One last point, about why value judgments are crucial to social practice. Here's a quote from the (Australian) *Smash Hits* penpal pages, 1988:

> *Calling all gorgeous guys on Earth who are 14 or older. We are two 15 year old chicks who are absolutely in love with Guns N' Roses, Mötley Crüe, Bon Jovi, Poison, and stax more! Interested?*

Now there simply *must* be disagreement over the value of Guns N' Roses et al. For if everyone liked Guns N' Roses, this call would be worthless.

To say that value judgments are crucial to social practice is to say that disagreements are crucial to social practice. Of course, that would be so obvious as to be a platitude *except* that the social "sciences" tend to imagine that agreement will or should be the ultimate goal of the social-science discourse, that disagreements will eventually be resolved. Whereas in pop, agreement is not expected and is not the goal.

I Love Everything chatroom, September 8, 2002

[I was surprised that no one hit me with the claim that loving Guns N' Roses can be a matter of taste rather than value. Indeed, hypothetically *it can be, except it almost never is. Even if you intend "gorgeous guys" and "absolutely in love with Guns N' Roses" to be no more than expressions of your personal taste, the world takes them as value judgments. And the world is right.]*

CHAPTER 20

PHOTO DISREGARDS ITS NEGATIVE

"What are the biggest assumptions and misconceptions about dance music that a person writing about it must challenge or at least consider?"

Assumptions to challenge: that dancing is visceral rather than intellectual, that technology is "cold," that "dance music" is only for dancing, that disco was just fluff and fun for the pop marketplace, that disco and rock have nothing to do with each other, that disco and hip-hop have nothing to do with each other, that other musics (e.g., rock, teen pop) are less scene-oriented than rave is, that techno and house are better than Europop, that techno and house are more innovative than pop is, that techno and house are more disco than teen pop is, that disco lyrics don't matter, that disco lyrics are no good, that Kraftwerk is more important than Boney M, that you can't understand the music if you don't get high. To expand on a few of these points, here are some thoughts I had after reading Jon Pareles a couple years ago comment in the *New York Times* on the twentieth anniversary of *Saturday Night Fever*. I was noting in general the tendency of professional intellectuals (though not necessarily Pareles, who's normally pretty smart) to get it all wrong, to project the wrong grid, not to mention the most schoolmarmy one. I'm thinking here of their need to debunk a supposed "rockism" and "essentialism" and _____ (fill in the buzz word) and to extol disco as a trivial, "inauthentic," celebration of artificiality—and thereby portray disco as simply a photonegative of rockism.

(a) There is too much emphasis on the "simplicity" of the disco beat—I don't think disco's one-two-three-four was necessarily any simpler than swing's one-two-three-four or the Velvet Underground's one-two-three-four. It would have been simple only if the one-two-three-four were the *only* rhythm going on.

(b) There is too much emphasis on the rock-vs.-disco divide and hence on disco's supposedly being artificial or synthetic in relation to rock. I have all sorts of problems with this emphasis. First, I don't know if anyone who isn't a critic or an academic sees it like this. Was a rock fan's antagonism towards disco based on his perception of the music's being artificial? Did he really think in such terms? (By the way, as a rock fan myself at the time, I didn't see disco as any kind of a threat; I saw "soft rock" as a threat.) Second, no matter how the rock fan saw it, the disco-goer most likely did not see disco as synthetic in relation to rock. I wouldn't say that disco *never* saw itself in some sort of relation to rock, but I don't think it particularly saw itself through the eyes of rock. So to overemphasize "artificiality" is to not see disco on its own terms. I think that the disco synth (other than for comedians like Kraftwerk) was more about mastery and creativity than artificiality. And then there's the whole gospel aspect of disco, which had nothing to do with artificiality. And the sex aspect, which for some people was absolutely meant to be as spiritual as the gospel (and for others was meant to be as spiritual as pudding).

I saw disco's gaudiness and glitz not as "artificiality" but as *reach*, something similar to Dolls glitter or the Warhol superstars: three-chord glamour that anyone could play, if you say you're a star, you are. And then for some it just plain *is* glamour. Most commentators would be more comfortable if it were merely *about* glamour.

(c) In discussing the differences between disco and rock, there is usually a misinterpretation of the meaning of "live performance." Which is to say, there's talk both of rock musicians constructing the music in the studio to make it *sound* live, to cover their tracks, to not emphasize the studio (is this even true? think of *Electric Ladyland*), and of rock musicians really playing their instruments in live performance (vs. disco divas singing to backing tracks or simply lip synching). Whereas, in fact, it's *disco* that assumes a live setting—a dance—a public space. Disco is much more the live music, and disco records are raw material for this live show.

Rock has an advantage as a commodity, in that a rock record is more likely than a disco record to be used for private listening as well as dancing; and it's in private listening that the listener is most likely to need to perceive a human within the music—a star or a singer or a composer or musician—a hand behind the text, as it were. On the dance floor we've got each other. (Which isn't to say that people don't dance in private, or listen to dance records in private while not dancing. And certainly, when listening alone, people nonetheless may have a sense of community or at least of other listeners "out there," and radio is a medium for suggesting such a world out there. And of course "dance" isn't the only live setting for prerecorded music. Car radios, supermarket speakers, living rooms with more than one person in it, movie theaters.) My guess is that, of the musics that use prerecorded music in a live setting, even though disco managed to garner a large audience first, hip-hop as a genre has been better able to manage to be both a live medium and a medium for private listening. Club records have usually struggled commercially.

Amalgam of a couple of emails to John Wójtowicz (Oct. 19, 1999, and July 20, 2000) and a contribution based on those emails to "Writing About Dancing: Disco Critics Survey," *rockcritics.com*, March 2001

CHAPTER 21

THE PSYCHOTIC CARNIVAL

In *WMS* #7 I wrote:

> *The idea that the teacher should teach kids the subject matter leads to the general demand that a lot of what goes on in the classroom contribute at least in some way to the learning of the subject matter. (This obviously can include naps, jokes, tangents.) The stronger demand, that everything at every moment that happens in class be shown to contribute to the learning of the subject matter, would be quite psychotic. It leads to the demand not so much that kids learn the subject matter but that they visibly engage in activities that people associate with "learning the subject matter."*

My argument here is that the psychotic classroom has the symbol stand in for the effects—out of nervousness and superstition, I suppose. My villain is the classroom as an area of well-regulated space where everything has to be justified in advance. It's a nightmare world where every little detail is examined and told, "If you're not part of the solution, you're part of the problem." Obviously, such a classroom is anti-intellectual, since it forbids you to fool around and experiment and discover the value of things.

You can have a psychotic carnival, which is the same thing as the psychotic classroom except that you've plugged "having fun" in place of "learning the subject matter." A lot of pop is this sort of anticlassroom, and that's why it's so boring. Or you could plug in "playfulness" or "open-endedness" or "disruption" or "sensuality" or "excitement" or . . . well, just about any value from any putative "discourse." What bugs me about postpunk, about academic postmodernism, about anything that contains the word *situationist*, is its underlying puritanism.

Movie critics have been pretty good on this subject; they've taught me. Manny Farber's a big source:

> *The idea of art as an expensive hunk of well-regulated area, both logical and magical, sits heavily over the talent of every modern painter, from Motherwell to Andy Warhol.*

> *Most of the feckless, listless quality of today's art can be blamed on its drive to break out of a tradition while, irrationally, hewing to the square, boxed-in shape and gemlike inertia of an old, densely wrought European masterpiece.*

The three sins of white elephant art (1) frame the action with an overall pattern, (2) in-
stall every event, character, situation, in a frieze of continuities, and (3) treat every inch
of the screen and film as a potential area for prizeworthy creativity.
—Manny Farber, "White Elephant Art vs. Termite Art"

And of course, as I said, you can substitute almost any value terms and still get
the same listlessness: "social-meaning song" for "densely wrought European
masterpiece," "attempt to decenter the text" for "overall pattern," "frieze of dis-
continuities" for "frieze of continuities," "disruptive desire" for "prizeworthy
creativity." The problem isn't this or that term of justification, but the attempt
to enforce it with a mad, unsleeping watchfulness.

The enforcement procedure is a process of subtracting things, and it is super-
stitious. E.g., my follow-up sentence in *WMS #7*:

People learn from experience that a lot of medicine tastes bad, and they come to think
that "tasting bad" is the active ingredient in medicine. So, when their medicine isn't
working, they think that by subtracting the sweet stuff they're making it more medicinal.

In my letter to [Michael] Freedberg, my worry is that the life gets subtracted
from disco, not that something inappropriate gets added. And, finally, referring
to your previous letter: Yes, intellectual concerns—hell, social-worker concerns,
too—can enrich the site of pop music, and initially they did via Jagger, Dylan, and
Rotten. But in total, so far, they've impoverished the site, subtracted more than
they've added. Since the concerns are good ones that I won't abandon, we've all
got to look real hard at what we're doing. The first *Why Music Sucks* started with
the claim, "_WE_ are doing something to kill music." Lots of people read this and
many tried, as vigorously and unconsciously as possible, to change the subject.

from letter to Simon Frith, June 23, 1991

A TRIP TO THE MOUNTAINS

SCOTT: Okay, well talk a bit about you and Chuck. There did seem to be a moment, in the mid-'80s or late '80s when something kind of exciting seemed to emerge—I mean, obviously you had been around for a while, but to people like myself, I had heard about you through *Spin* or something . . .

FRANK: Probably through Chuck.

SCOTT: Through Phil, I think. But something exciting had emerged and it was popping up in all these places like *Spin* magazine, so go back to that idea maybe, you know, it's not happening anymore. There's still great stuff going on, in fact there's probably more now than there was ten years ago if you look at this kind of little network of like, *Radio On*, *Why Music Sucks*, and I'm sure there's other 'zines that you're interested in or whatever, but . . . what happened?

FRANK: There's definitely something overall bad that's happening which I didn't think was happening ten years ago, certainly wasn't happening in *Fusion* or *Creem* 20 years ago, or 25 years ago. And a lot of people will say, "Oh well, everybody's now concerned about selling product." And this doesn't quite get the problem—it has something to do with the problem, but the problem isn't that *Spin* will say "Oh, our demographics show that blah blah blah people in Tulsa want to listen to the Stone Temple Pilots or"—well, not Stone Temple Pilots, that's a bad example 'cause you can get away with writing bad reviews of them [laughs]—but you know, "People wanna hear Pearl Jam so we better run a good review of Pearl Jam." I don't think they think that way; it's not this sort of conspiracy or something like that.

SCOTT: It seems like tepidity—if that's a word—on the part of the writers.

FRANK: Yeah. What I think is going on is something worse, it isn't that people are trying to sell the product or have to give a good review because that's what the readers want to read or something like that, but it's much more along the lines of they have to sell the subject matter as something worth reading about to the reader. And this is where I think something really evil has kind of overtaken.

A couple examples I keep held in my head: Maybe about two years ago I was in a doctor's office reading *Interview* and there was an article about Jodie Foster, and it seemed like every other paragraph was some quotation from some person who was identified, an important person in Hollywood says that, "It's really important that Jodie Foster is making her own movies." And it was just one thing after another. Rather than say, "This is the sort of movie that Jodie Foster makes and this is what it's like" and assuming that if you write it the reader should be interested in what you say, it's almost like you've got pages and pages of tributes to Jodie Foster, and the point is to tell the reader that the subject matter is worth reading about. It isn't that you're trying to sell Jodie Foster because you're on Jodie Foster's payroll, it's that you're trying to sell the idea that Jodie Foster is worth reading about, and therefore you should be reading this paragraph or this column, this article. And then there was something else where someone in the *San Francisco Examiner* was writing about the Kronos Quartet and it was the same thing, you know, here were a bunch of important people who were identified as important people, like blah blah blah, who's the head of the conservatory or blah blah blah bullshit or something like that says that the Kronos Quartet is doing something extraordinary, and it was like the first half of this thing was establishing the importance of the Kronos Quartet, and therefore establishing that, yes, this is something you should be reading about. This doesn't *always* happen. The same person who did the Kronos Quartet piece actually just did an interview with Mary Gaitskill, and you know, with Mary you don't have to do that because all you need to do is say, "So Mary, you said that when you worked in strip clubs you found it empowering," then you've got people who will read it anyway [laughs], you don't have to prove to people that she's important, since she's got something else you can sell. And to me that's much more interesting. I don't mind the fact that people are selling something if they're selling romance and adventure and sex, even if it turns out that they're reviewing this new group and they're making this group seem really daring and adventurous and romantic and witty and all that, and then you buy the record and it's bullshit. It's still an interesting . . . I mean I wouldn't deliberately lie as a writer—if the writer did something worthwhile in the world by presenting something on the page that was interesting . . . But just to sort of present, "Well, important people say this is important"—it's just awful.

In rock criticism it's like, you know, the pull quote will be something like, "Three years ago, PJ Harvey was milking cows in bars in the south of England, and now her third album has gone platinum." Or something like, "Frank Kogan is this obscure Basque sheep herder, except important people like Chuck Eddy or blah blah blah blah climb the Pyrenees to visit him." [laughs] That'll be the whole thing, we'll sell Frank Kogan by the fact that important people have come to visit him, rather than saying what Frank Kogan said and *allowing* the reader—well, not allowing them, just sort of letting the reader decide for himself whether he's interested in Frank Kogan or not, rather than having a bunch of testimonials telling you that if you're interested in Frank Kogan that's a good thing because Frank Kogan is important so you're not wasting your time, or for someone who isn't interested, well you *should* be interested in Frank Kogan because important people are and he's important.

And this cuts to the bone of not just rock criticism, but even of what I think is wrong with *rock*. There's a sense in which—I think the way I put it in some of my pieces is that I don't want to tell the editor or the audience that the subject matter is important, I want the audience to figure out their own importance. This is how journalism—cultural criticism—is doing a big disservice to the reader. One thing I imagine in my fantasy is that what Iggy was trying to do for the audience is in a sense put them on their own to decide, rather than come in a package that says "Iggy is important." I think a lot of the readers want to be told that, "I'm important through this thing I like"—it's very human—but I think this is something that—excuse the expression—it's important to deny them. I think readers do want to read testimonials to some extent, but being a good parent isn't always giving in to what your child demands, and this is something where you don't give in to the readers' [pause] insecurities. Their own importance is a trip that they've got to follow themselves, and whether they find Spoonie Gee or Teena Marie, or all these other people I've championed, interesting and of value to them, I want to put Spoonie Gee and Teena Marie on the page, I don't want to put the fact that other famous people were influenced by them.

from "Pushin' Too Hard: an interview with Frank Kogan," *Popped*, 1997

CHAPTER 23

HERE WE GO

My thoughts on this being the Year Of The Bubblegum (or whatever Metal Mike Saunders called it in his B*witched review): *Every* year is the Year Of The Bubblegum—I remember one of my roommates in San Francisco being upset to learn, in 1991, that in a poll of kindergarten kids in Los Angeles the category MY FAVORITE PERSON was won by Paula Abdul, with "Mommy" finishing a distant second. If this is the year of B-gum in P&J it will only be by default; i.e., it's not obviously the Year Of Something Else.

I suppose it's the Year Of The Bubblegum on *Billboard's* charts, with teen-associated acts in four of the top five spots (and Shania Twain, the lone non-teen-directed act in the Top 5, getting huge teen support). But then, "teen act" and "bubblegum" are ever more arbitrary categories: which is to say that the Backstreet Boys happen to be huge on Adult Contemporary radio, something that had never happened to Tommy James, Napoleon XIV, Ohio Express back in the day—I remember in 1968 my mother hearing "Yummy yummy yummy I've got love in my tummy" on the car radio and exclaiming, "That's obscene!" (I, at age fourteen, thought it was too stupid to be obscene.) And Backstreet Boys, Britney, Ricky, and 'NSync probably do way better among people over thirty than, say, toughs like DMX or Eve or Jay-Z or Juvenile do (or than Led Zeppelin and Def Leppard and Guns N' Roses and Bon Jovi and the Rolling Stones did when *they* first went Top 40). So "bubblegum" and "teen" (and "pre-teen") don't just refer to the perceived age of the audience but also to the style of the music, the demeanor and age of the performers, and something vaguer, say the general sense that this is the sort of music that is teenish and bubblegummy because it reminds us of the sort of thing we think of as being teenish and bubblegummy. Which isn't to say that the following definition isn't useful: "sweet, poppy-sounding songs, and also ballads, that appeal to teen girls and pre-teens." It just doesn't encompass all the people that the music appeals to or all the music that appeals to teen girls and pre-teens.

But anyway, I like the following fine (roughly in this order): "Livin' La Vida Loca," "Genie in a Bottle," "Tearin' Up My Heart," "I Want You Back" (I'm not sure it was a single, but the kid upstairs plays it all the time), ". . . Baby One More Time," and no doubt all the others that are getting votes. But I don't like them more than "Wannabe" or "Lollipop (Candyman)" or "Straight Up" or "Bad Bad Boys" or "Jump" or "Cars with the Boom" etc., so I don't see what's so special about this particular year—except maybe, as I said, the former set is *perceived* as teen music, while not all of the latter is. I don't remember Paula Abdul being considered a teenybopper act; just a general pop act (that happened to appeal to a lot of teens and pre-teens). And the teen appeal of Britney Spears and Christina Aguilera is based on their age, not their sound, which is not much different from the adult sounds of Celine Dion and Mariah Carey—who also have done well among teens.

The point I want to make is that to think of "fluff" and "fun"—terms used by Mike McPadden in some article that Chuck emailed to me (bubblegum did well among Mikes this year)—as defining what's for the kids simply does not take into account what kids want, what they really really want, or how they interpret or use what they really really get. It's an adult construction of kiddom, a cliché. Not that I in particular know what's going on. For example, to me, the Spicies were glitter-glam factory girls on their night out, and I simply don't know what to make of the fact that their audience was almost entirely girls under the age of fifteen. And I don't know what to make of the fatassed louty Spice sluts being superseded by skinnyass ex-mouseketeers; I know what I think, but I don't know what the prime audience thinks. I played the "Genie in a Bottle" video for my girlfriend's children: Lia (age seven) loved it right off, and said that she hoped she looked like that (like Christina Aguilera) when she got older (Lia is already far more beautiful than Aguilera, though she hasn't a clue yet about her own beauty; in her mind she's a doer, not a looker); Michaela (age nine) despised the video and said, "What, you want to look like a freak?" And then kept muttering, "She's a freak, she's a freak," which almost drove Lia to tears until we explained to her that Michaela was talking about Aguilera, not her. Jordana (age five) had immediately announced that she loved the song, then when Michaela started slagging it announced that she hated it, and Lia said that it wasn't very good; then when Michaela left the room Lia and Jordana agreed that the song was great. Jordana likes what she likes, what she really really likes, even if she superficially pretends to go along with what other people are saying. She's the only one to stick with the now-passé Spice Girls. Michaela got tired of the Spice Girls a year ago, probably of her own choice though maybe influenced by friends; Lia gave up on them too, partly from peer pressure—some neighborhood boys were over and they and Michaela must have badmouthed the Spicies, because the next day Lia gave away her own Spice Girl dolls to Jordana—but also because she cares more about 'NSync.

[Several months after Pazz & Jop, Michaela explained why she didn't like Aguilera: "You can tell from the way she sings that she thinks she's just SO great." Presumably Michaela was referring to Christina's show-off vocal wiggles. At the time, not only did Michaela's show-off younger sister like Christina, but the cool show-off pop fans in Michaela's fourth grade were shunning Michaela's best friend, leaving Michaela with a stark choice: her friend or the cool crowd. (She chose her friend.) I can't tell you if these were factors in her dislike of Christina, but they resonated for me when I heard Michaela's critique.

By the way, I haven't liked much beyond "Genie in a Bottle," and the trouble, actually, is that Christina doesn't think she herself is so great, she thinks MARIAH is great. And what is wiggly, assertively alive in Mariah comes across as self-abnegating in Christina.)]

Of the songs I've taped for the girls, the ones they love most are Boney M's "Rasputin" and Millie Small's "My Boy Lollipop," with an honorable mention to L'Trimm's "Cars with the Boom." Joyous stuff, but not *merely* joyous. Michaela was all set to do a research project on Lincoln, but then she heard "Rasputin" so decided to do it on him, though in then doing research (the story of Rasputin must have baffled her) she decided that she was more interested in Anastasia, the beautiful princess who got shot. Anastasia was easier to identify with.

The main appeal of "Eleanor Rigby" seems to be that Paul pronounces church "chuhch."

Lia likes "Here We Go" by 'NSync because it allows her to chant "here we go!" I think she likes the word "go." It suits her. During Britney Spears' "Crazy" she has me lift her up over my head whenever Britney says "Crazy." I don't know if I dare tape Debbie Gibson's "Shake Your Love." It might be perfect for her, a lift on every "shake," but I'm not sure I'd have the energy. Michaela likes ". . . Baby One More Time" but declares "Crazy" to be "the world's most boring song." I said, "I thought you liked the song?" "Not thirty-four times in a row."

Lia doesn't like to hear the name *Xuxa* (pronounced "SHOO-shuh") because it reminds her of sushi, and she once got sick eating sushi.

excerpts from "Pazz & Jop ballot 1999," January 14, 2000

CHUHCH AND GO

(letter to Geeta Dayal, at the time a journalism student)

I'm curious what you think about journalism. I don't hate newspapers per se, and I think it crucial that the *NY Times*, for instance, continue to do a good job chronicling the totalitarian impulses of the Bush administration and the potentially disastrous effects of Bush's tax cuts. But "journalism" has had an awful awful awful effect on criticism, has developed rules and prejudices that are dysfunctional and anti-intellectual and that produce continual stupidity and shallowness. One example: that we're supposed to report the news, not make the news ourselves. Why? As it is, rock critics are forbidden to write about each other and about each other's work. Imagine if chemists were forbidden to conduct experiments and forbidden to discuss each other's ideas, and were slammed as self-indulgent whenever they did so. Yet if you use music in your prose as you would in your life, and comment on how other people use it in their prose, then you're a wanker, either a weirdo rock-critic geek or a gonzo wild thing, a beatnik, a "personal journalist." Or a diarist, a blogwriter. And if what interests you in the life of the music doesn't match up with the standard idea of newsworthiness (e.g., doesn't tie in with some reportable trend or connect to some newly available commodity or recent disaster), then you're just plain off the map.

When Christgau excerpted from my [1999 P&J] ballot, of course he couldn't use all my comments, but the ones he chose were telling: He used the sentence about "teen act" and "bubblegum" being ever more arbitrary categories, and Backstreet being huge on adult contemporary radio; and he used the anecdote where Lia wanted to look like Christina, and Michaela retorting, "What, you want to look like a freak?" (but Xgau cut it off before Lia was driven almost to tears, that is, before it *really* became about the interaction between Lia and Michaela). And those two excerpts were the two that counted most as conventionally newsworthy, that is, were about the teen-pop phenomenon and girls' self-image (and connected to what other people were saying in Pazz & Jop about the relation between teen pop and girls' self-image); and with these excerpts being taken out of my context, my point was lost: that kids use music in ways that simply don't register in the adult discourse of "What kids are doing when they're listening to music." To me the best passages were the ones where Lia likes "go" and makes me raise her up over my head whenever Britney says "crazy," and that Paul says "chuhch" instead of "church," and that Xuxa reminds Lia of the fact that she got sick eating sushi.

To me this *is* the subject matter—"chuhch" and "here we go!"—eight million stories in the naked city, sixteen million hands, everybody grasping the music and each using it in his or her own way, finding his or her own "go," each discovering a "chuhch" to wonder at, no one's experience duplicated by the next person's but each drawing on the sounds and the people in the immediate environment—EXCEPT IN MAGAZINES, which are devoid of "chuhch" and "go," because the editors and maybe the readers too, the chuhchgoers themselves, don't want to see it in print. But damn, if I were an editor I'd want it in print, people's various, multiple, and creative chuhches and here we goes, and I'd want it in with no preconceived notion of what counts as "chuhch" and "go." It can be little girl action, kids jumping and dancing and joking and fighting, it can be gossiping and flirting, but it also can be Simon Frith, writing in dead encyclopedia prose (but in obvious long-term wonder and amazement nonetheless) for the *Encyclopædia Britannica* about how in 1962 Ray Charles set the pattern for the rock ballad with his gospel version of the country song "I Can't Stop Loving You": "Charles's emotional sincerity was marked by vocal roughness and hesitation (unlike the Italian balladeers), and, if his tempo was slow, it was nevertheless insistent." (A very simple sentence, but I hadn't connected the power ballad and the Mariah ballad to Charles until Frith did it for me, so Ray Charles is now one of my "chuhches"; and one of my "goes" is to wonder delightedly, given the fact that Charles knocked down the barrier between gospel and Garland; and Whitney, Mariah, et al. knocked down the barrier between soul and Streisand; whether Shakira, coming out of god knows where—Iglesias and Led Zeppelin and Colombia and Arabia?—is obliterating the wall that was supposed to separate Streisand and Celine from Dylan and Joni. Wouldn't that be a mindfuck! She's the only singer I can think of who could pull off convincing versions of both "My Heart Will Go On" and "Like a Rolling Stone.")

The thing is, most of the commercial publications out there—the altweeklies and the music mags and the dailies—have thrown in the towel completely on such things, if indeed they'd ever picked it up in the first place. The rock press is a chuhchless and goless landscape, and the readers themselves, despite their being the origin of chuhches and goes, seem not to want much chuhch and go, since chuhching and going *are* a challenge to readers, challenge their sense of what's important. But the music itself makes such a challenge—the *music* says that "here we go" matters, that it's a real "go," something that speaks to the inner Go. And there used to be mags that trusted the reader, thought that, though they were challenging and upsetting the reader, something within the reader would welcome the challenge, would prefer disturbance to stasis, didn't want the "go" safely at a fictional distance in pop songs or merely in his or her own life, but wanted it projected onto the public page, along with the joking and flirting and fighting that accompanies it, when different people throw their various and individual *go's* up against one another.

My principle is this: We can't convey the romance and the adventure of music unless we're willing to convey our own romance and adventure. And if we want to continue on with the so-long-ago ideals of the music ("Don't follow leaders" someone once said)—if we want readers to be inspired by the music, not subordinate to it—then we must set the example and not be subordinate to it ourselves.

email to Geeta Dayal, June 25, 2002

CHAPTER 24

AND *YOUR* BIRD CAN SING
(REVIEW OF RICHARD MELTZER'S *A WHORE JUST LIKE THE REST*)

There's creation and there's listening—one has eight letters and one has nine.
—Richard Meltzer

For what it's worth, Richard Meltzer is the greatest rock critic so far, and over the years he's developed an ability to write—to get the prose alive on the page—that probably surpasses Burroughs's or Twain's or Faulkner's. But hey, maybe this is only faint praise, and *not* because *rock critic* is a pejorative, but because as Meltzer has improved his writing he's let his thinking—at least about rock 'n' roll—go into reverse. And so much of his writing comes from anger, he's gotten such energy from it, that to accommodate the anger he's allowed his ideas to go stupid. So anyway, now he's a great writer, a great word-on-the-page man ("A powerful, scabrous work . . . by one of the great stylists in English"—*Birdcage Weekly*). Rate his collection, *A Whore Just Like the Rest*, an A PLUS. But that grade conceals several Everests of ambivalence.

For one thing, to get to the thought behind some of Meltzer's early work—which contains his first real flow of brilliant ideas and the purest joy he's ever felt in the subject matter, but which is also *very* elliptical and cryptic—is like trying to stare through to the other side of hieroglyphs. And this book's most crucial stuff, his great ACTING OUT of his ideas in the early '70s, tends to be trash-it-out, mannered flippantry. So you get the full voice of Meltzer later and the full ideas of Meltzer earlier, but you rarely get them together. And anyway the ideas are just a start; Meltzer never finished them. Profound contradictions are left unexamined, social ideas are stated in unwieldy philosophical terms, and, though he's written more and better social detail than any sociologist of music has, social *analysis* is nonexistent (unless you count, in his later writing, his calling fellow critics shills and whores or his taking sub-sub-sub-Frankfurt School clichés almost down to the moron level; e.g., his calling post-'60s rock "crowd control for the post-puberty (under 40?) masses").

So lately—and this includes the little intros he's tacked on before each of the old pieces—he's been doing a real shitsucky version of presenting his own ideas. For example: When he says, "I aspired to the SPIRIT of rock," he's just going along with the vague mysto-sentimentality of his most thoughtless fans. Yes, spirit is nice (rah-rah), but Meltzer also—once—aspired to the *mind* of rock 'n' roll, chose rock 'n' roll as his *intellectual* activity—chose to do rock 'n' roll on the page, since what rock 'n' roll did was to mix up, flummox, challenge, test everyone's sense of what was relevant or irrelevant in the world; to create a space where just anything could be pertinent. (Isn't this what real thinking is: to test what's pertinent? To question what matters? To act out your questions? To flummox, test, reinvent social relations? And if you're a thinker, isn't testing your own ideas what *rocks* you?)

As an undergrad student of artist Allan Kaprow's at Stony Brook, Meltzer noticed that environmental art and happenings did with great effort what rock 'n' roll simply *did*, which was to include the context—and therefore the audience—in the artwork. Context includes "money, competition, survival, acceptance by adolescents, reaction by standard adults," not to mention screaming teenies, fan magazines, girls holding signs ("We Love You Paul"), radio countdowns, marketing strategies, etc., and when you add to this *people's lives* (I dare you *not* to listen to music in the context of your life), it also includes joking and gossiping and flirting and fighting and whatever (e.g., there's this pet bird that likes to hear this Johnny Rivers song, and the girl who owns the bird has nice tits). And it also includes the listener *who writes about music*, e.g., Meltzer or me or you, who—duh!—has the same right as any fan or musician to use music in any way that he or she wants, to create context in any way he or she can; which in Meltzer's case, after rock seemed to him to have calmed down and normalized itself in the late '60s, meant mangling, altering, reinventing, and *being* the context. On the page, in his writing. And if the rock 'n' roll mind had gone dead in the music—pertinence now seemed to stay where it was told—pertinence could still be anywhere he wanted on *his* page. For instance:

MELTZER AT THE METROPOLITAN OPERA: "Real pindrop conditions and somebody rattling keys was told 'Stop rattling those keys' and another somebody really worked overtime slowing down a fart." These are social points, obviously, and obviously relevant. The transgression against standard journalism isn't that Meltzer includes farts but that in doing so he includes his own stance towards the subject matter and includes enough info for the reader to infer Meltzer's own stance towards him or her and for the reader therefore to (involuntarily, spontaneously) react, to come up with his/her own attitude towards not just the subject matter but towards Meltzer. All of which is as relevant as the fart, if you want it to be.

MELTZER ON THE DOORS: "*Absolutely Live* is a great party album. And what makes parties what they are? Food, mostly." Then he gives recipes for dishes to accompany the album, e.g., "Vomit à la Vitamin Pill" to go with "Soul Kitchen" (ingredients: "vitamin pill, any size or potency; Venetian blind cord"), "TV-Guide

Pizza" (staple remover optional) to go with "Who Do You Love?" ("Dump the liquid grease all over [the pizza] and stick it back in the oven until it reaches desired crispyhood. And you can stick the staple remover on there too if you go for that. Yum-yum.") Here he's not reporting a context but creating one, though one obviously appropriate to the Doors. (Which makes this piece probably rock-magazine acceptable. When I read it as a teenager I was hit with this epiphany: Historians and archaeologists/anthropologists of the future would understand more about the Doors from this piece than they would from a description of the Doors' music. Of course, there's no reason they couldn't learn from both—and a critic who could convincingly draw a connection between the musical notes and the vomit pill would be a great critic.)

MELTZER QUOTING HIGHWAY PATROLMAN SGT. JACK BERRY IN REGARD TO THE TRAF-FIC-JAMMED-AND-ABANDONED CARS AT ALTAMONT: "It's really a beautiful sight to see, nothing moving except the people themselves, and it's just like the cars are part of nature too, or art, like in a museum. It's beautiful, really, and I sure hope the people don't distort this in the press because it really shows us what travel is all about. These kids are hiking over there to the rock and roll, the music, but I can't really understand why they don't just stay here and have a party around the cars." Meltzer made this quote up, made up the entire piece, fiction, avoided mention of the Rolling Stones, Jefferson Airplane, stabbing deaths, or anything else that made Altamont newspaper-important. No, there was one mention of the Stones: "Even after the Stones were finished and most people were home in bed there were still parties going on. The Bellport Country Club was the scene of a gay glamorous party as members of the Bellport Chamber of Commerce gathered for their annual dinner-dance." And Meltzer did describe the perfor-mances of the Guess Who and Joe Cocker (neither of whom actually played at Altamont). So: imaginary context. Context completely at odds with the sense of importance attached to the main event. The context of the context: readers (and publishers) looking for insight on tragic event. Meltzer's act: not to cooperate with their sense of what's important, not to cooperate with their sense of the subject matter.

MELTZER ABOUT HEROIN: "And they oughta recycle all the used [fingernails] and use them in natural backscratchers. With replacements for when they get worn down and you could buy them in either sharp or dull as you all know even the dull ones get the job done too." Well, the first three paragraphs of the piece had been about heroin, and then Meltzer just veered away to chewing nails and scratching backs. He doesn't collapse the distinction between importance and unimportance so much as he simply walks away from the issue, leaving you to do the same, if you want. The walking away in the Altamont piece was still shaped by—was a reversal of—what was being walked away from (rock show to parked cars, freak party to chamber-of-commerce party). Whereas the heroin piece is more like: Any subject contains a multitude of tangents just waiting, like rabbit holes; here's one, and down we go.

MELTZER'S REVIEW OF AN ALBUM BY NED: "Asphalt can be used to cover cobblestones. It can be taken home (if no one is lookin'). Asphalt should not be confused with, with, with, with . . . asbestos. Confuse them at your own risk. Insects will sometimes live in cement but never asphalt. Asphalt soup tastes like tar. Asphalt soap does not clean especially well. Asphalt dopes are QUITE dopey. They know nothing of asphalt (having never seen it); some live in Alaska." And now, here, the subject matter is simply gone, erased; it's not even a point to be walked away from. The screen, camera, page is blank, and Meltzer is just writing. How does it feel to be on your own?

The Village Voice, July 4, 2000

CHAPTER 25

SUPERWORDS REVISITED

SUPERWORDS

I was clustering a group of related behaviors in my idea of the Superword: a word that causes controversies, that gets fought over, that sometimes runs on ahead of its embodiments; a word that seems to jettison adherents.

I'm restating the idea of *Superwords* here to highlight some points that might have gotten buried in chapter 7. Recall that a Superword is a word like "punk," which is, among other things, a battleground, a weapon, a red cape, a prize, a flag in a bloody game of Capture the Flag. To put this in the abstract, a Superword is a word or phrase that not only is used in fights but that is itself fought over. The fight is over who gets to wear the word proudly, who gets the word affixed to himself against his will, etc. So the *use* is fought over, and this—the fight over usage—is a big part of the word's use. That is, we use the term in order to engage in arguments over how to use the term. So meta-use is use.

But a Superword isn't simply fought over; what makes a Superword really super is that some people use the word so that it will jettison adherents and go skipping on ahead of any possible embodiment. Like, no one and nothing is good enough to bear the word "punk," and I wouldn't join a punk band that would have someone like me as a member anyway. "Rock," "pop," "punk," and many other genre names can act as Superwords. So "punk" (for instance) can be an ideal, and every single song that aspires to be punk can fall short in someone's ears. But for the word to be super, not only must people disagree on the ideal, but some people must consciously or unconsciously keep *changing* what the word or ideal is supposed to designate so that the music is always inadequate to the ideal, even if the music would have been adequate to yesterday's version of the ideal. And the music then chases after this ever-changing ideal. Words bounce on ahead, and the music comes tumbling after.

Yet this "bouncing ahead" often has its eye on the past. The argument over who gets to be punk in the present is often also an argument over who was punk in the past. Sterling Clover posted on *I Love Music*:

One key part of what constitutes a superword, I think (punk and metal being almost categorical examples), is the constant rewriting of history and restructuring and stream-

lining of the canon in the course of the combative evolution of a superword genre. . . .
For superword fetishists influence runs backwards and chooses its heroes in the process
of defining the genre (i.e., "the ultimate metal album doesn't yet exist, but if it did, it
would take these elements from the past and put them together—hey let's start a band
like that!").

Another way to work the mechanism is to put the ideal hopelessly and inaccessibly in the past: e.g., we realize that there's no way, even if we copy the notes and the look, that we could ever be what the Stooges were in '72 or Britney was in '99, so we look for or try to be something that is different but equivalent. See my "fuck machines and razor blades" rant in part six, where I'm contending (or dreaming) that the next Stooges won't arise from the closed world of "punk rock" but from postdisco musics like freestyle, where the Stooges aren't an influence but where, unlike in punk rock, participants can nonetheless just naturally dance themselves into Stooges-like fuckeduppedness.

You know that a genre term is a Superword if someone declares the genre dead and locates the real hip-hop/punk/disco in a lost golden age. And just as the Protestant reformers used the idea of a golden age (early Christianity, before corrupted by Catholicism) to progressively modify their conception of what a Christian Church could be and to create religious ideas that had never existed before, *Creem* magazine in the late '60s called itself "America's Only Rock 'n' Roll Magazine" while extolling music that had little to do with what had previously been called "rock 'n' roll." Interestingly, the Creemsters appropriated the term "rock 'n' roll" at a time when "rock" rather than "rock 'n' roll" was the generic term for the music, and "rock 'n' roll" was being used *only* to designate music from the antediluvian pre-1964 pre-Beatles era. But in *Creem*, the golden age was more likely to be 1966 ("Wild Thing" and "96 Tears") than 1956, even though in 1966 itself, *no* pop band would have called itself "rock 'n' roll," a term that was obsolete, square. Several years later, putting the "roll" back in "rock" was a countercool move in opposition to the counterculture's serious rock worship. But the *Creem* ethos didn't lead people to make music that sounded like '56 *or* '66 but rather to musics such as glam and metal and punk that progressed in their own ways, even while shunning the word "progressive." For that matter, the basic musical vocabulary of many of the mid-'60s "punk" bands (as they were only called in retrospect)—i.e., the garage bands and the Velvet Underground—was derived from the Yardbirds rave-ups. The garage-band kids were snobs who worshiped the Stones and Yardbirds and sneered at the Beatles as too pop (except for the ones who didn't) and were likely to think of themselves as experimentalists. (Ken Emerson: "The Yardbirds were too manic to be consistent, but their adventurousness exemplified all that was 'progressive.' They anticipated the freak-outs of psychedelic San Francisco, pioneered what later would be dubbed 'heavy metal,' and dabbled in everything from ersatz Gregorian chants to Mideastern reels.") One could say that the progressive rockers were inspired by the Yardbirds' guitar solos, while the garage rockers were inspired by the Yardbirds' rhythms. But in fact the garage rockers went for the solos as well. It was only in 1970s retrospect by snobby antisnobs that the garage bands were rehabilitated as nonsnobs and antiprogressive primitives. And the subsequent punk guitar sound of the Stooges and Dolls and Sex Pistols wouldn't have happened without the innovations of progressive FM radio heroes such as Cream and the Airplane and Hendrix. (Cf. James Williamson's opening guitar riff on the Stooges' "Search and Destroy" and Jorma Kaukonen's near-identical opening to the Airplane's "Have You Seen the Saucers.") So in some respects glam, metal, and punk were modifications of progressive rock. The punks initially looked "back" as a technique of progressing away from progressive rock.

So in the '50s rock 'n' roll declares itself the new and is haunted by its future, a specter it chases. But in the late '60s, having been superseded by the even newer "rock," it reappears—or something else appears, bearing its name—but this time carrying within itself the idea of a Fall from grace. So it not only chases the future, but chases the past into the future, as well.

Words can go from super to nonsuper depending on the time and situation, and words can gain or lose super status. Not all hot-button words are Superwords. For instance, Thomas Kuhn has described how the words "planet" and "motion" were the subject of great controversy during the several centuries' changeover from Aristotelian to Newtonian cosmology. But the controversy was one that had to be resolved. To disagree over "punk" is a normal way of relating to other punks, of being a punk. Whereas to disagree over "planet" or "motion" is to be unable to carry on a common enterprise of physics with the guy you're disagreeing with. So unlike punk, physics strives to resolve its basic disagreements.

This doesn't prevent its resolutions from eventually leading to new disagreements (and anyway I'm talking through my hat when it comes to physics, and basically just taking Kuhn on faith). I'll go off-topic for a moment to point out that the difference between science and music is social, not ontological; that is, physicists don't come to agreement because they're scientists with a method; they're called scientists because they come to agreement. However, a difference's being social rather than ontological doesn't make it less of a difference. And the fact that people can't and don't have to agree about such basics as whether, say, the audience screaming at 'NSync shows is part of the music or not (i.e., don't agree about what "music" is) doesn't mean that they don't *agree* about a lot of things—e.g., to report 'NSync in the music section rather than the sports section.

Genre names would be neither hot-button words nor Superwords if people didn't use them to differentiate themselves from each other. We differentiate from each other by using words differently (just as we differentiate by pronouncing words differently, by dressing differently, etc.), and we differentiate by *categorizing* each other as different. So we jigger the Superwords when we want to escape being identified with people who tend to be categorized as like us and when we want to be identified with people who tend to be categorized as unlike us. As Tracer Hand says, "I think one of the curses of being a superword is that your niche is never fixed, you have to keep packing stuff back into boxes and moving to a new place, even if it's just down the street. Sometimes you get to stay in the same apartment but the walls all have to move like 2 inches to the left. What a pain in the ass!"

That you can use "punk" as a Superword doesn't mean that it's *only* usable as an ideal. In fact, basic language skills demand that people use such words in a multiplicity of ways, sometimes even within the same breath (e.g., my complaining back in 1985 that "punk isn't punk anymore"). Someone might object to, for instance, the contention that Metallica is a metal band while Poison is a *pop*-metal band, given that Metallica is actually more popular, hence more deserving of the epithet "pop." Yet this person would have no problem directing a customer ("my nephew would like me to buy him some vintage 1980s pop metal") to bands like Poison, Crüe, Warrant, Cinderella, and Leppard (and would have no trouble understanding that "hair metal" refers to Poison but not to Metallica, despite Metallica's being hairier).

"Pop—glossy glorious robotic energetic teenage all-age singing dancing pop— is dead," Tom Ewing wrote in 2001—and subsequently went right on using the word "pop" to refer to music that didn't resemble his glorious dead era of She'kspere, Max Martin, TLC, Britney, "Bills Bills Bills," "Everybody (Backstreet's Back)." Tom explains (some) of his usages as (1) what's on the charts, regardless of quality, unless other considerations override this ("I'd sooner call MBV 'indie' or 'shoegaze' or something even if their record is in the chart because calling them 'pop' feels like a violation of meanings 2 and 3"), (2) the specific current style of pop, (3) "a personal ideal of mine, a kind of music which individual records and even periods of Pop(2) can live up to but which Pop(1) as a whole cannot," and (4) "one end of a continuum of images, stances, and actions relating to the presentation and production processes of an artist and their music; i.e. heavy marketing, major label support, not writing one's own music etc."

THE GREAT WRONG ARGUMENT

I want to emphasize here the basic normality of the Superword process. So I won't push the analogy between "church of Christ" and "punk" *too* far, since the Reformation took Christianity and Europe through great changes, whereas punk isn't doing anything remotely comparable, as far as I can tell. Most Superwords are part of everyday flexibility, may change something but rarely change an entire sea. In fact, if you look at what I wrote above about "motion" and "planet," it was because those and related hot-button words were *not* Superwords—within the relevant intellectual community the different usages ultimately could not co-exist, but rather new usages developed that entirely superseded the old—that the Copernican Revolution was a paradigm shift.

The reason I've put this chapter in the Great Wrong Place is that I don't want the concept *Superword* to get sucked into the Great Wrong Argument. Here's an example of what I mean:

In the margin of the college paper in which I'd originally worked out my idea of Superwords (I was using the word "freedom" as my example), the teacher wrote, "A structuralist might call this a form of deconstruction or de-centering; there is no longer a central core of meaning, but only little meanings, each of which is a variant repetition of the other, but none of which can point back to any single originating center." This went over my head at the time (1975); now it just seems incoherent. If you can't point back to a single originating center—and I think this is right, not just for Superwords, but for all words—then you can't say that there's *no longer* a core of meaning, or that you've *de*-centered anything. There was never any center in the first place, and the idea of a central core of meaning is simply irrelevant. I don't see why a structuralist would call this "de-centering" any more than an atheist would claim to be moving away from God. Actually, I'll say this more strongly: An atheist still has to contend with a world that *believes* he's walking away from God, even though he himself has dispensed with the concept; whereas the structuralist, if he were for real, could just ignore the concept of "core of meaning," since it hardly carries much cultural weight.

I think that in order to believe that "de-centering" or "deconstruction" is a big deal, or that "meaning" in the abstract is a socially important issue, you have to hold two basically incompatible positions at once: (1) that a word or a statement has something called "its meaning" that is self-contained and independent and not itself a word, sentence, or sign (making it a what? a physical object? a state of affairs? a set of sense impressions? those sense impressions as ordered by the psyche?—and can't those things be signs themselves, as smoke is a sign of fire, and fire a sign of dry weather, of lightning, of arson?) and (2) that a word, statement, object, or event has meaning only if there's some difference between its existing (or occurring) and its *not* existing (or occurring)—which makes "meaning" dependent on something's relation to what it is not, a matter of its contrasting with *other* words, statements, objects, and events, which in turn contrast with yet other words, statements, objects, and events, and so on, rather than centering on a "core." But position 2 doesn't announce the *absence* of some "core"; it simply makes no use of the concept "core," which therefore is neither present nor absent, just irrelevant. Position 1 demands that "meanings" be self-contained and isolated, whereas position 2 tells you to ignore anything that's self-contained and isolated, as it can't possibly matter—hence the two positions' incompatibility. I realize I've condensed a lot of yaddayadda in the previous few sentences, and I'm using the word "position" for convenience—I don't mean it to imply any great precision. "Tendency" might do as well, since, of the few people who care about the "positions," fewer still try to think them through; most just waft hopes and dreams in their direction. As for position 2, I'm really saying no more than, e.g., that a volcanic eruption is only significant if there's a difference between the volcano's erupting and its not erupting, and that the *sentence* "The volcano is erupting" is only significant if there's a difference between its being written/uttered and its *not* being written or uttered—so in general here, to understand the significance, you're looking not for cores but for alternatives, for causes, for effects, which can be many. Position 2 only gives you the conditions under which we call something meaningful; it doesn't offer (or require) a general theory as to what words, sentences, objects, or events mean. And as for the significance of, say, the sentence "an event has meaning only if there's some difference between its occurring and its not occurring," it's just a truism and barely meets its own criterion for being meaningful. Although I agree with it, its only useful role in the world is to point out that searches for a core of meaning are unnecessary—a role that I consider pathetic, given that "core of meaning" is irrelevant to the position itself. And, to elaborate on a point that Mykel Board made back in *Why Music Sucks #7*, the sentence really needs to be "a phenomenon has meaning only if there's a *meaningful* difference between its occurring or not occurring," which reduces the statement to a near tautology, telling us no more than that something matters if it matters. And who decides? (Mykel's example: "In English some folks say the word 'spot' with a little puff of air after the 't,' like the 't' in 'tuff.' Others stop abruptly after the 'o,' choking the sound off in the back of their throat. Others pronounce the 't,' but without the puff of air (almost like a 'd')—like the 't' in the word 'stop.' The sounds of all these t's are different, but the meaning of 'spot' does not change because of that difference. In English, these variations are not meaningful. In Hindi, on the other hand, there is a big difference if the equivalent of our 't' is said with or without a puff of air.") You'd have to be a kind of a mugwump, believing that you believe in position 2 while still searching for "a meaning" according to position 1, to think that position 2 changes anything, or matters.

I'll spell this out: If difference is the condition of our calling something meaningful, then you get meaningfulness as soon as something differs from something else, right off the bat, as long as the difference matters to you. Meaningfulness is not postponed, but rather grows as differences accumulate. However, if you're looking for a super-independent, super-self-contained something-or-other that's fixed and stable to a degree that's far beyond any normal standard we have for fixity and stability, well then, yes, the super-stable something-or-other will be endlessly sought but never found. So don't look for it, and don't consider it a "meaning."

Position 1 belongs to a very esoteric conversation, which is why it carries so little cultural weight. For example, the believer who (therefore) believes that the atheist is walking away from God isn't, however, likely to believe that the atheist is abandoning a specific metaphysical God—i.e., a God who is an unmoved mover, transcending time and space. Most believers don't even know that any theologian has posited such a God, and most wouldn't care even if they did know. Likewise, when someone says to me on the phone, "Speak louder, the neighbor's dogs are barking and I'm having trouble hearing you," I do indeed think that in using the words "dogs" and "barking" she's talking about dogs and their barks—but this is unrelated to any opinion I have as to whether dogs and barks have cores or whether those words and those cores have an originating center, can stand alone, etc. That I think my friend is talking about barking dogs is not a primitive version of position 1; it's not a position at all, and depends on no theory of meaning. Nor is it contradicted by position 2, which tells me no more than that being a dog requires the possibility of there being nondogs. (And I'm blissfully free of any opinion as to whether "speak louder" has referents or whether the dependence of a dog on nondogs and "louder" on the not-so-loud means that either concept will undergo change sometime in the future.) Position 1 makes "meaning" into the equivalent of the metaphysical God, makes it a transcendental signified, an unmoved mover that draws us to represent it but that has no dependence on the representation or on anything else and has no other relationship to representations or to anything else, either. In other words, position 1 demands that a "meaning" be *so* independent of what it isn't—e.g., words, statements, signs, other entities, other meanings—that the meaning itself would be unchanged if these other things did not exist (though, I suppose, the meaning itself would no longer be a "meaning," since the word, sentence, or sign that represents it would not exist). This isn't how we generally use the word "independent," by the way; normally, independence is a relative concept. (E.g., the U.S. is independent of Britain, despite Britain's still existing and still having an impact on the U.S.) Very few people actually hold position 1 anymore, much less do anything with it, even if many students and teachers have a vague sense that position 2, by blowing position 1 out of the water, undermines the foundations of something or other and is therefore threatening or liberating. But position 2 is only good for tearing apart attempts to ground "meaning" in an unmoved mover. If you're not searching for such a ground, then position 2 doesn't affect you. And this point can be generalized: Whatever the concept—e.g., "meaning," "presence," "origin," "center," "reality," "male"—if you're not trying to make it a transcendent, super-independent unmoved mover, then it's not a candidate for deconstruction.

So, although position 2—whatever you want to call it (structuralism or relativism or pragmatism or contextualism or holism)—is right, it's inconsequential here. If volcanoes, quarks, events, and all other things, including words, get their meanings from their social lives, as it were—in differentiating from other words, activities, volcanoes, etc.—then one wouldn't expect or need a word to have an essential or original core or for the word to hook onto some independent signified, and the absence of such core/signified would be of no import and would have no bearing on when and whether centers held or fell apart or constructs adhered or crumbled to dust, or whether or not you arrived at what something means.

Wittgenstein made the case against "cores of meaning" better than anyone, e.g., in his discussion of the words "tool" and "game." ("Imagine someone's saying: '*All* tools serve to modify something. Thus the hammer modifies the position of the nail, the saw the shape of the board, and so on.'—And what is modified by the rule, the glue-pot, the nails?—'Our knowledge of a thing's length, the temperature of the glue, and the solidity of the box.'—Would anything be gained by this assimilation of expressions?" And "Look for example at board-games, with their multifarious relationships. Now pass to card-games; here you find many correspondences to the first group, but many common features drop out, and others appear. When we pass next to ball-games, much that is common is retained, but much is lost.—Are they all 'amusing'? Compare chess with noughts and crosses. Or is there always winning and losing, or competition between players? Think of patience. In ball games there is winning and losing; but when a child throws his ball at the wall and catches it again, this feature has disappeared.") Yet despite this "missing" core, the words "tool" and "game" generate few controversies. A non-Superword such as "window" is (for the moment) consistent and boring in what it designates while still being just as relative and socially dependent as Superwords like "punk rock," "femininity," and "Christian"—that windows function as windows depends on their being distinguishable from walls and ceilings, after all. And non-Superwords such as "hot" and "up" are, if anything, far more variable and flexible than "punk rock" etc. without causing fights or undergoing a dynamic of degradation/progression like the one that Williams used with "church of Christ." E.g., a cold star can be a couple of thousand degrees above zero, and a high-temperature superconductor a couple of hundred below, without this making the terms "hot" and "cold" controversial. "Superword" is meant to distinguish some words ("punk," "femininity," "Christian") from others ("traffic light," "hot," "elbow"), rather than to invoke a principle that applies to all words.

And that's another reason why position 2 is of so little consequence: It applies across the board. Back in "Roger Williams" I said, "Hard rock was born in flight." Now, isn't position 2 saying the same thing, but about *everything*, that all phenomena are born in flight, that is to say, are born responding to a world of shifting social relations? Well, yes . . . but only if you set "stillness" at absolute zero, in which case all indeed is in motion, from Eeyore to Antarctica to the coldest intergalactic space, and all social relations are always in flux, no matter how imperceptible. But this simply jumps us back to position 1, makes transcendence and self-sufficiency our ideal, as if Eden were set in colder than cold space and all actual existence were the Fall. (And you don't have to be strange to be strange, as even the barest breeze puts you into unsteady, drifting relations.)

But then, if you want your words to matter, and want to differentiate, say, rock 'n' roll from moonscapes, you don't set stillness at absolute zero, or at anything, but let it be a relationship; so in the 1960s, rock is soaring, swing has lost its swingset, and country is taking careful steps so as not to lose the chip that it's precariously balancing on its shoulder.

I assume, by the way, that if "Superword" makes it into the lexicon, it will be a comparative term, like "hot" (i.e., a word will be super in comparison to the other words you happen to be comparing it to at the moment, and there won't need to be a set of words that everyone agrees are super any more than there needs to be a set of temperatures that everyone agrees are hot), whereas I wouldn't expect "Superword" to become a Superword itself, though you never can tell.

Words used strictly as value judgments—"good," for instance—aren't Superwords, despite their being constantly deployed in controversies. I mean, that's a value judgment's *job*, to be deployed in controversies, and no one but a cultural retard would expect consensus on what the term "good song" designates. Superwords tend to simultaneously be value judgments and descriptions, which gives them a useful tension in that you're expected to disagree about the first but not necessarily about the second. Arguments over what's a *good* hip-hop song aren't as heated as arguments over what's a *real* hip-hop song. (This hardly exhausts the topic, since "good song" can be an insult as well as a compliment, just as "good girl" can be an insult and "bad girl" a compliment—and as such, "bad girl" *can* be a Superword, just as "punk" became a Superword as soon as it became a praise word. Note that "bad girl" is both a value judgment and a social category, and that the judgment and the social category don't necessarily coincide. And note further that "bad" never simply reverses itself, never becomes a *simple* compliment. As an insult, it's a tool for disagreeing with others; as something of a praise word, it's a tool not only for disagreeing with others, but for disagreeing with oneself. See chapter 26.)

To give a boring and tautological answer to the abstract question, "What does something mean?": The *meaning* of something is whatever answers the question "What does *this* mean?" (or a similar question). And the answer depends on the situation and on what particular type of thing you want to know in that particular situation. E.g., "It's sunny and 37 degrees Fahrenheit" means that little Rosalind isn't going to get her wished-for snow day but instead will have to go to school and take the arithmetic test for which she is ill-prepared. "Should I, um, the, you know?" means—or meant in 1989, when I said it—"Should I get the second bottle of pancake syrup out of the refrigerator?" (Leslie understood this and said, simply, "No").

In general, "meaning" and its variants are nonproblematic terms used in requests for further information or in attempts to remove confusion. E.g., you want to know the consequences or implications of something ("Get out of here, you blithering idiot, you're fired." "Does this mean I don't get a letter of recommendation?"), you want clarification ("When you say 'He killed her,' do you mean that he caused the end of her life by shooting her, stabbing her, poisoning her, or something of the sort; or do you mean he made her double over with laughter?"), you want the definition of an unknown word ("What do you mean when you say 'We glocked them'?"), you want to know what distinction is being made ("It's hot in Denver." "You mean in comparison to how it normally is in Denver? Or do you mean in Denver as opposed to San Francisco? Or in comparison to what you were expecting this morning, when you dressed and, as it turns out, overdressed, which is why you feel hot now? Or what?"). An originating center is not even being sought; it's not at issue, and is no more relevant than the tooth fairy. Nor are "core of meaning" and "its meaning," for that matter.

Of course, questions such as "Does this mean I don't get a letter of recommendation?" "What do you mean by 'we glocked them'?" etc. often generate other questions, and you ask as many or as little as you want, depending on what you want to know. But your wanting to ask a further question doesn't necessarily mean that your original answer was inadequate, or that meaning is somehow escaping you. For example, once you've learned that "Glock" is an Austrian-made firearm, you can probably figure out that "glock" is slang for "shoot"; but if you don't figure it out, you ask another question; and, satisfied with the answer, you might nonetheless want to know what someone's using the term implies about his social stance, thereby expanding and enriching your sense of what's going on. But that doesn't mean there was something fundamentally insufficient about the statement "'glock' is slang for 'shoot.'" Sufficiency is always ad hoc. (Of course, if you didn't know what "shoot" and "gun" meant, and what fighting was, then the explanation wouldn't have done enough. All explanations demand knowledge on the listener's part. To know something, you've got to know something else, often a profusion of things. This fact doesn't make knowledge elusive, however, but abundant.) When "meaning" becomes controversial, this isn't due to your failure to finally arrive at an originating center or a core of meaning—what could those terms mean in such a context?—but rather to your success at uncovering a conflict. E.g., back to our Superword "hip-hop":

"You got any hip-hop?"

"Sure. Do you want to hear 'Girls Girls Girls' and 'Hot in Herre?'"

"Hey, I mean *real* hip-hop, not the Gay-Z Nelly faggot shit."

So in this instance, the statement about meaning doesn't provide clarity so much as it reveals a battle. "What do you mean?" can start a fight as soon as it touches value judgments and personal and social differentiation—though the fight can often be fun, something that's both battle and dance.

What's an assumed goal in some contexts and conversations—that *all* differences get resolved—does not pertain to popular music. But whether agreement is sought or not, the theoretical discussion of "meaning" is superfluous. You could say that Wittgenstein and crew decisively set aside the philosophical problem of universals but that this setting aside had little impact one way or another on actual disagreements regarding anything's actual meaning.

Of course, so far I've been sidestepping the fact that scores of otherwise intelligent people *do*, still, consider abstract "meaning" a critical issue. They're being mugwumps; but mugwumpery doesn't just happen for no reason, as some random intellectual mistake.

Consider the word "core." It can mean several things, e.g., can mean "crucial," as in "core values" ("in Community X, honesty is a core value, congeniality not"); but as my teacher was using it, it meant "transcendent" and "immutable." But if we foolishly link "core of meaning" to "originating center" (and to the transcendental signified, and all that), our core meanings are not the ones that are crucial, which'd be those linked to crucial *words*, but are merely the fairy godmeanings that are supposed to give content to *every* word (or every statement, at least). But I wonder if my teacher would have used the word "core" at all if the first meaning—"crucial"—hadn't exerted a subliminal pull. This first sort of "core" can exist, no problem: For a given purpose, some things are crucial, others less so. Say a community values honesty far more than congeniality; the former would be a core value, the latter not. However, when a community—via hot-button or Superword mechanisms—progressively changes what it means to be honest, or what it means to be congenial, or what it means to be feminine or Christian or hip-hop, it's progressively changing its values. The meaning of "Christianity" is a genuine social issue. Although a relativistic position like position 2 has nothing to say about such changes and issues (given that it applies to all phenomena, to windows and games as much as to femininity and hip-hop, whether they're undergoing change or not), people nonetheless jump sideways into a discussion of "core of meaning" and the like out of a false sense that in foregoing the transcendent we're either weakening the crucial or dislodging the conventional, and that when we discuss meaning we're somehow being more precise and rigorous than when we discuss "value"—"value" being, you know, kind of squishy. And here people fall into a basic misreading of Wittgenstein, Kuhn, et al. What Wittgenstein said about games and Kuhn said about paradigms implies nothing one way or the other about whether we should change our referents and vocabulary or should stick with the tried-and-tested. All it says is that when we *do* use the tried-and-tested, we're doing so via resemblance, so our use of a particular word A in situation C can resemble how we'd used it in similar but not-quite-identical situation B.

Obviously, the people who fall into the misreading want more from philosophy than they can get. I spoke above about wafting one's hopes and dreams in the direction of a relativistic position such as position 2. The position is adopted for its supposed implications and consequences. In effect, it's a hairstyle. Let's say that word A and related situations feel like a trap. This feeling may draw you to position 2, and you might kid yourself that, as a logical consequence of the position, you've upended A, B, and C. But really, the position is the consequence, not the cause: You set yourself against A, B, and C, and adopt position 2 as symbolizing their demise.

As for the trap: Sonia Pai, a high-school senior in 1999 at Cherry Creek High School in suburban Denver, whom I interviewed at the time of the Columbine shootings, described the social landscape of her school as it had been several years earlier:

> *There are preppies and there are skaters, and if you're a preppie that meant like you could not ever buy anything that wasn't from Gap or Abercrombie and you ate in a different cafeteria. And then the other group was the skaters, named because some of them—maybe one out of hundreds of them—actually skateboarded. My friends were skaters even though they didn't know how to skateboard. Going to middle school we were all preppies and all of a sudden we just decided . . . going to high school we just decided, "Yes, maybe we'll be skaters." And with that came this whole idea that you don't care about the school and that it's cool to do drugs.*
>
> *You had to go off campus to smoke, and a lot of people would come back in a dazed state and get hit by cars, crossing the street, so [the school] made two designated smoking areas. And most people would just smoke cigarettes, and there would be a security guard, and a few people would do drugs, but that was really cool, to go there! . . . and stand*

there! . . . and know *someone who was smoking! Not all of my friends thought that was cool, but some of them would go there and stand around just so that they could be associated with those people. They thought that it was time to rebel, and that we should do this. So I stopped being friends with them. And so freshman year is horrible.*

We ate in this cafeteria that's called I.C. And that was the skater cafeteria. And they're also called stoners. And that cafeteria was in the location where you need to pass through to get to other places in the school, but our campus is such that you can get anywhere by walking outside as well as inside. And people would just build up all this hostility saying that like, "Oh, people that eat in West"—which are the preppies—"would never walk through here. They always walk outside, even if it's snowing, because they don't like how it smells in here." Then I remember one of my friends, who happened to be black, went into West because she had to walk there for some school group, and she's like, "Everyone was like staring *at me, I just know they were laughing at me . . ."*

Now, if you're someone who wants to break *out* of that sort of world—the world of preps vs. skaters—you might find it enticing, once you're in college and having "theory" served to you, to believe that (a) the words "skater" and "preppy" have, or aspire to, something like "cores of meaning" and (b) there's a tool—de-centering, deconstruction—that dismantles those cores or makes them unattainable, thus freeing you from those words' dominion. And this is why intelligent people fail to notice the incompatibility of positions 1 and 2 above: 2 seems to represent a breakout; but to believe that it breaks you away from anything, you have to believe in 1. Whereas, actually, 2 merely tells you that preppies and skaters get their power from the world, not from their nonexistent cores. But 2 tells you nothing about how to break the power.

Richard Meltzer once wrote (*Aesthetics of Rock* p. 170): "Bob Dylan's greatest initial dive into the rock 'n' roll domain, 'Like a Rolling Stone,' represents an attempt to free man by rescuing him from meaning, rather than free man through meaning." If Meltzer'd written such a sentence *now*, it'd just be pseudointellectual posturing. In its time (mid-'60s, Meltzer in his early twenties), it was a potentially interesting way to jar us out of standard folkie social-protest or high-school English class ways of interpreting Dylan. What it didn't do though—what Meltzer didn't do—was to give us any idea what it was that Meltzer (or Dylan) was trying to break free of or what one achieves by being so freed. And the problem here is that his use of the word "meaning," as an abstraction, made it a big bag of nothing, a nonissue, neither threatened nor a threat.

Except for occasional bouts of actual posturing on the subject ("Nobody's more scathingly honest than Darby and Chris, who know in their bones that in a cultural U.S.A. gone terminally berserk the language of reason and empirical facticity is just a bottomless crock of merciless ruling-class hype, that classy straight-forward poesy is just so much suburban formica"), and unlike several thousand others, Meltzer hasn't subsequently dived into such theoretical issues but instead has danced straight into battle: "Shit, if you wanna go Orthodox New Wave on me and claim there actually *is* such a thing [as new wave] lemme just say the Topanga Canyon incarnation (getting *merely* generic this time, I know it's tiresome, but perhaps they're actually from Malibu) is, if possible, even more corrupt, gawky, and anachronistic than such regional stalwarts of '60s-revisionist NW as the Pop, the Naughty Sweeties, and 20/20." Not that Meltzer's done a superb job of choosing his battles or identifying his real enemies. But he's still more or less on the actual battleground—where the issue is Topanga Canyon and ilk, not "meaning."

The latter discussion—the meaning of "meaning" rather than the meaning of "Topanga Canyon"—simply evades the issues, and represents a persistent refusal to work out the causes of one's discontent, to figure out what one is really trying to get out from under.

THE GREAT WRONG PLACE

The obvious next thing is for me to say just what it *is* that we're trying to get out from under. But there can be a multiplicity of answers, since people are trying to get out from under quite a lot, different people from under different things—and philosophy, as an all-purpose filibuster, is an engrossing way to evade a whole bunch of stuff. I'd recommend that people go back to the impulses and experiences that made them retreat to the filibuster in the first place, and start from there.

Of course anyone who's read through to this chapter will already know what *my* crucial issues are. There's a self-hate that makes us seek ulterior justification for ourselves and our critical practice in terms that are PBS. "Theory" is a campus version of PBS. Here I'll emphasize that certain behaviors were *standard practice* long before we tried to justify them: "Met a guy, his name was Tussy/Took him to my house and he ate my pussy" (sung by two 12-year-old girls, overheard by Leslie at a Cala supermarket; the couplet is a variant on a Too Short lyric, or vice versa); Lia disliking the name "Xuxa" because it sounds like "sushi," and she once got sick eating sushi; "Well, my name is Vicki and I'm pretty bored, and I need someone to write to. I don't care how old you are, and I don't care where you're from, either. I hate Kylie Minogue. She is so stuck up. I love Alex Papps and Joey Tempest—they're so cute! And I also think Annie Jones is so cool. So if you like what I like—even if you don't—write to me. Please!"; basketball fans who serenade the losing team with "Na na, na-ah na na, hey hey-ey, goodbye"; guys at NWA shows who wear Chicago Bulls T-shirts and who beat up the guys in Raiders caps; fans of Tiffany who beat up fans of Debbie Gibson (only in my dreams); girls screaming for boybands and then passing rumors to each other about them (unpublished letter to *Smash Hits*: "Please say it's not true. Someone told me that the singing Bros collapsed onstage, had his stomach pumped, and in his stomach they found . . . his other brother's sperm"). This is all business as usual. It doesn't result from collapsing the relevant-irrelevant dichotomy or from deconstructing the concept "music" or from music's appropriating its margin. "The irrelevant helps to constitute the relevant; therefore, the irrelevant is relevant." That's just a word game. Anyway, Tussy-pussy etc. are central, not marginal. Central to *me*, anyway, since music has a life in the life of the world, and we get to create the life of the world; and I'm not trying to de-center music but rather to center on what I care about. What makes Tussy-pussy, sushi, etc. problematic is that they've been excluded from the official classroom discussion, either excluded altogether by music departments or made a subject matter to be examined but not engaged in, as in sociology and cultural studies. But someone's belief in a core of meaning (a.k.a. "transcendental signified") doesn't account for his excluding Tussy and sushi—it's not as if teachers and editors think that what music is can be separated from what it does and on that basis they therefore forbid me to use music as source material for my life; rather, they don't want me to live my life on the page, and this is because they're afraid of what I'll do, or repelled by it, or bored. And conversely, if you *are* bored by me, there's no philosophical theory that says you shouldn't be. My considering the concept "transcendental signified" irrelevant doesn't justify my including Tussy et al., or explain why I want to—which makes the concept *really* irrelevant, doesn't it! And this is the point I alluded to in "Presentation of Self" ("a lot of us will retreat to irrelevant arguments against someone like Plato or Locke or Husserl"): By attacking the philosophical rationalizations/excuses that someone gives for his policy, or the ones you've projected onto him, you don't touch his actual socioemotional reasons for the policy, hence you won't be likely to change the policy. And by loading your own prose with philosophical rationalizations and excuses for flouting the policy, you may gain yourself some space, but you won't really engage the issues, won't even work out for yourself what they are, and won't come to an understanding of your own motives. If you say your critical practice is based on position 2, or on something like it, you're a liar.

I won't leave it at that, however, since I don't think I've done right by the human story, the hairstyle story. Even *bad* arguments can be a big deal for their participants and can affect other folks as well. For instance, few of the people who argue for or against Darwinism have any real familiarity with the evidence for it, and most don't even know the theory; the argument, nonetheless, has real social consequences. And anyway, most people suck at theory—few who go on about "meaning" are actually doing anything as coherent as "holding two incompatible positions" or even holding any positions (much less the two I presented); they're shuffling buzz words in vague proximity of what they imagine are the theoretical ideas. This irritates the hell out of me, but doesn't always have bad results. "We believe [insert vacuous gobbledygook], which undermines the dominant paradigm; and, with the paradigm undermined, I can go out and write the criticism I want to." The criticism therefore comes enveloped in a fog of excuses; but this is better than no criticism at all. The mugwump who misreads Meltzer's "pertinence can be just anywhere at all" as meaning "pertinence *is* just anywhere at all," or who misreads Derrida's "différance" as meaning "all meaning is deferred," can nonetheless use these misreadings as an excuse to expand and enrich his idea of the subject matter. My dime-store-sociology explanation of "theory" in WMS #7 was that people got the shit beat out of them back in school or wherever and as a result now load their writing with empty philosophical platitudes in an attempt to blow smoke in the eyes of the internalized teacher or antiteacher, who's still in there bashing. The worse the philosophy, the more expressive it is, perhaps. Contrary to what I wrote above, position 2—*as long as it is misunderstood*—has many useful roles: as affirmation, hairstyle, bogeyman, red herring, camouflage, self-expression. The key word in Derrida's phrase "play of differences" is "play," not "differences," even though "play" has nothing to do with the principle. Rather, it's a passive-aggressive way of fighting for the right to party. Philosophically, "the ongoing slog of differences" would have been just as accurate, but that wouldn't have done the social trick.

Position 2 apparently eliminates starting points and fixed grounds—that is, eliminates them if you're pathologically extreme in your demands upon the terms "starting point," "fixed," and "ground"—but the phrase "no starting point and no fixed ground" evokes fears and hopes. "If there are no fixed grounds, then I am unmoored." "If there are no fixed grounds, then you have no right to tell me what to do."

And you might well ask me why, since I seem to feel kindly towards the Superword process, I think there's anything *wrong* with making pathologically extreme demands on the terms "starting point," "fixed," and "ground," not to mention on "meaning" as the mugwump construes it (always sought, never found, the epitome of the Superword). I'd reply that these words might once have been interesting as Superwords, back when it was the person who *aspired* to priority and grounds who nonetheless made such extreme demands on "priority" and "ground" that he denied himself easy priority or any grounds, much like Roger Williams. I certainly can admire the positivists in their failure. The trouble is that if you persist in extremity you eventually take yourself out of the game, which is what philosophy has done. E.g., as a proponent of position 2, I can say, "Nothing exists in isolation," and two hours later say, "I grew up in an isolated village," without contradicting myself, since the standards for isolation are different in the two sentences. The former has no bearing on the latter, just as a discussion of whether there can be *any* heat in deep space has no bearing on whether Antarctica is cold, and the discussion of whether there can be a first word ("And God said, 'On the contrary, let there be light'") has no bearing on whether or not to discuss, say, Newton's laws in isolation from his predecessors or from his personality or from his metaphysics or from his social status, a choice you'd make on the basis of what in particular you were trying to achieve on a given day.

But in its "theory" version, "isolation" has degenerated from being a Superword to being a Superword's stupid cousin—a *stupor word*, let's say. Ditto for "meaning" in its position 1 version. Neither is something that we aspire to while continually putting it just out of reach, so neither feeds our own creativity. Rather, it's a patsy, a straw man, only set up to be knocked down, a standard that almost no one sets or seeks for himself but the seeking of which is projected onto others in order to denigrate *their* authenticity, their autonomy, their significance. Worst-case scenario on campus would be one group of people invoking position 1 as a way to bully you into always treating Newton's physics in isolation from everything else, and another group invoking position 2 to bully you into including Newton's social status even when it's inapplicable to his physics and to your purposes and bores you silly. So freshman year is horrible. This wasn't particularly my experience, by the way, and I haven't been a student in twenty-eight years. But there was, and is, real exclusion, sometimes legitimate, often appalling. And you know that, where justification and "grounds" are at issue, terror and social division must be hanging around nearby.

There's a double contamination of academia, just as there's a double contamination of suburbia: In order to protect the intellect from terror and social division, academia excludes too much of life and, in doing so, itself becomes an agent of social terror and social stratification. It may have no alternative, but it feels at odds with itself anyway, contaminated by a self-imposed provincialism that runs counter to its own principles. And it's because of this sense of contamination from the top—in academia and elsewhere—that illegitimacy becomes a criterion and that terms such as "bad girl" and "punk" reverse themselves in the first place, become Superwords, semi-praise words that have to keep running, lest they be overtaken by mere badness, or goodness.

CHAPTER 26

SOMETIMES GOOD GUYS DON'T WEAR WHITE

I have seen a great many very bad movies, and I know when a movie is bad, but I have rarely been bored at the movies; and when I have been bored, it has usually been at a "good" movie.

—Robert Warshow, Author's Preface to *The Immediate Experience*, October 1954

But Warshow's quotation marks around "good" cause the sentence to start unraveling, so the emphatic "I know when a movie is bad" begins to waver. Warshow implies near the start of the sentence that not being boring does not in itself make a movie good (given that most bad movies have this attribute too), and at the end that being boring does not in itself make a movie bad. But with the quotation marks he's implying that maybe good movies that are boring are not so good. This is not altogether a *logical* contradiction (since not being boring could be a necessary but insufficient criterion for being a *really* good movie). You could say he's simply implying that a good movie might be better still if it weren't boring, and that bad movies for all their badness may have something that a good movie (at least a boring good movie) could use. But I think he's pushing further. He's using the phrase "bad movie" to indicate his judgment that the movie is really bad, but he's using "'good' movie," with "good" in inverted commas, to indicate that the movie belongs to a sociocinematic category, "the 'good' movie"—like "the 'art' cinema," another phrase of his that he decorates with inverted commas, implying that he doesn't quite assent to the terminology there, either. And I think he's also saying that some "good" movies aren't good, in fact some *boring* good movies are bad, and maybe bad movies are better than boring good movies. So the term "bad movie" wavers, just as the term "bad guy" in a western wavers if you decide the bad guy has admirable qualities that the hero lacks. The generic role and the value judgment don't always match, and moviemakers can make hay from this discrepancy.

Warshow wrote good criticism, not despite the contradictions but because of them. I think a *physicist* who used such slippery terminology and made such wavering judgments would be a bad physicist, at least if he didn't eventually try to work his way out of those contradictions (though I wouldn't be surprised if a physicist making conceptual changes in his field probably *did* slip and slide in his language, at first, until he'd evolved new concepts that satisfied him). Whereas

I'd say that a movie critic who did *not* have Warshow's conflicts and tensions and wavering and slippage would be a bad critic, a shallow one.

Read any metal 'zine and you'll see a pile of letters written supposedly to praise some drab-looking band like Metallica but really to proclaim the author's belief that (1) Poison, Guns N' Roses, Skid Row, and Enuff Z Nuff are faggots and pussies, (2) so are the people who listen to the bands, (3) girls who like Poison are sluts who probably lick each other's pussies, (4) Poison have small dicks, and (5) it's music that's important anyway, not hairstyle. Then there are answer letters: (1) Metallica are ugly and boring and can't sing for shit, (2) Poison are not fags, (3) I want to sleep with Poison and that doesn't make me a slut, (4) there are thousands of girls like me, and (5) even if Poison are fags, that doesn't matter, because it's the music that's important.
—Frank Kogan, "Let MTV Ring," *Village Voice*, June 5, 1990

So here's a conflict: Looks do matter, but they don't, but they do; the music itself is the final criterion, but are looks and sexual allegiance *part* of the music? This conflict doesn't get resolved. Even if I'm pro hairstyle, how far does this go? Does good hair compensate for boring rhythms and stupid lyrics? (*I* don't think so.) And someone on the other side, who claims that music is all that matters, and that's why he listens to jazz (for instance), will then say that boybands are no good because the boys smile a lot and are only liked for their looks and their nice teeth. (So is this a criticism of the music?)

Is there a way not to *care* whether looks matter? Does the discourse permit you not to care? Well, I suppose that there *could* be a magazine—academic, presumably—that runs only formal analyses of the music and covers all music: popular, classical, indie, etc. But I doubt that such a magazine would exist, since I doubt that a person analyzing pop music and African music and so forth would be willing to leave out the visuals. And whether those writers leave the visuals out or include them, they'll still worry about whether the decision was valid.

You little fuck, I got money stacks bigger than you
—Jay-Z, "Takeover," 2001

Jay-Z means this to affirm the value of his music. In the Jay-Z Nas Throwdown [an *I Love Music* thread], some people accuse Jay-Z of being too pop, the assumption being that "pop song" and "hip-hop" are mutually exclusive. And other people counter this argument without necessarily challenging the idea that "pop" and "hip-hop" are at odds; they say that Jay-Z *has* to go somewhat pop if he wants to sell in the suburbs; and at least some of these people are saying that one of the roles of hip-hop is to make money—not just that selling a lot is a *sign* that the music is good, but that selling a lot *is* a good feature of the music. And then the first set of people point to high-selling hip-hop (Nelly, for instance) that they assume *no one* in the conversation could possibly like. And fortunately there will be people on the thread who do like Nelly, though not enough of them. And then there will be those who claim that Jay-Z is selling well because he *sounds* better and that this matters more than the serious ghetto content of the non-Jay-Z's.

The positions I've stated are hardly the only ones. For instance, some people argue in essence that pop music is for girls and that (therefore) Jay-Z is selling out to the girls.

It might make sense to say that the discourse is structured around such arguments. Well, the word "structured" has an air of pseudoprecision that I don't like, but I can't think of an alternative at the moment. I hate the word "discourse," too, for *its* phony precision; I'd use "language-game" instead, but it would be baffling for those of you who haven't read Wittgenstein. Maybe I can just say that the argument is a good deal of the conversation, that some key assumptions are uncertain for many or all participants, and that the argument tends to revolve around the uncertainty (and flexibility) of these assumptions. For instance, it might be that *no one* has a stable sense of where the boundary between pop and hip-hop is and that some people may question whether there is or should be such a boundary, but they all can nonetheless get into arguments over how you decide who's a real hip-hop performer and whether someone's being or not being "pop" is a drawback or a virtue and whether it jeopardizes or enhances his status as a real hip-hopper. In the Throwdown we don't simply have some people who believe selling a lot of records invalidates Jay-Z (as too pop) and others who believe it validates him (as a big man who can live large): Many people are drawn both ways, or have different reasons for calling him too pop, and Jay-Z himself is drawn more than one way. So to be part of this conversation is to be pulled into several related conflicts, though not everyone in the conversation will feel the *same* conflicts: That is, someone might find it irrelevant how many records Jay-Z sells but will care a lot about whether Jay-Z is being true to the ghetto—but will nonetheless be torn about whether "being true to the ghetto" means bragging about dealing and hustling or means denouncing dealing and hustling (and again Jay-Z himself is torn). To participate in the discussion is to have certain tensions, but different people don't necessarily feel each particular tension to the same degree. Part of the argument could be over *which* tension is worth discussing—an argument between arguments, as it were, over which arguments are the real ones. (The competition between arguments need not be stated as such, and usually isn't. But notice that the Poison-Metallica fight is partly about what the letter writers should be fighting about.) Within the overall discourse about hip-hop, you've got arguments between arguments, and no doubt *some* people differing in assumptions, and some misunderstanding each other; but I don't feel that this gives us conflicts between *different modes of thought*, as you'd get in a science undergoing a paradigm shift, since as I said the conflicts in music help structure the modes of thought. A lot of the "incommensurability" (if the term is relevant to music criticism) will be internal to the normal discourse.

In rock criticism in its *normal* state some basics are at issue, but this doesn't have the destabilizing effect it would have in physics. In fact, these basic disagreements may help to hold the discourse together. But nonetheless, some people will argue about music in a rock-critic way, and others not used to such discussions simply won't get it.

We need to be real loose and pragmatic here about what counts as "basic" and "within an overall discourse" and "internal to a mode of thought" etc. I'd *probably* say that hip-hop and classical are different discourses, despite hip-hop's being willing to draw on classical. We can compare the assumptions and conflicts (and conflicts between assumptions) that are big in hip-hop to those that are big in classical. ("I know Stockhausen especially needs to do somethin or he ain't gonna be makin no $ after that ballerina shit at Summerjam. No one needs to die but somethin bigger than 'Fuck you!' 'No fuck you!' 'Oh yeah well you a bitch!' needs to go down for anyone involved in this to have any more cred. For example, Xenakis fucked Boulez up in a fight in QB a few years ago and that jus shut down Boulez's cred and took another wannabe out of the business.") But shouldn't I also try to make something of the fact that in the educational system as a whole (though not everywhere within it) classical is considered real music and hip-hop isn't? Suppose a curriculum committee is deciding whether courses in hip-hop should go in the music department or in the English department or in the cultural-studies department (if there is one) or nowhere. Would you say that these are arguments *between* discourses? But then, isn't the hip-hop "discourse" itself influenced by the fact that from some authority's viewpoint hip-hop is not legitimate, and that this official illegitimacy has some effect on what "keeping it real" and "being ghetto" mean? Notice that the type of hip-hop that's most saturated in classical—the slimy thuggy sexy Dirty South/crunk/Ca$h Money stuff—doesn't symbolize "classical" at all, so its classical leanings fly in under 'most everybody's radar.

But classical music itself is influenced by the fact that it's a genre facing commercial extinction whose survival depends on subsidies. Hence for it to continue to be *the* real music, and therefore deserving of subsidies, it's got to continue to sharply differentiate itself from popular forms. Yet, if it wants a broader audience—or just happens to have composers and musicians into a range of music beyond the old "classical"—it may well start to take in some of the popular forms: rock, hip-hop, techno, and so on. But in doing this—and hence acknowledging the legitimacy of these other forms—won't it be undercutting its own case for special treatment?

If rock criticism were to undergo a period of "revolution," this would be a period where not only its assumptions are in question (since in the normal music discourse, some basic assumptions are always in question), but where its conflicts are themselves in question: Arguments compete and argue with each other, but to a more drastic extent than normal (since arguments argue with each other in the normal course too). Rock criticism doesn't have shared paradigms in the Kuhnian sense of "shared" paradigm—which is that *everybody* in the field shares it—so it won't undergo a Kuhnian paradigm shift leading to a new shared paradigm; but nonetheless it could undergo major shifts that would drive some people out of the discussion and bring new ones in, or the discourse would break into several different discourses, with different participants. I don't really have anything in mind here—maybe current tensions would be replaced by different tensions.

I'd asked above if there was a way not to *care* whether looks matter. Does the discourse permit us not to care? Can we simply ignore the question of whether how the bands and fans look is a valid criterion for judging a band? Although both sides in the Poison-Metallica spat claim that looks don't matter, each judges the bands on appearance. Of course, you can say, "Excuse me, Frank; these people are not great thinkers," but I'd counter by saying that I've got the same "contradiction" too—not that I think that hairstyle both does and doesn't matter, since I know it matters; but I'm uncertain how much. A "revolutionary" shift in music criticism might be if no one even cared one way or another whether looks mattered. (I can't imagine this.) If you want more contradictions from me, here's one: I think that good music can have bad effects and that bad music can have good effects, but I also think that what music *does* is part of what music *is*. I mean, can you call something a good dance track and then say that many people have tried to dance well to it but none have succeeded? (It's got a good beat and no one can dance to it. I'll give it a 75.)

> *Calypso engineered for mainlanders is usually played on a chromatic scale with divergences no bolder than a flatted minor third. [Whereas] these chaps are playing out-of-tune and raggedly because they are laughing while playing, or else they are speaking unspeakable lyrics into the mouthpieces of the horns they blow. They are just being swept along with the calypsonian into the making of a calypso's goal, a fully rounded pear-shaped atrocity.*
>
> *. . . Within the spheres of various art forms, the deliberately perpetrated atrocity is rare. Passing quickly over the pedantic point as to whether or not calypso is music, and all music art, one emerges with calypso, this singular example of perversion.*
>
> —Liner notes, *Disco Atrocities*

I want to say that this quotation speaks for itself, but that's because anything I have to say about it will be both obvious and inadequate. The musicians referred to are islanders playing on the islands, not on the mainland. The writer doesn't merely both accept and reject mainland standards, and doesn't merely express ambivalence towards calypso. In his account, calypso itself is ambivalent, and he embraces the ambivalence wholeheartedly. Ambivalent towards ambivalence? Not he.

adapted from an email to Mark Sinker, March 27, 2002

PART FIVE

STUPID STORIES

CHAPTER 27
THE CONVERSATION

"Put the set on the bumpee."

He didn't move from where he was standing, holding the box of checkers, wondering if he'd heard her correctly.

"Put the set on the bumpee," she said again.

"I don't understand what you want me to do."

"I want you to *put the set on the bumpee.*"

He considered repeating, "I don't understand what you want me to do," just to prolong the stalemate, but instead told her, "I don't know what you mean by bumpee."

Frustration was in her face. "A bumpee is a . . ." The words could hardly come out. "A bumpee is a bumpee." She looked appalled. "Just put it on the bumpee."

He stared around the room. "Should I put it on the table?"

She was almost in a rage. "I said *bumpee*, not *table*. What's wrong with you? If I'd said, 'Put it on the table,' and you'd claimed not to know what a table was, I wouldn't be able to explain what I meant either."

"It's the thing standing over there with legs."

"*You're* the thing standing over there with legs," she said. "You'd probably tell me that you didn't see anything with legs except you and me, since if you were pretending not to know what a table was you'd also pretend not to know what a table leg was."

"I'm going to put the set on the table."

"No! Put it on the bumpee!" She was almost screaming.

"You'll have to show me what the bumpee is and where it is, since I obviously don't know it myself."

"If I get up and do that, I might as well put the set on the bumpee myself."

"That would be a good idea," he said.

She got up. He held the set out so as to give it to her, but she didn't take it. She formed her hand into a fist and hit him.

March 2000

CHAPTER 28

MAYBE THAT'S WHAT THEY MEANT

"Hi, Jack," Reggie said. "How are you doing? How are your shoelaces?"

"I'm fine. My shoelaces are fine, too. How are you?" Jack continued. "And how are *your* shoelaces? Are they bearing up well, being tied and untied and all that?"

"My shoelaces are fine," said Reggie. "Why this sudden interest in my shoelaces?"

"You're the one who brought up shoelaces."

"Yes, but I wasn't *interested* in them. I was just being polite. I don't *care* how your shoelaces are doing. I really don't."

"Well," said Jack. "No need to be brutal." Then, directing his voice towards his feet, "Come on, laces, let's go to my cubicle and get away from the mean man."

In his cubicle, Jack started his computer and, while waiting for it to load, took off his jacket and checked his phone messages. He decided to work quietly, without announcing his presence, to get some tasks out of the way. Once he was connected to the server, he ran searches on several documents that he suspected of not incorporating the latest changes. A few minutes into this he heard Brad calling over from the next aisle: "Niggly, you settled in yet?"

"Sure, Frosty," said Jack.

"I'm coming over," said Brad. He came in with a small stack of papers. "They left these on my chair, said these had the latest revisions. I wouldn't believe them."

"I don't," said Jack. "I've just been running searches on those things and I've already found a heap of mistakes."

"By the way, Niggly, how're your shoelaces?"

"Fine," said Jack. "You've been talking to Reggie."

"Reggie thought that your laces had been giving you trouble."

"Well, I'd led Reggie to believe that he'd hurt their feelings, but . . ." he cupped his hand to his mouth and said in a low voice, ". . . I don't think that my shoelaces have a nervous system, so I don't think that their feelings *can* be hurt. That's a general rule, I'm told: no nervous system, no hurt feelings." After a pause: "And don't tell anybody about this . . . this deficiency, this lack of a nervous system. I wouldn't want people to take pity on me for having retarded shoelaces."

"In high school, the girls always told me I had retarded shoes," said Brad, "but they never mentioned the laces."

"Well, maybe that's what they meant," said Jack.

March 2000

THE GREAT RAINSTORM

JOE HARDY [*excitedly*]: "It's raining. Do you know what that means?"

FRANK HARDY [*helpfully*]: "Um. Drops of water are falling from the sky?"

JOE: "Ha ha ha. That's very funny. No, it means that we have to unload my umbrella stash. Come help me."

FRANK [*not moving*]: "Oh. I thought it meant that we had to cancel our picnic."

JOE [*impatiently*]: "What picnic? I didn't know we'd planned a picnic. What are you talking about?" [*Goes over to a closet and rummages around.*]

FRANK: "Well, we hadn't planned a picnic. But if we had, we'd have to cancel it. [*Brightens up.*] Unless we chartered a plane to some place where it wasn't raining."

JOE: "Help me with these umbrellas." [*Lugs a box of about 30 umbrellas.*]

FRANK [*still not moving*]: "However, in weather like this, I suppose everyone will want to charter an airplane."

JOE: "Frank, stop babbling and help me with these. I'd bought them real cheap for just a situation as this. We'll go out and sell them on the street for four times what I paid. We'll make a bundle."

FRANK [*slowly walking over, grasps one end of the box, helps Joe carry it to the door*]: "And with the profits we can charter an airplane, so we won't have to give up our picnic."

[*Joe rolls his eyes.*]

FRANK: "I feel that I've been deprived of a picnic."

[*Exeunt, with umbrellas.*]

June 2003

PART SIX

REVIEWS AND CRITICISM 1985–1990

FUCK MACHINES
AND RAZOR BLADES

SPOONIE GEE

"Spoonin Rap" and "Love Rap" by Spoonie Gee are my favorite American-made records of the last ten years. They came out about five years ago, "Spoonin Rap" in late '79 and "Love Rap" in '80. I've never read a review of either—

Rap music centers on the human voice. The voice is a rhythm instrument as well as a melodic one, capable of emphasizing beats as if it were a set of drums. Spoonie Gee bears down hard on the words, achieving a mesmerizing intensity akin to hard rock—yet he also puts a hanging drawl in his phrasing. So he sounds tough and funky/graceful simultaneously. His first producers, Frank Johnson and Peter Brown of Sound of New York and Bobby Robinson of Enjoy Records, were smart enough to emphasize Spoonie's voice: "Spoonin Rap" is just bass and drums, sound effects and voice; "Love Rap" is just voice, drums, and percussion.

On the basis of his voice alone, the way it balances coolness with angry passion while keeping a dance beat, Spoonie is a major artist; in addition, he's a writer. His lyrics are as intense as his rapping, and embody the same tensions. Example: Both "Spoonin Rap" and "Love Rap" start with detailed and explicit bragging—about how cool and sexy he is, about how the girls go for him, how they're impressed with his rapping and his car. He puts on his eight-track. He makes love to the girl in his car. In his Mercedes. The seat's so soft, just like a bed.—At the moment of sexual triumph the lyrics make a jarring change, as if there's a second song hidden behind the first, as if the bragging is a set-up for something else. "Spoonin Rap": "Then I got the girl for three hours straight/A-but I had to go to work a-so I couldn't be late/I said 'Where's your man?' She said, 'He's in jail'/I said 'A-come on baby cuz you're tellin' a tale/Cuz if he comes at me and then he wants to fight/See I'm a get the man good and I'm a get him right.'" "Love Rap": "When I got into my house I drove the female wild/The first thing she said is 'Let's have a child'/I said 'No no baby I only got time/To make a lot of money and to save my pride/And if I had a baby I might go broke/And believe me to a negro that ain't no joke'/People smile in your face and talk behind your back/And when you get the story it's nothing exact/Some say they're your friends but they really are not/Because they're only out to try to get what you've got." And then it's like the first part of the song, but turned inside out—the guys and girls are drawn to his flashy clothes and car only so they can rip him off and leave him in the gutter. The girls are gonna play him for a fool. Then it shifts back to what a great lover he is, nice descriptions of his girlfriends. "Spoonin Rap" shifts around in the same way. It's about how cool he is, about how sexy women are; then it's about don't do dope, don't steal, you'll go to jail and they'll fuck you in the ass. Then it's about jumping the turnstile and the cop pulls a gun but he doesn't shoot.

—There's a lot of precedent in black lyrics for jarring emotional juxtapositions—in the blues particularly, also in Smokey Robinson's deliberate paradoxes. But the nearest emotional equivalent to Spoonie isn't in black music, it's in punk—early Stones, Kinks, Velvets, Stooges, Dolls—where a song will seem to be one thing, then be another. The ranting part of "Love Rap" could be Lou Reed in one of his bad moods—except that, unlike a Jagger or a Reed, Spoonie hasn't calculated—may not even be aware of—his juxtapositions. Which adds to his power. The feelings have great impact because they come from an unexpected source. If Spoonie were in punk or rock his alienation and rage would fulfill an expectation of the genre. In disco, they seem truer.

Spoonie Gee's later singles don't match the first two. His subsequent record labels, Sugar Hill and Tuff City, don't trust the human voice; they burden the records with heavy-handed funk arrangements. And Spoonie Gee's voice is reduced to a slowed-down drawl. It sounds like he's aiming to be a love man, and suppressing everything else. The lyrics are toned down, too, though "Spoonie's Back" has got a surprising section about his mother's death.

Spoonie update #1: After sending off the above article, I got "Street Girl," Spoonie's newest. It's the best thing he's done in five years. It's a piece of woman-hating. There's nothing like hatred to bring out the art in Spoonie Gee. A real punk.

Spoonie update #2: "What he thought was real turned out to be fake": What seems so real in "Street Girl" is Spoonie Gee's voice, a slow sexy bedroom purr, sounding so full of sympathy, like someone so caring and "supportive." The lyrics are brutality expressed in the language of sentimentality. The street girl (who could have been a "sweet" girl) breaks the heart of her lover ("somebody's son"), making him kill her. She took his money, she left him, so it's her own fault she got shot.—I've seen this movie before; the plot was old sixty years ago. So it's impressive the amount of feeling Spoonie gets out of it. He's the best man alive right now at matching voice to words and words to details, and at making it flow. On "Street Girl" he's helped immensely by Davey DMX's instrumental arrangement. A simple percussion rhythm and counterrhythm, similar in structure to Run-DMC's "Sucker MCs," is matched to soundtrack-like orchestral (or synthesizer) riffs. Norman Whitfield's arrangement of "Papa Was a Rolling Stone" is an obvious predecessor; so is Isaac Hayes's "Shaft." But this is the first use of movie-like riffs on a hip-hop beat-box record, and it's a breakthrough.

Spoonie Gee has made some great records and an equal number of mediocre ones. I think he's a genius, but I don't think he knows what he's doing. He's drawn to a vision of the world as a fake and treacherous place. Maybe something's bugging him. Maybe unconsciously he feels that it's not only the world that's fake, or women that are fake—it's himself.

Spoonie's not one of us. He has nothing to do with punk or postpunk culture. I don't know if I could carry on an interesting conversation with him, if we could find any cultural or moral common ground.—But there is a common ground, that part of the intellect called the "emotions," where I do my deepest analysis of life. However much I admire current heroes like Mark E. Smith and Ian Mackaye, people I identify with, I know they don't make music as strong as this. Listening to Spoonie is like hearing my own feelings, and I have to confront my fear. This means maybe that I'm not really unlike him. Maybe I'm more like him than I am like you.

Reasons for Living #2, June 1986 (written in spring and summer 1985)

SEX DON'T LOVE NOBODY

Spoonie Gee's new 12-inch single, "The Godfather" (Tuff City), is obviously conscious of its funk roots—it even has a James Brown–style bridge (as in "Take it to the bridge"). Yet it effectively deals in sounds and feelings that The Godfather of Soul might find foreign. The Godfather of the title is Spoonie himself, The Godfather of Rap.

"The Godfather" is produced thick (by Marley Marl)—a giant brick of sound, enhanced by repeated three-note horn bursts. It's like they took Fela's African horn and guitar riffs, which were often stretched-out JB-style riffs anyway, and condensed them back to JB length. (Is it really African? Caribbean? How would I know, I'm just a *rock* critic!) Some instrument enters halfway through—it would most likely be designated "guitar"—sounds like a lawnmower.

You could have any Joe Blow mouth the words and the effect would be powerful. Instead you've got Spoonie Gee, a great mouth—seductive, with a hanging sense of aggression. And Spoonie's a gut-level poet, one who makes concrete the oft-cited (among "poets") and often vague sex-death connection. "If I had a baby I might go broke," a sharp statement that cuts right through, in 1980's "Love Rap." Economics is a connection; broke means humiliation. Pain and death follow sex as if attached to it by a rope. In 1979's "Spoonin Rap," he has sex with a "girl," and his mind conjures up the image of her man coming at him with a knife. This time out, Spoonie barely brushes against these themes. "Young ladies, no babies, and marriage is out" slides right by. The song is really about sound more than words. But it's interesting: The Godfather of Soul was never openly afraid to make babies. The Godfather of Rap is.

I transport myself into rage a lot. I don't know if it's stimulation or catharsis or fun or just time taken from my life. Anyway, rage is a home I go to and rage is a kind of music. And rage is accompanied by music. When I was a teenager I'd put the Rolling Stones on the record machine and pace or run around and dream of destroying my enemies. Still do it—to the Stones, Stooges, Sex Pistols, Big Youth, Spoonie Gee. This month it's Kool Moe Dee on the rage machine.

Not that the LP *Kool Moe Dee* is mainly or only rage. Other things predominate: humor, audacious rhymes, invented words, preposterous boasts. "Go See the Doctor" starts as penis waving, then venereal disease comes along as a joke played on the penis. Like, he fucks the girl, then runs out to tell the boys; but—ha ha—three days later, go see the doctor. Joke's on you, sucker. "Dumb Dick" (self-explanatory) is another one, a joke on a guy who thinks with his penis.

This is rap music, everything stripped down to the rhythm. The voice is slow and clear, rapping on a single tone, so you hear each word. The rhythm tracks have a bright and bouncing backbeat; Kool Moe Dee's own vocal rhythms are buoyant, his tone jaunty. Despite or because of this, and despite Kool Moe Dee's always creative intelligence, some of the record sounds dreary. Too stripped-down, too plain. It's much less exuberant than the Treacherous Three, Kool Moe Dee's old group. But sometimes it works—when voice and rhythm interlock, when he gets himself mad—which he does on the best song here, "Do You Know What Time It Is?" Rage gets him going—it's not a joke on his penis anymore—he is the penis. The joke of life becomes the pain of life. The prick's a weapon; he uses it to beat up on women (psychologically). "I'm gonna run you around, take you up and down/Turn you out and leave you in the lost and found." And "Time to make sure that the girlie stay poor/String 'em out so they will always want more." And on like that, virulently and relentlessly.

The average *Voice* reader might (ought to) consider Kool Moe Dee a dickhead, and me a dickhead for liking him. Nonetheless, the music rocks and rages, and if you're like me, it will rock and (en)rage you. Anyway, there are a few things to consider:

Boasting is Kool Moe Dee's shtick, his genre. Boasting requires exaggeration, hence detachment. The boast is something you do, not something you are. I feel weird listening to him brag in his jaunty voice about how cold and loveless he is. It's all on the surface. Is this song a boast? A joke? A cry of pain? I listen for a crack in the surface, something that lets you see the man inside—some word or line of regret, perhaps—regret that sex (reputedly a pleasurable experience) has become this defensive, dumb war-between-man-and-woman thing.

The crack in "Do You Know What Time It Is?"—it's just a hint, almost thrown away—comes about three-quarters of the way through: "I made a little system so I can tell/Doesn't always work, but what the hell/Don't ask me for nothin', and don't give me nothin'. . . ." What's he trying to tell? What doesn't always work? It's not clear—but the feeling of resignation sure is.

It's been said that sex is Kool Moe Dee's only great subject. But sex isn't Kool Moe Dee's subject. The subject is fear. Fear of sex. Sex that leads to love that leads to dependence that leads to vulnerability that leads to loss of control. That leads to hurt that leads to defense that leads to cold, hard (penis-hard) rage. Hip-hop sound is sexy-voluptuous; the voice is part of that sound. But the voice also adds a detached edge—irony (the way he says "Go see the doctor"), or toughness. If your art is good enough you have your voluptuous sex-fear and have your detachment from it too. Via words you escape from your rage by exaggerating that rage. Escape from the boasting competition by exaggerating the boast. Then, if you're really good at your art, you do everything so convincingly—boasts, comedy, rage—that your listener experiences you as more than real, and all detachment is moot. (A favorite of mine is "I'm Kool Moe Dee": The joke here is that he's an icon of worship, Moses or God or something—it's a *joke*, but the sound and vocal isn't a joke, it's real enough to be scary.)

"Do You Know What Time It Is?" is so strong that it skews my attitude towards this album. Those of you less into rage may be most impressed by the wordplay—the way he rhymes "a dime a *dozen*" with "I never ever *was in* a situation," "disrespect you" with "intellectual," "cult" with "ultimate"—"I'm an auto-hypnotic, reverse psychotic/That'll make you feel, if you want it I got it"—"Love me or hate me, agree or debate me/Watch the suckers gather 'round, bow down and fellate me"—but for me it's at its most intensest, leaves me defenseless (sorry, it's catching), when the venom sound goes "Maybe you can be down—maybe you can be down—maybe you should be down . . ."—right to an angry feeling, 1966 ("Under My Thumb," "96 Tears"), me pacing around, a bitter message that's too familiar: You have to kill your feelings in order to live. It doesn't always work, but what the hell.

The Village Voice, September 8, 1987

SPOONIE GEE *THE GODFATHER* LP

"Take it off" says rap artist Spoonie Gee. He really pushes the words, like he thinks he can strip the clothes off her just using his voice. He raps all about love and sexual prowess, but his voice gives you frustration. He mixes, like, eighteen emotions at once. He's been punched out—his words tell you that in so many ways. He wants to be a lover, but it's a fight.

Spoonie Gee's voice is a great rhythm instrument. But his rhythm just drives forward, doesn't respond to or direct anything outside itself. It has nothing to do with funk music's underlying call-and-response. The only way to produce him is to augment what he does or get out of his way. So when producers Marley Marl, Aaron Fuchs, and Teddy Riley bring things down to the rhythm, they bring it down to his voice. Fuchs and Marl go for immediate impact: a loose charging funk, usually; or some mesmerizing reggae. Riley's more subtle: His arrangements kind of dance around Spoonie Gee's voice. The voice stays center. The words stay center, too. The words are drums; they have beats: "He'll pop you, stop you, then he'll drop you." That's heavyweight Mike Tyson. "This girl ain't gonna/Make me or break me/She might shake me." That's Spoonie's girlfriend. "You'll wind up flat on your back like the canvas is your bed." That's if you go against Tyson. Go against Spoonie, girl, and your bed is the canvas.

Spin, April 1988

FUCKED (PAZZ & JOP 1987)

The future of music may well be world beat, as may be the future of my music enjoyment. I keep tempting myself to say "Fuck everything else" and just start buying that stuff, nothing else, at least no "rock" shit. But I haven't admitted defeat. I think the Stones-Stooges knew something that James Brown didn't know and that Brown's musical descendants (and world beat's musical descendants) are going to need to know. "Funk" needs "punk" as much as vice versa. In general, Greg Tate and Harry Allen, too, lie to themselves too much—they're just too committed to portraying black American music as an expression of Pan-African mental health. They overlook black music's very American fucked confusion. Which fucked confusion may at times be a strength. That we were fucked and making an issue of it was, I think, one of the strengths of punk.

excerpt from "Pazz & Jop ballot 1987," January 1988

MY DREAM DATE WITH TEENA MARIE

Naked to the World—that ridiculous title—this record has nothing to do with Teena Marie being exposed to the world. It's more like the world is naked to her, and she slurps it all up. She pulls in whatever she can. "You don't have to play *everything*!" an exasperated Miles is supposed to have said to Coltrane. Well, Teena has to play everything; she has to sing everything, a big EVERYTHING: styles, cultures, races, emotions, sex, pop music—sounds she hears, things she reads, phrases she remembers. All into her music.

Her voice goes all over. She sings all these different notes but also all these different timbres and note bends and wails—she stretches the words or clips them short or runs them around the block or reduces them to rhythm or just talks them or chants them—the gamut of recent (mainly black) vocal mannerisms—she crams it all in, without disjunctions. But that's just musical technique. It doesn't really explain the . . . whole THING.

I'm in awe of Teena Marie. If I were a young musician just starting out, I would go search out Teena, and place myself at her feet, so to speak—in a subtle, unapparently fawning way. I'd say, "Teach me what you know." What I need to learn—her knowledge—it's not the technical stuff, the Sarah Vaughan notes she's memorized, the P-Funk bass lines she's figured out—I don't give a fuck about technique as such. I want to learn how she does it as a big, oh gosh, kid in front of the record bin, POP thing. She grabs hold of "jazz" like it's just another present under her Christmas tree. She blasts off and away from Authority, Dignity, Integrity, Elegance, and other straitjackets. She wails, she rocks. Two years ago she did "Lips to Find You"—the most blistering rock 'n' roll of the '80s. You know, in so-called "punk rock" we want to make the most blistering rock 'n' roll song, so "Okay, let's concentrate everything on blistering rock 'n' roll." Teena tosses off blister like it's mere background throb.

On the new LP's "Crocodile Tears," she's got the irony of '70s black rock, which she intersperses with soul-style (unironic) commitment. "Owwww"—she flows into sex sounds. The moaning wail, then the laugh. The main thing is "Look at me sing, look at me, no hands, Ma, look at me, I'm flying" as her voice swoops all over. She puts in this absolutely convincing hurt wail, and this comedy commenting on the ridiculousness of the wail—how could she ever have gone out with this jerk; then she does this wicked sample on the word "tears"—she's razzing the jerk, "t-t-t-t-tears, t-t-t-t-tears"—and then she goes off buddy-buddy into the sunset with her boyfriend's other girlfriend. Female bonding. I think she saw *Outrageous Fortune* or something. In the rhythm—"huh chuh huh chuh huh chuh"—it's probably a percussion instrument, but it sounds like human breaths. She's breathing the rhythm. Incredibly sexy.

I've got eight album covers, and she looks different on each one. I wouldn't recognize her if I saw her on the street. But hearing her, I hear a body. A BIG body. (What is she? Five feet tall? A thin five feet? But I mean her sound.) The voice will move. It will search. Teena can be empty and at the same time voluptuous. It's really very, very attractive. My dream date with Teena Marie: "If I give you this number, would you call me?"—Teena has a guy ask her that at the beginning of *Robbery*. If she were to hit me with that line, I wouldn't answer. I wouldn't call. She's not one of us.

Teena can be such a NITWIT. When John Lennon died, she wrote a song for him. When Marvin Gaye died, she wrote a song for him. Maudlin gibberish. "Soon you will see a pretty rainbow shining through the clouds." She gives us greeting-card sorrow—she leaves out the terror and the piss. Now, I don't go out with people who make greeting-card music. There's a social gulf. Janis Ian could write a song about it. Well, hell. Fuck. What would she think of my T-shirt? "My grandparents went to Auschwitz and all I got was this lousy T-shirt." *Naked to the World* has got "Opus III (the Second Movement)," for Marvin Gaye (again), Donny Hathaway, Minnie Riperton. Here we have one of these mammoth paint brushes dunked in syrup and tears. My girlfriend and I were listening to it, we were laughing—this was beyond giggles, this was gales of hysteria. It was too stupid. I'm sorry. Maybe if I'd known Minnie Riperton, I wouldn't have been laughing.

But then—second listen—the music was this nice faucet full of pretty good sound, actually, and this voice coming out doing Minnie Riperton. Teena pulls off that shrill vocal descent from "Loving You." And the bird cheeps! I like it that Teena Marie doesn't always have the discernment . . . she doesn't know what works and what doesn't. There's a wire running from the name "Marvin Gaye" to her tear ducts. When Whitney Houston or Michael Jackson get sappy, I want to fart in their faces. Their sentimentality is worse than plastic. But I let Teena get away with it, and not simply because she "means it." Maybe if this were all she did, these mawkish little elegies, I wouldn't be able to stand them. I like the sap; it's part of a likable whole, an unbounded whole: Let's see what she can gobble up next. You don't know. You can't separate the sentimental shit from "Let's launch into this guitar solo and sear you." It's the same impulse that wants to sear you with the guitar and wants to blubber over Marvin Gaye.

Teena Marie doesn't suffer from good taste. Her intelligence is her excess. Pulling in the whole world—the vocal stuff, all those dips and swirls: Sometimes she's really wailing, other times she's just running her workout. But . . . what I'm trying to say . . . not just "the sum is more than the total of the parts" . . . not only are the flaws inextricable from the virtues, they enhance her virtues. They make her wider and bigger. I like it all, even the stuff I don't like. This is what R. Meltzer was saying about rock 'n' roll. This is what he and Lester Bangs were writing about. This is what those books are about. Making it bigger. . . .

The Village Voice, April 26, 1988

NEW PERSPECTIVES ON ORNETTE COLEMAN

Dear Ornette,

I like your music very much and so does my older sister and even my father says you're not bad. My friend Shelly just gave me a copy of *Science Fiction* for my tenth birthday. She says it is hard to find but she found it. It is my favorite album I think. I like Tiffany's album too but yours is better. Someone told me you were touring with Richard Marx and Jerry Garcia. My dad said he would take me if you played an auditorium so that they would let me in.

Best of luck,
Cynthia

Dear Ornette,

I have this argument with my brother. He says you have brown eyes. I say they're hazel. I'm sure I'm right. My brother is so obnoxious that he won't believe me. Would you answer this and tell him that I'm right and he's wrong?

I hope that Prime Time is doing well. Are you coming to Australia soon? Please come and play in Darwin. Not many bands play in Darwin because it's small, but we would like you very much if you did.

Big Fan in Darwin

Dear Ornette,

I am fourteen years old and I am seeing a man who is twenty-four. He wants to kiss me and go all the way. I am hesitant but I don't want to lose him. What should I do?

Waiting in Wichita

Dear Ornette,

You know what I hate? I hate *ectopussies*. These guys are even worse than pussies. They're lame on the outside like pussies. And on the inside they're such creeps. This guy named Wayne really is a "Wayne," if you know what I mean. We try to be nice to him and not be sarcastic or violent like everyone accuses us. Then he says something and you know he's a jerk.

Joe

Dear Ornette,

I feel that the world has turned into the world of mysteriousness. Things are happening but you don't know what they are. The sun's out and it's a normal day, the roofs across the street are normal as the sun hits them, there's a guy who just got a paper at the grocery store and he's now getting into his pickup, etc. But it's sssssoooo strange. I feel that I'm watching one of those movies on Nickelodeon where they've erased the old soundtrack and then put in new dialogue. Except Nickelodeon has people say silly things, while today in my life people are saying normal things that they normally say, yet it's like someone else is saying it for them. A friend of mine was Caller 20 on one of those radio contests, and that's when I stopped believing in things. I know you understand.

Patrick in Queens

Dear Ornette Coleman,

Please excuse how horrible my English. This is not good to say but everyone I know prefer Icehouse and Bon Jovi but I prefer you! I like too Frank Sinatra and Leonard Cohen. You see I like a lot and there is much happiness with me. You play violin too and trumpet. My teacher say you play for a very long time ago. I'm glad you continue.

An Ornette Coleman Enthusiast

[It says on the sleeve to *Virgin Beauty*, Ornette Coleman's new album with Prime Time, that you can write Ornette Coleman at: The H-Group Box 1377, New York, NY 10013. It does not say whether he will answer.]

Swellsville #8, 1989, written with Leslie Singer in June 1988

TO SCARE A TRENDY

The interview with Depeche Mode was fantastic, but I think you were mis-informed about something. Depeche is *not* a "teenybop band." They are cult or new wave or technopop, but *not* teenybop. Their fans are not teenyboppers; the real fans are the cult following. Depeche are not for everyone. A trendy would get scared at a concert because of the audience.

Kyla Sharron
McHenry, IL

letter printed in *Spin*, October 1988

The interview with Jim Jones was fantastic, but I think you were misinformed about something. People's Temple is *not* a "teenybop group." They are cult or new wave or technopop, but *not* teenybop. Their fans are not teenyboppers; the real fans are the cult following. Jim Jones is not for everyone. A trendy would get scared at a concert because of the audience.

Frank Kogan
San Francisco

unpublished letter to *Spin*, November 1988

NIETZSCHE WITH TITS

The Ladies of Love show in San Francisco was messy and wonderful and irritating and fabulous. The mess and irritation were caused by abysmal acoustics that went way beyond the usual big-hall stupid-mix wrong-volume stuff into a realm of abysmalness that I had never before experienced at anything calling itself a "concert," even CYO dances back in junior high. It was the building's fault, or the soundman's inability to adapt to the building. Pier 2 is really this big ex-warehouse or airplane hangar. The floors are concrete. I didn't check the walls, but they probably have steel in them. Everything echoes. I hoped that, when more people came, the crowd would absorb the echoes, but the place never got more than a quarter full.

As my girlfriend Leslie and I walked in at the far end, giant speakers about an eighth of a mile away were throwing big globs of bass at us. The higher notes rang away unclearly above it all. Even in back, the music was unnecessarily loud; close-up, it was painful. Leslie and I argued a bit—she wanted to back away, I wanted to stay close to the speakers of pain, to better separate "vocals" from the mishmash.

Well, I'm taking a while to get to the matter at hand, but, you know, if you see Shakespeare In The Park in the midst of a violent thunderstorm, you'll experience "thunderstorm" as much as "Shakespeare" or "acting."

"Put your hands in the air. I know you can party better than this." First group up was a local trio called Children Of The Night, each child about twenty years old. The lead singer was a heavyset guy named Kevin, with a real high voice, almost feminine high. Not bad standard-type soul-pop, it didn't galvanize the crowd, but how much were we hearing? "He's the singer, they're the curves," I wrote in my notebook. The curves were Phoenix and Octavia, the girl backup singers who (actually) were the center of attention. The biggest cheer came when they took off their jackets (backs to the audience, wiggling their asses), revealing slinky form-fitting dresses (and the forms therein). They did their slinky dances in unison, were well-rehearsed, and didn't fluff anything. They kept their spirits up, kept exhorting us to clap and party, which few of us did (airplane-hangar acoustics didn't help). Well, I was having a good time, writing in my little pocket notebook while curvy young women urged me to throw my hands up and clap. I asked Leslie if she found the heavy sex sell offensively submissive. "No. It's kind of aggressive—they're pushing it on you—she's making the first move."

Between sets I walked around, studying the crowd. It was mainly Latino, a good number of Filipinos, a few whites, a few blacks. They all looked good—stylish—and I felt stodgy. The majority were between fifteen and twenty-five. That's why they held it in this dumb place instead of a club. The speakers boomed out tracks by the likes of Sweet Sensation and the Cover Girls: really danceable, even with the high end lopped off. I danced to it. Most people stood around and talked.

Children Of The Night had done live vocals against taped accompaniment. That would be the evening's standard setup. But next on was The Answer, a real band, playing generic sort of Rick James sort of funk stuff. They had costumes, steps, attempts at a call-and-response; but clearly they were a band ready to play, expecting to get over on sound, and the PA wasn't doing anything for them. Maybe the band wasn't either. Though the acoustics made "melody" more a hypothetical construct than something one "heard," I could tell that the singer got farther and farther away from "in tune" with each note. They did their set, showing no outward frustration. It's a hazing procedure that opening bands have to go through.

Between acts the DJ played more Sweet Sensation, the DJ's voice coming on twice as loud in the midst of it (musical emphasis, perhaps) saying something that the reverberations turned into loud farts. Leslie looked at the teen girls around us. "They've got some good-looking hair."

Leslie Stoval (of KMEL), a buppie dressed for church, did the performer intros. She announced the next act; the sound system garbled it. "Rios"? "The Rios"? Should I ask someone? Suddenly I felt shy, like an outsider—didn't ask anyone. No one would know the name anyway (I rationalized); I've never heard these people on the radio. "These people," "The Rios," "The Wetchamacallits" were terrific dancers, two young woman from New York. "How you doin' San Francisco? We hear you know how to party." The crowd did little. The Wetchamacallits wore matching black two pieces, breasts highlighted in silver, skirts like see-through scarves. Matching hairstyles. Nice loose bodies, swinging as if wild, but in complete synchronization. This is what dancing is for.

Their first song was real spare, just voices against percussion. I thought, "They're doing something here, with the spareness." They had deep, powerful voices (I hypothesized) that the sound system shredded.

Their genre is "Latin hip-hop"—misleading name, because, except where the genre mixes with Miami bass, the music has no rap. I guess people are trying to avoid the avoid-at-all-costs word "disco"—but say it loud, this is disco and . . . proud? Proud! Proud??? It's "Latin" and maybe proud: the music of young Puerto Ricans in New York and of young interracial whatevers in Miami. It takes the fast technorhythms that Arthur Baker and John Robie borrowed from Europe in the early '80s (e.g., Freez "I.O.U.," Soul Sonic Force "Looking for the Perfect Beat," C-Bank "One More Shot"), giving them a more Caribbean-type syncopation/complication. On top you often get Supremes-style wails and whines—three out of every five songs derive from "You Keep Me Hangin' On" it seems—but sometimes with a Spanish feel. Melodies are minor or modal or something.

The Whoseywhats (turns out their name *is* The Rios—I just called Leslie Stoval at KMEL and asked) did their next song, "Hold Me": not as spare as the first and maybe not as interesting (who could tell?). They lifted up their skirts, and got their loudest cheers. They kicked their legs way up over their heads, as natural as waving their hands. "Hold me/Fulfill me/Possess me."

Stoval came out again—this time with a pile of Ladies Of Love T-shirts in her arms. The crowd came alive as it hadn't all evening. People started screaming. Hands reached out: gimme gimme gimme. Leslie (*my* Leslie, not Stoval) got pissed at this. Why go gaga for a fucking T-shirt when you've barely responded to the show the T-shirt is supposed to commemorate?

"Are you having fun yet? Is this a PARTY?" Corina came out in a black two-piece that looked like underwear. She sang "Give Me Back My Heart," tried to move the immobile crowd. She went to the back of the stage and brought back some giveaway posters; a sea of hands reached up for them.

Details of Corina's performance, like whether she had a thin voice or a husky one, escape me (might have escaped everyone else too, given the acoustics). I don't blame her for this. I don't blame the performers for anything. The thought "sounds like 'You Keep Me Hangin' On'" keeps popping in my mind, but I forget if it applies to Corina or India, the next performer, whose image has merged with Corina's in my memory. Both were anorexic-model-type skinny, and India's outfit also took the basic black underwear approach, this time with a silver-studded belt. I wrote "India—vocal descents" in my notebook, so she must have sung some.

Judy Torres was next, and she blazed. She loves to dance and move. She'd be doing this even if no one paid her. She broke the color pattern by wearing a dark-blue tunic over tight spandex pants. On the radio, her melodies had never seemed like anything special, and they didn't astound me here. Her voice did.

She has lungs. She'll have a career. As a singer, not a model. I thought she looked fine, and the audience thought so to, but she's too hefty for Pepsi commercials. She raised the issue between songs, described a typical reaction: "'Oh my God! She's so big!'—All right, I'm chunky but I'm funky." Huge cheers. Girls screamed for her.

Her second song was "You Keep Me Hangin' On" but with different words. She pulled a guy out of the audience, sang her heart out to him: "I've got to have you." The guy was a good dancer, lithe, kind of angular. He was shy, too; not wanting to outstay his welcome, he scampered off the stage, but Judy pulled him back up. They moved well, mirroring each other's motions, bumping asses, thrusting hips. The song ended to wild applause. "A night to remember," she said.

She announced "Come Into My Arms," and girls shrieked. People clapped to the music. "Say 'oh-oh,'" she demanded, and we said "Oh-oh." Finally, real call-and-response! Her voice climbed, climbed higher, and let loose, thrilling birds in the rafters. She got gigantic applause as she left the stage.

Leslie Stoval returned, asked us, "Do you like the boom?" More shrieks. The excited audience stayed excited. L'Trimm are these delightful or cloying (depending on your point-of-view) gigglepuss girl teens whose "We like the cars/The cars that go boom/We're Tigra and Bunny/And we like the boom" has been booming from Bay Area car stereos for the last month. Tigra and Bunny wore matching gold I-Dream-of-Jeannie two pieces. "We want all the ugly people to keep quiet," Tigra said in a voice full of her absolute delight at having uttered such an original line. All us beautiful people in the audience made noise.

Bunny is seventeen, Tigra sixteen, and, their world unmarred by worry or cynicism, each has spent the last fourteen years wiggling and showing off for appreciative relatives and anyone else coming to visit. That is to say, whether their charm springs naturally from their pure and gently mischievous hearts, or whether it's a desperate defense mechanism raised to an art form, onstage it is full-bodied and absolutely convincing. (Their *performance* was full-bodied; the girls themselves are actually kind of scrawny. They don't eat enough.) They're rappers, not much dependent on melody, so sound systems that go FLUMPFFF don't hinder them. Live, they enhanced the wondrously silly wonderfulness of their hits. "Grab it! Grab it like you wahhhnt it!" Like, what could be more fun than to want it! "Bunny, the people on my side can shout louder than the people on your side," gushed Tigra with joyous assurance, as if this weren't an ancient show-biz gimmick, but something thought up on the spot.

Next.

After Judy Torres's intense sincerity and L'Trimm's spirited, innocent (or "innocent") girlishness, what more could we want?

Debbie Deb bounded onstage. My girlfriend Leslie's jaw dropped. Debbie Deb is white. She wore a black leather jacket. (Leslie wears a black leather jacket.)

After the first song, Debbie Deb took off her jacket, to cheers. "Oh, you like my tits," she blurted out. She wore a skimpy black two-piece. Her "skirt" was a miniature hula thing dipped in black paint, fishnets underneath. For once we were seeing a woman of normal human weight—i.e., her flesh hung over her skirt a little bit. Her hair was a trash blonde semi-dye job, brown hair left deliberately visible underneath. She looked great. (This afternoon, KMEL's Leslie Stoval, undoubtedly a victim of eating disorders, who'd earlier won my heart by calling me "hon" over the phone and saying that "the performers gave their all," pissed me off—blew it!—by saying derogatorily on the air, "Debbie Deb has quite a tummy roll," and then opining that if you're not built for revealing costumes you shouldn't wear them. "You like her, Rick, because she was playing up to you," she told her colleague Rick Chase.)

Most Debbie Deb material was catchy disco pop, good melodies, I decided (such decisions, remember, were rather theoretical, given the acoustics), performed, it seemed (this evaluation being rather theoretical too, and influenced perhaps by her physical presence and onstage demeanor), with soulful grit. Anyway, it was straight-ahead disco, unabashed disco; between songs she *called* it "disco." Good for her. Honey disco, with Girlschool's personality, or Jean Harlow's, or Grace Slick's. (Vinegar disco.) Next she did "Wild Thing"—without the famous chord pattern; only beats and words. Eyeing someone in the audience, she breathed "I really need you," a tinge of sarcasm in her tone. To Debbie Deb's left was a curly-haired keyboard player—manager-boyfriend-husband, I imagined—of eastern or southern European descent, I imagined also, feeling (for the first time that evening) a rush of sudden, unexpected IDENTIFICATION WITH THE PEOPLE ONSTAGE.

She introduced her single "I'm Searchin": "You're waiting at home in bed, waiting for him to join you. He comes home at 4 AM, whiskey on his breath, the smell of another woman on his person. What do you do girls when he comes home with the smell of another woman upon him? Do you open your arms—your legs!—and say dive right in, the water's fine? NO! You say FUCK YOU!!! Then you put on your cocktail dress and your hat and go out and get yourself a real man, a true man."

"Did she say, 'a true man'?" I asked, feeling attracted to her—which was entirely superfluous, since she reminded me of my girlfriend Leslie, who was standing right next to me. By now Leslie and I were projecting wildly. Leslie: "She's being very satirical. She probably read Nietzsche in school. She was a philosophy major and she supported herself doing porno." Frank: "Let's say she went to Florida State. Yeah, she went to Florida State, then afterwards got thrown out of the Yale philosophy program for doing her master's thesis about *Soul Train*. She called her faculty advisor 'a cultural illiterate.' 'You guys don't know dick about anything.'"

What was the rest of the audience thinking? They were cheering okay, some of them "joining in" when called, though without the feeling of unity that had been there for Judy Torres. But was Debbie Deb trying for unity? I was noticing—enjoying—all these discordant elements (in my imagination?). Debbie was doing work-the-crowd routines, just like all the others. "San Francisco is one of my favorite places in the whole world." "Everybody say 'Owwww.'" And I was hearing this edge of deliberate insincerity. Or mixed insincerity and passion—really straining the distinction between sincerity and insincerity—evoking deep feelings in me because of the strain.

How far had I gone into intense overidentification with the performer? Here I was convincing myself that I was experiencing something truly awesome—the new Iggy Goddamn Stooge—while merely watching a (most-likely) normal foul-mouthed woman sing disco that I couldn't quite hear and carry on audience interaction that I couldn't quite interpret. Anyhow, her edge, her power: Like, she's communicating that these are just routines—this is just my job—and I fuckin' love this job. . . . She's sort of like Jerry Lee Lewis tossing something off, Elvis when he starts parodying himself: I'm just going through the motions—and I do the motions better than anyone on Earth, so suck on this.

Pause.

Top of the bill, headline act, was Sa-fire. Um, Polygram Recording Artist Sa-fire. She had two good hits on Cutting Records, both similar to "You Keep Me Hangin' On" but with aggressive guitar parts shooting out of really aggressive dance rhythms. She was now riding her new hit, the okay "Boy I've Been Told." I'd seen several pictures of her, and she never looked the same.

Sa-fire wore a form-fitting lime-green jacket over real short purple shorts. After her first song she ran to the side and put on her hat—a wide-brimmed thing with a purple flower on it. She's thin, strong-boned, round-eyed, gorgeous. Of all the performers, she was the one with the most Latina diction.

But . . . something wasn't connecting. It took me a while to realize that she was putting out, singing hard (out-of-tune, but that's okay). I felt this strange non-involvement. Maybe I was still reeling from Debbie Deb's anti-involvement.

"It's getting hot in here. Should I take it off?" I don't remember if this got a response. Under her jacket was a low-cut lime-green blouse. She started "Let Me Be the One" (version two of "You Keep Me Hangin' On") a cappella, unintentionally changing the key several times. The sound man seemed to be *adding* reverb. Like adding salt to the Dead Sea.

End of her set, she started to walk off, then remembered, oh! she was going to give away tapes of her new album. She got a few tapes, handed them out, and left again, not getting a huge amount of applause. I had the weird feeling that it hadn't quite happened. The sound system defeated her.

The morning after: The next day I wondered whether any of it had happened—I mean, happened as I'd constructed it in my mind. Decided to do some reality checking. Also, since the written account of nonwhite pop events tends to be done by literate (and white) ignoramuses, and since my radio listening, like a lot of my other work habits (e.g., writing, sleeping, working), is irregular, and there's no "hot" format station here anyway, and I'd never even heard Debbie Deb or Corina before Saturday's show . . . well, I bought some records.

I'd be happy to hear Corina's "Out of Control" on any dance floor, though I still don't think I could tell Corina from India in the dark—nor from a lot of other Latin disco divas. That's not necessarily a flaw, not in this genre. It does make it hard to develop "acts" and "stars."

Judy Torres blazes on record as well as onstage, and deserves to be a star. Perhaps I've slightly exaggerated everybody's melodic debt to "You Keep Me Hangin' On." For example, "Come Into My Arms" doesn't resemble any Supremes song; it resembles "It's a Sin," i.e., "Wild World." I played it ten times in a row today, so I guess I like it (or her, anyway) rather extremely.

I found two Debbie Deb singles but didn't find any eastern or southern European surnames on their credits, nor anyone named "Debbie" or "D." listed as a songwriter. It's possible that she's just another voice and a bod who's some producer's tool. (Rambunctious tool, no?) In any event, "I'm Searchin'" is a fucking Godhead of a record, and I'm not saying this just because I like her "goddamn titties" (as she referred to them onstage). She (or her producer) takes these pretty melodic elements and, instead of adding more pretty elements and coming up—voila!—with a pretty pop song, she concentrates on the thing, with this mesmerizing, relentless repetition. This tough black-like voice (reason Debbie's skin color provoked Leslie's jawdrop) on the borderline between sweet and blistering:

Tonight I want to take a chance on how I feel
But I don't know if what I feel is really real
He says he is the man I know that I can trust
But of course it could be love but then again it could be lust
'Cause I'm searchin' . . .

It's not amazing poetry or a breakthrough in modern psychology or anything, except for me right now it's EVERYTHING because I can feel her onstage living those lines every time she faces an audience.

Swellsville #8, 1989 (written in September 1988)

PUBLIC ENEMY (PAZZ & JOP 1988)

You know that Public Enemy are punk rockers because they're addicted to their own oppression. Those prison bars on the cover give their lives meaning. Those bars excite them. Those bars get them moving. On Ed Sullivan back in 1956, Elvis Presley introduced "Love Me Tender" by calling it "my newest RCA Victor escape . . . uh, release." That's classic. That moment of escape is a great rock 'n' roll buzz, but after a while you get so stuck on the thrill of the escape that you carry your cage around with you. You become a goddamn escape artist, and the routine gets old. It isn't old yet for Public Enemy, but it will be, and they'll have to be better than Houdini if they want to keep their music alive.

It's unintentionally poignant when Flavor Flav says, "I got a right to be hostile, man. My people been persecuted." This reminds me of Chuck Eddy's "the Bad Brains have earned their anger" accolade, and it has the same problems. Hostility is a feeling, not a right. But Public Enemy have to justify their hostility before they can feel it—or at least, before they can express it. Normal everyday hostility's not good enough—it's got to be righteous hostility. It's got to be world-important, or it's no good. So Flavor Flav's feelings are only real to himself in the context of "his people's" victimization. He needs that victimization; without it, his feelings can't live.

excerpted from "Pazz & Jop 1988" (written in January 1989)

GOING TO DIE

Here are Guns N' Roses in the Top 40: "She's got eyes of the bluest skies/As if they thought of rain." Those are lyrics a thirteen-year-old girl wants to hear? Hell, they're lyrics a thirteen-year-old girl *writes*. (Some thirteen-year-old girls, that is.) But then, suddenly, the mood changes for no reason. They feel trapped (our thirteen-year-old heroine and her beloved Axl). Axl sings "Where do we go, where do we go now" over and over at the end like a prayer, stretching the word *go*, pleading.

Axl will prowl through a song, carry a vowel sound into transcendence. Like, this moment, this sound is everything. Like Janis Joplin: "This one day is your life." He'll break his voice into rhythm, ride with that. Guns N' Roses evoke Zeppelin and Aerosmith, but there's more effort and, maybe because of that, more humanity or soul or beauty or reach or desperation.

Now, our heroine . . . I'll make her fourteen. She's looking out the window (of her house or her school). It's a peaceful day, the grass is bright green, the essence of super-green spring. Things look pretty well-ordered out there (let's say it's a suburb). A song rages in her mind—she's imagining the sound is out there in the silent green. "Welcome to the jungle," goes the song, about sleazy, scary L.A. But the girl knows where the real jungle is, the jungle's inside her.

"The sincerity of what we're doing," says Axl Rose, when asked on MTV to explain Guns N' Roses' popularity.

So Guns N' Roses call their new album *GN'R Lies*, a contradiction so big you could drive a truck through it. It's also as old as the hills or at least the Stones.

To note that rock 'n' roll has contradictions is to do no more than note that, say, roller coasters have inclines and boxers have fists. Contradictions are functional equipment, just like amps and drums. The more unlivable the contradiction, the better.

Every interviewer has commented on the band's honesty. The band is outspoken. They'll tell you whom they like and dislike, they'll rip the record company, one of them (at least) will tell you that he's been a junkie, they'll get sloshed in front of a reporter, almost get violent. We're ourselves and we don't give a fuck.

This honesty . . . it's a role. Axl is honest because he's unacceptable, real because he's going to die.

Lies? Is this title self-knowledge? Evasion? The first side is their indie EP from 1986, *Live ?!*@ Like a Suicide*. It's loud headbang stuff. Axl introduces the songs with helpful epistemological comments: "This song is about your fucking mother." It's okay, and would have been a blast to hear live, but what's obvious to me is that in the next year of drugging and fucking around horribly they found time to turn themselves into a good band, adding interplay, throb, contrasts, space, giving Axl's voice room to move in the music rather than screech on top.

The second side is major mindfuck: new mainly acoustic stuff that's beautiful and lush and rocks a lot harder than loud side one. The words have trap doors. Which make them better? fucked? thrilling? "I used to love her, but I had to kill her." Totally catchy. I play this for a woman friend, who laughs delightedly, "They're being so silly." Next, "You're Crazy," in a gentle, slow version, Axl's voice continuing its desperate search for El Dorado. Then, "One in a Million," a plaintive, haunting song, with hateful lyrics. He's mad at cops who rough him up, niggers who peddle stolen goods, immigrants who act like they own the place, faggots who spread disease. My friend goes, "What the hell is he doing? Where's his goddamn mind? These are lies for sure. Immigrants? Is he an Indian or something? He looks Norwegian to me." The words have more trap doors. "They cause so many goddamn waves," Axl complains. He can't be serious! In the rock world, it's *good* to cause waves. Guns N' Roses cause waves. (Is that his point? His tip-off that this is satire? Or maybe he's just stupid. I vote for stupid.) He sings, "It's been such a long time since I knew right from wrong." Cop-out. Fucking escape hatch.

"If you choose, try to lose," goes an old Lou Reed line. That's more applicable to *GN'R Lies* than are "bigot, racist" (though those seem applicable too). Axl sings, "It's all a means to an end now." No. It's all means and no end, except the one that puts you underground, poor guy.

A poor guy with gorgeous, chiseled features.

My friend, who fell in love with Axl on MTV, says, "Axl screams and makes his face like a monster. It's so cute. He's got a girlish-looking face and effeminate movements. It's especially cute when he tries to look like a tough boy, when he's just in jeans and T-shirt. If I had a little sister I'd want her to be just like him."

I know what she means, though I'd find it rough having a kid sister who was never happy.

The Village Voice, January 3, 1989

[Axl talks so many goddamn ways that I don't always hear him right. But in the rock world it's good to talk in accents. Guns N' Roses talk in accents. In any event, the line in "One in a Million" isn't "They cause so many goddamn waves" but "They talk so many goddamn ways," which doesn't change my analysis of the song at all, but I felt bad about the fuckup. It didn't cross my mind that I'd misheard. Doug missed it too. Also, I was so angry about the racism and homophobia that I didn't do justice to the way the song's a journey from nowhere to nowhere, a getaway that takes him from chaos to handcuffs, "Like a Rolling Stone" in glitter town. Heartbreaking. He hops a Greyhound, but whatever's dogging him hops it too. Axl was only a couple years away from shutdown. Fade to black. . . .]

SQUEEZED FROM THE TUBE

There's no word for "music" in Swahili. That's not true. I once saw an English-Swahili dictionary, and the word for "music" was "musiki." Anyway, music isn't a separate thing, you get costumes, sounds, and dancing, it's all the event. And that's what you get on MTV. You don't get initiation ceremonies or doing the dishes, which probably all come with specific music in parts of Africa. You don't get hog-tying contests, or the guy biting off chicken heads, or the ferris wheel (things you get in the "white" tradition of multithing events, like county fairs,

San Gennaro festivals). You don't get the girl throwing up in the corner or the guy hitting on you (part of the standard "bar or club" event). You do get the guy peeling the skin off the chicken (if you happen to be me peeling a chicken while watching *Yo MTV Raps*, which I was doing yesterday). You get Axl's face, Axl's cheekbones, Axl's tattoos, Axl extending his arm (like he's drying his nails), Axl wiggling his hips.

MTV is radio with pictures, essentially. It's moving pictures added to sound, rather than the usual vice versa (I have a friend who was told in film school never to do this, never add pictures to a song, never build a movie around a song). (That's why 95 percent of all art videos suck—art assholes never start with the music.)

In the "I Want Action" video, Poison look the way the Sex-O-Lettes sound ("Bay City Rollers play the Sex-O-Lettes"). They are (were) transvestites let loose in a kiddie clothing store. All those bright colors.

They never dared do it again.

Axl looked glitter, teased hair and that, on "Welcome to the Jungle." But GN'R and all rock bands are afraid to cross a sexual line that any old bo—Dolls, Bowie, Eno, Alice Cooper, Lou Reed, Marc Bolan—was expected to cross in 1974. Sex Pistols made punk safe for fag bashers (I'm sure this was one of the reasons for their success); the glam-metal bands are making glitter safe for fag bashers. Maybe. There's still something unresolved, I hope. I wish I could see something Sylvesterish in Jon Bon Jovi and Adam Curry, but I can't. (They should get Little Richard to Vee Jay.)

Once, when my mother worked for the Massachusetts Housing Authority, she went to see the mayor of Springfield. He boomed out across to her as she entered his office, "Mrs. Hogan, you don't look Irish, but I'm pleased to meet you."

They did business with this firm that my mother called "St. Louis Hit and Run" (real name was St. Louis Screw and Bolt).

This guy Anthony lived down the hall from me when I lived on Mott Street. He was shy and would wear his jacket all the time and look puzzled, except occasionally he'd get upset and I'd hear him stamping his foot and bellowing "Goddamn, goddamn" over and over. One bright day I wrote this poem:

Spring is here
The flowers are smiling
The buds are swelling
The Anthonies are bellowing
In the sun.

There's this bed that Kylie Minogue ("I Should Be So Lucky") flops onto and off, like it's there to be bounced on but she doesn't know what to do with it. (Needs someone to bounce with.) She looks like they squeezed her from the Pepsodent tube. She's staring in the bathroom mirror, holding her nail file. Then she tosses the file in the air, like, "What's the use?"

Why Mildred Skis (WMS #5), spring 1989

RAZE "BREAK FOR LOVE"

This is an oh-ungh-gasp orgasm song that's panted its way up the dance and 12-inch charts and onto a major label. It's got an eerie and gentle synth line that embodies that strange peace you feel after you've stayed up all night studying in the library . . . oops! That's a slip, I mean after you've stayed up all night *partying* in the *disco* and you're still buzzing and you go outside and whoa, the sun's coming up.

The ungh-gasp stuff is pretty eerie itself, since it has none of the warmth, the sensitivity, the *humanity*, of, say, Donna Summer; nor the spontaneity of . . . well, what I'm trying to say is that it's done by machine. By digital sampler. There are a few basic breath sounds and a female moan and a male groan. The "breath" sounds are played precisely as rhythms, while the "moan" and "groan" vary in length, pitch, and volume (it's great what you can do with technology), depending on how far along we've gotten.

The 12-inch contains four versions; on my favorite, the "Drop the Panties" mix, writer-producer-arranger Vaughan Mason says encouraging things like "yeah, rub up and down next to me," "let me do that for you," "let it go, let it go, oh yeah, don't stop," and the machine gets more and more excited.

Spin, March 1989

DONNA SUMMER

As for Donna Summer, she was a hero of mine through 1979, then she became . . . I don't know what she became. A singer with a strong voice and a "past." She reformed and stopped being a disco slut and never established anything else. An old article by Michael Freedberg says flat out, "No disco artist despised disco more fundamentally than Donna Summer." I actually don't believe that.

But no disco artist sang with such a raging coldness. Smart, funny coldness. In "I Feel Love" she was out there and gorgeous in synth-cold outer space and no one could touch her. If she felt love, it wasn't for me.

excerpt from review of *Another Place and Time, Spin,* 1989

LET MTV RING

When I was thirteen this song by Steppenwolf—first song to use the phrase "heavy metal," as far as I know—had a real clever line, "If the tune makes you smile/You were born to be wild." Actually, I'd heard it wrong (really went "Like a true nature's child" or something); this was good, since my version was more useful. I was a hemmed-in kid; no way was I a nature's child. I mean, in my house, on my street, in my school? By my locker? At my desk? You kidding? But "the tune makes you smile"—I can get there! From my smile to the wild. A first step, at least.

"I just want to rock and roll all night, and party every day." That's an old Kiss song. But back when the song was new and my wife Leslie was twelve years old (this was before we married), she heard it as, "I just want to rock and roll all night, and *part of* every day." OK. Again, a necessary mistake, to make the dream accessible—imaginable—to a twelve-year-old.

"Up all night, sleep all day," goes the song by Slaughter that's ruled *Dial MTV*, MTV's call-in request show, for the last month and a half. *Sleep* all day? For some readers, no doubt, those words are too much of a compromise (you don't even have to hear it wrong), not mitigated by the utopian "Maybe we can just stay up twenty-four hours a day" tossed off in the middle. But, see, if you're a bubble-metal band that wants twelve-year-old girls in your demographic, you've got to give them something in their range. At fourteen, Leslie wore black leather and cheered in homeroom whenever it was announced over the intercom that the school's football team had lost. When you're fourteen, everything's possible. But twelve-year-olds have a sense of reality.

Mark Slaughter has an ultra-pretty-boy face (also for the twelve-year-olds). The video's got a nice cum shot—a woman's walking along and then there's this big burst, courtesy of the water vent off a truck. The music is pomp and flourish brought down to a muscle-bound boogie, like Leppard. Leppard Lite. The vocals are Zeppelin brought down to a pretty-boy tunesiness, like Kix, like Crüe, like _____. The tune makes me smile.

The rest of their LP, *Stick It to Ya*, is pretty depressing: a couple more catchy tunes, and craft and care and many hooks, but embedded in too much uninvolved imitation and rote misogyny. Still, the single itself shines, and I like how, at its conclusion, the chant "Up all night" leads into (wafting through the video's morning sky) a singsong, "From every mountainside/Let freedom ring," as if the two ideas were indivisible.

There are people who take seriously clichés and lies like "up all night" and Skid Row's "youth gone wild," as if just over the near horizon these empty phrases have some content (other than "insomnia" and "change the diapers"). And I'm one of those people, sort of: I imagine that these phrases stand in for others just past the near horizon, and these other phrases themselves have imaginary contents galloping along just past the horizon after that, kind of.

Read any metal 'zine and you'll see a pile of letters written supposedly to praise some drab-looking band like Metallica but really to proclaim the author's belief that (1) Poison, Guns N' Roses, Skid Row, and Enuff Z Nuff are faggots and pussies, (2) so are the people who listen to those bands, (3) girls who like Poison are sluts who probably lick each others' pussies, (4) Poison have small dicks, and (5) it's music that's important anyway, not hairstyle. Then there are answer letters: (1) Metallica are ugly and boring and can't sing for shit, (2) Poison are not fags, (3) I want to sleep with Poison and that doesn't make me a slut, (4) there are thousands of girls like me, and (5) even if Poison are fags, that doesn't matter, because it's music that's important.

Then there's *Dial MTV*—shows the top nine requests, weekdays, 6 PM—which is dominated by metal bands who dress like faggots and pussies: in studs and leather and perms and—sometimes—makeup. Which is not to say that any of them are trying to stand in solidarity with gays and women—simply that, for a young white male, gay and female style is a move over the horizon, into flamboyance. And of course most metal bands would deny their girly roots—all except Poison, who opened their first LP with the drumbeat from the Ronettes' "Be My Baby," and who at that time looked like transvestites let loose in a kiddie clothing store: a move interpreted by a million or so teen girls as boy-cuddly, not homosexual ("girls like to lick our makeup").

On the other hand, a couple of years ago, watching Poison's video for "Nothin' but a Good Time," a fourteen-year-old girl shocked me by saying, "Those guys are grits." So, like some soldier said in Vietnam, if you're not confused you don't understand the situation. If you're not confused, you don't understand MTV.

Dial MTV, taking them one at a time:
Sinéad O'Connor "Nothing Compares 2 U." The camera stays close on her face: remorseless, like the song itself. Clearasil (soda pop version of "Da Doo

Ron Ron" in background); *Dick Tracy*; "White Water Falls" at Great America Amusement Park. Great White—live acoustic version of Led Zeppelin's "Babe I'm Gonna Leave You," Zep's imitation of "While My Guitar Gently Weeps." Lead singer Jack Russell wears his Ian Hunter sunglasses, an open V nearly to the waist, mondo-hairy chest. Classic Led Zep poetry: "Oh baby oh baby oh baby I'm gonna leave you oh babe sweet babe you make me happy every day, but I've got to go, oh mah mah babe, baby baby." Inspiring.

Aerosmith "What It Takes"—Steven Tyler minces around doing his usual who-gives-a-fuck comic parody of Mick Jagger doing a comic parody of himself and pretending not to give a fuck. Video has them in cowboy gear at a c&w bar, hiding behind chicken wire while a brawl erupts around them. Effect is improved immeasurably by Leslie reciting in my ear famous composer Glenn Branca's *Forced Exposure* interview: "The Dolls were my ultimate gods after Aerosmith . . . the Dolls were pure drag, Aerosmith was glitter." Skeptical interviewer Howard Wuelfing: "Well, [the Dolls] wore pants." Branca: "Yes, but they'd wear yellow pants like my aunt used to wear in the '50s, yellow clam diggers with little slits." On the screen, cowboys are knocking over tables and pounding each other.

Danger Danger "Bang Bang," pretty metal boys mildly dressed up. Topps baseball cards; some model named Gabriella for hair shampoo; Young MC for summer color Pepsi cans; Hawaiian Tropic tanning lotion; *Total Recall* with Schwarzenegger, by the director of *Robocop* (I want to see it). Madonna "Vogue." MC Hammer "U Can't Touch This"—strenuous fast dancing, shots of people on stairs (like Eisenstein), lots of bright colors (like a kiddie clothing store). New Kids on the Block to guest VJ on Saturday morning; feminine deodorant protection; oopee balls with bright colors; "my hair gets wet and my scalp gets drier," use dry scalp shampoo from Head & Shoulders; *Robocop 2*; *Who Framed Roger Rabbit?* on the Disney Channel.

Faster Pussycat "House of Pain," a godawful power ballad that I've come to like a lot, with a tearjerk video about this kid crying while his parents fight in the kitchen—telling detail of a kettle boiling and no one noticing. The life of a kettle is a lonely one. "There's no one home in my house of pain." I sing this to myself later that night after reading letter from a friend. No one understands me.

Mötley Crüe "Without You." Metal goes McCartney. Lots of pretty-boy chest shots. This time the chest is hairless. The video is set in an ancient Egyptian temple that's been made up to look like some movie lot in Arizona.

Kiss "Rise to It." A barely glammed Kiss sings a nondescript rock song. Don't know why anyone cares enough about this one to vote for it. MTV street party "four hours of house-shaking sound"; Playtex "a tampon's got to feel comfortable"; Little Caesar Pizza "I taught my dog to say I love you"; clarifying makeup acne formula; how to watch Nickelodeon's seven-day Donnathon; *Basket Case 2*.

L.A. Guns "Ballad of Jayne," pretty-boy metal band dressed in Haight-Ashbury death-rock gypsy bullshit; singer with bare chest (hairless) holds a rose. It's another godawful power ballad that makes girls' hearts flutter and does nothing for me. After hearing it for a month I'll like it—they've done tests with mice that prove this.

Dentyne; Barq's root beer with women weight lifters and calypso soundtrack; Chevy Chase in *National Lampoon's Christmas Vacation*; *Robocop 2* "Think it over, creep!"

Slaughter "Up All Night"—what a transcendent triumph! It soars, it sings. A model wears a black bra with studs. The bass player wears leather with studs. He reminds me of that hairy creep who appears in Sarah Palmer's hallucination (*Twin Peaks*) and may have killed her daughter Laura. He's kind of cute and goofy.

The Village Voice, June 5, 1990

REAL PUNKS DON'T WEAR BLACK

Fan mail to the cast of *Twin Peaks* received by ABC TV during the week that followed the premiere of that series:

To Sherilyn Fenn (plays Audrey Horne)
Dear Sherilyn,

I write to let you know what good impression you make on me with your character on the TV show. I am just moved to USA with my parents so words in this letter are probably not altogether correct. I applaud how there is many nuance on your face when you learn of your classmate's death. I say this about myself: I am a punk. I am shy and studious and do not resemble the look of a punk, but in deep reality that is what I am. And you are a punk too, though you as well do not resemble the look of a punk. I know you are actress but I know again that it comes from somewhere, inner experience or observation, it is achievement. With your face it is too good and teeth are too straight to appear conventional punk. You use oblique strategy as the only way.

Real punks don't wear black! The important is inside. I have killed many people in my mind, and though I have no worry of killing people in life, sometimes I wish my mind could rest. But there is a rage in the world and my mind will dance to that rage and will not sing it lullabies. I rage with hope and that's why your character is forefront hero. You are actress and by now you must receive many proposals of marriage for your face and way of standing and much fan mail from boys and girls with blank face and dimples and straight teeth who wish that they too could be blowtorch. They really should look to each other. So I write simply to congratulate your achievement.

Best wishes,

A fan

To the actress who plays Harriet

Dear Donna's Little Sister Harriet,

Yes, "the full blossom of the evening" is much better than "the blossom of the evening" or "the full flower of the evening." I am a poetess too.

In the damp dark, in the night
It is still
A rock in the woods
An unformed light reflected in the quiet stream
My face feels the air

Like you, I have an older sister. Like you, I live in a town that looks fine but is really very strange. I don't show anyone my poetry, though, especially not my older sister. Next year I can take a creative writing class. However, I don't know if it would be good for my poems to write them for a teacher. In the second episode you weren't there when James and Donna and Donna's parents had dinner. I hope this means you were babysitting or something and not that you've been taken from the show. I don't even know your name. It's not listed in the credits in *TV Guide.*

Yours sincerely,

Carolyn

[Editor's note: Harriet Hayward is played by Jessica Wallenfels.]

To Dana Ashbrook (plays Bobby Briggs)

Dear Dana,

We are two twelve-year-old girls who think that you are THE super babe. It's not just your looks, it's something deeper. There isn't much chance of you ever coming to Pawcatuck, is there? We've got some good swimming nearby. Since your show is new and it'll be months before we see you in *Superteen* or *Bop*, could you please send us your picture? We dream of you. Your hair is *so* black.

Thank you

Cheryl and Cynthia

Why Music Sucks #7, March 1991 (written in spring 1990)

FUCK MACHINES AND RAZOR BLADES

Disco managed to be audacious without being upscale in the usual sense. Its making room in its heart for cabaret, for opera, for kung fu, for anything, was simply that: making room for something and saying "You can be disco, too, all you need is a disco beat—and we can discofy anything." It's as if, in the early '60s, Hank Ballard, Chubby Checker, and Joey Dee had all found themselves in the same format, the same demographic. And maybe Ballard would be just as gritty, and Dee just as smooth and would-be elegant, and Checker just as teenybopper, but the distinctions wouldn't play as distinctions. In this way the whole thing could be upscale without leaving anything behind, without shedding its down-home mannerisms, so to speak. It could be down-home without being stodgy or reactionary. "Down-home" is probably the wrong phrase here. Like this: Elvis never stopped being a truck driver with dreams; the point is he dressed himself in the dreams, not in the overalls. I'm really not sure what I'm driving at here, of course. A disco is basically a Saturday night bar 'n' dance floor that doesn't know its place. But that doesn't make it a would-be supper club, dinner theater . . . It's got its own style of ambition. It's like Tony Camonte in the original *Scarface*, asking the sophisticate Poppy what she thinks of his jacket. "Kinda gaudy, isn't it?" she says, and he says, happily, "Yeah," oblivious to her sarcasm, and winning her over. But in my dream, disco doesn't ignore the sophistication and the sarcasm, but incorporates it, discofies it. Again, what does this mean????? How do we take sarcasm, knowingness, a sense of tragedy, politics, and make it gaudy, turn it into a circling disco globe? I'm working on it. A flash of glitter, glamour. The vision is made of scraps and probably won't amount to much in the daylight. But fuck the daylight, that's not what music's about. The point of having a vision is to use it, not to check it for accuracy.

Chuck [Eddy] tends to underplay the way that, for young unmarrieds, night life is, in its way, a *job*. That's not all it is, of course, but that's part of it.

One of the great '70s punk songs, "Lost in Room," by Alternative TV, has this line that goes (though I'm not sure about the first three words): "[DJ above me] played records all night/While I sat in the corner shivering from fright." That's certainly part of the disco experience, and I'm sure it was also part of the basic social experience of a lot of teens who grew up hating disco. And I can see how a musician could want the music—not just the metal detector at the entrance—to at least acknowledge this part of the experience. I think Talking Heads and Gang of 4 (boo hiss) aspired to make disco that took the terror into account; also I imagine that Psychic TV (whom I haven't heard) try to do something of the sort, and Mark Stewart, and PiL in its early years. But disco doesn't need terror infused into its sound, or a sense of tragedy. The terror is already there, from the eeriness of "I Feel Love" (yes, the song is funny, but it's hard, too, and Donna does not sound warm and easy to get, not at all) to the corrosive little dance tracks of Phuture. The smart artist brings terror and conflict to the party because he thinks it will make a better party, not to make the party more "realistic." And in the disco words—well, the subtext of "Get Into the Groove" is about loneliness, if you want it to be. The urgency in Strafe's voice: "Come on let's get this party started, RIGHT?" as if the thing needs to be jump started, forced, if it's to get moving. The desperation's there if you want it. And Debbie Deb: "Lookout Weekend," that wisp of a concept of a moment, isn't actually set in a disco, but in that uncertain time of anticipation. You get the idea that it's sung early in the evening somewhere, in a room, alone, and her voice sounds so poignant because the night is incomplete, and she needs it so much.

The first time my wife Leslie and I heard "Lookout Weekend," we thought it went:

Jumping music, slick DJs,
Fog machines, and razor blades

Patty Stirling heard:

Jumping music, slick DJs,
Fuck machines, and laser rays

If Chuck dislikes the world-beat influence (does he? I think at most he might dislike the use of world beat by semi-intellectual Americans as a kind of Music We Are Allowed To Dance To Because It's Not Trashy Like Disco, It's Ethnic) (or something), maybe it's because he realizes that all Americans are fucking crazy, and he's afraid the foreign stuff will dilute the madness.

Letter to Michael Freedberg, December 18, 1990

PART SEVEN

REVIEWS AND CRITICISM 1991–1998
ERNEST BORGNINE, SONGWRITER

Mariah Carey "I Don't Wanna Cry": A sexy waif, sitting in the corner, and her voice is a motherfucker, even if it doesn't signify (or communicate) "emotion." (7.0)

Martika "Love . . . Thy Will Be Done": The first word I learned to say as a toddler was "No." My mother said I had a will of my own, but she wasn't all that perceptive. I merely had a won't of my own. Anyway, they could have called this "Love . . . Thy Won't Be Done" or even "Love . . . Thy Won't Be Done Until You've Eaten Your Cauliflower" (and followed with "Love Thy Can't Watch TV Until Thy've Finished Thine Homework"). I don't remember hearing this, but I like the name so I give it a 7.0.

Whitney Houston "My Name Is Not Susan": Whitney's the prototype for the Mariah-Carey-great-motherfucker-of-a-misused-instrument vocal style that I praised in my previous letter; moreover, there's a basic animal *competence* that I always respond to. But "So Emotional" and "I Wanna Dance With Somebody (Who Loves Me)" were much better bits of simmering competence. And anyway, my name's not *Lisa*. To hell with Susan. (5.5)

Corina "Temptation": A concept song. The video's great. She makes love to a chair. The single's got this bondage photo on front, with her in handcuffs and a long explanation on the back which claims that it's not about bondage, at least not in the sexual sense, but about the terror of going to parties and having your life ruled by a Temptation (capitalized in the original) or an addiction. The song lyrics are all about sex. A previous single was called "Out of Control." She's got a Gabby Sabatini short haircut and Gabby's cheekbones, and my future ex-wife says the cover photo would go over great as an S&M poster at the G-Spot (local lesbian bar) (not to imply anything about anybody or anything). But, as I said, it's a concept song, like last year's "Seduction Theme" (10.0) by Seduction, where you get seduced by seduction ("it can be a look, a touch, or even a narcissistic projection of your own desires")—well, this year you get tempted by Temptation itself, rather than any particular tempter (though she likes the way he touches her). There's a whole concept-song tradition here: "Love Don't Love Nobody," also Bananarama's "Love, Truth and Honesty," which they were fools ever to believe in (again, not applied to any particular person or lover or statement). Christgau once complained that Axl's "Night Train" was about being in love with alcoholism, not alcohol. (I agree, but don't see why it's a complaint—Lou was in love with heroin addiction, not heroin, and that didn't bother Christgau, I don't think. Axl's in the wrong demographic, I guess.) So, let's see, my point? Be themed by theme parks? 10.0!

Mariah Carey *MTV Unplugged EP*: All through the video for her hit "I'll Be There," Mariah Carey's bubbling under: She's in a conventional passionate singing pose, eyes closed, brows wrinkled, fist clenched in effort—this probably helps her concentrate—yet from time to time you see her lips curling up into a totally inappropriate grin. And basically I sense this grin throughout the song, and it disturbs me, and I love it.

It's her animal grin, her self-indulgent grin, her happiness, her voice celebrating itself. She's not doing a "real" soul thing, since her vocal swoops don't come from her being possessed by the Holy Spirit and they don't reach up and touch God. It's really just like some damn horse being out for its run and enjoying its own gallop, not being responsible to the Jackson 5 song or its lyrics, not signifying a particular emotion. Her voice just goes.

Most people I know hate her. Her show-biz garishness irritates them. Too bad. They're missing the excitement. Chuck Eddy says that the cable kids' network, Nickelodeon, had a Mariah's Greatest Screeches countdown over Valentine's Day weekend. "The kid hosting told us to take off our glasses and protect our pets." And my friend Renée tells me that she goes around singing "Ben" (the theme to a movie about a screeching rat) whenever Mariah hits the high notes. Of course, Renée does this because she can't stand Mariah, and we argued. "Mariah has *inspired* you," I said. Renée doesn't want to give Mariah credit. She'd say that Mariah has goaded her. Let's say it's both, and either way Mariah has enriched my world. (8.0) [*This was my first attempt to write for the* SF Bay Guardian, *and my voice went a bit stiff.*]

Bonnie Raitt "I Can't Make You Love Me": There's an underplayed stillness here (which is the only intelligent way to play stillness, in my opinion). I'm thinking of the difference between Bonnie Raitt's "Love Has No Pride" and Linda Ronstadt's. It was Ronstadt, right? The one who got the hit with it? The Bonnie Raitt version had something in the sound that seemed to echo in the space outside the song. It might have been a catch in her voice or something in the arrangement—I don't remember, not having heard the song since 1972 when my freshmen roommate Kerry would play it ten or twenty times a day. I remember Raitt's straightforward, *factual* reading of the chorus, like love has no pride, it's just there, like Everest or Nob Hill or the big rock behind our house when I was growing up (as opposed to Ronstadt's emotionless wail, which wasn't behind our house). Anyway, it echoed in the facts of a room, or my room, or me sitting in my room. And what goes wrong in Ronstadt's version is like what goes wrong when you've got this room sound in your song, this space, and you send it to be mastered and it comes back without that sound—they got rid of the space, thought it was a mistake, would have been unprofessional to leave it in. Like what the hacks at *Request* did to my "misheard lyrics" piece—they took out hesitations, conjunctions, flow, left it with no sense of sound or speech. So Raitt factualizes the fact and lets it reverberate, Ronstadt merely illustrates. But in pop life, since Ronstadt got the hit, it's her version that echoed in the experience of jilted girlfriends and boyfriends all over the nation. The day someone heard that recording is probably richer than the recording itself; I suppose that that day is sufficient. Anyway, Raitt's got the room sound here again, finally, for the first time since her resurgence. (8.0)

Paul Young "What Becomes of the Broken-Hearted?": They write for fanzines, that's what. [not rated]

Mariah Carey "I'll Be There": Comparisons to the Jackson 5 version are beside the point, since Michael sings the song whereas Mariah stands next to it setting off rockets. And—if you're interested—the live unplugged version of "Can't Let Go" is a 9.0. Everybody loves it. I played it for my roommate Elizabeth who said, "It's . . . it's . . . it's that woman, isn't it?" Then she ran out of the room and disappeared down the hall, screaming, "I hate her, I hate her." She came back a moment later. "I just want to split her head open with a tire iron, in the middle of a brightly lit street. With witnesses." (8.0)

Sophie B. Hawkins "Damn I Wish I Was Your Lover": She throws her personality and bad poetry at us like it's some wonderful floppy fish or something, and she matters to me. She's an engaging mess. I think so far whether she hits or misses the emotional side of a barn door is fairly random. (And maybe once she gains focus and maturity she'll miss it with more consistency.) I admit I have trouble with a sex priestess being named "Sophie." Sophie's a name you give to someone's great aunt in Brooklyn. And maybe she's not so "engaging." Really, what she sounds like is an animated person at a party, center of a crowd, talking much too loud, but when you go up to her and try to be part of the conversation you realize that all she's doing is making uninterpretable, self-referential comments, that not only won't she ever really talk to you, she'll never ever really even talk about herself. Bad poetry is a form of fear: It's a filibuster, a withdrawal. There's a lot of it on the album. "It's in your solar system/It's in my superstar/There's nothing more persistent/Than the planet of our heart." Yeah, OK, but what does that have to do with, like, you and me, baby? Yet . . . yet . . . well, as I said, she matters, because even if she's unclear, even if I know better, she still manages to make it sound like she's throwing all caution to the wind, and it inspires me to want to do the same, with someone like her. (If she'd change her name.) And this rocks really hard, even though it's slow. It's got a *thwomp*. The trouble with a lot of the album, even somewhat on this track, is that despite all her emotional and heavy-breathing excesses, she too often pulls this trick of laying back heavily in the mix and mumbling and moaning and evoking back there with the munchkins and the druids. Nonetheless, anyone who can successfully work a sex lyric like "Come inside my jungle book" is a talent to watch. Whew! And on the LP she's got a song about having sex with her mother in a dream as the only way she could have of reaching her. "She was lonely like a woman/But she was just a kid." So Sophie's just a lonely kid, too, spouting one-body one-spirit one-breath one-God one-sex mumbo jumbo in the vain hope that all this oneness will get her across the divide. "Let's make love to exclusion." OK, I guess it's *not* a filibuster. The words do mean something. (8.5)

Miami Sound Machine "Primitive Love": She reminds me of Brazilian music—she floats so effortlessly across the beats that I find it hard to give a fuck, except when suddenly there will be something utterly inexplicably emotional. And then it just goes back to the float. What reaches me here is that there's enough *resistance* from the backing track, so her normal contained little voice actually sounds like it's doing something. (7.5)

The Rolling Stones "Heart of Stone": An important rock critic, I forget who (Reynolds?), said that the Stones had been doing a "camp version of r&b." This is like saying the Vietnam War was a camp version of the Korean War. I don't know why people say such things. Maybe it's a distancing device. Maybe the critic genuinely doesn't comprehend how anyone could have been moved to awe or terror by "19th Nervous Breakdown," ever. I can't imagine what would be a camp version of r&b. Barry White, maybe? I don't think the conditions for camp exist at the moment. Camp needs a closet. Camp is a way of appropriating someone else's ridiculous exuberance as your own, doing it in such a way that you yourself get to go over the top but get to remain *cool* about it, too. It's a way of saying that you're in control of the imagery, that the ridiculousness is voluntary and that you're at a remove from it; you're using it; it's not using you. Camp is for groups that are oppressed, silenced, underground, for situations of fear, where losing your cool means humiliation. Controlling the imagery that's trying to control you. Camp is dead because, in a positive way, the *idea* of being silenced is no longer accepted. Situations of fear and oppression and silence exist, of course, but not the idea of simply adapting to them. That's the positive reason for its death. The negative reason is that there *is* no sense of cool, of style. Traditions of cool and style have been shot to hell. *No one* is in control of the imagery.

I think maybe at first Jagger *thought* he was within a protected space, thought he was acting a role. "Heart of Stone" was conceived as a genre exercise, an r&b ballad. Each beat is broken up into slow triplets, the swing feel of a lot of ballads. But they flip it around. They play it hard; Charlie (or Brian) really whacks that tambourine. The way Keith plays his guitar lead, each note is a hard fast little pebble. I spent years trying to get that sound from my guitar. I memorized the solo. The way I played guitar would make her feel so . . . masochistic! And she would do anything . . . (Okay, that last sentence is untrue.) (10.0)

Plastic Bertrand "Ça Plane Pour Moi": This does (or outdoes) the Ramones trick of having some standard element (e.g., C. Berry guitar) become ENORMOUS upon entrance because of its previous absence. At the time, I thought this type of song was a dangerous distraction from real punk, which just shows how good the real punk really was for a brief period. But (it turned out) it was the real punk that ultimately distracted from real punk. (8.5)

Quarterflash "Harden My Heart": Talk about mishmash music—John Zorn's never approached this: blues boogie playing beneath "soft"-rock MOR pseudo-country that is played loud with rock embellishments and utterly square vocals. Unpretentious yet passionately in your face like it's no big deal to be passionately in your face. This song represents to me a whole ethos of irrelevant and totally expendable and unnoticed great artistry—unnoticed by most rock critics, certainly; or unwritten about, anyway, at least by me. (Not that this record is necessarily all that fabulous, mind you—among bands with "Quart" in their name, I prefer Quartzlock.)

"Harden My Heart" is on a set of Context of Alphabetical Order tapes from Chuck Eddy that has successfully remapped my post-'60s landscape. What I hear jelling in the '70s is the bottom end of progressive AOR rock meeting a kind of c&w or sideburned or several-years-behind-the-times bell-bottomed look that's basically MOR squareness uncertainly trying to rock: Three Dog Night and Doobie Brothers might be prototypes, maybe Heart, too, and Cher in her "Half-Breed" period, and Merrilee Rush—and then, when it uncertainly tries to dance itself into the '80s, there is dance-era Olivia Newton-John and

Laura Branigan and whoever preceded them in dance-oriented rock. My kind of hard rockers from the '70s (Stooges, Pere Ubu) were playing rock right at its limitations, contradictions, and impossibilities and almost certainly no longer believed in "counterculture" and possibly didn't even believe in "rock"—whereas these guys, metal people and AOR and ballad rockers, still believed in regular old rock as a viable something to shoot for or at least shake hands with (even or especially if they never lived rock culture from the inside and had not the foggiest idea what they were shooting for or where it put them). I guess I'm making them sound naive, and most likely they were—they didn't comprehend rock's utter destructive "fail-to-fail" thing. Nonetheless in their compromised way they found space where they could rock. And after a while the compromised stuff outrocked the real thing. I mean, who rocks harder, Foreigner (compromised) or Minor Threat (fail to fail)? "Music for stewardesses," wrote an awestruck Robert Christgau about Quarterflash. (8.5)

Tom Robinson Band "2–4–6–8 Motorway": There's a basic pub stodginess to this song, despite the gay subtext. It's comfortably dissolute in a way that won't threaten even the most adamantly antidissolute. It's a party song, and the party could go "crazy" but the craziness will never outstep the bounds of the party. (On the other hand, it never gets as precious as the B-52s' misnamed "Party Out of Bounds.") Yet maybe that's why it works okay—within its safe limits it falls all over itself, chairs tilted precariously backwards and the background yellers almost running off with the song and with the cash register—a nice almost horizontal sprawl layered over a music-hall bounce. The word *barrelhouse* could apply—not to the music style but to the environment. *American Heritage Dictionary*: "A disreputable, old-style saloon or bawdyhouse." However, there is something safely trad about it, like a movie version of the 1890s, or skiffle. Interesting occasional moments from the lead vocalist sound wearily evocative and have nothing to do with song or party. (7.5)

Diana Ross "Swept Away": Re the Nelson George *Voice* piece where he points out that the middle-class girl (Aretha) has got the down-home-in-the-Bar-B-Q rep while poverty-child Diana's got the slick fashion rep. As Chuck says, this song is a wet dream. It's heaven. This kid from the projects had dreams or she had nothing. Berry Gordy took a pass on Aretha and took Diana, thinking Diana'd be better for his sound. He knew what he was doing. Of course, this song is disco's dream as much as it's Diana's. Right, this rocks as hard as Teena, as hard as anyone. And, you know, it outpasses Aretha. Reveals the Godpussy to us. And it's got a good beat. You can dance to it. (9.5)

Azalia Snail "Another Slave Labor Day": "99 Luftballoons" played backwards, heard over the radio during an electric storm. You bought this for the melody, I bet. (6.0)

Mary Chapin-Carpenter "I Feel Lucky": She has a real warm voice. I wish she weren't wasting it on dime-a-dozen "country"-"rock" like this. I don't buy the line on the "new country"; I think it's nearly as pathetic as alternative rock. It's proud of its limitations. (6.0)

You know, **Garth Brooks's** "The Thunder Rolls" (8.5) is just a hair away from **Skid Row's** "18 and Life" (8.5), but the hair, or the makeup, or the cheekbone (Sebastian Bach's) is a big difference, and it bugs me that Garth won't cross that hairstyle line. ("The Thunder Rolls" is still one of the great songs of the last few years.) By "hairstyle" I don't necessarily mean length (old blunderhippie Charlie Daniels had length), I mean a whole attitude that goes with the Skid Row look, a whole basic gone and broken burnout—a world of cosmic burnout—that country won't consent to acknowledge or play. A world of *glittering, swishy* burnout. Sure, Merle Haggard and Waylon Jennings and David Allan Coe make a big deal of how fucked they are, but it's all on a personal level. "18 and Life" lives in a world that is *wrong* and we are fucked and wrong with it; "Thunder Rolls" is a world where you try and you fuck up and crack, but the world is intact. I'm sure that Chuck would argue with me here and win, about country living in the cosmic fuckup too; and we both point out, to anyone who would possibly listen, that dorks on "our" side of the Limits/No Limits barrier have been the ones playing the most frightened music these days. (The good people, Michael Jackson and Corina, for instance, don't even know there's a barrier.) I guess the problem is that the country singers weep to the fuckup when they should be dancing to it. By the way, to make this clear to readers who haven't heard the songs, "The Thunder Rolls" is about a guy who drives home in a desperate rainstorm and into the arms of his grateful wife, who then smells the wrong perfume on him, and she cracks, and she gets a gun and blows him down, and the thunder rolls. That's what happens in the video, anyway. In "18 and Life" a teenager gets thrown out of his house by his Pa (literally, through the window) and picks himself up and goes and gets drunk in an abandoned subdivision with his best friend, and then the drunk friend laughs and taunts him and gives him a gun and puffs his chest and dares the boy to shoot. And the boy shoots; and then the video ends with him in jail. (Some country guys have *lived* this, but how many have sung it recently?) Mary Gaitskill's got the video in her novel *Two Girls, Fat and Thin*. She describes Sebastian, "who looked as if the hard planes of his face were the direct result of the hard world in his skull." And "the video told the story of a boy named Ricky who had crossed over into the dreamy world of limitless cruelty with the blithe ease of childhood"—actually, I think it was the blithe ease of alcohol, and the video was great not for catching easy cruelty but for catching the adolescent posing that suddenly finds it can't turn back but has to become real. But—anyway—Brooks and Co. (and Coe) will walk near such a world, but they won't acknowledge it. I mean, it's not just the plot—"The Thunder Rolls" even *sounds* like "18 and Life." But not loud enough. The thunder should have rocked.

Whitney Houston "I Will Always Love You": I talked in *Radio On* #2 about her "animal competence," but really there's no animal in it, it's more like a jet engine preening and showing its parts. Which can be powerful enough. She kind of loses control about two-thirds of the way through this song, however—it's the section in the video where the camera moves in close and she smiles bright and meaninglessly and opens her mouth and lets loose while the camera pulls back again and you see her now sitting in a chair in the snow (!) wearing nothing but a thin suit jacket. And from here on she's just blaring away, trying to power all the windmills in Holland, and the song disappears in the whoosh. But before that, it's undeniable. Really, this song is now a feature of the world's topography, and there's nothing to do but accept it. (8.5)

RuPaul "Supermodel (You Better Work)"

> I doubt that RuPaul, tall and feminy
> Has lips as gay as sea anemone

(6.5)

Soundgarden "Black Hole Sun": John Lennon was putting all those filters on his voice because he didn't like the way his voice sounded. This guy's putting filters on his voice because he wants to sound like John Lennon—which he can't do, because he just doesn't have Lennon's haunting blues pang or really much of a voice at all, just the usual hardcore croak. The song is haunting anyway, filters and phase shifters and all. Is he saying "Wash away the rain" (as opposed to something normal like "wash away the pain")? Real apocalyptic, the wash that washes away the wash. Bermuda love triangle. The giggle, the golf club, the black hole sun. And this is the first single of theirs that really does sound like a garden. (7.0)

Los Fabulosos Cadillacs "El Matador": Argentinean alternative rock, charging-bull division. People are wearing elephant masks, tiger masks, Marilyn Monroe masks; faces distort into gigantic whistles; parade floats carry young women in hula skirts; scantily clad male dancers play hand-held bongos; other dancers jump back and forth, making the occasional heroic effort to suck on their big toe while not losing the beat; the strangely mournful singing is provided by the Parade Grand Marshal (who works weekdays as a travel agent); and the big blowout party spins on and on. (8.0)

Divine "Walk Like a Man": Fuckin' Gawd. The set-up here, the synthesized bass, is lifted whole from Donna Summer's "I Feel Love" and has the same hard coldness. The voice comes from I-don't-know-where; it's a horrendous rasp, the complete opposite of Frankie Valli's falsetto. It's scraping cardboard, and it does what Valli's didn't: It delivers the lyrics. Fuckin' Gawd, I never noticed them, they're so virulent. "No woman's worth, crawling on the earth." And they're complicated: The song's about a boy, but you never hear from the boy; the point of view shifts back and forth from a narrator to the boy's father, the latter telling the kid to lift himself up, walk like a man. But it hasn't happened yet. The narrator says "He'll tell the world, 'Forget about it, girl!' and walk like a man from you," so now the song's addressing the girl. But the kid hasn't walked, hasn't told anybody anything; as I said, we don't hear from him. He hasn't broken free. The fight's still on. (9.0) [*Well, in the original, by the Four Seasons, we* do *in fact hear from the boy; he announces: 'I'll tell the world, forget about it girl, and walk like a man from you." But he* still *hasn't actually done it. The fight continues. My copy of the Divine version, on a Mexican comp, fades out after the cowbell solo, so perhaps he switches to the first person later.*]

Meat Loaf "Why Are the Expired Items in the Refrigerator Not Disposed Of?": (2.0)

Joke:
Q: Why did the chicken cross the road?
A: I forget.
(I made up this joke myself!)

The *banda* song on Spanish-language radio where the singer sounds like a mouse and the horns play the riff from "There's A Place in France Where the Girls Wear Paper Pants," proving that you can play fast silly music without sounding the least bit techno: (8.0)

The maudlin, expressive song they played right after the mouse one: The singer is crying in his soup. He's so sad. He wipes his eyes with his tie, then he wipes his lips with it. He closes his eyes and dreams of faraway bunny rabbits. (4.0)

The song right after that one, which oom-pahs right along down the line to the chord pattern of "La Bamba" and "Louie Louie": Island horns play sweeping flourishes, try to persuade the singer to trade his jeans for shorts. But the singer tells them that he's a jeans man and that's it. The DJ interrupts the song several times to cackle at it. (5.5)

Another dreadful sad one. (3.0)

The song after that, which does some more oom-pah and also has techno beats and a fast sweet woman singer (she *sings* fast, that is) and other sweet women who help her on the chorus: She's singing about a *corazon*, but since I don't know the language I don't know if the *corazon* is brimming or breaking. These people may be Sparx, a girl group I saw on *Padrisimo* last Sunday. (7.0)

Another dreadful sad one. (2.0)

A throaty woman on the next one: She's lively *and* wailing in a *corazon*felt manner, as she rides along on wings of oom-pah. This'd be disco, except it's polka. (7.0)

After that, a bunch of guys sounding like they're riding horses: It's kind of hard to ride a horse and play trumpets and violins, but these fellows are doing fine. The sky was layered on with thick blue paint. The horses look orange as they canter under the blue-paint sky. The singer just sings along; he's unworthy of such horses. The horses wait for him to shut up, so that they can resume dancing. (5.0)

Cynthia "Change On Me": We loved, we no longer love, why did you have to change on me? All that's left is the pulse of a bass guitar, and the sorrow of a synthesizer melody. Oh, why? (10.0)

Debbie Deb "When I Hear Music": It's a normal evening. You're not expecting anything. Some friend talks you into going to a party. You climb the creaky stairway. You walk into the room . . . and you're surrounded by lights and beats and sound effects. Everything is done on the cheap, with borrowed bulbs and an extension cord run in from next door. But the effect is impressive. Lights criss-cross the ceiling. You see someone sexy. The lights flash into strobe. The sky is moving. You shiver. You step forward. (10.0)

Grade A "Strut On": Elizabeth told me about a guy at her job who would throw spitballs and hug people. He was finally fired for being too friendly. (8.5)

D.J. Hollywood "Shock, Shock, the House": Why did they get rid of barber poles? When I was young there were red-and-white-candy spirals. But then all the hip longhairs got afraid of barber shops. It was a time of warfare. Casey at Casey's Barbershop had been a jolly man who'd given us lollipops when he was done cutting our hair. But then he became angry and bitter. The Beatles and fairies took over. He couldn't adapt. He couldn't make the transition to hair salons. His bright lollipop pole design lost its vigor, became something I dreaded. (9.0)

House Master Baldwin featuring Paris Grey "Don't Lead Me," the Remix by Mike "Hitman" Wilson: She dresses in scraps and shards of steel and copper and manganese. Why doesn't she wear a barrel like the rest of us? Because her way is sexier? (9.0)

King Sun-D Moët "Hey Love": Can such a peaceful day be full of so much frustration? A walk in the park can become a bad dream: Antonioni put it into a movie, then Bananarama put it into a song. She's so serene, and she just stays that way. Isn't it just to torture me? But she's not torturing me, she's just admiring the scenery. I do it to myself. (8.5)

L S Fresh "You Can't Get No Pussy": I remember that when I was four or five some friends of my big brother convinced me to throw a dead squirrel at passing cars. This was a disturbing experience. Never throw a squirrel unless you *want* to, that's what I learned. (8.0)

Maribell "Roses Are Red": What if Jesus had turned water into cough syrup instead of wine? I mean, maybe he did it by mistake. Or he misjudged his audience, thought that they preferred clarity of gullet to cloudiness of mind. (7.5)

Phuture "Your Only Friend": This is Kogan speaking. I can make you do anything for me. I can make you cry for me. I can make you fight for me. I can make you steal for me. I can make you kill for me. I can take your car from you, take your job from you, take your wife from you, take your life from you. In the end, I'll be your only friend. (8.5)

> I'm a misty, baby, so why don't you kill me
> I'm a blue cheese, baby, so why don't you kill me

("Blue-cheese baby" as opposed to a "blue cheese-baby" = a cheese baby that is sad.)

Unidentified performers, field recording from Ibiza "El Cuantre": I'm not sure I can distinguish this as music; it seems more like a rhythmic throat-clearing contest. A guy hacks out his vocals, a woman answers with rattling, mirthless laughter, the kind of laugh you give when you've just been diagnosed with throat cancer. In rhythm, of course. (6.5)

I saw a movie in which **Ernest Borgnine** played a songwriter. Ever since, I've pronounced the phrase "Ernest Borgnine, songwriter" to my roommates whenever our world seemed too well-ordered. I myself would not have cast Borgnine to play a songwriter any more than I'd have cast Harry the Hairy Behemoth to be the tightrope walker in *Stone Over Water*, but what do I know about songwriting? In the movie, the title of which I've forgotten, Borgnine is Bickle of the songwriting team Hickle, Bickle, and Schnickle, who were famous showmen of the '10s, '20s, and '30s. I don't remember their actual names, obviously, or the names of any of their songs; but the movie was based on actual people from real life. In the movie, the part I saw—I caught the last half on AMC—Hickle goes off to Hollywood to kowtow to the big shots and earn fortune and celebrity, leaving Bickle and Schnickle in a pickle and his woman friend in the lurch. Bickle is a goodhearted lug who's a steadfast good buddy to the woman, and he and Schnickle try to carry on in the biz; but without Hickle's genius at arrangement their next show just sputters. Things are sad and the woman walks out onto the balcony and stares at nothing. But then Hickle comes back. He's tired of the big shots and the hoity toity. He's ready to roll up his sleeves and craft some *real* music; he's seen the road show, it's got promise, you just have to make the Third Act the First Act, and exchange the verse for the chorus, and add a bridge, and . . . So things fade out to happily-ever-after, and I hope you appreciate my restraint in not using the word *fickle*.

Gloria Grahame (10.0) in *The Big Heat* walks into Glenn Ford's drab hotel room and she immediately identifies the décor. "Say, I like this: early Nothing." So I'd misquoted her slightly back in 1991 in my review of Tom Petty's "Learning to Fly." Has it been five years? So much has happened, yet so little has changed.

Tom Petty & the Heartbreakers "Walls": "Half of me is ocean, and the other half of me is sky." He's telling us that he's not grounded. (4.0) (Phil, I jotted down these lyrics on the fly—it was a small fly and so I had trouble reading them, especially as I myself was just learning to fly—so they may be slightly off.)

Interface "Plastic Age": Typically stiff Eurovocals sung by the woman who works in Accounts Receivable. This is from one of those Singapore three-for-a-dollar dance tapes I got in Chinatown. It's been in my thoughts for several years, because I can't make out the last word in the first line and the last word in the third line and so keep rewriting them. One attempt is:

Nobody wants to determine fate
Living in the Plastic Age
Don't realize it's only a wait
Living in the Plastic Age

Another attempt goes "Nobody wants to turn the page" as in a page of history (and to correspond to this, "Don't realize it's only a stage," also of history; unless it's a cage). When will these shallow brainless pop groups just give up? (8.5)

Fortuna "O Fortuna": Oh damn, it's raining. And the *horse* is loose! And someone left the turn signal on! What is this, a fucking *sound-effects* record? In any event, the turn signal keeps the beat for mad, storm-swept nuns who wander the midnight hills, chanting eerily in a foreign language. They surround some sort of flat totem. An old derelict gesticulates angrily at them, but they don't seem to notice. They don't realize it's only a cake, left out in the plastic rain. (Notice how nobody chants in English anymore?) (7.5)

Sophie B. Hawkins "Right Beside You": Sweaty clomper, this Sophie woman, and she always draws a mixed response from me. I find the beginning of this just awful, with forest-being-reborn-in-the-spring keyboard cheeps followed by a deadeningly serious recitation of Cole Porter's originally quite funny lines from "Let's Do It": "Birds do it, bees do it, even sacrilegious trees do it." In general, I find her Earthy-Sex-In-The-Female-Gulch mannerisms really soggy and unsexy. I'm glad when the bassline and the song itself come in and obliterate the pastorale. Sophie's much sexier in the bar light than in the moonlight. She needs a dance floor. I'm still angry about all the stuff in the arrangement. Like someone turned on the fog machine, so we'd feel mystery. A good voice and an emotional yank in the hook: That should be mystery enough. Then all you need add are beers and beats. (7.5)

Tina B "I Always Wanted to Be Free": I've never been able to explain my concept in a way that makes the least sense to anyone, but this track is a supreme example of what I call "the disco rave-up"—*rave* meant to associate not with dance raves but with the Yardbirds of thirty-two years ago, their "rave-up" being an instrumental break during which the group would in effect abandon the song for a long vamp and crescendo. (A "vamp" is improvisation to a repeated riff or chord pattern.) The disco version, by analogy, is a track in which a vamp takes over a lot or all of a song. It's a gospel technique, originally, and James Brown used it a lot. In disco, there's often a point where the song climaxes and instead of getting on with the melody the singer abandons it—it's either given to the backup singers or jettisoned altogether—and starts improvising and expostulating, while backup shrieks and fireworks and drum fills and dinner bells accompany her. So in the disco rave-up pretty early in the song they go to one of these climaxes and then never return to the song but just rave on. Lewis Martinée in Miami was a master, though this particular record is by Arthur Baker, and what's interesting is that it doesn't even bother to have a song, it *starts* at the climax, everything breaking loose and all scenery being chewed, and then from there it's all climaxes and rhythm breaks, chants and incantations, wails and fireworks. Hard to pull off—since you have no song to carry you, you need a lot of variety and inventiveness—but really exciting when done well. And the form creates a space for ridiculous lyrics that might have been irritating (not to mention noticeable) in a more placid environment but are charming as they tumble forth from this chaos. "The colors of my dreams are painted on my walls." They're part of the track's audacity, which I appreciate, since, in general, nobody wants to turn a phrase, living in the plastic age. (8.5)

Back 2 Bass "I Wanna Be With You": This is Europop sped up to ridiculous speed, so now it accompanies delirium and drugs and dance frenzies. Michael Freedberg wrote in 1981: "To rock 'n' rollers, disco songs must sound as irruptive as trains sounded to the farmers whose grounds they passed through. No matter; many rockers find they must ingest disco's industrial, scientific tones if they're to bring about the miracle of dance. What they don't see is that the car age is over, and that in jets one doesn't feel he's moving at 900 miles per hour. 'DOR' [dance-oriented rock] runs as high as 160 BPMs. That's a good enough reason for its songs to last only two minutes." Really persuasive; and how was Michael to know that the 1990s would prove him wrong and that rock would become indie boys staring at their feet and disco would be the fast-beat, charge-off-in-all-directions sprint? I don't get it, actually; do people go out and dance "*all night*" to these things? In which discos? Where? (I think the answer is "Holland.") Do they dance *well*? I think the reason I'm able to like this song is despite the beats; I kind of stare through them like they're a haze through which I discern the actual song in its somber, noncrazed handsomeness. (8.5)

Whoops There Goes Another Rubber Tree (excerpted from Pazz & Jop ballot for 1998): In the spirit of Dylan's Albert Hall Bootleg, John Wójtowicz made note of the following new holy days, which are to be observed in the upcoming 1999 liturgical year (except that he only remembered a few of them, so Naomi and I had to come up with the rest, and then John had to add another one, and his friend Joe has a comment in there somewhere):

Our Lady of Indiscretions
St. Aloysius the Imprudent

St. Stanislaus of Maquillage

The Mortification of St. Masochistus

Fellatiary Sunday

The Feast of the Holy Catamites

St. Belinda Who Meows Too Much

St. Victor Who Meows Too Much and Is as Dumb as a Box of Hammers, and Is Bad-Humored to Boot

St. Jupiter Who Is Even Dumber than Victor, if You Can Imagine That

Subject: I've actually called David this for months and months, whenever his high horse gets too high

St. David of the Cloyingly Pompous

St. Andrew of the Common Condom

St. Andrew the Chased

St. Belinda of Pulchritude

St. Belinda the Pussy

St. Duryea of the Duryeas of New York and Newport, R.I.

St. Dusty Whom We Also Call Foghat Because She Sounds Like She's Quacking but Jennifer Didn't Understand When We Told Her this so She Used the Name Frogcat . . . Well, Anyway, Dusty Who Intimidates Belinda and Has a Scar on Her Face and Sounds Like a Duck but Fortunately She Moved Away

St. Dusty Springfield Whom We Also Call Foghat Because She Sounds Like She's Quacking but Jennifer Didn't Understand When We Told Her this so She Used the Name Frogcat . . . Well, Anyway, Dusty Springfield Who Intimidates Belinda Because of Her Orthodox Lesbian Lifestyle and Has a Scar on Her Face Even Though It Is Rumored to Have Been the Result of an Ill-Advised Visit to an All-Night Tattoo Parlor and Sounds Like a Duck (the Scar Not the Tattoo Parlor) but Fortunately She Moved Away

I wish I knew the context for the above. Besides, Foghat fucking RULED, man!

P.S. You should specify the dates of these feasts, e.g., the Feast of the Holy Catamites falls on the first Thursday after the Feast of St. Sebastian, etc.

Called David what?

I've lost track of what all/any of this is about.

I've actually called David for months and months but he's "high" on "horse" and that gets in the way.

Not only have I lost track of what any of this is about—I can't even remember to whom I'm writing this.

As my conscience wouldn't let me abandon the subject "Ernest Borgnine, songwriter," I did some research and discovered that the songwriters were DeSylva, Brown, and Henderson, the movie was *The Best Things in Life Are Free*, Borgnine was Brown, and Sheree North played the woman. Michael Curtiz directed, badly. I didn't get so far as finding out what songs the team wrote (the library closes early on Sundays), but I did discover the following palindrome on three different Websites: E. Borgnine drags Dad's gardening robe.

Mariah Carey "My All": Finally, I'd thought, with the most recent album, that I would get the chance to join Elizabeth in pouring forth hatred at the whole hideous Mariahness of this woman. Finally I felt revolted; finally I felt that she was ugly; finally I became appalled at the whole gelatinous breast thing, leg thing, whatever thing, the overproduced-orchestration thing, the overendowed-everything thing. And now, just in time for *Radio On*, she puts out a new single and it's hot and beautiful. What am I to do? I *do* think I'm starting to hate her, though. She's backing Someone-Or-Other Dupri on *his* single, too, and she's *good*, she rescues it from rap-r&b lifelessness, and *still* I don't want to look at her. I guess I've just burned out. (8.0)

1991–1998, assembled mostly from stuff written for *Radio On*; also from *Why Music Sucks*, *Tapeworm*, *Pazz & Jop*, the *SF Bay Guardian*, and letters to Chuck Eddy and Renée Crist

PART EIGHT

REVIEWS AND CRITICISM 1999–2004

LEGEND OF THE
GLOCKEATER

DAN DURYEA

The blurb for the Castro Theater's "Universal Noir" series says that in *Black Angel* Dan Duryea is "cast against type (well, sort of) as an affably alcoholic songwriter"—the "well, sort of" probably refers to his frequent casting as an affably gun-crazy sociopath. I caught him on TV recently in a couple of Anthony Mann movies: *Winchester 73*, where he's an affably leering gunslinger who paws at Shelley Winters; and *Thunder Bay*, which I glimpsed while channel surfing, where he plays an affably womanizing cad ("you know he's hit and run," Joanne Dru proclaims to a defensive Jimmy Stewart) who turns out not to be a cad after all. His easy way with a scam and a girl in so many previous movies had made him be suspect right from the start.

Also glimpsed amid my channel surfing was *Ride Clear of Diablo*, an interesting Audie Murphy western (AMC's been showing a lot of them, and they are better than I'd expected: Murphy's got a hard pretty-boy face that he uses to convey a temptation towards bitterness or obsessiveness within his usually good-guy characters) with Duryea as an affably contrary murderer who likes to side with underdogs just to keep gun battles from ending and everyone ill at ease. So he sides with good-guy Murphy for a time, for the fun of it, while Murphy does battle against organized evil. I couldn't hang around to watch the whole thing; I assume that eventually Murphy has to shoot him or, if he sticks with Murphy and crosses over into genuine goodness, that he has to die for it at the hands of one of the criminals. The genre demands that he die. But the genre also demands—this is why there's rarely a boring western—that there be some confusion between good and evil, that the good-guy hero must be hardened and twisted a bit by the violence he has to commit, that his psyche must be endangered. Duryea is smart casting as second fiddle because his happy attitude of "I'm just going my way having a good time causing trouble" makes *him* more immediately attractive than the dogged hero Murphy, and the audience can have its own fun enjoying this sadistic appeal yet can then safely snuff out this feeling when the character himself gets snuffed at the end.

In a lot of his best parts Duryea seems hardly to be acting at all but just lounging about doing the Mr.-Congeniality-with-a-Razor-Blade routine, and the charm/tension in him is his *inappropriateness*. In *Winchester 73* he's inappropriate as a charmer (because he's really a meanie underneath), but he's inappropriate as a badman too, because as first underling among the outlaw gang he frequently gets distracted from the business at hand by the ladies, by the need to gab, by the urge to just buddy up to whomever he happens to be standing next to.

When Duryea puts the make on Deanna Durbin in *Lady on a Train* it seems like chivalry—as if he felt that a heel like himself were socially obligated to put the moves on a dish like her, and the fact that he believes she's just inherited the loot and that she's doubly loaded is beside the point. (His relaxing presence isn't enough to distract either Deanna Durbin or the movie as a whole from being unswervingly, unspeakably perky—he'd been paired with Durbin at the insistence of Universal's poetry department, which heard rare euphony in the juxtaposition of their names.)

In *Pride of the Yankees* he's a cynical newsman who refers to people as chumps and says that Lou Gehrig is a bore. If he'd been more fairminded he'd have said that the movie was a bore and not have blamed Gehrig. Fellow newsman Walter Brennan's role in debating Duryea is to, in effect, argue down the naysayers, the guys in the back of the room whispering impatiently or playing with their hair or making wisecracks to their buddies. But since in this movie Duryea's given no buddies and no world for him to have an impact on, Brennan's victory is meaningless—there's really no choice but for Gehrig to be Gehrig and for everyone to applaud his steadfastness and rectitude, and the movie itself is steadfast and narrow, a sentimental clunker.

As Jim the radioman in *Sahara*, Duryea's an everyday Joe helping to guide a tank that's cut off from its unit behind enemy lines. Here his congeniality/distractibility is a kind of courage. He's a take-it-as-it-comes guy, sticking to his everyguy rituals, such things as his constant little side bets with his pal Waco (tank crew and friends are the usual war-film goulash of national and ethnic types) no matter what the danger. The bets are about whether the sergeant will get the tank to start, whether the sergeant will abandon the Italian prisoner to die of starvation, and so forth. There's an interesting division of labor between Duryea and the sergeant (Humphrey Bogart, the film's star): Bogart makes the action while Duryea makes bets on it. This is a prototype for Duryea's later sideman roles. Even when he's in the thick of things, other characters drive the plot forward while Dan sort of bounces along next to it. So he becomes a connection to the world beyond the main characters' self-induced dramas, to the ongoing life suggested but not shown on the screen, and to the world outside the movie altogether. This gets real interesting in movies other than *Sahara* because he plays so many creeps and chiselers that his presence suggests the existence of a whole substratum of lumpen wise guys—bars and cities full of them—just beneath the edge of the frame.

The way he rides in the jeep at the beginning of *Foxfire* is a good picture of his role: He moves to the back seat to make way for Jane Russell, then he's basically along for the ride. He plays an affably alcoholic doctor who's continually and brazenly pursuing his best friend's wife (Jane Russell's fairly great herself as a feisty, needy, but ultimately solid-headed woman whose husband Jeff Chandler doesn't know how to tell her he needs her). A line of Duryea's, while he's slightly tipsy: "You're a beautiful dancer. Do you do other things as well as dance?" Duryea pulls off this overwritten line because a come-on like that is almost a formal requirement for his type of a character. Again, it's chivalry, and it's a warning to the solid-citizen males in the audience that if they don't give their women warmth and flash then some punk will.

In truly nasty roles Duryea's affability can make him really snotty, wheedly: Like, hey, I'm just being *friendly*, how can you take it amiss? And this carries over to his good-guy roles, where his friendliness can seem a little unsettling, as if he's sneaking something by you. But *strain* too is an important part of his style. Affable, easygoing, but with a kind of puzzlement, worry, that makes him not at ease. He's uneasily easygoing because something inside could always snap, impulse could take over, or the outside world could snap him in two, when he suddenly fails to fit.

In *Thunder Bay* he carries within him a sense of wildness and unpredictability, and it seems at first as if he's the one who will send everything haywire, getting into brawls, romancing some kid's fiancée. He's assisting Jimmy Stewart in setting up an offshore oil rig; Stewart's got the drive and the ideas; Duryea is the regular guy who manages the crew and can fast-talk money and cooperation out of the local fishermen. There are two contrasting acting styles, Stewart doing a good "I'm-burrowing-into-my-own-internal-weariness-and-obsessiveness" routine; while easy, chatty, ongoing con-boy Duryea is actually a bridge to reality, bridge to the outer world, and he sort of becomes the point of view for the audience. Duryea's smart enough to see that Stewart's monomania gives Duryea himself and all the oil workers a framework and a sense of purpose; but he knows that he and the workers have to breathe the air of the world, too. So his impulsiveness becomes a form of sanity.

As the lead in *Al Jennings of Oklahoma* he's an affably hotheaded frontier lawyer (really—he can't stop himself from slugging opposing attorneys in court, but then he'll turn around and cheerfully argue legal points with the judge who's fining him for contempt) who's forced by treachery, bad breaks, and his own hotheadedness to run with a bunch of outlaws. This allows the movie to do the mingling-of-good-and-evil theme except that, strangely, the evil hardly takes place. The movie refers to his outlawry while rarely showing it; and the guys he rides with aren't ruffians or scum in any way. The best is one who, at the beginning, shows up driving a horse and buggy, chats pleasantly with the Jennings brothers, and then pulls a gun and holds them up when he learns they've got money. Duryea is more bemused than upset by this; he tells the guy that it's odd for a bandit to use a horse and buggy, might make for slow getaways. The bandit explains that that's just why he tried it: because no one in the world would expect it. Duryea *does*, after that, shoot the gun out of the man's hand but then lets him go, because he's charmed by the guy. Unfortunately, from here on the film spends too much time on the Duryea character's basic good-guy-ness and not enough on banditry, and there's no more of this pleasant nonsense.

The Underworld Story is a good little movie from out of nowhere that pastes an underlying dread onto its spirit of adventure. It starts with shots from the crime-movie handbook: utility poles, car going into tunnel, lines of fate, guy getting gunned down on the steps of the Hall of Justice. But actually the Duryea character is way too loose-limbed and sassy to be glued to any kind of fate—he thinks so, anyway. He's all over the place, penned-in by nothing. He's a newsman who thinks of journalism as a combination freakshow and shakedown racket (hey, we'll find stuff out about people and then have them pay us not to print it!). He gets run out of the big city; his bosses like him when his sleazy tactics make money for them but not when he gets caught at it. The thing is, the Duryea character doesn't know he's in a crime melodrama. He thinks he's riding the breeze and has control of the breeze and that he'll ride out with a lot of dough—whereas I, watching the screen, know that there's a bomb ticking within his personality, that his plans will whirl out of reach, and the world will close in. When it happens, when the world does close in, he actually—surprisingly—finds his moral center. This is surprising because a happy ending is not built into this genre: You know that decency will be redeemed, at least nominally, but you don't know that it'll be the Duryea character who achieves decency.

He has alighted in a slow-moving suburb where he takes over a failing paper and hooks up with a bunch of do-gooders (he thinks there's money in it for him) in championing a black woman who's been accused of murder. Interestingly, the do-gooders abandon the woman once they learn of *Duryea's* sleazeball past, their solid-citizen instinct being that the black woman is fine when she's just a victim to champion but not when defending her mixes them in with the messy, ugly world. The do-gooders do good out of habit; Duryea penetrates to the *reason* to do good. There's an interesting balance: For the Duryea character, adventurousness and being a guy on the make eventually need an internal engine, or heart, or purpose. But there's a corollary too: There's an old guy who runs the printing press and has the look of a fuddy-duddy, but he knows right off that Duryea is a schemer, and he quietly gets a kick out of it. He likes it that this operator has come in to liven up his little town. As I said, sidemen and bit players give a movie its sense of psychological space, a sense of the worlds and lives that exist beyond the concerns of the main characters. So the scene with this white-haired print-ing-press guy is nice: He's already let Duryea know that he's onto his scams, and Duryea's just rushed into the office to get everyone (i.e., the press guy and Gale Storm—at this stage in the movie she's the perpetually aghast and uncooperative love interest whose disapproval Duryea takes with affable unconcern) to help on some wheeling-dealing, and the old guy simply says "Okay, boss"—it's his use of the word *boss* that signifies, as if to say, All right, we need someone here in charge, to rev things up, I'm with you if you can do it. This gives the sense of his needing Duryea for reasons that have nothing to do with how Duryea came to be there. But in doing so, the old guy provides the movie's endorsement of Duryea, without waiting for him to become "good."

In general, Duryea's threat and his appeal are not a form of cool. He's not hanging back sardonically or with quiet menace like a Mitchum; he's someone who can be penetrated and someone who can explode. In this sense he's like Cagney; but unlike Cagney he's weak and changeable, easily pulled by impulses and pressures and dames passing by. Like both Mitchum and Cagney, he can bring his "bad" qualities into his good-guy roles. As a bad guy, Duryea is the wise guy on the corner, the casual opportunist, the main evildoer's distractible understudy. He's pretty much the same when he's a good guy, but his opportun-ism becomes ingenuity, his distractibility becomes openness, and as a wise guy he'll charm the pants off you.

from *O.K. You Mugs: Writers on Movie Actors*, 1999

MEDUSA AND CHILDE

Thighs are apt to play a great role in the new postwar art, which will be so eager for life.
—Leon Trotsky, Madrid, 1916

The new Sophie B. Hawkins LP, *Timbre*, has been in the can for a couple years, and a lot of the delay was because her record company, Sony, wanted "Lose Your Way" to be a single, but the song has a banjo, and mainstream radio won't play banjos, so Sony told her to redo it without banjo. Sophie refused. She'd written the song on banjo, she wanted the banjo. Eventually, she encouraged her fans to call, write, and e-mail Sony on behalf of the banjo. This worked. Sony gave in.

I'm sure there's more to the story than that, but I like it, and I like her for it. Her resistance is completely admirable. A radio prohibition against banjos? I wouldn't put up with that either. Even if it's real—even if the banjo sinks the song commercially—one can't tolerate such stupidity, a world that won't let a banjo in. Anyway, I don't think that written into the rules of mainstream rock/pop is the commandment that everything has to be balanced and bland. Streams, even main streams, have eddies, pools, rocks, character. All sorts of flora and fauna come in by way of tributaries, and the odd ones don't necessarily have to get fished out.

Yet I wonder about the psychology behind her refusal. Sophie is part of a songwriting tradition of poetic overspill; it starts with Dylan but then mainly gets taken over by women, who make it misty and sexually feminine—a sea of feeling. But basically I think that Sophie's *not* a natural, not the free spirit or the force of nature that she'd like to be. She doesn't have the Teena Marie ability to swoop her voice and personality all over everywhere, or the Stevie Nicks ability to have her femininity soak through the music. Sophie's fundamental voice is a husky burr—it's effective but not all that rich. When her voice goes into the higher register it can be quite beautiful, but only sometimes carries her personality with it. So she has to *work* for her voluptuousness, for female fecundity, for animal richness. She *makes* her music full-bodied. And so when a record company wants to take away a sound that she'd put into her song, it's not just an aesthetic or commercial disagreement, it's that they want to take away part of the blood and bone of her music. And so of course she's got to fight back, because the music *is* her body.

The promo packet quotes her saying, "The whole goal of this album was to make it resonate something really, really true that came from my body. There was no compromise. To me it was like playing the cello. When it's tuned so that it's ringing—singing against your sternum—you go for a tone that evokes the truth of your whole self. That's the timbre I'm talking about."

I have two contradictory responses. One, this is horseshit; the truth about yourself isn't in a feeling or a tone, it's what you do and why you do it. Understanding yourself involves probing and testing, comparing your memories and ideas to someone else's and asking yourself if why you think you did something was the real reason, and so on.

Response number two is that she's not so much uncovering truth as she is trying to *be* true to some things: to a sound, to a songwriting tradition, to a feeling in her sternum, to a bodily sense of life, to what she can do, to what music can be. In this sense *true* doesn't mean "accurate" so much as it means "being worthy."

I think she intends to do both: to dig inside, to reveal herself; and to create a full sound that's worthy of the musical impulse within her. She does much better at fullness than she does at self-revelation. This is because—simply—she has not thought through her ideas, thought through her lyrics. She has a talent for words—they're part of her abundance, an overload of images, a verbal too-muchness. Startling metaphors, mawkish clichés, feints at narrative, shock effects. But she's evasive: She retreats too often into vagueness and sentimentality and high-school girl twaddle, fake self-discovery.

She started in music as a drummer, and she has a good sense of how words sound, how they have beats and rhythm and tones. The first verse of "32 Lines":

> *I want your hand across my belly*
> *I want your breasts upon my back*
> *I want your pain to rip right through me*
> *I am your death, you are my wrath*

The words sound compelling: death wrath back, belly right through me, hand pain rip, I want I want I want. You think that there's an interesting drama being introduced, let's say a woman lover acting out Sophie's mute anger, Sophie in turn representing the woman's unacknowledged mortality. But if you're the listener you're going to have to provide such a drama for yourself, because Sophie doesn't. Instead, the song goes on, with more verses, more conclusions, a string of abstractions ("You are my fate, I'm your design," etc.), without answering the questions: Why wrath? Why death? What ripping pain? The words are hardly meaningless—there's a potential vision here, sex as not just something whole and wholesome, but as a dangerous sharing, shattering as well as unifying. But she doesn't know how to put the vision down into words, doesn't, as it were, give it a body. This is a great song nonetheless, sexy, a slow intense rocker not unlike "Justify My Love" but that manages to vary from whispers to wails without losing its intensity.

"I long to be your handsome woman," Sophie sings, and two lines later, apparently apropos of nothing, "I long to free Medusa's stallion." Trying to make sense of this has given me days of pleasure. Perhaps "Medusa's stallion" is just a slang phrase the meaning of which I'm not privy to (a Web search comes up with this, attributed to Freud: "If Medusa's head takes the place of the representation of the female genitals, or rather if it isolates their horrifying effects from the pleasure-giving ones . . ."). Or maybe it's an odd and inexplicable reference to Pegasus, the winged horse who sprang from Medusa's blood after Perseus had lopped off her head—but I wasn't aware that Pegasus needed freeing. I think Sophie just wanted to throw *Medusa* in with *stallion*, to cross female deadliness with wild male sex—she wants to unleash both, maybe wants to be both. As my girlfriend said, just listening, not seeing Sophie's picture: "I'll bet she has flowing, wanton hair." Like the snake-haired Medusa.

Typically, the rest of the song doesn't have much to do with this image; you've got "I find your lips, they give me peace" (sappy), "I need to die in your embrace" (no thank you), all mixed in, sex and death and horses.

But then, as I've been saying, her sound is better than her sense. And the range of instruments and styles is important: She isn't just using synths and steel drums, jazz moods and rock guitar, for the sake of variety, she needs the extra colors—well, timbres—to give the sound the depth she wants. Even the couple of songs I don't particularly like on here—the high-voiced, gentle, sentimental ones—have a solidity that prevents them from being utter piffle.

My favorite song on the LP is "Your Tongue Like the Sun in My Mouth," a slow build on a base of acoustic Celtic guitar plinks, with dense electric drones working their way into the background. It compares favorably with anything I've heard by the Fairport Convention. And when Sophie gets to the chorus/climax, she lets go in a pop diva way, which gives an emotional payoff I've never gotten from Richard Thompson or Sandy Denny. The guitars and strings do a wonderful romantic-agony riff into the fade-out. It's quite thrilling, honestly. The words are provocative, elusive, silly: the usual Sophie mixture. It's about sex, first woman-to-woman, then woman-to-man. "I was young in his eyes, I was sweet on his thighs, I was profound." "Your tongue like the sun in my mouth" is a risky image, it sits there glittering and potentially absurd, promising more about sun and heat and tongue than the song actually delivers. And later on the inscrutable simile, "He fit my body like a one-horse town," again, potentially meaningful but only if decipherable.

My friend Rob says, "Sophie B. lyrics (by which I mean vocals—she only writes to give her voice something to make a mess about) are sexy . . . scary/creepy, but creepy in a light and sexy and decorous way."

But she doesn't simply write to give her voice something to make a mess about. She not only means her lyrics to be taken seriously, she puts them forward in such a way that you have to take them on—especially in "Darkest Childe," which is more like declamations and incantations than regular singing. The "e" in "childe" (which I find unbearably precious) invokes a time when life was darker and more demonic, when it held earthy mysteries: a time of emotion, shadow, romance. "You fly through the night into the dreams of ancient ruins and make them sing." If her creepiness lacks genuine menace, this isn't due to decorum but to laziness. She's too lazy to give evil, darkness, wilderness—the demon "e" in "childe"—much in the way of vividness and specificity. In any event, frighteningly or not, she puts violence into her sensuality: "Fucked the man immobile" is not a rape by legal definition, but she calls it a rape and makes it feel like one, as if the wild girl has the knife to the man's throat. It's not just moist sex in the warm female gulch, this time; now she's the handsome lover too, and the stallion and the aggressive Medusa terror face.

The Village Voice, July 27, 1999

LEGEND OF THE GLOCKEATER

Drunken Tiger is a rap duo, DJ Shine and Tiger JK, I think from L.A., where they record—but they rap mostly in Korean and the album's out on a Korean label. People in the U.S. can order *The Great Rebirth* on the Web at turborecords. com, though I got it from a Korean store in Aurora, Colorado, so if I can get it out there you can get it in New York City. An interview with them on the Web seems to indicate that English not Korean might be their first language, though I'm not certain how to interpret the interview since it was first translated from English to Korean and then from Korean back into English (I'm serious; this seems to be what happened) with who-knows-what changes along the way—this is the sort of thing that Mark Twain would do, except he's dead and anyway doesn't know Korean so he'd do it in French. But from the interview I gather or guess that when Drunken Tiger began rapping in Korean they chose the words first and then tried to figure out how to pronounce them. ("The hardest part was to be able to find the words to flow that are Korean. Since we're not both fluently enough to speak Korean, and can't enunciate correctly.") Which reminds me of Selena, though she's dead too and also doesn't sing Korean.

Anyway, Drunken Tiger's hip-hop is the real deal, "real" not necessarily meaning "better" but meaning "sounds like real American hip-hop." Wu-Tang Clan is an obvious influence, with a couple of tracks that use a RZA-style simple eerie piano figure, wide reverberating bass, easy flow. I taped "Wu-Tang: 7th Chamber" for a friend and put a Drunken Tiger equivalent called "The Movement" alongside it, and the Drunken Tiger track held its own. Probably more than the particular style, though, Drunken Tiger gets from Wu-Tang a general sense both that less is more and that more is more too—which is in fact the general hip-hop aesthetic, which is that you can use any damn sound you want. So they build one track around Mexican resort-city spy music, another around blues-metal guitar, and so forth.

What should make them matter most, though, and not just to their own ethnic group, is their use of exquisitely beautiful Korean pop music—or maybe I should say their exquisitely beautiful use of Korean pop music, since I get the sense that some of the pop melodies might be sickly sweet in their original versions but that the rapping and devil-may-care carousing that overlay the pop on this album mitigate the sweetness so that what you hear is gorgeous. (I'm not at all sure what I mean, actually. In my notes I have the sentence, "Such words—though not to be used as weapons—ought to be spelled correctly." I have no idea what I was referring to.) Interspersed are "skits," which on this LP are a series of phone calls, a man talking to a woman about I-don't-know-what since it's in Korean, except that the man gets progressively drunker with each call, and his speech gets interrupted by burps and farts, until the final call, in which his end of the conversation is almost entirely burps and farts. (Such burps—though not to be used as weapons—ought to be spelled correctly. An international conference to fix their spelling is planned.)

There's a martial arts flick called *Legend of the Drunken Tiger* about a master who gets better as he gets drunker (which is not the strategy by which this review is being composed, though you might think otherwise).

Anyway, if you're a five-year-old Anglo girl and you're down in the rec room putting on a show for your mom and her friends, and the show consists of dancing and lip-synching, how do you lip-synch to Korean when you don't know Korean? Easy. You just move your lips to the sounds. (Problem solved.) But if you don't know what the words mean, how can you act them out—you know, like when dancing to Britney's "Lucky," you know to cry and pout when Lucky is sad and to pat your cheeks when Lucky puts on her makeup? Well, for these Korean words you can *guess* what they might mean, and when one of your mom's weird friends says that a song has "big Wu-Tang beachball beats," whatever those are, you can decide that the music sounds the way that the Powerpuff Girls look. So you're round and you can zap people. You know how to do that; you've practiced in front of the TV. And when the words break into English and you still don't know what they mean since they are "glock" and stuff . . . what's glock? A chocolate bar? Could be. (Make like you're stuffing food in your mouth.) "Packin' more heat than the sun"? Grab the sun, pull the suitcase lid up with one hand, push the sun into it with the other, close the lid, blow on your hands afterward. And remember those skits where the guy talks on the phone and burps and farts a lot? Well, you've already taught yourself to burp on command, so you don't even have to wait for those parts, you can do them early. OK, what about the song with that insanely pretty melody that repeats and repeats? It's like the song that Jigglypuff sings and makes everyone fall asleep. But how do you dance when you're supposed to look asleep? I don't know. (Pause.) *Sleep dancing!* Which is when you make your arms and legs go all rubbery.

SO THIS GUY WALKS INTO A BAR . . .

Lifter Puller's *Fiestas + Fiascos* can probably be designated "emo" for sounding simultaneously bulky and flouncy. ("Emo" is short for "emology": "The study of music that's simultaneously bulky and flouncy.") The vocals come across as spiels overheard in bars: come-ons, scams, scores, threats, boasts. The singing isn't singing so much as it's ranting (and declaiming, boasting, enticing). And the ranting has a barroom feel of struggling upward: up through the noise and up through the spieler's own emotions, like it's struggling to be heard and struggling to be believed. The milieu reminds me of the Springsteen of *The Wild, the Innocent & the E Street Shuffle*—except that Bruce had a literariness that put the stories off in the distance, whereas this guy, singer Craig Finn, pushes his spiels right against your nose.

Taylor M. Clark at pitchforkmedia.com says, "You know that guy nobody likes who absolutely *has* to chatter for hours about the wild, crazyass party he went to the other night? The very same guy who was always totally getting checked out by this hot chick but he couldn't talk to her because they totally had to bounce right away to go to this other intense party? He's the lead singer in Lifter Puller now." Clark finds the whole thing repellent, but I really like it, and I'd say simply that the words succeed in pretending not to be poetry, hence their immediacy. The music is grindingly melodic guitar, heave-up-the-Hefty-bag bass, etc. My favorite song here has a '60s organ—a Paul Revere style of riff—and in the din you hear Craig raving away: "I want everybody who's been eyeing my girl to slowly close their eyes and think about what you've got, compare it to what I've got, and ask yourself what do you think my girl wants."

Chuck Eddy tells me that Lifter Puller remind him more of the "verbose babbling of the Fall" than of Springsteen, though (he also tells me) it's not as if the Fall babblement and the early Springsteen babblement have nothing in common. I wasn't initially referring to the sounds of Craig's/Bruce's voices but to subject matter: local boy trying to be someone who cou-ou-ounts in the hick-city night. But I do hear a similar sound in Springsteen and Lifter Puller: Both are passionately oververbose, as opposed to the Fall's Mark E. Smith, who's pugnaciously oververbose. Anyway, both Bruce and Craig write dialogue songs. Craig: "We mixed the Ripple and the champagne, and then things got kinda strange. She said, 'My name is Juanita, but the guys call me L.L. Cool J, 'cause I've been here for years. And you can't call it a comeback if you never even been away, and I ain't ever been no place." That reminds me of Springsteen: the conversation, the young woman with the Spanish name, the setting (seaside town after Labor Day).

The band name "Lifter Puller" makes me think it's from the punch line of some joke—like "Dead Milkmen"—except no one's told me the joke. The statement

"Lifter, puller, throw 'er on the floor" keeps popping up in my brain, I don't know from where. (Well, from my brain, obviously . . .) I like the promo sheet, too. "*The City Pages* also recently quoted Joe Strummer as saying 'It's Lifter Puller's world . . . We just live in it,' in a story about the Clash. Of course, that same evening he was overheard saying to Craig, 'You guys are going to be bigger than Blur, or Pavement . . . [pause] . . . or Blur,' so take that in mind. With *Fiestas + Fiascos* I fully expect to get more press than Blur or Pavement. Or even Blur!" Well, I'm trying to do my part. (The rock critic came out of the bar, walking carefully. Everything was a blur. He rubbed his eyes, looked down at the pavement. The pavement was a blur.)

The promo sheet for the Distillers' first album says, "Don't try to make the pigeon hole for the Distillers smaller than 'punk.'" They're asking for it, aren't they? OK: There's more variety in thirty seconds of the first Pere Ubu album than in all of *The Distillers*. Blondie, the Contortions, the MC5, the Raincoats—they represented an ocean of possibilities, while this, this, this little barnacle, this seaweed, this discarded shell, this straitjacketed pigeon . . . actually, I like this record a lot. It's a sliver of a flake of a stereotyped version of a sound that was born a decade before lead singer Brody Armstrong was, but she's good, being young enough to do this old thing as if it had spit forth from her cranium this morning. As if she didn't know she was singing a closed world. (And maybe that means it's not a closed world.) A nice, tuneful screamer. "Hey, ah-ah-yeah! Hey. Fuck you. And I'll fuck you. Fuck you." But tunefully. Hey, big guy, want a nice tuneful fuck? Want some nice Jett-Courtney throat-retch? I'm functional, like a wall-bed (what are they called?) clanking down on your skull. (Not really; I just felt the need for a simile.) Squalling vocals. Stormy vocals. That seems so quaint, to have vocals that one could describe as "stormy." His beautiful but stormy wife, Isabella . . .

Track 10, "Red Carpet and Rebellion," has the lyric "colossally mistaken," which is a great lyric, though I don't know what it's about. Bloodshed, puritanic shit, ain't no money ain't no time, I'm out of my mind. St. Petersburg 1905—Yeah yeah yeah, and after that a shock of pogroms and my great-grandparents and their children fleeing for their lives. (The Distillers' actual lyrics seem not to co-alesce into anything colossal, or even understandable. "Oh Serena, I know what they're saying about you. It's not true." But what *are* they saying about her? That she's a ditz, a frivolous airhead? Whereas we know that she's really Sailor Moon, the girl who will protect humankind from the evil forces of the Negaverse? But the song says nothing of the sort. The song says, "Night irreverential, the time, carneleby is a bit of you." I'm not making this up.) "Gypsy Rose Lee": A pretty song. Brody Armstrong is scratching at the cracks in her voice, like Patti Smith, like Joe Strummer. She's not as brilliant as Joe, but like him she finds beauty amidst the ruin of her vocal cords. The joy of anguish.

Leatherface's *Horsebox* is yet another roar of beauty. Or beauty of roar, except it's a barely implied beauty of a would-be roar. I'm not sure how much I like it, but I keep listening out of curious fascination. The singing (by Frankie Stubbs) has scratch and ruin all right, but when you dig into it for a voice you get nothing. It's like listening to someone with laryngitis. Yet somehow it lifts itself—lifts its nothing—into melody, into a kind of sketchy transcendence. Two or three of the songs, anyway, could rank with "Suspect Device" and "Alternative Ulster" by Stiff Little Fingers. Which is pretty damn good, though with phlegm in place of the Stiffies' little screech. So I *do* like this album. "This is the spilt milk stench of wretch, an average cold walk home, avoiding sunspots, soundbites like snowstorms." That's telling 'em.

The Village Voice, December 19, 2000

GORE GORE GIRLS

Detroit's Gore Gore Girls sound totally ripped and fried, not like go-go girls—at least not like go-gos onstage, though maybe like go-gos after stage, their minds fried and battered. Everything about the Gore Gores' *Strange Girls* is fried. My eardrum got fried listening to them. They all seem to be playing Telecasters with the treble on superbright, the woofers and tweeters all torn up, the CD recorded in the girls' lavatory at Detroit's East Central Death And Atomic Warfare High School. The microphone has marbles in it. Occasionally, the girls grow weary of shredding their vocal cords, and come through with sweet, clear harmonies while the electric storm swirls around them. Since the sound is essentially slash-your-face-and-throw-rocks-at-the-window, it all registers as extreme punk; but the musical underpinnings come from several different sources: high-wailing girl group, early-Kinks freneticism, garage rock, rockabilly, girlabilly, rockagirly. And despite all the wind and sleet, there *is* form and beauty, amidst the gore. The ongoing storm has diminishing returns, however—with the needle always in red, a lot of the sound is muffled. But three songs stand out as incredible energy and great songwriting—I might compare the Gore Gore Girls to a certain great, long-defunct Detroit band that many groups are compared to but none *really* sounds like, and indeed the girly Gores don't have the whole dance-around-and-toss-the-notes-back-and-forth *motion* of said mythical band; but nonetheless on these three songs guitar-player Amy Surdu proves she's mastered James Williamson's fast guitar vamps and lightning melodies. Damn exciting, for those three songs, and restlessly sweet on many of the others. I'm curious what they'd do with a recording budget.

Gore Gore Girls are just one of a slew of mostly female mostly good mostly retro punk bands I've been enjoying lately: Fabulous Disaster, Candy Ass, Mensen, Thug Murder, the Color Guard. Now, punk women back in the day like X-Ray Spex, the Slits, Siouxsie and the Banshees, the Raincoats, etc. took the lesson of bands like the Clash and Sex Pistols not to be "sound like the Clash and Pistols" but rather "invent your own sound." The Slits, for instance, at first made me think of escaped madrigal singers from the zoo, and it took me many days to figure out what the hell they were doing and how great they were. Whereas now we have all these noninventors going back 20, 30 years for their sound, yet sounding good too. There's no law that says they *can't* sound good. And maybe bands like the Gore Gore Girls imitate an old sound of unruliness and recalcitrance and somehow come up with the energy of that unruliness, even if they do seem to be following punk rules and don't seem to have paid attention to any music from the last 30 years.

It seems to me, though, that the styles that these new retro gals are going back to had never been all that firm and established back in their original day. So the retro bands are not maintaining old ways but rather reasserting ways that never quite happened. Which is to say that they go back to moments of transition that in history had never been the transition to anything—or perhaps had been the transition from lashout to lifestyle. But lifestyle is a disappointing outcome for punk.

In inventing their own music, real post-Pistol punks like the Raincoats had inspired thousands of bands to make bohemian music for living your life rather than for changing your life—which in the long run has led to music that's disappointing in comparison to the promise of punk's early years. So you could say that maybe some retro punk is going back further, back to the promise, and maybe in copying old sounds it *is* somehow getting that promise into the music. But promise of what?

The Gore Gore Girls seem like the band that actually lives emotionally in the long-lost era of not-there-yet-and-straining-to-break-through. Which is to say that maybe they're real punks. And maybe they could develop their music in unexpected ways, given that they haven't yet integrated their various song styles, unless you count playing everything through ripped speakers as a form of integration. I'm wondering what happens if somehow the James Williamson guitar-chording can connect itself to the various other styles that they heave their noise at: Kinks, Crystals, Sonics, and so forth. And what would be the musical result (or even the social result)? Can unreconstructed retro-punk brats actually move their sub-sub-sub-microworld off its duff?

excerpted from "Return to Whenever," *The Village Voice*, August 21, 2001

[Shortly after this review, I got an email from the Gore Gore Girls' new drummer, Monica Breen. "So listen, we're going into the studio to start the second album tonight. The article was perfect to help boost our self esteem right now. Thank you, thank you, hope to see you in New York one day. P.S. We don't have duffs, we have big, cute butts!"]

AN ONLINE EXCHANGE

Brevity = energy, foax
— mark s, July 27, 2001

Britney = energy, fox
— Frank Kogan, July 27, 2001

I Love Music chatroom

ON-RAMP TO STYLE

At first glance, the cover of the *Gentlemen of Leisure* CD seemed like a boring attempt at "style," but now it strikes me as a charmingly austere attempt to pretend to evoke opulence—the two gentlemen, each wearing an expensive dress-up suit, are standing next to an automobile that would have seemed futuristic in a low-budget 1960s British spy film, though the car is actually a Delorean. Its doors open out into strange wing-like flaps. You expect it suddenly to go airborne, or to launch natty spies with parachutes. The gents and the car are next to what seems to be a highway on-ramp, and that's all you can tell, pretty much, because they and the car and the on-ramp are all that's in the picture, signifying perhaps that if one is a gentleman of leisure, one has no need of scenery, since one carries one's landscape of style within oneself. (Is this what the young and the leisured do in their spare time, stand by highway on-ramps?)

The expensive suits are cleverly incongruous in this context (i.e., a modern-day dance LP that plumps for leisure), given that no one wears such a suit in his leisure hours anymore. Suits are the work uniforms of corporate employees or are brought out on state occasions, or for eightieth birthdays and opening nights at the opera. The suits seem humorous to me. The whole getup is humorous: the suits, the car, the highway. The inner photo has the two gents striding through an airport. I imagine that they're pretending to be the jet-setting equivalent of beach bums: We're just sashaying around in airports being, you know, stylish.

The Gentlemen of Leisure are Karl Heinz and Dieter Muller. Karl, a Capricorn, was born in Hamburg. "No one has a better sense of humor than that Capricorn." Dieter is from Stuttgart. As a youth, he made spontaneous trips to the many natural hot springs that litter the area. Turn-offs include veal and cheap denim. (This is so you don't mistakenly think he was ever in Norwegian "gay" punk band Turbonegro, who proclaim, "Turbonegro wear Levi's Denim or they wear nothing at all.")

Karl's turn-offs include saxophones (for not being as funny as tubas, presumably).

The lyrics fall likably between tenuously emotional and casually ad hoc—that is, between (1) We Are Displaying Our Finely Tuned Emotions, and (2) If Songs *Must* Have Words, I Suppose We Should At Least Make Them Rhyme. So you get the preposterously metaphoric ("You're sweet and tender driving my desire/Pull out the blowtorch and light my fire"), the functional ("When the party's just begun/You know you'll be the only one"), the not even functional ("I see you movin' in those tight blue jeans/You get the point, you know what I mean"), and the cheerfully beside the point ("Southern seas, ocean breeze/The letters that you sent to me").

I'd call the vocals "fey," though "fey" might just be strategy for a couple of guys with high and not-at-all-powerful voices. "Fey" is preferable to plaintive, if one is a gentleman of leisure. As for the music itself, it's excellent—early-'80s dance-wave and electrobeats and Europop riffs, sweet melodies, catchy rhythms, nine good songs out of nine tracks (plus one authoritatively inept "skit" that has the gentlemen, speaking in ridiculously fake sophisticated accents, at a retail counter, buying a wallet: "Is the leather textured? I wanted the more textured look"). With all the lameass quasi-electro stuff out now, this is a record you might actually want to play next to Kraftwerk or Human League or Soul Sonic Force or the Flirts.

"I wanna be your boy toy/Won't you be my boy toy?" So, as Karl and Dieter commit themselves to poignantly uncommitted sex, the background blips go off dancing tunefully on their own. (Germany, land of the rising blip.) I'd say the "style" and "sensibility" are mainly pretexts to allow these two fellows to indulge their gifts for melody: melodies sung, melodies buzzed, melodies beeped. Melodies up with the vocals, melodies down with the synths, melodies in with the whooshes and off with the whirrs. But then, the melodies add flair to the whole image. And so what initially looked glum, turns out to be glam.

The Village Voice, September 3, 2002

QUIET DESERT STORM

Toby Keith has a strong rich voice, but he lets it sit easily—so easily that it's easy to overlook what a good singer he is. In this he reminds me of Cary Grant, who excelled at light comedy and therefore never pulled off the sort of bravura performance that would garner him an Oscar.

The ease of Toby's singing doesn't make his music low-impact so much as it makes his impact low-profile; there are no giant crater walls announcing "Toby Keith struck here." Which makes his recent bellicose single [insert name of recent bellicose single . . . (sigh) all right, it's "Courtesy of the Red, White and Blue"] atypical. So how about if we ignore it, OK? It's track one on his current album, *Unleashed*. The next single, "Who's Your Daddy," is track two; summertime and the singin' is back to easy. And the woman is knocking on Toby's door because all the college boys have left for holiday, leaving the field clear for full-time man Toby. This song *could* be about his being merely the consolation prize, a substitute for the good stuff that's gone. But the way he sings it—the ease of his voice, the confidence—he's bragging. He's here and she needs him, and presumably the college boys know nothing anyway, or they'd have hung around.

Track three, "It's Good to Go to Mexico," is set in the chill of an Oklahoma November, and Toby is inviting a lady to come with him to Mexico, so the charms of Mexico are something of an advertisement for *his* charms. "It'll be just you and me and moonlight dancing on the sea/To Spanish guitar melody of a mariachi band." Wait, Toby, it's not just you and she, it's you and she and the *guitar player* and the *horn players* and the *drummer*. (Romantic movie scene I'd like to see: The woman and the man are on a wild stretch of beach, the sunset coloring the air around them, strings swelling in the background. "We're alone now," the man bends to kiss her, she stops him with her hand and says, "Wait! Who's that?" "Who's what?" "Well, if we're all alone, who the hell is playing the violin?") But

Toby's still up in Oklahoma, importuning her to get off the phone, put on her shorts and sandals, and fly south with him. (Maybe with modern communications and all, she could take the phone with her and still conduct business between guitar licks. Hadn't thought of that, had you Toby?) And on the *next* track he has her *turn off the news* so the two of them can get to smoochin'; so those are three songs in succession where you tune out or hang up on the outside world, or clear the area of college boys—anything to stanch the information flow.

All right, next song, track five . . . Wait, I suppose we have to go back to that bellicose track one; since if there's a giant pink bellicose in the living room, you can't just pretend it isn't there. You've probably heard about it anyway, unless you live in a cave in Afghanistan or somewhere. It's Toby's heartfelt response to 9–11, his tribute to the flag, to fighting for freedom, to slaughtering people. Actually, the famous line, "We'll put a boot in your ass/It's the American way," is pretty mild, all things considered (though I read an unhappy teen girl in one country music chatroom lamenting that, because of the dirty word, her parents wouldn't let her listen to the record). What piss me off are the lyrics "Man, we lit up your world/Like the Fourth of July" and "It'll feel like the whole wide world is rainin' down on you," with no thought to the identity of the "you," of the people our rain is actually choppin' down, which in this war is damn problematic. But of course, I myself might threaten to knock people down, for instance when someone cuts in line at the supermarket. And conversely I can listen with equanimity to Johnny Cash singing "I shot a man in Reno, just to watch him die." No, not with equanimity—the line scared the shit out of me when I first heard it, sounding like bullyboy wiseass toughness that I've always wanted to avoid all contact with, except when it thrills me in music or when I feel like embodying it myself, when someone cuts in front of me. But whereas I think bullyboy toughness deserves expression in song, I don't like it packaged as patriotism and turned into public policy. I'm glad Toby and his ilk respond to the world when it comes crashing in on them; I just get irritated by the moral laziness, by the fact that his response is to turn off his mind and start blasting.

But then there's the music, which is extraordinarily pretty: As the song winds down, the bell chimes for liberty, and the sound is sweet. This album puts a glaze of sugar on everything, the way the guitars ring out. Samples from my written notes: "Nice bells." "Good riffs." "Really sounds nice." "Consistently pretty." "Again, here's a pretty one." "Weeping steel, but pretty nonetheless." Fits well with the ease of his singing—and manages to disconcert me, since everything feels so damn comfy, despite the social insecurity that underlies his lyrics. The best song is "That's Not How It Is," which in a more open world would get play on the urban AC stations (what used to be called "Quiet Storm"), since in its sweetness and quietness, it nonetheless contains disturbance, sorrow: "I used to steal your breath away with just one little kiss/Me and you were so in love back then, but that's not how it is." And the easy singing and gentle jazz-blues lines really do sound like latent power, leashed-in and desperate. The main defect of this LP, actually, is too few strong melodies like this one (about four). Nonetheless, there is care and artistry throughout. I guess my real sadness is that the smarts of his small ideas don't make their way into his bigger ideas. Really, political songs should be smart. But that's not how it is.

The Village Voice, November 5, 2002

COUNT FIVE, HAVE A PSYCHOTIC REACTION

I checked the Oxes' press kit online—pictures of the band cavorting, but it didn't tell me what I most wanted to learn, which is why they eschew the old Anglo-Saxon "oxen" in favor of the not-yet-English "oxes." I prefer the old myself, and if you disagree I'll poke out both your eyen. (Maybe the group were originally Foxes, but after years of hard living and trying to play in 7/4, they were no longer foxy.)

The Oxiness of their song forms is that instead of going verse-chorus-verse-chorus, or Part A/Part A/Part B/Part A (known to aficionados of song form as AABA), the Oxes go ABCDEFGH, or variants like ABCDAFGCAH. Or ABCDguitarplaysAwhileotherguitarplaysCthenguitarplaysEwhileotherguitar-playsDthenFGH. The Oxy ones deal with the question "How come there are no good rock singers anymore?" by not having a singer, and they deal with "How come there are no good rock instrumental soloists anymore?" by not playing any solos. And they deal with "Who gets to play the main melody?" by not having main melodies. Just riffs and power chords and drumbeats. This is so no one will mistake them for a jazz band. The instrumental parts roll and slide and scrape by each other in counter-rhythm, so that you don't mistake the Oxes for a punk band either. But you might mistake the Oxes for a punk band nonetheless, because they *are* a punk band—though one with a slide-scrape-and-roll pit instead of an old-fashioned slam pit. And when dancing with your honey you can slip and trip too, if that's your thing, since the Oxicles intersperse 5/4 and 7/8 rhythms with their 4/4s. (Slip-and-trip is more punk than slam is, anyway, since slam dancers merely slam *to* the music rather than against it, while slip-and-trippers get to dodge and entangle themselves in the beat, as the music stalks them and laughs.)

"Russia is HERE": Drums roll in the distance. Different rolls in different speakers, like two armies approaching. Half a minute in, one drum stops rolling and starts beating; twenty seconds further, a guitar heralds a second guitar, which fires a volley of fast notes, while drum #2 just keeps rollin' along. So guitar #1 whines tunefully, and the rolling drum drops out (leading to a life of crime, poverty, and indolence). Some of this is in 4/4. Some is in 5/4. Then, for no reason, a jig from one of the guitars; and then, out of nowhere, chiming guitar chords (they get the chime effect by playing the "do" and "so" notes of the chord but not the "mi"—you didn't need to know that, but I thought I'd tell you anyway). A squalling guitar squalls all over his chiming comrade.

"Half Half & Half": The flight of the heavy-metal bumblebee. This should be in 3/2 time, if I understand the title, but instead it seems to alternate 3/4 and 7/4.

"Tony Baines": Real *heavy* swamp riffs, in 6/8. Then acoustic anemia guitars playing the same riffs but taking nine beats rather than six to get through. Then back to the electric riffs in 6/8. Then different riffs in 6/8. Then more rhythms and riffs, none of which are from the original bogstomp. Then a pretty coda.

"take & free Miami": As time signatures are to the Oxes' music, capitalization is to their song titles: varied. A scratchy oxylicious guitar rhythm like the one Destiny's Child sampled from Stevie Nicks's "Edge of Seventeen," but the Oxxers keep interrupting it.

"boss kitty": A circling little riff, and to hell with specifying time signatures (he says, while hearing a solid 6/8).

"Bees won": Fast strum. (I'm trying to remember the violin name for fast bowing: tremolo?) They abandon the tremolo soon enough, but a minute later it returns (our motto: Back to Tremolo)—but not played for tremulous effect; rather, for scraping the barnacles from your soul (or the plaque from your teeth, at any rate) (speaking of "rate," they seem to be scraping around in 4/4). Suddenly, this is all replaced by a pretty keyboard. Pretty, that is, if you're a male car alarm hearing the mating call of a female car alarm across forest lakes.

"chyna chyna chyna": This is *all* nice prettiness. Chyna chyna chyna indeed! I'm giving up counting time, I swear. By the way, they've turned on the distortion and turned off the prettiness, gone to speed riffing. Then back to the pleasure plink. In 4/4. ("Patient resumes compulsive counting activities; recommend placement in experimental medication program.")

"Kaz Hayashi '01": They *count off* 1, 2, 3, 4 and waltz right into 3/4, then break into 4/4 but in "swing feel" (which means that each main beat subdivides into three beats) (oh shut up).

In short, I would recommend this album to anyone with an interest in propulsive overload and elementary arithmetic.

FODDER BITES CANNON

Living Things' "Bombs Below," the first track on their *Turn In Your Friends & Neighbors* EP, has a sound that's both hard and defeated. It's as good hit-your-fist-into-the-wall music as you'll ever get, but its condition of existence is that the wall stays intact. And the music feels ageless; it's so spare that it could be categorized as metal or punk or just plain hard rock, since there are not enough signifiers to make the distinction. Such a song could have emerged at any time from 1969 to the present; so even though the style goes way back, the song doesn't sound like a throwback (don't call it a throwback, it's been here for years).

The EP packaging identifies President Bush as a tyrant and uses as a backdrop the Declaration of Independence whose values Bush is in danger of eviscerating. But in the song lyrics themselves, the politics are but half-expressed; the person singing has impulses that he can't turn into ideas, and rather than fake the ideas, he just gives you the impulses. "Where do all the dead boys go?/No solution just bombs below." I can't tell who's narrating: In the first half of the song, the "we" seems to be stoner boys who are being harvested for cannon fodder; in the second half, the "we" is the old warmongers sending the kids to die. But that's just one way to interpret it. The sound subdues any extended interpretation. Read the news, feel rage, make a fist. No solution. No future.

The Village Voice, August 11, 2003

ALONE AGAIN, NATURALLY

After a half-year build on indie label TVT, Lil Jon and the Ying Yang Twins are ruling the hip-hop zeitgeist with "Get Low," the low of which isn't just dance-'n'-sex low, it's Baker-Robie low, Miami-bass low, car-boom low, down-into-the-whirlpool low.

As for *Me & My Brother*, the Ying Yang Twins' own LP, it stays accessible while being as dense with overshifts and undertows as any music I've ever heard *and* sounding more committed to the ping and whirr of electro than even New Orleans bounce is. *And* it pulls in movietrack-doomtrack moods while maintaining the feel of a whoot-whoomp yuk-it-all-up and blat-till-you're-blotto party. So the Timbaland-Gotti genius stuff that ten minutes ago sounded state-of-the-art now feels bare in comparison—producer Beat-In-Azz runs his tides and eddies deeper. Though maybe Lil Jon's LP does better with the gang shouts.

The lyrics are basic raunch and slurp that only get complicated by accident, no deliberate attempts to shake up the complexities à la Eminem or Black Flag ("I got a six-pack and nothing to do/I got a six-pack and I don't need you"). But the complexities are there nonetheless, of their own accord: "The nigga's so drunk he'll fuck the floor—fuck the *floor?*—fuck the floor," on the heels of which achievement they tell us to "Put your middle finger up, if you don't give a fuck/Get your head back down and finish the cup." The idea is old hat but still potent, to link being alive and defiant with drinking yourself into dysfunction and stupor (being alive equaling being comatose), though here this profound paradox is but another bubble in their barrel of yuks. "Naggin'" is an obvious and safe single, with the melody to "There's a place in France where the girls wear paper pants," which they get unexpected beauty out of by way of deep-growl voices and quasi-baroque keyboards, not to mention unintended poetry by substituting "kiss my pants" for "kiss my ass" in the radio version. But the best tracks are the dense party throbbers like "What's Happnin!" and "Grey Goose" and "Hanh!"—the latter of which seems to be an eccentric spelling of "WAAAAAAH!!!" In "The Georgia Dome" they lay down some crazy Strunk for the hipsters: "I smoke by myself. I drink by myself. I fuck these hos by my goddamn self." (Meaning, like, without a spotter?)

Drinking by yourself: What an admirable thing to brag about! They do it in two different songs. What's so bizarre is that however you interpret "by myself," it doesn't work for the entire passage. It can't mean "all alone," since, while that applies to the smoking and drinking (as if to say "I can party even when no one else is around"), it doesn't do for the ho-fuckin'. But neither can it mean "without any help" (e.g., "I'll fuck all the hos myself, rather than fucking A though L and leaving M through Z for my assistant"), since one generally doesn't ask for aid in drinking and smoking. "Here, um, sir, will you pull open my mouth for me, so that I can get this liquor in, please?" (Their previous album contains the explanation "I was born by my goddamn self," which is also incorrect, as he's forgetting the stork, among others.) The doing-it-alone stuff might be the ultimate way to pretend that you can desire yet remain unbeholden and invulnerable to the person you're desiring (which is what hip-hop's P.I.M.P. thing is all about, really). And maybe to the extent that these guys are aware that they're alone, they're aware of the pretense.

The only track that dulls out is a spare one called "Hard," which stays ghetto-real and Glock-tough in its suspense-soundtrack way, with boring words to match. "'Hard' is a dick that's erect." Yeah, and hard's the floor you're fuckin'. So what? I suppose that it's just two sides of the same shtick, to think that you're most real when you're dead to sentiment and that you're most alive when you're dead to the world, but fortunately these guys know which side their shtick is buttered on. So they stick to the sunny side of life—or the party side of death, at any rate—and make most everyone else sound immobile.

The Village Voice, November 11, 2003

DEATH TAKES A HOLIDAY

The title cut on the Black-Eyed Snakes' *Rise Up!* manages to simultaneously pound you down and lift you up, like a cross between Living Things' "Bombs Below" and Black Flag's "Rise Above"—though if anything, "Rise Up!" is the one that slugs hardest.

It's sung through a filter, so I can't really make out who's supposed to be rising over whom, but since Day of the Dead skeletons parade across the album cover, maybe they're the ones on the rise. The music emerges from primordial late-'60s Blue Cheer proto-metal, an ancient land of giant riffs and drum 'n' bash. Unfortunately, the rest of the LP is true to its actual home in present-day noise bohemia, so despite being a visceral mix of blues skronk and rock 'n' roll, it's as feckless and distant as most other indie rock. I'm used to this: the musical vocabulary dying in our hands yet then, momentarily, inexplicably, returning to life. Indie rock has been suffering from dry rot for more than two decades, but this has been an OK year for it. You never know.

The Village Voice, November 18, 2003

SCARRED OLD SLAVER
(COUNTRY MUSIC CRITICS POLL 2003)

My P&J comments were short and boring, so I'm posting my country music ballot instead (that I'd drawn up for the *Nashville Scene*'s Country Music Critics Poll).

I find the idea that I'm a country-music critic hilarious, since I'm so ignorant of the genre. But I suppose at this point the idea I'm a *rock critic* is just as hilarious. I mean, I can't remember if I've ever heard a blink-182 song. And I *know* I've never heard a Cradle of Filth song. Seriously, can you call someone a rock critic who's never heard Cradle of Filth? (Answer: Uh, I don't know. I've never heard them.)

Exclusively for *ILX*, not only am I posting the ballot, I'm posting a version with the *typos corrected*. Then I'm posting Josh Kortbein's reaction to the ballot. And then (to round out the box set), I'm posting the letter to Geoffrey Himes in which I ask him to correct the typos if he prints any of my ballot. (In the original I'd written "Hear 'em whip the women just around midnight" when in fact I should have written "Hear *him* whip the women just around midnight.") I believe this letter expresses my true personality better than anything I have ever written for publication.

As you'll see, I created a few award categories of my own.

BEST COUNTRY ALBUMS 2003

   1. Dwight Yoakam *Population Me* (Electrodisc/Audium/Koch)

   2. Winfred E. Eye *The Dirt Tier* (Luckyhorse Industries)

   3. Deana Carter *I'm Just a Girl* (Arista)

   4. Gary Allan *See If I Care* (MCA)

   5. Toby Keith *Shock'n Y'All* (DreamWorks)

   6. Brooks & Dunn *Red Dirt Road* (Arista)

   7. Drive-By Truckers *Decoration Day* (New West)

BEST COUNTRY SINGLES 2003

   1. David Banner "Cadillac on 22's" (Universal)

   2. Faith Hill "One" (Warner Bros.)

   3. Bubba Sparxxx "Deliverance" (Interscope)

   4. Bubba Sparxxx "Comin' Round" (Interscope)

   5. Deana Carter "There's No Limit" (Arista)

   6. See first vomit song below (but don't give it any points from me, thank you)

   7. Dwight Yoakam "The Late Great Golden State" (Electrodisc/Audium/Koch)

   8. Dixie Chicks "Travelin' Soldier" (Sony)

   9. Montgomery Gentry "Hell Yeah" (Columbia)

  10. Kenny Chesney "No Shirt, No Shoes, No Problems" (BNA)

DUO/TRIO/GROUP

   1. Montgomery Gentry

   2. Brooks & Dunn

   3. Dixie Chicks

MALE VOCALIST
1. Toby Keith
2. Dwight Yoakam
3. Gary Allan

FEMALE VOCALIST
1. LeAnn Rimes
2. Deana Carter
3. Martina McBride

OVERALL ACT
1. Montgomery Gentry
2. LeAnn Rimes
3. Toby Keith

BEST SONG TO MAKE ME THROW UP
Toby Keith "Beer for My Horses" (DreamWorks)

MEDIOCRE SONG THAT ALSO MADE ME THROW UP
Gary Allan "Tough Little Boys" (MCA)

CRUCIFIX RESTING AGAINST HER SEXY BREAST
Faith Hill

HER NAME WAS PAULINE AND SHE LIVED IN A TREE
Tim McGraw

IF I WERE JESUS I'D SAY FORGIVE HIM 'CAUSE HE DOESN'T KNOW WHAT THE FUCK HE'S DOING
Toby Keith

SHE'LL DO ANYTHING FOR LOVE, BUT SHE WON'T DO . . . WELL, ACTUALLY, SHE'LL DO ANYTHING, OR SO SHE SAYS
Deana Carter

COUNTRY COMMENTS

A song counts as a single for 2003 if that's the year that the song lived its life as a single or a radio emphasis track. Obviously, some of these were on albums released in 2002. Really, I only worry about release dates when I'm in prison.

Chuck Eddy has in fact seen a CD-single of "Comin' Round," though it's maybe a promo and hasn't yet been hawked to the radio.

My list isn't meant to comment on what is or isn't "country." It might do so accidentally. I vote for anything I like that visits or inhabits the socioemotional turf within the country contours of my headbox, or, when I like a song but it's not on that turf (e.g., LeAnn's disco records), if it's on the cw turf of enough other people's headboxes (or sandboxes, or record-store bins, or publicity sheets). In other words, I vote for what I want to, and find a way to rationalize. "Comin' Round" would be country on many people's headboxes, if the country chaps got a chance to hear it. "Deliverance" would be novelty in the country arena but is countryish nonetheless. "Cadillac on 22's" is almost beyond category: The chords resemble "Lay Lady Lay," and the delivery is vaguely soul, I guess (or just plain vague, dreamy, eerie), but lacks the many soul shouty-n-melisma signifiers that you hear on (for instance) the Lee Greenwood LP and the Faith Hill, neither of which has remotely the feel of "Cadillac on 22's."

But anyway, hip-hop having reared its happy visage on my list, let's talk about it. For all of country's confusion about whether it could or should be rock or pop or disco, one thing country is sure of is that it's not hip-hop. The hip-hop mess is what the woman leaves Montgomery for in MG's "She Couldn't Change Me"; hip-hop is the destination that Cledus T. Judd imagines for the Dixie Chicks in his malicious kiss-off "Martie, Emily & Natalie"—which is absurd, since it's not the Dixies who are in hip-hop's range, but Brooks & Dunn in their crowded rhythms (on *Steers & Stripes* more than *Red Dirt Road*) and Deana Carter and Toby Keith et al. when they talk their songs. This hardly makes Carter and Keith hip-hop—while the Deana-Toby talk style shares some ancestors with hip-hop, it doesn't take in hip-hop. Brooks & Dunn, on the other hand . . . well, I bet if they called Tim and Missy, the answer'd be "We're coming right over."

So here's Bubba Sparxxx. He's unmistakably in hip-hop, he's accepted in hip-hop, and he's rapping in a voice whose cadences come from where southern white and southern black mix, one of his backing tracks is country (but with the hip-hop beats), and another is a kissing cousin. And as far as the country audience is concerned, so nothing. So far. We'll see.

As for pop—and Faith: Yeah, pop sounds may be inundating country, and I don't believe this is a bad thing, and this sort of pop 'n' soul was somewhat shaped by country in the first place, and it's nice that country lets women roam the world, even while it requires men to stay home and tend the hearth.

Now about rock: Yeah, rock is pouring into country. Rock guitarists find a home in country for their licks, rock formalists find a home for their songwriting. I have only a few qualms about calling Montgomery Gentry the world's greatest rock band (they sure *rock*). Etc. etc. etc. But, well, here's the hesitation: Even while Brooks & Dunn can prosper and gain kudos for making an album that resembles the sixteenth-best Rolling Stones album and that quotes platitudes from the seventh-best song on the nineteenth-best Rolling Stones album, and even as B&D endlessly and creatively run the riff from "Brown Sugar" (best song on the fourteenth-best Rolling Stones album), they simply won't let their music do what the Rolling Stones would do. I'm not sure how best to convey what I mean, but notice the *lyrics* to "Brown Sugar": "Gold Coast slave ship bound for cotton fields/Sold in a market down in New Orleans/Scarred old slaver knows he's doin' all right/Hear him whip the women just around midnight." And that sadistic slaver inhabits and contaminates every sex act in the rest of the song. And this stoking the fire, pulling the rug, yanking up the floorboards, is just what Brooks & Dunn won't do, with either their sound or the words. Not that they're required to, any more than the Stones were required to reincarnate Howlin' Wolf. I'm just pointing out what's missing, where the real barrier is. And hell yeah, sorry for wimping out, they *should* cross the barrier, or someone should, 'cause if they or Montgomery Gentry or some other performers of that caliber *don't* cross it (this feeling of mine colored by the fact that Toby's horse-vomit song cited earlier, which came within a hair's breadth of endorsing lynching, lived high on the charts), the genre will continue to be a fake moral, fake rowdy, bullshit lie. (But not an uninteresting one.)

Sincerely,
Frank Kogan

From: "Josh"
To: "Frank Kogan"
Sent: Tuesday, January 06, 2004 1:38 AM
Subject: Re: Frank Kogan's Country Music Critics ballot 2003

"Frank Kogan" sez:
"the genre will continue to be a fake moral, fake rowdy, bullshit lie."

surely you must know this is the most tendentious and contentious thing in your whole ballot. the one where the ballot should start, the one where the thinking should start.

happy 2004, frank.

From: "Frank Kogan"
To: "Josh"
Subject: Re: Re: Frank Kogan's Country Music Critics ballot 2003
Date: Thursday, January 08, 2004 11:53 AM

Giving me a taste of my own medicine, eh?

From: "Frank Kogan"
To: "Geoffrey Himes"
Subject: country music correx

Geoff—Don't know if it's too late to fix typos on my poll ballot, but my two proofreading buddies, Anal Spice and Pedantic Spice, inform me that "countours" should be spelled "contours" and that in "Brown Sugar" Mick is singing "Hear HIM hit the women," not "Hear 'EM hit the women." (And truly, it would be pointless for Aunty Em to hit the women.) I think the chances are miniscule that you'll be quoting those bits, but just in case. (Oh, and *Steers & Stripes* takes an ampersand, and I don't know why I put a hyphen between "sadistic" and "slaver," and I'm just wasting your time telling you this, but I'm compulsive and can't stop myself.)

But also, given the apparently real—and wonderful—possibility that David Banner's "Cadillac on 22's" will place high enough to get printed among the top singles, I want to say that I got the title right: It's "Cadillac" in the singular, despite how your other voters seem to have spelled it. (See your reminder email of a few days back.) It SHOULD be "Cadillacs," because that's how Banner sings it, and that's why everyone gets it wrong. But there's only one Caddy in the title.

Thank you for your attention to these earth-shaking matters.

P.S. I *won't* ask you to correct any of my mistaken IDEAS. That would be cheating. (I got hyperbolic and inarticulate there at the end of my comments, didn't I? 'Tis what happens when one waits until the last minute.) But you might be interested to know that a friend of mine who read my spiel pointed out that when she'd seen the Chicks perform in London (six months after the famous concert), Martie'd said between songs that they'd listened to a lot of bluegrass while making *Home*, but that now they were listening to a lot of Eminem and Missy, and she couldn't predict what the next album'd be like. So you never know. (Hear Em whip the dixie chicks just around midnight.)

Frank Kogan

Yikes! I just noticed that in my letter to Geoff I kept saying "hit" when I meant to say "whip."

original ballot submitted January 5, 2004, expanded version posted on *I Love Music* chatroom on February 13, 2004

NASHVILLE STALWART DONS ROSE-COLORED GLASSES FOR MISS EMILY

Most of John Conlee's hits are about totally screwing up or being totally screwed over. In one of the few exceptions, 1983's would-be smug but completely unconvincing "Common Man," John, just a beer-drinkin', truck-drivin' Nashville fellow, says "highbrow people lose their sanity"—and believes his life's better than that. But thanks to the miracle of this *Classics* CD's near-chronological programming, it comes right after the hilarious "I Don't Remember Loving You" (also 1983), featuring lowbrow John in a *mental institution*, crayon in hand, suffering from the amnesia he'd induced in himself to forget the pain of his last breakup. So there you are.

Deliberate self-deception is a longtime country staple: making believe you love me, making believe I don't love you, making believe I never lost you, making believe I never cared that I did. But in country all this deceit is delivered with such good-natured self-mockery that it acts as a bond between singer and audience. Yeah, isn't it funny, the way we make such dopes of ourselves! Conlee's first big hit, "Rose Colored Glasses" ("they keep me from feeling so cheated, defeated, when reflections in your eyes show me a fool"), could be classified as a sad song, but I doubt that anyone feels sorrow while it's playing. So his music only *seems* to be about defeat.

And anyway, Conlee generally chooses to wallow rather than dissemble. His basic theme is not getting over it (the nuthouse song being the apparent exception that very much proves the rule); this can mean being true to a true love, but more often it means not letting go of a lost love. In "Miss Emily's Picture"—a song that's far more maniacal than the one from the psycho ward, though nothing about its words or their delivery indicates that anyone involved in creating it finds it the least bit abnormal—poor forsaken John is perpetually straightening the long-absent Miss Emily's picture: the one by his bed, or the one on his nightstand, or the one on his wall. Or he's pulling Miss Emily's picture from his billfold, to show to the boys at the bar.

It's in his perseverance—in the face of disaster and in *being* a disaster—that he's triumphant. "Clinging to the broken heart inside my head"! The arrangements are heavily orchestral, and since he sings in a high nasal heartbreak that's rich but not too rich, he comes across as a regular guy swamped in large emotions. And with quasi-gospel background vocals, lots of this feels like a sing-along: a community of feeling. You get buoyed up, in that sound, in that community.

Except "She Can't Say That Anymore," a song I love unreasonably, the one here I'd take to a desert island: It's beyond category and beyond comfort. It defies musical description. I can say, "Oh, it's countrypolitan with disco strings and a hint of disco spaciness," which is correct but conveys *nothing* of what it's like. The opening steel-guitar line could be one of those sad, repeating architectural riffs that Tom Verlaine would build songs around—but instead, the song goes on its country oompah way. The lyrics don't really give you the plot. You get a detail here (she's fumbling for her keys), a metaphor there (she jumps the fence but doesn't get free), a snatch of conversation ("Mama insisted that I stay awhile"), and you have to connect the dots yourself. "She's breakin' in a new routine for the man who walks the floor." I guess it just means he's home alone, pacing, while she's working up her alibi. But with the background singers whispering "she said" into an echo chamber, it all sounds ghostly. "Walking the floor" feels like walking the plank. And you've got percussive orchestral riffs that had originated in disco, disco-pomp, except there's neither pomp nor dance here, just the empty floor and the man who walks it. Spooky.

The Village Voice, May 25, 2004

TOP 11, 2004

SINGLES
1. Don Yute f. Ying Yang Twins "Row Da Boat"
2. Kardinal Offishall "Bang Bang"
3. David Banner "Crank It Up"
4. Westside Connection "Gangsta Nation"
5. Ying Yang Twins f. Trick Daddy "What's Happnin!"
6. Method Man f. Busta Rhymes "What's Happenin'"
7. Crime Mob "Knuck if You Buck"
8. M.I.A. "Galang"
9. Jay-Z "Dirt Off Your Shoulder"
10. Miss B. "Bottle Action"
11. Toby Keith "Whiskey Girl"

ALBUMS
1. Big & Rich *Horse of a Different Color*
2. Various Artists *Rio Baile Funk: Favela Booty Beats*
3. M.I.A. *Piracy Funds Terrorism Volume 1*

4. Various Artists *Crunk Classics*
5. Yolanda Perez *Aqui Me Tienes*
6. Notekillers *Notekillers*
7. Courtney Love *America's Sweetheart*
8. Gene Watson . . . *Sings*
9. The Hold Steady *Almost Killed Me*
10. Country Teasers *Full Moon Empty Sportsbag*
11. David Banner *MTA2: Baptized in Dirty Water*

'Twas a happenin' (and happnin!) year in hip-hop.

ACKNOWLEDGEMENTS, THANK YOUS, EXPLANATIONS

"Please help me to distinguish between Frank Kogan and Chuck Eddy" was the desperate plea put forth on the *I Love Music* chatroom, April 16, 2003. After several tentative starts (kogan = calvin, eddy = hobbes; kogan = celine, eddy = dion; eddy = marsupial, kogan = reproduces via infecting victims with hallucinogenic spores), it was determined definitively, by Scott Seward, that "one is tigra and one is bunny but i can't remember which is which."

Well, Chuck is Tigra, and I'm Bunny. This is *so* obvious.

OK, maybe it's not all that obvious, but examine the evidence. Chuck is 55% frothy and 45% sly, while I'm 55% sly and 45% frothy. (We're each 100% funky fresh, however.) Chuck sees so many kinds and doesn't know where to start, while I like them dumb and I like them smart. So *right off* he's trying to take everything in, while I'm there making invidious distinctions. Tigra Chuck is 55 parts curious to 45 parts relentless; Bunny Me reverses the ratio. Now, we both like the boom—that's a given—but for Chuck *that's* the biggest part of it (again, 55:45 ratio; I'm not going to keep repeating it; but yes, we're not either/or, we can both talk and chew gum at the same time). When Tigra Chuck blasts the boom out of his window, this is because he really likes the boom a lot, or finds it a fascinating boom, and *he wants you to hear it, too.* Whereas when Bunny and I blast you with our boom, we're speaking *through* that boom—that boom is our voice—we've got a point to make. Hell, we'd boom you even if we *didn't* normally like the boom, so long as the boom served our purpose in that instance.

So when Chuck cranks the stereo, with his windows down and his system up, it's because he really wants you to hear that record, and the next record, and the one after that. The most important term in the subtitle to Chuck's *Stairway to Hell: the 500 Best Heavy Metal Albums in the Universe* isn't "heavy metal" but "500": And sure, Chuck is delighted to fuck up and discombobulate your notion of heavy metal, but still, that's not the point. 500 albums is the point. And so his strategy as to what to include in the book isn't based on any particular argument about what heavy metal is, but rather on *every* argument about what heavy metal is. A particular argument will include some music and exclude other music, but what Chuck does is to take all the arguments and include any record that any argument would include, while setting aside the fact that each argument excludes a lot of what the other arguments include. So if Teena Marie records a side of hard funk and metal guitar, she's in the book. Whereas when *I'd* brought Teena into the discussion, I'd said "'Billie Jean' rocks as hard as any '80s 'rock'; 'Lips to Find You' rocks harder," and this didn't mean "include Michael and Teena within the genre 'rock'" but rather, "if you want rock, you gotta go to nonrock to hear it." So I wasn't including Michael and Teena in rock, but excluding rock from rock, and saying that if rock were to reconstitute itself, this would happen outside of rock. A year later I claimed that the girl-twirl disco of Company B and Sa-Fire and Vivien Vee and Exposé was the only possible future of punk. (Yes I did; you can look it up. I'm also the guy who told Selznick that he'd lose money on *Gone With The Wind*.) So one of my *goals* was to fuck up your idea of rock—"think of rock as an idea without an embodiment"—get you thinking about genre, call into question the rules of the game. I'm the one who spins out theories about Superwords. And Chuck will use the theories, but always to bring you back to the music (which is good for me, since he often brings me to the music that challenges the theories).

Not to overdraw the distinction. The abundance/free-lunch stuff in my Disco Tex Essay may have been a continuation of my thoughts on how to get out from under the context of our appreciation/justification ("there's a self-hate that makes us seek ulterior justification for ourselves/our music in terms that are PBS"), but it was also a rhetorical device that allowed me to throw together a bunch of things I wanted to say about Slade and Dylan and "Louie Louie" and "Smooth Criminal." And conversely when Chuck brought the awesomeness-triviality conundrum to Gladys Knight & The Pips, he came up with a much better way of expressing the idea than Meltzer or I had. And sure, I'd *said* that disco naturally danced itself fucked (so that you don't have to *add* tragedy to disco, rather, just extrapolate from what is already there), but Chuck's the one who spelled it out in detail in the *Flashdance* chapter of *Accidental Evolution of Rock 'n' Roll*. ("Dave Marsh . . . wrote in his usually much smarter *The Heart of Rock & Soul: The 1001 Greatest Singles Ever Made* that since Madonna's ghostly 'Live to Tell' is sung from the point of view of an abused child, the material girl has therefore earned the right to party. Ouch! Talk about working for your weekend!!") Still, I'm the one who's going to keep asking "*Why* does triviality protect awesomeness? Why does it need to? What's the social process here? What are we trying to get out from under?" Chuck's the record-list geek and I'm the social-science geek.

Which brings us to the beginning. My dad, Norman Kogan, poli sci prof, wrote (*The Politics of Italian Foreign Policy*, 1963): "The principal issue in Italian foreign policy is whether to preserve or change the domestic social structure." You can hear echoes of this throughout my writing ("the lyrics make a jarring change, as if there's a second song hidden behind the first"), the frequent asking of what's the music's social life.

Go back to the Kogan family sitting 'round the dinner table having discussions on whether to preserve or change the domestic social structure, my mother, Meryl, exasperated, telling me I would no doubt grow up to be a lawyer: She says now that I am fundamentally a philosopher, which is true if by "philosophize" one means "likes to argue." I recall that at the family table I would sometimes throw food. My brother, Richard, sometimes the target of this philosophy, has since been stalwart in his encouragement, as has Nan, his wife. Their children David and Bobby have been a continual inspiration.

So much of this book is about where I come from. Thanks to Tom Olds and Tina LaConte ("dweeb of misery I seemed to be"—no, Tina, dweeb you were not) and Leah Schmidt ("I can't say I remember my favourite album being *Tapestry*, but if you say so . . .") and Larry Groff for letting me invade their privacy, and Mrs. Trevithick and Mrs. Singer, and Fred Smith, and Maureen Nolan, if she were still alive (died last year of cancer, and I regret the reductiveness and inadequacy of my portrayal of her in the Dolls piece), and Jay Carey, of course, who's been a consistent champion . . . well, this book was written over thirty-five years. How to summarize? Start with the music:

Dylan and Grace gave me words when I didn't have my own; also gave me the courage to follow language into Wonderland. The Yardbirds, the Velvets, and Dylan (again) became models by finding a repetitive little blues vamp or rave-up bit within a song and extending it to make it a container for references, puns, gags, doohickeys, crescendos, wheelbarrows, mannequins, theories, etc., a strategy obviously adaptable to writing. Isaac Hayes added the idea that such a structure can come from anywhere within the culture, from rock, soul, jazz, muzak. (I probably would have gotten this same message from Shakespeare and Faulkner if I'd understood them better.) James Brown is absolutely crucial for knocking down the final barrier in my brain between foreground and background. A revelation was hearing "Get It Together" and finally, viscerally, *getting* that music is a conversation, that r&b and pop are a chatroom. The Stones and the Stooges were a model for my fanzine practice of taking the writer-reader-editor-letter-writer-call-and-response thing and turning it into a come-on and a brawl. (One of the drawbacks of this book is that you don't see the call-and-response world we created in *Why Music Sucks, Swellsville, Radio On, Kitschener,* and *Tapeworm.* You're only hearing one of the singers in the shouting match.)

The Rolling Stones are huge. In 1993 I wrote a 41-page letter to Renée Crist where in the middle I became Mick Jagger: "I knew I couldn't do the sweet emotion of heartbreak straight. The guy couldn't *say* he was broken, or else it'd be just a lame old heartbreak song that no one believed anymore—*even though it's true.* So the guy would deny it. He—I—the singer—would pretend to have the heart of stone. I'd be proclaiming my stoneness even though the whole situation I was laying out would say otherwise. We'd point our finger in the direction of the sweet heartbreak song, but we wouldn't have to actually do it. In the background singing we brought in real beauty that was better than any we'd done before, and it worked as beauty because the song was somewhere else and the beauty was almost beside the point. But if the listener just says, 'Oh, I get it, he's saying he's hard but he's really in love,' then the song is still boring, and why should the listener continue to care? What I've learned is that I have to absolutely commit myself to what the narrator says he's saying, even if the idea is that the song is pointing somewhere opposite. You see, as soon as you say where you're aiming, as soon as you make a point, then the song is dead. So you make sure the song doesn't have one point, doesn't go in just one direction. If you keep the song equivocal, if it's not a message but a struggle, then the song can still matter, for years, even when everyone's gotten used to how it sounds and even when 'hard' no longer sounds hard. This was accidental. The song got away from us, fortunately. And it was dynamite. As the songwriter I put cracks in the song, holes for emotion, reasons to rebel against the singer. But I sing the song like . . . well, like *I'm* singing the song. Sometimes when I hear the song unexpectedly I say, 'Who is that motherfucker?'"

Richard Meltzer's a hero and nemesis; he's all over this book. In 2000 I had an advance copy of *A Whore Just Like the Rest* sitting in my apartment for three months before finally opening it, was afraid he'd come across as nasty and as compelling as ever and that his words would control mine. (Basically, after reading Meltzer I can't write for a day without taking on his style, it's so strong.) And fundamentally I just don't know how to live with this man's on-page personality, it's a threat, whatever part there is in my superego that is labeled "Meltzer" and tells me I'm an asshole for not being more like him.

Lester Bangs. His response to Steven Tyler's proclaiming "I'm back in the saddle again": "So what?" The most articulate of the *Creem* and *Fusion* writers in his distrust of "progressive rock," and then of "rock" in general. A lot of the early *Why Music Sucks* was my turning around and aiming that distrust onto punk and its progeny, and trying to make it more articulate still. Lester knew my friend Charlotte, played with my friend Rob. I'd assumed we'd meet . . .

I was imitating Ring Lardner long before I'd read him; he may have been the first crucial pre-rock rock critic, predating even Otis Ferguson. His early '30s radio reviews in *The New Yorker* read a lot like Meltzer's early '70s rock reviews, Lardner going after the music with blowtorches and noisemakers, making the story not just the sound but what you do with and to it.

My first rock-critic hero was Ken Emerson; extolled singles in the (supposed) album age of the late '60s, was a gentler guide than Meltzer to reordering importance and unimportance ("without the Zombies, rock would be no different; just poorer"). Was nice enough to reply to a letter I wrote him freshman year in college.

Simon Frith and Robert Christgau were friends of mine decades before they ever heard of me. A lot of this book might be seen as my end of a conversation with Simon about how the world creates music and about how, within the worlds that the music goes on to create, there are listeners and dancers who create the music anew in their lives. A man who listens not just for the sound but for the reverberations, sound *as* a reverberation.

It's late spring of 1974, during the year I'd attempted to drop out of college; I'm now living in a walkup in NYC near Hell's Kitchen, cockroaches scurrying around inside my trash bags; the phone rings, and it's Maureen, her voice in total joy: "I just got *Creem*, and Christgau gave *Too Much Too Soon* an A PLUS." [The second Dolls album.] And she proceeded to read me the review. (To really appreciate this, you'd have to have experienced the utter disdain most of the rock press of the time had for glitter and for the Dolls.)

Probably most good critics would assent to Meltzer's "pertinence can be just anywhere at all," but while for Meltzer "anywhere at all" means bottle caps and bugs and Buber, for Christgau . . . well, he's as bonkers as the rest of us, but it's Bonker Man In Record Land. Even though Bangs and Meltzer are the *official* wild creatures in the game preserve, They Who Have Collapsed The Distinction Between Relevant And Irrelevant, the Christgau Consumer Guide is in fact every bit as audacious and lunatic, as well as being more systematically so. E.g. (as Chuck's pointed out to me), in *Christgau's Record Guide: the '80s* there are *seven* entries for Joe Jackson, none higher than B or lower than C PLUS, one grade actually having been altered from B to B MINUS. Talk about roaming around in the Who Knows Where in search of the Who Knows What! A man who thinks good music can come from anywhere and that even if you've checked the ground, that doesn't mean you shouldn't check it again. And then you speak with honesty, no matter that the money guys wish you were saying something different.

Greil Marcus. Read this passage (*Creem*, June 1975), then go to "Death Rock 2000": "It's as if the Stones went after a sound they thought they heard in Chicago blues, Chuck Berry, early rock and roll, but in truth heard something else—heard what the music reached for and what it only implied—and went past their idols to a sound no one had really gotten before . . . I mean a hardness in the music you can reach out and touch. The difference between the Stones' truest music and anything else is the difference between hitting a softball and a baseball. And from the side the Stones are on, it must be the difference between throwing them."

Movie critics. "Think instead of music as an activity in which people participate"; how I do so comes in part from Otis Ferguson, Robert Warshow, and Manny Farber thinking about how people participate in the watching as well as the making of movies. Ferguson is as big an inspiration for me as Bangs and Meltzer and Dylan and Jagger and Johansen, and I return to him a lot more frequently. *The Film Criticism of Otis Ferguson* is the best book ever on the subject. What he says about Cagney applies to himself: "In spite of writers, directors, and decency legions you are going to see the world and what it does to its people through his subtle understanding of it." My chapter on how music creates ideas is something of an outgrowth of Ferguson and subsequent auteurists exploring how movie makers create thought through sight; especially useful is Andrew Sarris. E.g., free lunch, in the Sarris version:

What Ford had been evolving all through his career was a style flexible enough to establish priorities of expression. He could dispose of a plot quickly and efficiently when he had to, but he could always spare a shot or two for a mood that belonged to him and not to the plot.

Context of abundance:

There is a fantastic sequence in The Searchers *involving a brash frontier character played by Ward Bond. Bond is drinking some coffee in a standing-up position before going out to hunt some Comanches. He glances toward one of the bedrooms, and notices the woman of the house tenderly caressing the Army uniform of her husband's brother. Ford cuts back to a full-faced shot of Bond drinking his coffee, his eyes tactfully averted from the intimate scene he has witnessed. Nothing on earth would ever force this man to reveal what he had seen. There is a deep, subtle chivalry at work here, and in most of Ford's films, but it is never obtrusive enough to interfere with the flow of the narrative. The delicacy of emotion expressed here in three quick shots, perfectly cut, framed, and distanced, would completely escape the dulled perception of our more literary-minded film critics . . . If it had taken [Ford] any longer than three shots and a few seconds to establish this insight into the Bond character, the point would not have been worth making. Ford would be false to the manners of a time and place bounded by the rigorous necessity of survival.*

Philosophy. Chapters 3 and 4 of Richard Rorty's *Philosophy and the Mirror of Nature* are important not merely for his demolition of philosophy, but for the never-quite-articulated question, "So why do these guys care?" I like Rorty's vision later in the book of the postphilosopher: "the informed dilettante, the polypragmatic, Socratic intermediary between various discourses. In his salon, so to speak, hermetic thinkers are charmed out of their self-enclosed practices. Disagreements between disciplines and discourses are compromised or transcended in the course of the conversation." (My mission once this book is published is to get someone to back me financially on starting a Department of Dilettante Studies somewhere, sort of the Son of *WMS*, maybe, or an *ILX* that pays.) I've been disappointed by Rorty's follow-through: The time wrangling with Hilary Putnam, Donald Davidson, et al. would have been better spent finding a way to re-engage the creeps who beat him up in high school. I've long had a dream of forcing Rorty at gunpoint into a room with Richard Meltzer, allowing neither to leave until each is convinced that the other understands him. The hope is that Rorty strips Meltzer of what's left of his philosophical façade, and then, with façade stripped, Meltzer (who's never stopped being a junior-high-school creep) shocks Rorty out of his vague and cheerful blah blah blah. (Sorry about the gun. I guess I was a charm-school dropout; but do you know of any other way to get these guys together?) Not that I expect the Rorty types to read this book, but in the event one of them does, I'm doing my job if I get him to pause before writing inexplicably retarded things like (from *Mirror*, a couple pages beyond the dilettante vision):

> *Normal discourse is that which is conducted within an agreed-upon set of conventions about what counts as a relevant contribution, what counts as answering a question, what counts as having a good argument for that answer or a good criticism of it. Abnormal discourse is what happens when someone joins in the discourse who is ignorant of those conventions or who sets them aside.*

The problem is that Rorty's concept "normal discourse" has little to do with actual normal human discourse, most of which falls outside both "normal" and "abnormal" as Rorty's defined them. Would he claim that the kids who beat him up were ignorant of the conventions of high-school discourse, were setting them aside? Or conversely that in hitting him they were following agreed-upon conventions as to what counts as a relevant contribution? Agreed-upon by whom? Rorty is trying to generalize Kuhn's distinction between "normal" and "revolutionary" science, but the distinction won't carry beyond the hard sciences (except maybe to organized sports), since normal nonscience doesn't act like normal science. For instance, in normal music discourse Patty can say, "The Smiths are godlike, but XTC sucks shit in the mud," and John can retort with "XTC is fabulous." No convention has been set aside here, but no one is agreeing on what counts as "answering a question" either. Someone who thinks otherwise would himself be ignorant of the conventions.

Thank-yous also to: Leslie Singer for living through my writing terrors with me, acting as de facto editor, unpaid, and continually coming up with ideas I swiped, I can't tell you how many (Leslie, as we're listening to Julee Cruise's droning methadone-clinic vocals in the roadhouse scene in *Twin Peaks*, says: "This is bullshit. These people aren't the punks. Real punks don't wear black. Audrey's the real punk"; the phrase "methadone-clinic vocals" was also Leslie's), and if there's an interesting visual detail in anything I wrote through 1991, it was probably Leslie who pointed it out; Patty Stirling for asking me in 1985 to write about Spoonie Gee and for loving and hating music with me ever since (she's the friend quoted in my GN'R review); Aaron Cometbus for his great zine and for being one of the first to print me; Jim DeRogatis, who published my Spoonie Gee piece when *Puncture* demurred; Doug Simmons and Joe Levy for being brilliant editors who encouraged me to take risks; Eric Weisbard for persuading me to rewrite the second paragraph of my Mariah review; **Black Type** a.k.a. David Nichols for doing the letters at *Smash Hits*; Luc Sante and Rob Sheffield for being longtime friends and inspirations and for making sure I didn't turn my face to the wall in the early '90s (a thought for Rob's late wife Renée Crist, whose words were an important presence over this last year while I was reviewing our correspondence in the compiling of this book); Scott Woods and Phil Dellio for providing me a forum whenever I crawled from my tent, and whose rhetorical devices I frequently imitate; Elizabeth Shaw for holding my hand through late-period *WMS* and acting as yet another unpaid editor; and loads of people from the Greater *Why Music Sucks-Radio On* Metropolitan Area (Mykel Board, Pennie Stasik, Alan Korn, Steve Kiviat, Jack Thompson, Sarah Manvel, Liz Armstrong, Zeb Olsen, Chris Cook, Chris Buck, Arsenio Orteza, too many others to mention) and loads more from *ILX* (Josh Kortbein, Tom Ewing, Sterling Clover, Jess Harvell, Ally Kearney, Tim Finney, Tracer Hand, the Pinefox, the Artist Formerly Known As Ramosi, Martin Skidmore, David Howie, Tiit Kusnets, Julio Desouza, plus another several zillion) for stirring my mind and creating a world for my ideas; also Derek Krissoff, who when he was an acquisitions editor at the University of Georgia Press read a posting on *ILX*, laughed, searched for more by the writer who'd posted it, laughed again, and got in touch; Andrew Berzanskis who shepherded the book through the review process and who shared thoughts via email about PBS and David Allan Coe; Jennifer Reichlin, project editor who saw the book through publication and had to wrestle with lyric permissions and with my idiosyncratic formatting; Steve Barnett, who copyedited the manuscript and cheerfully assisted with the wrestling; Anne Boston, who designed a terrific cover; John McLeod, David Des Jardines, Allison Reid, and Alison Lerner, who engineered the publicity that brought this book to your attention; and others unknown to me who put their time and effort and courage into what must have been an unusual project; Ken Freed and Jill Rothenberg for contract advice; Sherry Handlin, my neighbor and friend on Mott Street who back in 1985 took the photo we're using on the cover (when Tina LaConte learned we'd chosen this photo, she was reminded of the day she and her father were walking through Boston's Combat Zone; her dad pointed at the girlie photos outside the strip clubs and said, "Yeah, that's what they looked like *twenty years ago*, maybe"); Andrew Klimek, Andrew Palmer, and anyone else in the world named Andrew; the lion on p. 223; the recording crew and staff at Super Lotto Records; and Tom Barrett, Charlotte Pressler, Tim Gilbride, Mark Edwards, Betty Hellman, Craig Seligman, Mary Gaitskill, Liz Hartka, Jody Friedman, Joanne Piretti, Ames Vincent, Cindy Ehrlich, Naomi Ryerson and her children Jordana and Lia and Michaela, Michael Freedberg (the freshest, least predictable disco critic ever), Simon Reynolds, a special shout-out to Don Allred for decades of conversation, Suzanne Haraburd, Bill Routt, Bryan Wolf, Roni Manner, Margaret Plank, Georgina Kleege, Richard Campo, anyone else named Richard, anyone named Emily, anyone named Sarah or Sara, Bob Galipeau, Kevin Jordan, Michael Hersh, Nina Fonoroff, Linda Heiss, Mark Hatton, Sheldon Brown, James R. Paul, Fish, Mark Fenster, André Radatus, Mary Frances Nevans, Phyllis Brock, J.C. Adamson, Kara Lukin, Keith Howard, Chuck Nefzger, Steph DeRosier, Leslie Tyson, Lee Merrick, Barbara Wolter, Marge O'Mara, Elizabeth Mallory, Freddy Bosco, Phil Hoyle, Don Webster, Pam Goodfriend, Sue Mellows, Grete Reed, Eugene Wrayburn, Archie Goodwin, Thomas Magnum, Angela Chase, Rayanne Graf, like omicron is the fifteenth letter of the Greek alphabet or Sarah Vaughan is like jade, Jessica Lange became Frances, and Dunaway and the word respect go together like hand in glove. They are just being swept along with the calypsonian into the making of a calypso's goal, a fully rounded pear-shaped atrocity. I cannot use the word eye anymore. Alas, did Iggy writhe in vain? To the intellectuals and commentators of Bombay, Calcutta, and other great cities of the East, Frank Kogan was a man of strength and mystery . . . to the music fans deep in the bohemian jungles, he was a god, gifted with supernatural powers . . . but to himself, he was a coward! Fortunately, I've had the continuous encouragement of John Wójtowicz and Mark Sinker whose words and ideas permeate this book, often uncredited. And Mark has consistently made time to listen to my barely formed notions, to comment on drafts, to extrapolate or challenge my contentions, and to welcome my relentless questioning. And once again to Chuck Eddy, who, when I withdrew from the commercial press in the early '90s, kept sending me cassette tapes, promos when he had duplicates, old records, everything, in the hopes that I'd consider writing about them somewhere, anywhere, if not for the greater public then at least for fanzines, and if not for 'zines then at least in letters so that at least *he* could read my ideas; finally, dragging me back in front of the public. Also, there are Chuck's ideas themselves, his constant prodding, "The desire for 'community' has never made a lot of sense to me, at least from an aesthetic standpoint. Elvis and the Beatles (apparently) 'dissolved boundaries' and united factionalized factors, but that doesn't make their *music* any better, only more 'important' (historically)." "Your prescription that we oughta be treating music 'as an activity' strikes me as completely vague and empty. How are we not doing that already? Do you mean a creative activity, an entertainment activity, a communication activity, an 'artistic' activity, a sociological activity, what?"

I would like to thank those who allowed substantial quotations of song lyrics. Select lyrics from "The Lonesome Death of Hattie Carroll" are reprinted by permission. Copyright © 1964 by Warner Bros., Inc.; copyright renewed 1992 by Special Rider Music. All rights reserved. International copyright secured. Select lyrics from "Visions of Johanna" are reprinted by permission. Copyright © 1966 by Dwarf Music. All rights reserved. International copyright secured.

The phrase "the Great Wrong Place" was taken from W.H. Auden, his characterization of the corrupt milieu of Raymond Chandler's Los Angeles. "The Presentation of Self in Everyday Life" was the title of Erving Goffman's sociological study of how people present themselves to others. My thoughts about how social categories evolve in high school ("these people don't live according to the prep-vs.-skater social split, and if *that* split wants to maintain itself, and the preps and the skaters want to defeat the freaks, the preps and skaters have to absorb some freak characteristics") owe a lot to Penelope Eckert's *Jocks and Burnouts.* The first section of my Oxes review models itself on David Howie's review of the same band in *Freaky Trigger.*

The quote in chapter 26 about Stockhausen et al. is from jsidway, a guy on an *I Love Music* thread, though since I was quoting from memory I may have gotten some of the names wrong. The review of Phuture's "Your Only Friend" in part seven simply quotes the lyrics to the song, except that I deliberately misidentify the speaker.

In the version here of my letter to Michael Freedberg ("Fuck Machines and Razor Blades") in part six I added two sentences ("Fuck the daylight . . .") from a Corina review I wrote several months later for the *Voice.* This brings us to an interesting issue: Given that most of these pieces were originally printed elsewhere, some many years ago, changing or improving the prose would have been cheating. So, did I cheat? You bet! But not a lot. I was willing to make an ambiguous sentence clear by changing or adding a word or two. But if clarity would have required a lot of changes, that was because I didn't know what I was saying in the first place, and I let my confusion stand. I occasionally inserted a couple of words to make a cross-reference intelligible, or deleted several unintelligible cross-references, but most of my unintelligibility was retained. Rock criticism is built on unintelligible cross-references.

I also allowed myself to replace a few words that clanked, or to rewrite or eliminate altogether a passage that was mud, but in general I didn't try to give the writing a lilt it hadn't originally had or try to remove a self-conscious swagger it shouldn't have had. Where I ran excerpts, I sometimes had to rearrange paragraphs, add headings, and so forth.

What I didn't do was to change my bad ideas to good ones. E.g., in "Death Rock 2000" I embarrassed myself by describing Eminem's vocals as "a slow talk, unlike 'real' rap not heavily into rhythm and rhyme," even while "Forgot About Dre" was scooting around the charts. My excuse is that I was thinking only of "My Name Is." Even so, a couple of sentences on I quote him rhyming "tits off" and "Kris Kross," so where was my brain?